*Understanding and Teaching
the Cold War*

The Harvey Goldberg Series
for Understanding and Teaching History

The Harvey Goldberg Series for Understanding and Teaching History gives college and secondary history instructors a deeper understanding of the past as well as the tools to help them teach it creatively and effectively. Each volume focuses on a specific historical topic and offers a wealth of content and resources, providing concrete examples of how teachers can approach the subject in the classroom. Named for Harvey Goldberg, a professor renowned for his history teaching at Oberlin College, Ohio State University, and the University of Wisconsin from the 1960s to the 1980s, the series reflects Goldberg's commitment to helping students think critically about the past with the goal of creating a better future. For more information, please visit www.GoldbergSeries.org.

Series Editors

John Day Tully is a professor of history at Central Connecticut State University and was the founding director of the Harvey Goldberg Center for Excellence in Teaching at Ohio State University. He has coordinated many Teaching American History grants and has received the Connecticut State University System's Board of Trustees Teaching Award.

Matthew Masur is a professor of history at Saint Anselm College, where he has served as codirector of the Father Guerin Center for Teaching Excellence. He has also been a member of the Teaching Committee of the Society for Historians of American Foreign Relations.

Brad Austin is a professor of history at Salem State University. He has served as chair of the American Historical Association's Teaching Prize Committee and has worked with hundreds of secondary school teachers as the academic coordinator of many Teaching American History grants.

Advisory Board

Leslie Alexander Ohio State University
Kevin Boyle Northwestern University
Ross Dunn Professor Emeritus, San Diego State University
Leon Fink UIC Distinguished Professor of History, University of Illinois at Chicago
Kimberly Ibach Meeker High School, Meeker, Colorado
Alfred W. McCoy J.R.W. Smail Professor of History, Director, Harvey Goldberg Center for the Study of Contemporary History, University of Wisconsin–Madison
David J. Staley Director, Harvey Goldberg Center for Excellence in Teaching, Ohio State University
Maggie Tran McLean High School, McLean, Virginia
Sam Wineburg Margaret Jacks Professor of Education and (by courtesy) of History, Director, Stanford History Education Group, Stanford University

Understanding and Teaching the Cold War

Edited by

MATTHEW MASUR

The University of Wisconsin Press

Publication of this book has been made possible, in part, through support from the Anonymous Fund of the College of Letters and Science at the University of Wisconsin–Madison.

The University of Wisconsin Press
1930 Monroe Street, 3rd Floor
Madison, Wisconsin 53711-2059
uwpress.wisc.edu

3 Henrietta Street, Covent Garden
London WC2E 8LU, United Kingdom
eurospanbookstore.com

Printed in the United States of America

This book may be available in a digital edition.

Library of Congress Cataloging-in-Publication Data

Names: Masur, Matthew, editor.
Title: Understanding and teaching the Cold War / edited by Matthew Masur.
Other titles: Harvey Goldberg series for understanding and teaching history.
Description: Madison, Wisconsin: The University of Wisconsin Press, 2016. | Series: The Harvey Goldberg series for understanding and teaching history | Includes bibliographical references and index.
Identifiers: LCCN 2016016546 | ISBN 9780299309909 (cloth: alk. paper)
Subjects: LCSH: Cold War. | World politics—1945-1989. | United States—Foreign relations—1945-1989. | Soviet Union—Foreign relations—1945-1991. | Cold War—Study and teaching. | World politics—1945-1989— Study and teaching. | United States—Foreign relations—1945-1989— Study and teaching. | Soviet Union—Foreign relations—1945-1991— Study and teaching.
Classification: LCC D842 .U53 2016 | DDC 909.8/25—dc23
LC record available at https://lccn.loc.gov/2016016546

For Jenn, Ben, and Bernie

Contents

Contents

Contents

Acknowledgments

I am deeply indebted to the contributors who have generously shared their insights from years of studying and teaching about the Cold War. Three anonymous readers offered additional suggestions that improved the final product. I am also grateful to John Tully and Brad Austin, coeditors of the Harvey Goldberg Series for Understanding and Teaching History. Their guidance, support, and friendship were indispensable in bringing this book to fruition. It has been a pleasure working with the staff at the University of Wisconsin Press, particularly Matthew Cosby, Sheila Leary, Andrea Christofferson, Adam Mehring, and Carla Marolt. Dennis Lloyd, the director of the University of Wisconsin Press, has been enthusiastic in his support for the Harvey Goldberg Series. I could not ask for a better editor than Gwen Walker, who has patiently guided this project. Anyone who has worked with Gwen has benefited from her impeccable editorial instincts.

I am fortunate to be part of a thriving academic community at Saint Anselm College. I am surrounded by colleagues, particularly in the History Department, who are devoted teachers and accomplished scholars. My students continue to impress me with their curiosity and enthusiasm. They may not realize it, but they were the inspiration for this project. Saint Anselm College provided helpful financial assistance for this volume through a Faculty Summer Research Grant.

This book—like all the projects I undertake—could not have been completed without the incredible support I receive from my family. Jennifer Walton has given me intellectual guidance and emotional comfort for almost twenty years. Ben and Bernie haven't been around quite so long, but their support is no less crucial.

*Understanding and Teaching
the Cold War*

Introduction

MATTHEW MASUR

On December 17, 2014, Alan Gross was freed from a Cuban prison and returned to the United States. At the same time, three Cuban prisoners in the United States were returned to Havana, and an additional American agent held captive in Cuba was released. The prisoner exchange, with its echoes of the Cold War, was a precondition for reestablishing diplomatic relations between the two countries. The announcement that the United States and Cuba were taking steps to normalize their relationship signaled that a chapter in the Cold War was finally coming to an end. But it also highlighted the fact that, more than twenty-five years after the fall of the Berlin Wall, the Cold War was still being fought, at least in some parts of the globe.

US-Cuban relations illustrate the value and the limitations of viewing international affairs through the lens of the Cold War. The dispute between the two countries is undoubtedly a part of the decades-long rivalry between the communist bloc and the "free world" after World War II. But, as recent events show, the tensions between the United States and Cuba continued long after the Cold War ended. Additionally, the differences that divided the United States and Cuba predate the Cold War by at least a half-century. In other words, the US-Cuban relationship can be understood both as an event that embodies the Cold War and as one that transcends it. In this regard, the history of US-Cuban relations is not unique. Other issues of great importance in current international relations, such as the US rivalry with Russia and China and tensions between North and South Korea, can be traced to the Cold War. At the same time, these issues have causes that extend beyond the Cold War and influences that have endured long after the Cold War's end.

3

The end of the Cold War led to a period of soul-searching for historians of American foreign relations. With the conflict over, historians had a weaker claim for the importance and relevance of their research. Moreover, the end of the Cold War coincided with a scholarly shift away from the study of diplomacy and state-to-state relations. Even the very name that scholars used to identify their field—"diplomatic history"—seemed outdated and old-fashioned. Indeed, historians of American foreign relations wrote countless articles and participated in numerous panel discussions about strategies for remaining relevant in a changing academic environment. These discussions contributed to important changes in how historians researched America's role in the world.

So the end of the Cold War, rather than spelling doom for historians of American foreign relations, led to a renaissance in the field. Indeed, even if the academy is sometimes hostile to the study of foreign affairs, the public has an insatiable interest in America's relationship with the wider world. Influential figures in the government, from the national to the state level, also see the enormous value of understanding the history of America's global activities. More and more, colleges and universities are being tasked with preparing students to live in an interconnected world. At a time when colleges and universities are constantly trying to prove their usefulness, the study of the Cold War is an ideal topic to show not only the relevance of the history of America's place in the world but also the value of history as a discipline.

For many of our students—and even a growing number of teachers— the Cold War is a relic of the distant past. Today's students still occasionally live in fear of America's enemies, but they are more worried about terrorist attacks than about nuclear annihilation and World War III. They are unlikely to perceive communism as an existential threat to the United States, seeing it instead as an antiquated and misguided ideology that survives in a handful of countries. Where communism does exist, it bears little resemblance to the principles of Marx, Engels, and Lenin. Students are much more likely to hear a political candidate described as "soft on crime" than as "soft on communism." I still sometimes slip up and refer to present-day Russia as "the Soviet Union," eliciting quizzical looks from my students. For them, the Soviet Union—like Prussia or Siam or Rhodesia—exists only in the history books.

And yet, more than twenty-five years after the fall of the Berlin Wall, the Cold War continues to exert its influence on the modern world.

North and South Korea remain bitter rivals, with North Korea enjoying the (sometimes grudging) support of communist China and South Korea relying on the protection of the United States. The antagonistic relationship between the United States and Cuba shows signs of improving, but the two countries remained locked in a Cold War struggle for years after the collapse of the Soviet Union. The United States still looks warily on Chinese and Soviet—I mean Russian—power, competing with both countries for influence around the globe.

This book is predicated on the fact that the Cold War is a topic of immense historical importance for scholars and teachers alike. For almost fifty years, the Cold War was a defining feature of the international environment. Participants included the United States and the Soviet Union but also their allies around the world. The literal battlegrounds of the Cold War stretched from Korea to Cuba to Afghanistan to Angola. Metaphorically, the fighting extended even further, with the two sides competing for economic, technological, and cultural supremacy. Countries that tried to remain neutral were no less affected; indeed, identifying as a "nonaligned" country was an acknowledgment of the Cold War dynamic. Understanding the Cold War in all of its complexity is crucial for understanding nearly any topic in post-1945 world history.

The Cold War, then, can be understood as more than a single, discrete historical event. Rather, it is a framework or narrative that can be used to explain or understand a multitude of historical events in the modern world. This is not to say that the Cold War is the only framework—or even necessarily the best one. As the twentieth century fades from view, historians are better equipped to understand the long-term trends that define the recent past. Some historians might argue that colonialism and decolonization provide a better "grand narrative" for understanding the recent past and contemporary global affairs. Other historians might focus on industrialization and technological innovation as forces that have exerted the most influence on the world. Still others might argue that identity—the way people understand themselves as part of certain racial, ethnic, national, and religious groups—is the key to understanding modern history. These frameworks are not mutually exclusive. Colonialism, industrialization, and identity formation overlapped and intersected, influencing and being influenced by one another. By the same token, all of these processes affected and were affected by the Cold War. Just as it would be impossible to understand late-twentieth-century

5

anticolonial movements without understanding the Cold War, it would be misguided to study the Cold War without acknowledging the importance of decolonization.

The Cold War is also a useful topic for teachers who want students to think more broadly about *why* it is important to study the past. When I ask my students why we study history, they almost always say that knowledge of the past can help us address dilemmas in the present. For those students, the Cold War offers numerous "lessons" that can guide us as we navigate the challenges of international relations in the twenty-first century. For example, students often think that America's relationship with the Soviet Union can be used to understand its relationship with any number of current rivals or enemies. But many teachers, myself included, want to disabuse students of the notion that history is useful because somehow the past provides easy lessons when we think about the present. If anything, the Cold War offers numerous examples of how this sort of simplistic historical thinking can create a host of new problems. Therefore, teachers can use the Cold War to explain to students that the past can often seem familiar, but they should be attuned to the characteristics that make it distinct and unique. Having students try to understand how the Cold War world was *different* from the world of the twenty-first century will force them to hone their analytical and imaginative skills. Ideally, students will gain an appreciation for the potential lessons that the Cold War offers but also the limitations of these lessons. This is, at its essence, a key element of the "historical reasoning" that we want our students to grasp.

The very qualities that make the Cold War an important topic of historical study—its geographic, chronological, and thematic breadth—make it difficult to cover in a single volume. This collection, therefore, is not conceived as a comprehensive guide to teaching the Cold War in its entirety. Some regions or themes are treated briefly or omitted entirely. This is not to suggest, however, that those topics are not important to the Cold War or that our students do not need to understand them. As with many other historical topics, teachers must make difficult choices about what to emphasize, what to downplay, and what to omit entirely. This volume reflects one effort, however imperfect, to make those difficult choices.

The introductory chapters in part one of this volume highlight the fact that the story of the Cold War cannot be understood by looking at the role of the United States. Contributors Carole Fink and Warren I. Cohen are distinguished scholars with decades of experience researching and teaching the Cold War. Fink, a specialist on European diplomacy, provides a general framework for understanding the Cold War as it unfolded in Europe. Cohen, a historian of Asia, argues that the Cold War is necessary for understanding modern relations between the United States and China. Their pieces are especially helpful in framing the Cold War for teachers and in establishing the broad chronological and geographical scope of the conflict—something that can be lost when we focus on the specific details of such a vast topic.

Subsequent chapters in this volume reflect the most recent and influential features of Cold War historiography. Early scholarship on the Cold War sometimes tended to approach the topic moralistically, in particular by either praising or blaming the United States for its role in the origin of the Cold War and for its foreign policy as the conflict dragged on. More recent scholarship is less likely to see the Cold War in such black-and-white terms, instead scrutinizing both the United States and the Soviet Union for their actions during the Cold War and avoiding conclusions that are overly celebratory or condemnatory.

The chapters in part two reflect this stance in examining topics that have long been of interest to historians of the Cold War. Jessica Elkind's piece on the origins of the Cold War and Mario Del Pero's chapter on the end of the Cold War will help teachers bring much-needed balance to these topics. Shane J. Maddock's chapter on nuclear policy during the Cold War takes a topic that was central to Cold War tensions and presents it fairly and dispassionately. Anthony D'Agostino's chapter will help teachers to understand that Soviet perspective(s) on the Cold War need to be taken seriously, while being viewed with a critical eye. Finally, David Bosso's chapter on teaching the Cold War in the post-9/11 era gives teachers useful ideas about how to reach a student population that uses different resources—conceptual and technological—when grappling with global issues.

Studying the influence of the Cold War on American society—and vice versa—is not exactly a "new" trend in the historiography. But the interaction of the Cold War and American society has equaled and perhaps eclipsed more traditional diplomatic topics as a subject for Cold War historians. As a result, Cold War historians are as likely to use films, music, architecture, consumer goods, and literature in their research as they are to use official documents from the White House or the State

Department. The chapters in part three illustrate a variety of ways that teachers can incorporate these topics into their classes on American history. Kenneth Osgood's chapter on Cold War propaganda shows not only how propaganda was an important tool in the Cold War but also how analyzing propaganda can help students to become critical readers of other sources. Molly M. Wood uses movies and literature to explore ways in which powerful nuclear arsenals affected the mindsets of Americans who lived through the Cold War. Laura A. Belmonte's piece on American Cold War culture, like Wood's chapter, identifies movies and other nontraditional sources that will capture students' interest and help them to analyze nonwritten primary sources. Finally, teachers who want to show that the Cold War had a profound impact on American society can draw on Brenda Gayle Plummer's chapter on the civil rights movement and on Thomas Zeiler's piece on the intersection between sport and the Cold War. Both of these chapters suggest that the Cold War was inextricably linked to trends in modern American society, particularly the critical topics of race relations and racial equality.

The Cold War was not simply an American phenomenon, nor was it simply the story of US-Soviet relations. The Cold War by its very nature linked events that were taking place across the globe. To cite but one example, the Suez Crisis involved not only regional actors like Egypt and Israel but also Great Britain, France, the United States, and the Soviet Union. Moreover, it coincided with the Hungarian uprising, and the two events, though seemingly disparate, exerted an influence on each other. By the same token, the 1954 Geneva Agreements regarding the French conflict in Indochina were influenced by the relative military and economic strength of the French and the Viet Minh but also involved diplomatic maneuvering by China, the United States, and the Soviet Union. Each of these actors, in turn, was influenced by domestic pressures, other strategic concerns, and its relationships with the other players.

While the Cold War often linked events in far-flung parts of the globe, historians have also become increasingly attuned to the local context of the Cold War, especially in developing parts of the world. Historians with in-depth knowledge of the third world have shown that, in spite of the inordinate power of the Cold War's main antagonists, local conditions and local actors are indispensable for understanding the Cold War. Returning to the example of Vietnam, scholars with expertise in Vietnamese politics, society, and culture have persuasively demonstrated that the Vietnam War was as much an intra-Vietnamese struggle as it was a conflict between the Vietnamese and American outsiders. This is not to suggest that the Vietnam War was a local dispute and not a Cold War one. Instead, it shows that the local context is necessary for understanding how the Cold War played out in Vietnam. The opposite is also true: Vietnam area specialists are wise to understand how local Vietnamese affairs became enmeshed with the larger global Cold War struggle. The intersection of local and Cold War influences is apparent in any number of other events: the Cuban revolution, the Korean War, the Solidarity movement in Poland, and the Soviet invasion of Afghanistan, to name a few. Historians studying these events, often benefiting from new sources that were unavailable to earlier scholars, are less likely to depict these "secondary" Cold War players as either emblems of heroic resistance or examples of passive victimhood. In other words, recent scholarship on the Cold War portrays all the various participants with subtlety and nuance, eschewing simplistic caricatures.

The chapters in part four offer helpful tips for navigating the sometimes complex global and local currents in the Cold War. Philip Pajakowski highlights the essential place of Poland in the early Cold War. His piece also offers a nice complement to chapters on American culture by demonstrating how the Polish novel *Ashes and Diamonds*—and a subsequent film adaptation—can be a useful tool for understanding the Cold War. Along with Pajakowski's piece, J. Simon Rofe offers ideas for teaching about the Cold War in Western Europe that are especially useful for classes on Modern European history. Building on Warren Cohen's introductory chapter, Hiroshi Kitamura explores one of the most volatile and violent regions of the Cold War: East Asia. Andrew Kirkendall's chapter on Latin America and the Caribbean examines a region that was of particular interest to American policymakers, while Ryan Irwin's chapter on Africa explores a continent that seemed only gradually to get drawn into the Cold War—but that was a critical region as the Cold War heated up in the late 1970s. Finally, Mary Ann Heiss's chapter on the nonaligned movement shows how the Cold War exerted a strong pull, even on those countries that wanted to "opt out" of the conflict. Combined with the chapters on Africa, Latin America, and Asia, it offers a useful resource for teaching about the Cold War in the developing world.

For teachers who want their students to read and interpret primary sources, the Cold War offers a treasure trove of materials, many of which are conveniently available online. Part five of this volume highlights three essential collections that can easily be woven into various classes and that can be used as the basis for student research projects. Christian Ostermann outlines the Cold War International History Project (CWIHP), an effort to collect, analyze, and digitize archival materials, especially from the former communist-bloc nations. The CWIHP has dramatically influenced Cold War historiography and is thus dramatically reshaping the way the Cold War is taught. Marc J. Selverstone's chapter on the White House recordings highlights an indispensable resource that can be used to bring students into the Oval Office to eavesdrop on some of the key presidential conversations that took place during the Cold War. Finally, M. Todd Bennett explains how teachers can introduce students to the *Foreign Relations of the United States (FRUS)* series, a primary-source collection that has long been integral to any research on American foreign policy in the Cold War period.

Teaching the Cold War is both necessary and challenging. The chapters in this volume will help teachers navigate the vastness and complexity of the Cold War, provide them with ideas about integrating the Cold War into their classes, and suggest strategies and tools that can be used to help students understand this difficult topic. The authors of the chapters are scholars who have contributed up-to-date research on the Cold War. They are involved in the academic discussions and debates that define the field of Cold War history. They are also experienced teachers who have brought their knowledge into the classroom, determining through trial and error the best way to help students to understand the history of the Cold War.

PART ONE

The Cold War and the Classroom

Teaching the History of Cold War Europe

CAROLE FINK

Europe's Cold War—marked by the almost (but not completely) impenetrable barrier that divided the continent from the Baltic to the Adriatic—has had both a personal and a professional impact on my teaching. In 1961 I witnessed life first-hand in the Soviet Union, Poland, and Czechoslovakia and also saw the construction of the Berlin Wall; in the 1980s I took part in several conferences in Moscow on the history and prospects of East-West collaboration; and after 1990 I was able for the first time to do research in Polish and Czech archives.

Similarly, my teaching career, which commenced in the late 1960s and extended through the decade after 9/11, reflected three stages of Europe's Cold War history. At first our emphasis in the classroom was on Europe's descent into war and barbarism and its division and control by the United States and the Soviet Union after 1945. By the 1970s, however, we began to focus on the recovery of Eastern and Western Europe, on their diverse peoples and regimes, and on the historic and cultural ties that still bound the continent. And after the revolutions that took place between 1989 and 1991, our task was to examine not only how and why communism was established and crumbled in Europe but also how the continent shaped and was shaped by the Cold War.

Today teaching the history of the Cold War in Europe is exceptionally challenging. To be sure, there is a rich selection of documents, enabling students to examine texts, images, and sounds on their computers. However, professors are now speaking to a generation that reacts incredulously to the Berlin Wall and also has no memory of its breach in

November 1989. During my recent guest professorship at the University of Jena, in which I taught master's and doctoral students from several European countries, the history of the Cold War was barely present in their personal and intellectual landscape.

Nonetheless, the distinctive European experience contributes substantially to our understanding of the Cold War. It shifts the emphasis from the US-Soviet conflict that for more than four decades engulfed the entire world and focuses instead on the specific site where the superpower rivalry began and ended. It includes a *longue durée* encompassing earlier cold wars between religious, ideological, and national rivals. It also offers nuanced and occasionally paradoxical details overlooked in the bipolar and global narratives, for example taking account of economic, technological, cultural, and social forces; acknowledging the permeability of seemingly ironclad physical and political boundaries; recognizing the robust interplay between center and periphery, including diverse manifestations and limitations of power; and, above all, paying close attention to the unforeseen ideas, individuals, and events that can disrupt an existing order. It is in this spirit and framework that I propose thirteen teaching units as well as suggestions for sources and discussion.

The European Past

Although the world's second smallest continent, Europe for almost four centuries played an outsized role in world history because of its military advances and overseas expansion, its science and technology, and its political and ideological innovations. It is thus useful to begin with maps from as early as the fifteenth century and to bring the picture up to date to illustrate the continent's principal physical characteristics and its ethnic, religious, and political divisions along with the vast empires it created on land and overseas. In this first part, we not only gain familiarity with Europe's contours—this small, jagged peninsula that juts out of the western end of the Eurasian land mass, lying mostly in the temperate climate zone and possessing rich farm lands, mineral wealth, and numerous navigable rivers and deep-water ports as well as vast plains and lofty mountain chains—but also learn how political frontiers were created, shifted, and even disappeared and how humans were affected by these changes.

Thanks to the abundant resources on the Internet, this long sweep of Europe's history can be supplemented by documents and visual materials that illustrate some contrasting themes: statistics describing Spain's immense imperial wealth in the sixteenth century and also depictions of its Armada's defeat in 1588; the Treaties of Westphalia of 1648, which enshrined the principles of unimpeded state sovereignty and also lay the ground for the protection of religious minorities; the Declaration of the Rights of Man and the Citizen, which revolutionized the concepts of citizenship and human rights, and also Marx and Engels's *Communist Manifesto*, which made demands on behalf of the working class; the conclusions of the Berlin Congress of 1884–85, which established the ground rules for the partition of Africa, but also the Treaty of Versailles in 1919, which imposed contested borders in Europe and large parts of the colonial world; excerpts from the Freud-Einstein correspondence seeking peace after World War I and also Hitler's *Mein Kampf*, which set out a design for global conquest.

By delving into Europe's past, we may recognize continuities as well as change. For example, earlier East-West political and religious divisions provide background for our understanding of the post-1945 borders; the two world wars shaped the mentalities of postwar Europe's leadership and population; and the vast destruction of people and property between 1939 and 1945 and the forced migration of millions of Europeans altered the continent's political landscape. We can also examine contested symbols—words, such as "Munich" and "Yalta," and images, such as those of Verdun and Auschwitz—to gain a deeper understanding of the diversity of Europe's memories and mentalities.

Europe Remade by Others: Tehran, Yalta, and Potsdam

Following earlier prolonged struggles against imperialist powers, coalitions have sometimes grasped the authority to rearrange borders without consulting the affected populations. Thus, the Grand Alliance of Great Britain, the Soviet Union, and the United States, preparing for the defeat of the Third Reich, whose frontiers had once stretched from the English Channel to the steppes of Russia, remade the map of Europe. Moreover, as happened to earlier ad hoc alliances, as the war turned in their favor the Big Three's divergent views on Europe's future

15

came to the surface during their deliberations at Tehran (1943) and Yalta (1945), and their postwar meeting in Potsdam (1945) exposed fundamental differences in their visions of what Europe's future should look like.

There are abundant sources through which to examine World War II diplomacy between 1939 and 1945: speeches and photographs, maps and films, and, of course, letters, diaries, and conference proceedings from all three sides. From this distance we can evaluate the Grand Alliance's success not only in defeating Hitler but also in setting up the postwar Allied Control Councils in Germany and Eastern Europe, founding the United Nations, and creating the world's first International Military Tribunal at Nuremberg, which prosecuted twenty-four Nazi leaders and seven organizations and produced an unprecedented and voluminous historical record of aggressive war, state violence against combatants and civilians, and crimes against humanity. On the darker side, in addition to establishing Europe's de facto borders and regimes, the Big Three also approved major programs of ethnic cleansing in Poland, the Baltic states, Ukraine, Hungary, Czechoslovakia, and Romania that drove millions of Germans, Poles, and Hungarians from their homelands.

The unraveling of the Grand Alliance at the end of 1945 was a perhaps inevitable development among three partners of disparate size, wealth, and wartime casualties, but other unforeseen factors also came into play: the disappearance of the two of its major figures, Roosevelt and Churchill; America's use of the atomic bomb against Japan; and the unexpectedly chaotic conditions in Central, Eastern, and Southeastern Europe, which, as various entities attempted to fill the vacuum, led to a resurgence of East-West ideological differences. It is useful to read George Orwell's October 1945 article in which, using the term "Cold War," he deplored "a peace that is no peace" and predicted a world divided by "two or three monstrous superpowers" that would ensure conformity and stifle dissent.

Europe Divided, 1945–53

For Europe the high Cold War that lasted until Stalin's death was a time of peril and violence for which we have ample documentation from newspaper accounts and photographs, diaries and memoirs, and speeches and diplomatic gatherings, as well as from all the materials that became available in the former communist archives after 1989.

To be sure, the division of the continent was a gradual one, completed in 1949 with the creation of two German states and preceded by communist takeovers in Bulgaria, Albania, Poland, Hungary, Romania, and Czechoslovakia on one side and the removal of communist ministers in the coalition governments of France, Italy, and Belgium on the other. In this period the US-Soviet rivalry—bolstered by nonstop espionage and propaganda—reached its frightening climax during the Berlin blockade between 1948 and 1949, which even threatened a nuclear confrontation.

Nonetheless, the onset of the Cold War did not solidify Europe into two frozen blocs. Not only were Austria and Finland able to escape Moscow's grip and Josip Broz Tito to defy Stalin in 1948; the persistence of religious, scientific, cultural, and athletic connections across the Iron Curtain ensured that Europe, even in its most polarized years—and despite Orwell's dire prediction—maintained its distinctiveness and cross-border links as well as a measure of independence from full superpower control.

Hungary

It can be exceedingly difficult to convey the shock of the Soviet invasion of Hungary in November 1956. Images of Soviet tanks rumbling through Budapest, speeches and newspaper accounts, and statistics of massive casualties (including Hungarian leader Imre Nagy) and refugees help create the picture of Europe's most violent episode since 1945.

The suppression of the popular revolt in Hungary marked a new stage in the European Cold War. For the Soviet Union it represented a revival of Stalinist repression but also a display of its realm's fragility; after 1956 the mercurial ruler Nikita Khrushchev would accumulate critics and rivals while also being forced to pacify millions of disgruntled Soviet and East European subjects with "goulash communism." Washington's response balanced public outrage with official prudence. Despite its vows to "roll back" communism in Eastern Europe (and its radio broadcasts that up to the last minute encouraged the Hungarian rebels), the United States feared nuclear war more than it feared a divided Europe.

Europeans also experienced the events in Hungary in two different ways. For East Europeans, for whom the Iron Curtain had been confirmed by force, they would usher in period of somewhat better housing and consumer goods; in contrast, for West Europeans, Marxist and Liberals alike, they brought the realization that, however heavy America's political and economic hand, their lives were freer than those of people living in the East.

Suez

The Franco-British-Israeli invasion of Egypt at the end of October 1956 to topple Gamal Abdel Nasser (who was being armed by the Soviet bloc and had nationalized the Suez Canal) occurred almost simultaneously with the Soviet invasion of Hungary. For Moscow it provided welcome cover for the invasion and also spurred Khrushchev to bluster with nuclear threats against the three Western powers. President Dwight Eisenhower, who grasped this opportunity to align the United States with the outraged colonial world, joined the Soviet Union in pressuring the three to withdraw (although he would soon lay the groundwork for usurping Britain's commanding role in the Middle East).

For West Europeans the Suez episode had major consequences. Khrushchev's threats emphasized their vulnerability; the split in the NATO underscored the alliance's weakness; and America's commitment to defend them was shown to be uncertain. The humiliation at Suez also heralded Western Europe's retreat from empire in Asia and Africa, which had already begun in India and Indochina and would now proceed rapidly. On the other hand, from the shock of the Suez crisis emerged the West German–French bargain that gave birth to the European Economic Community (or Common Market), which, despite (or perhaps because of) Britain's absence until 1973, created practices and institutions that not only benefited its six original members but also exerted a strong influence across the Iron Curtain.

The Wall

With the August 1961 construction of Cold War's iconic symbol, the last exit from communist Eastern Europe was sealed, and the US-Soviet standoff over Berlin reached its climax in a twelve-hour tank confrontation in October. There are numerous visual and written accounts from this period that depict the human and political drama of the enclosure of West Berlin with almost one hundred miles of barbed wire and concrete along with guard towers, mines, and trenches. But, behind the sensational headlines, it was also evident that both super-powers in 1961 were determined to defuse the "German question" and build a more stable Europe: the Soviets by bolstering East Germany (which had been hemorrhaging its young, well-educated population and demanding the Kremlin's support to maintain its political legitimacy) and the other side through President John F. Kennedy's acceptance of a Wall rather than face a nuclear war.

The Wall's impact fell unevenly on the continent. Eastern European leaders, now backed firmly by Moscow, allowed a brief cultural "thaw" that included an outpouring of film and music and also increased contacts with the West. But for West European leaders the Wall became a spur for more independent action vis-à-vis their problematic US protector. French president Charles de Gaulle began building an independent nuclear force and moved closer to West German chancellor Konrad Adenauer (who also hoped to join the atomic club), while West German mayor Willy Brandt, distraught over US inaction, challenged Adenauer's failed policies and called for "Change through Rapprochement" (*Wandel durch Annäherung*) as a means of eroding the Iron Curtain and eventually securing German unification.

The Prague Spring

The 1960s in Europe remain an object of fascination, enshrined in photographs, magazines, and newspaper and first-person accounts. In the West student protestors, garbed in jeans and t-shirts and sporting long hair and beards, took to the streets to denounce the US war in Vietnam and their own "repressive" governments and institutions and to demand greater personal freedom. In the East dissidents risked beatings and imprisonment to demand that their governments respect the various nations' constitutions and provide freedom of speech, religion, assembly, and movement.

To be sure, a mental Iron Curtain separated the protesters in Paris, Rome, and West Berlin, who identified with the third-world leaders Che Guevara, Mao Zedong, and Ho Chi Minh, from their counterparts in Moscow, Warsaw, and East Berlin, who aspired to live in a liberal, pluralist democracy.

Early in 1968 the government of Czechoslovakia, once the most loyal of Soviet satellites, was transformed from above when the Soviet leader Leonid Brezhnev placed a Slovak loyalist at the helm to rescue its failing economy and to kindle popular support. Instead, Alexander Dubček inadvertently authored Eastern Europe's most dramatic reformulation of communism: a "socialism with a human face," the six-month-long Prague Spring (named after the country's increasingly cosmopolitan annual music festival), which aimed to grant a vast amount of personal, political, and economic freedom without a formal exit from the Soviet bloc. When Moscow hesitated to use force, Czechoslovakia's neighbors, terrified by the fear of contagion of Dubček's reforms, demanded his overthrow. On the night of August 21–22, Warsaw Pact troops invaded Czechoslovakia; subsequently, the Brezhnev doctrine asserted the Soviet Union's right to crush any threat to a fellow communist regime.

Once more the Soviet Union and its hard-line satellites were the ostensible victors, having restored order in Eastern Europe. Moreover, Washington, requiring Moscow's help to end the Vietnam War, and NATO, fearing further Soviet expansion, were silent. Nonetheless, there were popular protests not only in Western capitals but also in Moscow and Kiev, Warsaw and Budapest, and even East Berlin. And in Beijing, Mao—now a rival of Brezhnev—castigated the Soviet leader's doctrine. The crushing of the Prague Spring dispelled East European hopes for a peaceful reform of communism or for help from the West. For West European realists, on the other hand, it reinforced the conviction that the Cold War could be overcome only through active and non-threatening engagement with Moscow and its satellites.

Détente

After long and difficult negotiations, the Helsinki Accords were signed on August 1, 1975, by thirty-two European countries along with the Soviet Union, the United States, and Canada. It was a long-sought goal of the Soviet Union: Helsinki recognized its post–World War II annexations and the borders of a divided Europe; ensured non-interference in the signatories' internal and external affairs; and opened the way to trade and technology transfers from West to East.

However, on the insistence of the smaller West European governments, the Helsinki Accords also contained provisions relating to humanitarian and cultural cooperation (the so-called Basket Three), binding the signatories to grant their citizens "fundamental freedoms, including freedom of thought, conscience, religion, or belief" and to promote and encourage "the effective exercise of civil, political, economic, social, cultural and other rights and freedoms all of which derive from the inherent dignity of the human person"; it also provided for follow-up meetings to implement these pledges.

The Helsinki records, now available from both sides, reflect the ambivalent characteristics of European détente. On the one hand, Georges Pompidou and Willy Brandt (who came to office as president of France and chancellor of West Germany, respectively, in 1969) held more dynamic views of East-West détente than did the Nixon administration in Washington, which was restrained by ideological reservations and also by congressional and press opposition to "appeasing" the Soviet Union. In particular, Brandt's pragmatic *Ostpolitik*—aimed at gaining security for West Berlin and eventually eroding the Iron Curtain—minimized Germany's national claims and human rights violations and included major concessions to the Soviet bloc: not only Bonn's renunciation of nuclear weapons and its acknowledgment of all the lost German territories (which it vowed not to reclaim by force) but also its disavowal of claims to represent *all* of Germany (the Hallstein doctrine) and de facto recognition of communist East Germany along with support for major private and governmental trade and investment arrangements to bolster the communists' economies. According to Brandt's critics, *Ostpolitik* replaced principled opposition to communist dictatorship with cynical deals that betrayed the East European opposition and extended the life of an enfeebled and unpopular Soviet bloc.

On the other hand, Helsinki both acknowledged the reality of a divided Europe and also revived the Prague Spring's ideals in the text of the Basket Three. Although neither superpower took these clauses seriously, many Europeans did. After they were published, West European nongovernmental organizations (NGOs), such as Amnesty International, and East European and Soviet dissidents, including the Czech and Slovak founders of Charter 77 and the Moscow Helsinki Watch group, invoked the Basket Three to demand political and religious rights, exit visas, and the release of political prisoners.

Solidarność

In Poland, the Soviet Union's most defiant satellite and the scene of major protests in 1956, 1968, 1970, and 1976, Solidarność

(Solidarity), the communist world's first free labor union, was founded in 1980 in the port city of Gdańsk. In alliance with KOR, a group of dissident intellectuals, Solidarność organized strikes and issued political demands that by 1981 threatened to topple the economically fragile and highly unpopular Warsaw government. When the Soviet Union threatened to invade, the United States and its West European allies adopted a strict noninterference policy and also granted substantial loans to stabilize Poland's communist leadership.

The rich amount of documentation that has been published by the Cold War International History Project has furnished crucial details of the Kremlin's tense deliberations, its reactions to NATO's signals, and the ailing Brezhnev's decision *not* to invoke his doctrine and to appoint the Polish loyalist General Wojciech Jaruzelski to stifle Solidarność by imposing martial law and arresting its leaders. Only then did the new US president, Ronald Reagan, retaliate by imposing stiff economic sanctions against both Moscow and Warsaw and also by prohibiting the export of American technology for the construction of the Soviet gas pipeline to Western Europe.

West European leaders, although shocked by Jaruzelski's crackdown, were unconvinced that economic punishment would alter Soviet policy or alleviate Poland's problems, and they imposed far milder sanctions than Washington's.

But once more the Soviet Union suffered a setback, forced to prop up a failing satellite and purchase high-priced grain on the world market while pursuing a costly, unwinnable war in Afghanistan. Under pressure from the Polish pope John Paul II, criticized by Western Socialists and labor leaders, and hurt by US sanctions, Jaruzelski soon had to end martial law and the repression of Solidarność. But, while Reagan stepped up his anti-Soviet policies, Western European governments quietly maintained and even expanded their economic, cultural, and political ties with the East.

The Gorbachev Phenomenon

At age fifty-four, the young and vigorous party loyalist and determined reformer Mikhail Gorbachev became secretary general of the Communist Party of the Soviet Union on March 11, 1985, and during the next six years changed the history of his country, Europe, and the world. Margaret Thatcher, the British prime minister, who had met the new Soviet leader on the eve of his appointment and was impressed by his pledges to end the arms race and his references to Europe as a "common home . . . and not a theater of military operations," stated that here was a man with whom the West could "do business." But Reagan, unimpressed, promoted his Strategic Defense Initiative to protect the United States from a surprise Soviet attack.

Europe's optimism was dampened on April 26, 1986, when one of the four nuclear reactors in Chernobyl, Ukraine, exploded and, without any warning from Moscow, sent megatons of radiation westward, affecting millions of people. Nonetheless, a resolute Gorbachev moved forward, with *glasnost*, which ended censorship and the jamming of foreign broadcasts, released dissidents, and opened Soviet-era archives, and with *perestroika*, the restructuring of the failing Soviet economy. Even more daring in his foreign policy, Gorbachev pressed for an arms control agreement with the United States, took steps to end the war in Afghanistan, and, emphasizing his European credentials, established close personal relationships not only with Conservatives such as Thatcher and Chancellor Helmut Kohl of West Germany but also with the Social Democratic prime minister of Spain, Felipe González.

If today we see the Gorbachev phenomenon through the lens of a collapsed Soviet Empire and a more aggressive Russian state, there are excellent contemporary sources that capture the "Gorby-mania" of the late 1980s: the surprise and excitement stirred by this remarkable leader. Gorbachev's most impressive moment occurred on December 7, 1988, when, in his address to the UN General Assembly, he declared the end of the Cold War, renouncing not only the Yalta settlement but also the ideological struggle between the Soviet Union and the West that had existed since November 1917. Moreover, he explicitly repudiated the Brezhnev doctrine: "Force or the threat of force neither can nor should be instruments of foreign policy. . . . Freedom of choice is a universal principle, which knows no exception." In addition to pledging a halt to the arms race and cutting five hundred thousand men from the Soviet army, Gorbachev announced the withdrawal of fifty thousand soldiers and five thousand tanks from the Soviet forces in Eastern Europe. From the *New York Times* came the conclusion: "Perhaps not since Woodrow Wilson presented his Fourteen Points in 1918 or since Franklin Roosevelt and Winston Churchill promulgated the Atlantic Charter in 1941 has a world figure demonstrated the vision Mikhail Gorbachev displayed yesterday at the United Nations."

The Wall Falls Down

A quarter of a century later, in teaching the heady days of the end of the Cold War in Europe, it is exceedingly important to stress its *noninevitability*, to use contemporary sources to sort out the major elements both chronologically and thematically. Few Westerners, although they welcomed Gorbachev's words and reforms, foresaw the extraordinary events that occurred between 1989 and 1991: the liberation of Eastern Europe from Soviet control, German reunification, and the disintegration of the Soviet Union. To be sure, in most of the world the appeal of Marxism had been supplanted by a resurgence of religion and nationalism as well as by fascination with Reagan and Thatcher's neo-liberalism and by the phenomenal economic achievements of the four East Asian "Tigers" (South Korea, Taiwan, Hong Kong, and Singapore). The Soviet Union, with its polluting heavy industries, technological backwardness, and plummeting gas and oil prices appeared extremely fragile. Nevertheless, in the late 1980s Western pundits continued to accept the permanency of Europe's division (one even predicting the decline in an overextended United States). Thus, when the Czech police in January 1989 cracked down on peaceful Prague demonstrators demanding reforms, neither West European leaders nor the new Bush administration in Washington took special note or protested.

Gorbachev, on the other hand, convinced that top-down domestic reforms would rescue socialism and attract Western aid, was allowing the Soviet satellites unprecedented leeway to experiment (later popularized as his "Sinatra doctrine," from the song "My Way," allowing each to determine its own future). This message spread to two of the Kremlin's most rebellious satellites, Poland and Hungary, whose failing economies Moscow could no longer sustain.

The Western press paid less attention to these quiet reforms than to the horrific events in China. On June 3-4, 1989, only two weeks after Gorbachev's visit, the government ordered a military assault on peaceful demonstrators who for a month had occupied Beijing's Tiananmen Square. East Germany's hard-line leader Erich Honecker applauded Deng Xiaoping's "victory over counterrevolution," but Gorbachev immediately condemned the use of force and reasserted his commitment to our "common European home."

To be sure, another essential element in the transformation of Eastern Europe was the persistent and courageous human rights activists in almost every communist country. By late summer of 1989 the spotlight focused on East Germany, where tens of thousands of citizens had been fleeing to West Germany through Hungary and Czechoslovakia; in Leipzig, in contrast, the weekly candle-carrying marchers were chanting "We are staying here" and demanding Gorbachev-style reforms to rein in the secret police (the infamous Stasi) and to grant the freedoms promised in the Helsinki accord. When these demonstrations spread to the entire country, Honecker contemplated a Tiananmen solution.

Gorbachev, who arrived in East Berlin on October 9 to celebrate East Germany's fortieth anniversary, warned his comrade to heed the people's needs "before it was too late" and ordered Soviet troops to remain in their barracks (a move noted critically by one of the KGB's recruiting officers in Dresden, Vladimir Putin). To stanch the refugee flood and defuse the protests, the East German leadership replaced Honecker and announced a spate of reforms. But it was too late to save the regime and, indeed, the Soviet empire in Eastern Europe.

In one of history's significant chance events, on the night of November 9, 1989, a misinterpreted government announcement on lifting travel restrictions to the West brought huge crowds to the Berlin Wall, forcing the guards to open the gates. Masses of people flooded into West Berlin, where they were received with champagne and flowers, and within hours the world's televisions showed exultant Berliners standing on and dismantling the Cold War's foremost symbol, one that had divided Germany for twenty-eight years.

The fall of the Wall precipitated a cascade of changes in Eastern Europe. Under pressure from popular forces, the communist leadership in Poland, Hungary, Bulgaria, and Czechoslovakia surrendered their power, and only Romania succumbed to violence. Thereupon, political prisoners were released, free elections held, and within two years six countries had removed themselves from Soviet control.

The swiftness of German reunification caught many observers by surprise. Forged in 1990 by two determined collaborators, West German chancellor Helmut Kohl and President George H.W. Bush, it was greatly facilitated by Gorbachev's growing weakness and East Germany's economic collapse and also by an outside event (Iraq's invasion of Kuwait in August 1990) that enabled Bonn to overcome its neighbors' and Moscow's objections, add sixteen million people and forty-two thousand square miles to its territory, and also remain in NATO.

The Soviet Union's collapse may or may not have been inevitable. Scholars are still debating whether a more decisive leader, major structural reforms including the federal solution offered by Gorbachev, and/or greater foreign support could have saved the regime (which many Western leaders until the last minute still preferred), and there is as yet no conclusion. But for Europe, the largely peaceful end of the Soviet Union on Christmas Day 1991, accompanied by the independence of its fifteen republics, ushered in a new stage in its history.

Aftermath

Post–Cold War Europe experienced an eventful decade between the demise of Soviet Union and the attack on the Twin Towers in New York on 9/11: the United States became the world's sole superpower and China commenced its remarkable economic ascendance; some former Soviet republics and countries in Africa and Asia erupted in violence and a militant Islam spread to every continent; technology and globalization transformed the world's economies and markets; and environmentalists issued warnings about climate change and dangers to the earth's air, ground, and water. Within Europe itself, the wars in Yugoslavia and also the expansion of NATO and of the European Union (EU) tested the region's cohesion.

The disintegration of Yugoslavia between 1991 and 1999 exposed the disunity of post–Cold War Europe. Not only was there disagreement among Britain, France, and Germany over recognizing and supporting the secessionist states of the former Yugoslavia and between West European governments and the United States over taking military action to halt Serbian aggression, but also Russia's support of the Serbs placed it at odds with its new Western partners, reinforcing its resentment of the new Pax Americana, which was manifested by NATO's 1999 bombing campaign against Belgrade on behalf of the separatist movement in Kosovo.

NATO expansion stirred additional Russian resentment. The admission of the Czech Republic, Hungary, and Poland to the defense organization in 1999, followed by the entry of Estonia, Latvia, Lithuania, Bulgaria, Romania, Slovakia, and Slovenia in 2004, placed the alliance directly on Russia's borders and raised protests from Moscow of "encirclement." The subsequent proposals to place missile defense systems in Poland and the Czech Republic evoked angry criticism from the Kremlin.

Unlike its negative stance toward NATO expansion, Russia had initially raised no objection to EU enlargement, conceivably in the hope of increasing the presence of pro-Russian sentiments in Brussels. However, by 2004 Moscow's attitude had changed dramatically. It was suddenly faced with the prospect of border controls that would sever its land connection with Kaliningrad; of an enlarged EU Council, where its former satellites criticized its human rights violations in Chechnya; and, especially, of an EU Eastern Partnership program that threatened to include the former Soviet republics of Georgia, Moldova, and Ukraine. After Putin's reelection to the presidency in 2004, charges of EU expansionism became routine in Moscow.

A "New Cold War"?

Relations between Russia and the United States also deteriorated after 2004, and within a decade both sides exchanged charges of inciting a new Cold War. Putin (and also Gorbachev) accused the United States of interference in Russia's internal affairs, starting a new arms race, and "hegemonic" behavior in the Middle East and North Africa. Washington, in turn, chastised Moscow for its stepped-up espionage and military buildup, its human rights violations, and, especially, its aggression against Georgia and Ukraine, and its intervention in the Syrian Civil War. The United States and its allies revived Cold War–era forms of retaliation, including the imposition of sanctions, export bans, and the suspension of collaborative arrangements between Russia and NATO, the European Union, and the G-7 group of advanced industrialized nations.

European leaders, once more at the center of an East-West conflict, gave diverse responses to the chill in US-Russian relations. Several former communist countries on Russia's borders underscored Moscow's violation of the Helsinki principles—the guarantee of territorial integrity and the sovereign ability of every country to choose its alliances—that lay at the core of European security and called on their allies to treat Russia as both "a strategic competitor in the EU's neighborhood" and a "spoiler on the global stage." Others, among them German chancellor Angela Merkel and French president François Hollande, while disapproving of Russia's behavior and also imposing sanctions, did their utmost not to isolate Moscow and to keep diplomatic talks proceeding. In the meantime, in 2014 Crimea was incorporated into Russia, and the eastern provinces of Ukraine became the site of a brutal civil war with more than nine thousand casualties.

Later historians may well incorporate this twenty-first-century Cold War revival into the longer history of Russia's fraught relations with the West, one in which periods of peace have alternated with decades of antagonism. But at least one Cold War lesson can be applied to this latest East-West flare-up: the importance of striking a balance between establishing rules of international conduct and recognizing great-power interests. And from Europe's Cold War, there is also the legacy of the unanticipated: of unexpected economic downturns, of bold leaders who resolved seemingly intractable differences, and of courageous, persistent activists who brought down seemingly impenetrable barriers.

Reflections
on the Cold War in Asia

Then and Now

WARREN I. COHEN

When my book *America in the Age of Soviet Power* (1993) was published, David Reynolds praised it for not being Eurocentric. Ernest May wondered how I could write a history of the Cold War without mentioning Jean Monnet or giving Konrad Adenauer more than a passing reference. Clearly I had failed to conceal the fact that I was more interested in East Asia than in Europe.

I had served as a line officer in the Pacific Fleet in the late 1950s. When I returned to graduate school in 1959, I studied Chinese-American relations. My intended dissertation topic was an attempt to discover when and how the US government had realized that the Chinese Communists were likely to win their struggle against Jiang Jieshi's (Chiang Kai-shek's) Guomindang regime. Failing to obtain research support, I wrote *The American Revisionists* instead but quickly resumed my study of Chinese-American relations, leading to my *America's Response to China*, first published in 1971.

Struggling unsuccessfully to read Qing documents, I found it much easier to read Chinese Communist documents of the 1920s, '30s, and '40s. I chose to focus my research, therefore, on Chinese-American relations during the Cold War. A year after I began teaching at Michigan State, I was fortunate to be shipped to Taipei to teach at National Taiwan University. I was there for two years, improving my Chinese-language skills and teaching American history in general and particularly American diplomatic history to Taiwanese and overseas Chinese students. Not the least of the benefits of my time in Taipei was temporary access to the archives of the Republic of China's Bureau of Investigation, which contain a magnificent collection of Chinese Communist publications and documents captured during the Chinese civil war.

My research in Taipei, supplemented by materials I found in Hong Kong, allowed me to trace the attitudes of the Chinese Communists toward the United States through the 1920s, 1930s, and 1940s, in both published and internal Party documents. I wrote two articles for *Orbis* in 1966 and 1967, unwittingly beginning the debate over the so-called lost chance in China: Could the United States have acted differently toward the Chinese Communists in the 1940s and kept them from becoming an adjunct to Soviet power? I concluded that although the Chinese Communist Party mistrusted the Soviet Union, ideology dictated its choice of sides in the emerging Cold War—that liberal, capitalist America could not likely have outbid Stalin for Mao Zedong's support. That debate raged over the next several decades as documentation from American, Chinese, and Soviet sources became available, especially after the end of the Cold War.

My teaching in Taipei, explaining American foreign policy to Taiwanese and "mainlanders," the young men and women whose parents had fled the mainland during and after the civil war, was also a very rewarding experience. It began, amusingly enough, when my course listing offered only my Chinese name (Kong Huaren) and attracted a CIA operative eager to learn how a Taiwanese or Chinese professor would teach American policy—he never returned for the second lecture.

America's war in Vietnam was intensifying while I was in Taiwan from 1964 to 1966, and I found that Chinese intellectuals who had come to the island from the mainland were highly critical of the burgeoning antiwar movement on university campuses in the United States. They equated the movement with communist subversion on campuses in China. I devoted many an evening to arguing that American dissenters were not communists. But I also met a number of Green Beret officers in Taipei for R&R and was surprised and favorably impressed by their concern for the Vietnamese they perceived themselves as defending. It was not until the Tet offensive in 1968 that I understood that we had failed.

Returning to the United States in the fall of 1966, I found greatly intensified student interest in American-East Asian relations—an interest generated by the escalation of the war in Vietnam. I was involved frequently in on-campus panels discussing the war, and I usually found myself in the center between one colleague who was a leading member of the American Friends of Vietnam, an organization supportive of the Saigon regime, and another colleague who was vehemently antiwar—all wars. I designed well-attended courses at both the graduate and the undergraduate levels that focused exclusively on the historic role of the United States in East Asia, with particular emphasis on the post–World War II era.

It was opposition to the war in Vietnam and claims that it had to be fought to contain the Chinese Communists that politicized the debate over American policy toward China in the late 1940s. Beginning in 1950, as the Korean War brought the Cold War to Asia—and especially after the People's Liberation Army intervened to drive back UN forces—conservative critics of the Truman administration claimed that it had "lost" China, that it had not offered Jiang the support necessary to prevent a communist victory in the Chinese civil war. But in the 1960s, many liberal and radical critics charged Truman and Dean Acheson, his secretary of state, with giving Jiang too much support, failing to respond to opportunities to keep China from allying itself with the Soviet Union. They argued that the administration had driven Mao into Stalin's arms and had lost the chance to establish useful relations with the People's Republic of China. Had American policy not been so intensely anticommunist in the 1940s, they maintained, the United States would not have to be at war in Vietnam to contain China.

In the late 1970s, as Department of State and White House documents for the late 1940s were declassified, it became apparent that Truman and especially Acheson *had* intended to recognize and work with Mao's regime and that their declared policy *had* in fact been to prevent that regime from becoming an adjunct to Soviet power—that they had tried to keep the Cold War out of Asia. That story was presented definitively in *Patterns in the Dust* (1983) by Nancy Bernkopf Tucker (a brilliant young scholar who years later became my wife). Since I had written a brief essay of similar purport, the explanation she offered became known as the "Tucker-Cohen" thesis. The issue will doubtless be argued until the end of time, but materials that eventually became available from Chinese sources confirmed Mao's lack of interest in working with the United States in the late 1940s.

In the 1960s, after the Cuban Missile Crisis, President John Kennedy and Soviet premier Nikita Khrushchev succeeded in taking modest steps toward easing Soviet-American tensions. Mao, on the other hand, ridiculed Khrushchev for condemning Stalin and for backing off in the confrontation with the United States over Cuba. By the mid-1960s, in the context of the Sino-Soviet split, the American national-security apparatus perceived China as the greatest threat to world peace. Simultaneously, leading nongovernmental authorities on foreign affairs and policy toward China in particular, including George Kennan and A. Doak Barnett, were critical of both the war in Vietnam and the efforts to isolate China. Voicing their concerns publicly at open sessions of the Senate Foreign Relations Committee in 1966, they called for "containment *without* isolation." In 1972, on the eve of President Nixon's historic meeting with Mao, Senator William Fulbright (D-AR), chair of the committee, invited me to testify about the history of the relationship.

Nixon's trip to Beijing in 1972, not long after the publication of the first edition of *America's Response to China*, created opportunities for me to travel, to work with Chinese scholars, to interview Chinese officials, and eventually to gain access—limited, to be sure—to Chinese diplomatic documents. I toured China for the first time in 1979, accompanying the governor of Michigan and a delegation of Michigan businessmen. For years afterward, I traveled to China frequently, on behalf of either the state of Michigan (in 1982 I negotiated a Michigan-Sichuan sister state agreement) or Michigan State University's burgeoning empire in China. Chinese newspapers referred to me as a friend of China. That love affair ended with the Tiananmen massacres of 1989.

Cold War tensions in East Asia dissipated after the opening to China and the subsequent end to America's failed effort to halt Hanoi's forceful unification of Vietnam. The normalization of relations between the United States and China was delayed until December 1978 by the Watergate crisis and other domestic political affairs. In January 1979, Deng Xiaoping, de facto ruler of China, carried out a triumphal tour of the United States. The euphoria lasted less than two years, shattered by president-elect Ronald Reagan's threat to reestablish relations with the Republic of China, which had been terminated as a condition of the establishment of diplomatic relations between Beijing and Washington.

As president, Reagan backed away from policies that would have shattered the tacit alliance between China and the United States that had emerged from their shared enmity toward the Soviet Union. He even went to China and had a wonderful time, and for most of his administration Chinese-American relations prospered. Many American analysts, in and out of government, marveled at Deng's economic reforms as China moved toward a market economy (albeit "with Chinese characteristics")—and imagined a liberal democratic China in their lifetime. This was what the historian/journalist James Mann called "the China fantasy." For most Americans, the dream of a China recast in their image, a China that would work with the United States to create a liberal democratic world order, vanished with the events of June 4, 1989. As the Cold War ended in Europe with the collapse of the Soviet Union, the seeds of a new one in Asia were planted in Beijing.

In 1986, I was invited to Beijing to give a series of lectures on Chinese-American relations after World War II. My audience consisted of young officials and intellectuals from all over the country. In return I was given the opportunity to interview a number of Chinese who had played major parts in that relationship. On one occasion, I was summoned to meet with former foreign minister Huang Hua. One of his secretaries— not on the class list—attended my lectures and reported back to him. He called me to his home to "correct" some of my misunderstandings. He, too, saw no lost chance in the 1940s, contending that his meetings with the American ambassador early in 1949 were designed merely to prevent US intervention in the civil war, to try to ease American concerns.

While I was living in Beijing I had many opportunities to drink beer and discuss China's future with Chinese intellectuals. The young ones— those who had been spared the Cultural Revolution of the 1960s and early 1970s—were highly optimistic that political reform would follow economic reforms and were eager to participate in the democratic processes they saw on the horizon. They were dismissive of my fears that the Party would never surrender its monopoly of power—or that they could find themselves in serious trouble if they pressed their views. Soon after I left, Deng ordered another of those campaigns against "bourgeois liberalization." And on June 4, 1989, he met student protests with lethal force.

Some of us had been forewarned. In 1986, a group of American scholars had been invited to Beijing to meet with their Chinese counterparts in the first Chinese-American conference on relations between our two countries from 1945 to 1955. After the conference, we met with Li Peng, then state councilor for education. He welcomed the contributions American scientists were making toward China's modernization. When Harry Harding, speaking for us, remarked that we were *social* scientists, Li said we were welcome also—but that China would never accept American values. It was Li who carried out Deng's orders to send the troops into Tiananmen Square in 1989, after replacing Zhao Ziyang, who had opposed the use of force.

After the Tiananmen massacres, relations between the United States and the People's Republic were strained. President Bush imposed sanctions on China but secretly assured Deng that he still understood the importance of the relationship. Many Americans, including presidential candidate Bill Clinton, were critical of Bush, raging against the "butchers of Beijing."

The Cold War was over, but the question remained as to whether two countries, one a liberal democracy and the other a one-party authoritarian dictatorship contemptuous of liberalism and democracy, could co-exist. The Soviet Union was gone, but China was rapidly increasing its power, becoming a threat to American interests.

The ultimate concern of Clinton as president was the revival of the American economy. To that end, he put aside campaign rhetoric and did everything he could to stimulate trade with China. Sanctions designed to force Chinese respect for human rights were dropped. Permanent most-favored-nation treatment for Chinese goods, once conditioned on Beijing demonstrating improvement in its human rights record, was granted. Clinton appeared to accept the idea, strongly supported by the business community, that more economic exchanges with China would bring that country closer to capitalism—*and* that democracy would follow.

Chinese-American trade and investments are presumably good for both counties—and enormously important to both. In the early twenty-first century China's economy grew with remarkable speed. Its GNP is expected to pass that of the United States before mid-century. At the same time, funds for China's military modernization became readily available, and the People's Republic created a formidable armed force, including a nascent blue-water navy.

The most obvious source of tension between the United States and China in the decades after the normalization of relations in 1979 was American support for the government of the Republic of China on Taiwan—considered by Beijing to be part of China, a renegade province. That government was a remnant of Jiang's Nationalist regime, which had control of the mainland during the civil war of the late 1940s. When I lived on the island in the mid-1960s, Jiang's administration, run by refugees from the mainland, was repressive and resented by the native

34

Taiwanese. I was hostile to it and was once warned by an American military intelligence officer that I was on a hit list—a threat that greatly exaggerated my importance. I had no regrets when the Carter administration abrogated the mutual defense agreement with Taipei in 1979—a condition of normalization of relations with Beijing. Congress, however, passed the Taiwan Relations Act, requiring the United States to sell Taiwan whatever arms it needed to defend itself, outraging Deng and his comrades.

Against my advice, Nancy Bernkopf Tucker chose to write a history of US-Taiwan relations, and, after our marriage, when she became the world's leading authority on the subject, she constantly dragged me into Taiwan affairs. Happily, the Taiwan government morphed into a democracy, and I joined most Americans, liberal and conservative, in wishing it well and hoping for its continued autonomy.

At the turn of the century, the Taiwan Strait was widely viewed as the most dangerous place in the world, the point at which two major powers, China and the United States, might be dragged into a military confrontation. This was especially true when the Democratic Progressive Party pushed a pro-independence agenda early in the twenty-first century.

Perhaps fortunately, the return of the Nationalists to power in 2008 led to an easing of tensions between Taipei and Beijing. The Cross Strait issue did not disappear, but the men and women who dealt with it in Washington were able to relax. Hopes for a smooth integration of a rising China into the world order were quickly dashed, however, when Xi Jinping, China's new leader, chose to pursue a more assertive foreign policy.

It quickly became evident that Xi's China intended to become the dominant power in the Western Pacific and that it was unwilling to accept a continuation of the role the United States had played in the region since the end of World War II. Chinese planes and ships harass American military operations in international waters. Xi wooed South Korea, hoping to weaken Seoul's ties to Washington. He and his colleagues made extravagant claims to waters, islands, and rocks claimed by neighboring states. They intensified long-standing tensions with Japan over islands the Japanese called the Senkakus and the Chinese insisted were the Diaoyus.

Perhaps most troubling is mounting evidence that Xi's regime is more repressive than the Hu Jintao and Jiang Zemin administrations that preceded it. Censorship of the Internet, "the Great Firewall," prevents most Chinese from access to sources of information other than those approved by the Party. Dissenters, including human rights lawyers, are routinely imprisoned on trumped-up charges. The Nobel Peace Prize winner Liu Xiaobo rots in jail while police torment his wife. It is a government that challenges the patience of even the most dedicated American apologists. And yet the United States and China must find a path to what Soviet and American analysts once called peaceful coexistence.

Although few among us predicted the collapse of the Soviet Union and although some prominent specialists on China believe that it will collapse before it equals the United States in power, the twenty-first century is most likely to be marked by constant Chinese challenges to American primacy. A military confrontation is not inconceivable. But the threat from China, the threat of a new Cold War, is very different from the threat posed by the Soviet Union at the peak of its power. China gives no indication of seeking world domination. It no longer has an ideology that it seeks to plant across the globe. Its goals, expressed principally in nationalist terms, are to restore China's historic place among nations and specifically to dominate East Asia and the Western Pacific. It will frequently seek to undermine American interests and influence, but it is not likely to pose a threat to the security of the United States.

To live in peace with the new Chinese empire, Americans will have to learn to live with a contemptible government—and hope that, as with the Soviet Union, change will come from within.

PART TWO

Traditional Topics, New Perspectives

Origins of the Cold War

JESSICA ELKIND

W hen did the Cold War start, and who was responsible for its onset?" "How did the origins of the
Cold War shape international relations in subsequent decades?" These
are complicated and somewhat loaded questions. Whenever I pose such
questions to my students—whether I am teaching an undergraduate lecture course on twentieth-century American foreign relations or a graduate seminar on the United States and the Cold War—I always receive a
diverse array of answers. The seemingly straightforward query about
when the Cold War began elicits responses that range from the final
months of the First World War to the late 1940s or 1950. Even after discussing the various possibilities for some time, my students rarely agree
on a year, much less a specific date, for the inception of the prolonged
superpower conflict that characterized so much of the twentieth century.
They also disagree on which factors or individuals caused the Cold War
and how simple but fundamental differences among the large powers
manifested as tension and competition in every corner of the globe. And
that sense of complexity regarding the early Cold War is exactly what I
hope to convey.

In teaching about the Cold War's origins, I have three major goals.
First, I try to frame the Cold War period as one that consisted both of a
continuation of policies and behavior set in motion decades before the
1940s and also of significant departures from the established world
order. Rather than present the early Cold War entirely as a break from
past developments, I encourage students to consider similarities with
earlier periods and ongoing trends. Doing so provides a deeper sense
of historical perspective and allows students to understand the Cold
War within broader transformations in international relations. It also

allows students to think about some of the intellectual and pedagogical problems inherent to "origins" narratives and the limitations of "the Cold War" as an analytical category. Students may be asked to consider whether the very idea of the Cold War should be viewed primarily as a construction of policymakers and scholars rather than as a description of reality. Second, I hope to dispel any assumptions that the Cold War was inevitable. I stress the contingency of the various actors involved by focusing on individual decision making. I urge my students to consider how leaders on each side of the "Iron Curtain" played a part in escalating tensions. Finally, I present the Cold War as a global phenomenon, which from the outset had far-reaching implications for people all over the world. Although many students conceive of the conflict as an ideological, military, and economic contest between the United States and the Soviet Union, I contend that it was far more multipolar than such a simple formulation suggests. Not only were individuals and groups from other countries directly affected by the policies and behavior of the superpowers, but also many participated willingly in the struggle and contributed to political polarization domestically, regionally, or internationally. Intricately linked with the mid-twentieth-century process of decolonization, the Cold War concerned and affected a huge segment of the world's population from its inception.

There are many primary sources from the early Cold War period that are readily available and accessible to students. I rely heavily on the second volume of *Major Problems in American Foreign Relations*.[1] Like the other volumes in this series, each chapter contains well-selected historical documents as well as a series of short essays written by preeminent historians. Not only do I assign the chapter that specifically focuses on the origins of the Cold War; I also ask students to read documents and essays from earlier chapters, many of which are directly relevant to the causes and significance of the early Cold War. Although I use other sources to supplement the *Major Problems* text, this collection provides a single volume with many documents that are central to understanding the origins of the Cold War.

Continuity and Change

My lectures on and discussions of the origins of the Cold War focus heavily on events that occurred during the 1940s. However, I also encourage students to look for the pre–World War II foundations of the conflict and to think about the Cold War era as one characterized by continuity as well as rupture.

In terms of the pre-1945 roots of the superpower contest, one logical starting point is to consider American responses to the Bolshevik Revolution of 1917 and the subsequent Russian Civil War. Just as the Cold War had foreign and domestic implications, American responses to the Bolshevik Revolution manifested at home and abroad during the late 1910s and early 1920s. For example, American support for the White Army, particularly in Siberia and Czechoslovakia, fueled Soviet suspicions that the United States and its European allies were seeking to weaken the nascent government in Moscow. On the domestic scene, the First Red Scare can be seen as a precursor to the discriminatory practices and repressive policies of the McCarthy era. As a way of encouraging students to think more deeply about antecedents of the Cold War, I often ask them to compare and contrast the First Red Scare and McCarthyism. They find many parallels, including US officials' intolerance for any criticism, their profound distrust of expressions of radicalism, and their explicit attempts to weaken the American labor movement. But there were also important differences, especially regarding the sophistication and coordination of the various government agencies involved in identifying and punishing suspected subversives. And these distinctions can lead to fruitful discussions about the evolving nature of the state and its role in American life. For example, considering the Federal Bureau of Investigation's activities invites students to think critically about the expansion of state power in the 1940s and 1950s and the implications for Americans' freedom of expression and privacy.

Although tensions certainly existed between the new Bolshevik government in Moscow and US policymakers, there were also important instances of cooperation and attempts made by both sides to coexist peacefully in the decades following the First World War. When discussing international cooperation during the 1920s, I include an overview of US foreign assistance programs to the Soviet Union. For example, in 1927 the US government sent a group of advisers to "modernize" Russian agriculture and to introduce Russian farmers to industrial agriculture.[2] I also explain that the Soviet Union was one of sixty-two nations to adopt and sign the Kellogg-Briand Pact. Although the Kellogg-Briand Pact fell far short of its lofty goal to outlaw war, Joseph Stalin's endorsement of the Pact suggests his interest in having the Soviet Union included in the international community. By the end of 1933, the United

States and other major powers, including Great Britain, France, Germany, and Japan, formally recognized the Soviet Union. And contact and cooperation occurred in the private sector, as well. Several American corporations did business with the Russians, and some even opened factories on Russian soil during the 1920s and 1930s. Perhaps the most noteworthy example of this trend is the 1929 agreement between the Ford Motor Company and the Moscow government. According to the arrangement, the Soviet Union would purchase millions of dollars' worth of cars and automobile parts from Ford in exchange for technical assistance on the construction of an automobile manufacturing plant at Nizhny Novgorod (or Gorky, as it was known during the Cold War). I hope that these examples of US-Soviet cooperation encourage students to think critically about the issue of inevitability and to consider alternative ways that the superpowers might have related in the years after 1945.

In addition to discussing specific aspects of Soviet-US relations from 1917 on, I ask students to think about how the attitudes and approach of US policymakers in the early Cold War represented a fundamental acceptance of previous American leaders' vision about the role and responsibilities of the United States in the world. For example, when discussing Franklin Roosevelt's assumption that the United States would serve as an international leader during and after the Second World War, I remind students of Theodore Roosevelt's belief that the United States should act as a global police force. I also invite students to compare and contrast imperial projects pursued by the United States and other powers in the late nineteenth and early twentieth centuries with American efforts during subsequent decades. Many students see significant overlap between various tools of empire and policies introduced during the 1940s and 1950s. For example, like the civilizing mission of Western colonial powers in the late nineteenth century, American modernization efforts in the early Cold War resulted from a strong sense of cultural superiority and a "developmentalist" instinct.

One document I use to encourage my students to think about earlier models for Cold War policy is Franklin Roosevelt's 1937 "Quarantine Speech."[3] In October 1937, a few months after the Japanese initiated a full-scale invasion of China, President Roosevelt delivered an important address in Chicago in which he condemned Japanese expansion. Roosevelt argued that "international anarchy" and aggressive nations constituted "a matter of vital interest and concern to the people of the United

States," that that they threatened "the very foundations of civilization." FDR's recommendation for how the United States should deal with such behavior relied on a medical metaphor, in which he described "world lawlessness" as an epidemic, and depended on active intervention in international affairs as a way to contain the spread of that disease. As Roosevelt explained, "When an epidemic of physical disease starts to spread, the community approves and joins in a quarantine of the patients in order to protect the health of the community against the spread of the disease." When read next to sources such as George Kennan's 1947 "X" article, FDR's Quarantine Speech appears to be a strong model for containment policy. For a more detailed examination of Kennan's use of illness metaphors, as well as gendered rhetoric in early Cold War discourse, teachers and students might also consult Frank Costigliola's 1997 article "Unceasing Pressure for Penetration."[4]

Contingency and the Role of Individuals

Many scholars argue that US-Soviet relations began to unravel even as the Allied powers worked together during the Second World War. Although the wartime partnership represented the high point of Soviet-American cooperation in the first half of the twentieth century, this was clearly an alliance of convenience resulting from a temporary alignment of interests. After the German army invaded Russian territory, in violation of the Nazi-Soviet Nonaggression Pact, Stalin had little choice but to join forces with the Allied powers and to cooperate with American and British strategists. Russian troops played a critical role in defeating the Nazis in Europe, and Stalin provided at least lukewarm support for Jiang Jieshi (Chiang Kai-Shek) at the expense of the communist forces led by Mao Zedong in China. But relations among the Allies were fraught with tension and were characterized by mistrust and suspicion on the part of the leaders involved. This was especially true in the case of British-Soviet interactions.

In teaching about US-Soviet relations during the early 1940s, I focus in particular on wartime diplomacy among the Allied leaders, especially the "Big Three": Franklin Roosevelt, Joseph Stalin, and Winston Churchill. Considering the wartime conferences among these leaders, as well as other conferences at the foreign-minister level, encourages students to think beyond the US-Soviet dichotomy and to consider the role and place of other powers.

The Allied leaders' disparate visions for the postwar world manifested in their discussions and decision making at the wartime conferences. This was particularly true in the case of the conferences dedicated to the creation of the United Nations, the new international organization designed to replace the defunct League of Nations. After explaining some of the debates over membership, powers, and responsibilities of the UN that erupted during conferences such as the one at Dumbarton Oaks in the fall of 1944, I ask students to read important sections of the charter of the United Nations.[5] Students then participate in an in-class activity in which I divide them into small groups and ask them to consider how the victors of World War II attempted to exert their influence and protect their core interests in the new world order. I also ask the students to discuss the advantages and challenges that membership in the United Nations presented to various nations. For example, students may conclude that a relatively weak state, such as Nicaragua or Poland, would derive significant benefits from membership. In cases like these, the international community might serve as a check on the influence of stronger regional powers, such as the United States or the Soviet Union. This activity encourages students to consider the competing interests and priorities of the major powers and also to think about how superpower rivalries might affect smaller, less powerful populations.

In addition to discussing negotiations and outcomes of the major wartime conferences, I use photos from those conferences to help illustrate the mood and relationships of the leaders involved. For example, photos from the Tehran Conference in late 1943 and the Yalta Conference of early 1945 show Churchill, Roosevelt, and Stalin seated together.[6] Not only do these photos humanize these larger-than-life historical figures; they also capture certain aspects of the dynamics at play among the leaders. While my students look at these photos on a large screen, I ask them to share their impressions about the men and their relationships. Students mention the fact that Roosevelt is always seated between Stalin and Churchill, and they sometimes comment that Churchill's expression indicates his discomfort with the situation. They often suggest that this seating arrangement can serve as a metaphor for understanding the dynamics of these complicated relationships, in which Roosevelt served as an intermediary between the other two and enjoyed a better relationship with both Britain and the Soviet Union than they did with each other. Some students also comment on the leaders' attire, which prompts a conversation about what military dress (in the case of Stalin and

Churchill) or civilian clothes tell us about each leaders' background and the relationship among the military, government, and society in the respective countries. Examining these photos also invites a discussion about the importance of individual actors and historical contingency— it is difficult to consider these photos without thinking about how particular leaders' proclivities, biases, and behavior shaped national policies and international relations.

1945 and Beyond: A New World?

Given the influence of individual leaders on international dynamics, students might be asked to consider whether Roosevelt's death marked an important turning point and how it contributed to the onset of the Cold War. The timing of Roosevelt's death, which occurred as World War II was coming to a close, likely added to the general instability at the end of the war. Although Roosevelt had cultivated a relatively good working relationship with Stalin, tensions were far more strained between the Soviet premier and FDR's successor. While Roosevelt displayed some understanding of Stalin's fear about a remilitarized Germany or unfriendly states on Russia's borders, Harry Truman proved far less sympathetic to Russian interests and security concerns. By 1946, the Truman administration's "Get Tough" policy had replaced FDR's attempts at accommodation with the Soviet Union.

As some scholars have argued, Truman's indifference to Soviet demands likely derived, at least in part, from his own insecurities and lack of experience. When Roosevelt died, in April 1945, Truman had been serving as his vice president for less than three months. For various reasons, including his declining health, his access to more-trusted advisers, and his autonomous governing style, FDR had done very little to prepare his new vice president to assume the presidency, especially when it came to foreign-policy matters. Truman's inexperience and distance from FDR's inner circle of advisers became particularly important in the summer of 1945, when American scientists successfully tested an atomic bomb.

In our discussions about the origins of the Cold War, I ask students to consider why Truman decided to use the devastating new weapon to end the Second World War and the implications of that decision. These questions could also be used as essay prompts on a midterm or final exam. I assign an excerpt from a report issued by scientists who had worked on developing the atomic bomb in which the group recommended that the United States stage a demonstration of the new weapon rather than a surprise attack on Japan. The Franck Committee's recommendations to Secretary of War Henry Stimson were clear—using the atomic bomb to end the war would have devastating consequences. The scientists argued, "If the United States would be the first to release this new means of indiscriminate destruction upon mankind, she would sacrifice public support throughout the world, precipitate the race of armaments, and prejudice the possibility of reaching an international agreement on the future control of such weapons."[7] In class, I invite discussion about why the Truman administration rejected the scientists' recommendations. Students consider the various options for ending the Pacific War that Truman had available in the summer of 1945, such as an American-led invasion of the Japanese islands, a blockade, a demonstration of the atomic bomb and a strongly worded warning to the Japanese leadership, or a joint US-Soviet military assault. I encourage my students to try to put themselves in Truman's shoes as we discuss the pros and cons of each scenario and debate why American policymakers settled on the surprise attack.

After the United States used the devastating new weapons on Japan in August 1945, the specter of atomic warfare only contributed to escalating tensions between the United States and the Soviet Union. Those tensions resulted in the security dilemma and a nuclear arms race. Leaders from the United States and the Soviet Union both claimed to act in defense of their nation's vital interests. However, each side viewed the other's actions as a fundamental threat. In order to illustrate how this cycle bred insecurity and increasingly confrontational behavior— and also to suggest the shared responsibility for the onset of the Cold War—I focus on a series of "crisis" moments and subsequent decision making by American and Soviet officials during the second half of the 1940s. I emphasize that both sides contributed to the rising tensions through their efforts to extend their influence throughout the world. And, whenever appropriate, I also include the behavior and policies of other actors to highlight the role of individuals outside the United States or the Soviet Union in advancing the Cold War.

In many ways, 1946 proved to be a pivotal year in the emerging Cold War. One of the key reasons for the deterioration of Soviet-American relations was the way that policymakers on each side understood (or misunderstood) the other side and its interests. Diplomats from the

United States and the Soviet Union played a central role in shaping how leaders and the public in both countries viewed their rival. Students can get a glimpse of each side's assessment of the other by reading a few primary documents from the time. George Kennan's "Long Telegram," which he sent to his superiors in Washington, DC, in February 1946, provides a good starting point for considering how Americans viewed their Russian adversaries.[8] Kennan served as a diplomat in the Balkans and in Russia during the 1930s and early 1940s, and he became one of the foremost American experts on Russian affairs. By the early 1940s, Kennan had become disillusioned with US policy toward the Soviet Union, arguing that cooperation between the two powers was unrealistic. In his influential "Long Telegram," Kennan provided a scathing explanation for aggressive Soviet behavior, which he argued resulted from a "traditional and instinctive Russian sense of insecurity" combined with a "dangerous and insidious" form of Marxism. Kennan concluded that Soviet leaders were "committed fanatically to the belief that with the US there can be no permanent modus vivendi," and he suggested that those leaders needed to destroy the American way of life and break the international authority of the United States in order to ensure their own security. Although he did not claim to have all the answers for how to address the challenges posed by the Soviet Union, Kennan offered some concrete suggestions for how the United States might respond without becoming engaged in a direct military conflict. Claiming that the Russians were both relatively weak and "highly sensitive to the logic of force," Kennan argued that strong and unified resistance from the United States and its Western allies would deter Moscow.

Students might also read part or all of Kennan's "The Sources of Soviet Conduct" (commonly known as the "X" article), which appeared as an anonymous contribution to *Foreign Affairs* magazine in July 1947.[9] This article repeated much of the analysis of Soviet behavior and policies that Kennan first presented in his "Long Telegram," but it also offered a more forceful prescription for how the United States might deal with Soviet policies. Describing the Soviet Union as "a rival, not a partner, in the political arena," Kennan argued that "the main element of any United States policy toward the Soviet Union must be that of a long-term, patient but firm and vigilant containment of Russian expansive tendencies."

As a counterpoint to Kennan's "Long Telegram" and "X" article, I ask students to read a cable sent a few months later by the Soviet ambassador to the United States. Ambassador Nikolai Novikov's assessment of American foreign policy reveals a perspective that is fundamentally different from that of US officials and sheds light on how Soviet officials viewed the United States as a threat to their interests.[10] Novikov describes how the American military buildup, secret agreements between the United States and Britain to divide the world, and internal political developments that sought to silence advocates for cooperation with the Soviet Union clearly indicated that the United States was "striving for world supremacy." After students have read Kennan's and Novikov's pieces, I invite a discussion of differences in how each side viewed its own interests and the ambitions of its rival, as well as how those assessments might have shaped policy. Students might also be asked to participate in an in-class activity in which they pretend to be American, Soviet, Chinese, or British advisers during the mid-1940s. On the basis of their reading of Kennan, Novikov, and other sources, the student-advisers could present their impressions of their rivals to their respective leaders (that is, the rest of the class and instructor).

I also ask students to read and comment on Churchill's "Iron Curtain" speech.[11] The former British prime minister, who was highly respected for his staunch opposition to the Nazis during World War II, delivered this speech in Fulton, Missouri, in May 1946. Relying on alarmist rhetoric, Churchill spoke passionately about the "difficulties and dangers" posed by the "expansive and proselytizing tendencies" of the Soviet Union. He told his American audience that "an iron curtain has descended across the continent" of Europe, and he warned of the "challenge and peril to Christian civilization" posed by communist "fifth columns" in other parts of the world. Reading Churchill's speech encourages students to think about how American allies contributed to rising tensions and played an important role in political and ideological polarization throughout the world.

During the years after 1946, superpower tensions continued to mount, largely as a result of American and Soviet policymakers taking more hard-line positions. Leaders in Washington and Moscow also put increasing pressure on their allies and client states, as well as on their own populations, to adopt their respective dogmas and beliefs. In the United States, this meant subscribing to staunch anticommunism even if that led to support for authoritarian governments or violated the professed anti-imperialist sensibilities of many Americans.

On the US side, I focus especially on the Truman Doctrine, the Marshall Plan, and the Point Four program. Each of these programs provided assistance to local pro-American forces. All three laid the foundation for one of the most important ways that the United States would wage its war against the Soviet Union in future decades—not through direct military confrontation but by propping up "friendly" governments, aiding foreign militaries, and attempting to "win hearts and minds" through economic development and technical assistance. In the case of the Truman Doctrine, I frame US financial support for anti-communists in southern Europe as primarily a reaction to decolonization and shifting regional power. Here I borrow from Thomas McCormick's interpretation that Truman's request for $400 million in aid to Greek and Turkish forces was largely a response to British policymakers' call for US assistance. As the British Empire crumbled in the Mediterranean and in the Middle East, officials in London and Washington became concerned with maintaining trading partners and securing continued access to resources, in particular oil.[12]

American efforts to aid in the postwar reconstruction of Western Europe polarized the continent and appear to have strengthened Stalin's determination to extend Soviet influence throughout Eastern Europe. In class, I read excerpts from Secretary of State George Marshall's graduation address at Harvard University in June 1947. In that speech, Marshall laid out the basic concept of the European Recovery Plan, without providing any particular details about how the program would function on the ground.[13] Marshall linked capitalist economic growth with political stability in Europe, and he argued that American economic and security interests were directly tied to the European recovery. He said, "It is logical that the United States should do whatever it is able to do to assist in the return of normal economic health to the world, without which there can be no political stability and no assured peace." Moreover, Marshall portrayed the program not as a challenge to the Soviet Union but as a universal offer of assistance. He claimed, "Our policy is not directed against any country, but against hunger, poverty, desperation and chaos. Any government that is willing to assist in recovery will find full co-operation on the part of the USA. Its purpose should be the revival of a working economy in the world so as to permit the emergence of political and social conditions in which free institutions can exist." After reading these excerpts, I invite a discussion of the Marshall Plan and its role in accelerating the Cold War. I ask students to consider the intended audience(s) for Secretary Marshall's speech, how Soviet leaders might have interpreted his remarks and the program, and how the Marshall Plan signaled American intentions in Europe and elsewhere.

Although students are usually familiar with the Truman Doctrine and the Marshall Plan, many have never heard of Truman's Point Four program before. I begin by outlining the first three major "points" in Truman's 1949 Inaugural Address, which deal with US support for the United Nations, the importance of European economic recovery, and the need for a collective security agreement for countries in the North Atlantic. Then I ask one student to read the fourth point in its entirety.[14] Doing so not only gives students a sense of Truman's vision but also reveals how confrontational American rhetoric had become by the end of the decade. In his inaugural address, Truman outlined his plan to use technical assistance and foreign aid to "modernize" underdeveloped countries and to fight the Cold War in the "third world." In effect, the Point Four program would extend the Truman Doctrine and Marshall Plan into the decolonizing world. Truman's focus on spreading American influence in formerly colonized areas suggests the global nature of the competition between the United States and the Soviet Union as well as the intersection between the early Cold War and the major transformations that accompanied decolonization in the mid-twentieth century. After listening to this portion of the inaugural address, I ask students to consider how original or novel Truman's proposals were, and I invite a discussion about the significance of American and Soviet attention to areas of the world that those powers had previously considered to be peripheral to their interests and security.

In addition to looking at American policies during the Truman years, I encourage students to consider how Soviet leaders, especially Stalin, contributed to escalating tensions and the security dilemma. A number of scholars have placed considerable blame on Stalin for igniting the Soviet-American rivalry through his expansionist policies in Eastern Europe, the Mediterranean, and East Asia, especially Manchuria. For example, I present students with the perspective of the historian John Lewis Gaddis, who describes Stalin as a classic imperialist.[15] In Gaddis's view, Stalin was motivated less by the revolutionary and anti-imperialist ideology of his predecessors such as Vladimir Lenin than by his own desire to extend Soviet authority and hegemony, as well as his belief that the Soviet Union had earned a place as one of the world's most powerful and important nations as a result of its sacrifices and contributions during the Second World War.

To illustrate Stalin's somewhat schizophrenic behavior, which was at once ambitious and risk averse, I provide a number of examples in which Stalin first pushed his advantage but then acquiesced to Western demands rather than confront the United States military head on. For example, I discuss the 1946 "Iran crisis," in which Stalin initially delayed removing Russian troops from Iran following the end of the Second World War. However, as Anglo-American pressure for a Soviet withdrawal mounted in the spring of 1946, Stalin backed down relatively quickly. The Berlin Blockade also illustrates Stalin's willingness to back down in the face of an American challenge. In retrospect, Stalin's decision to cut off the western portions of Berlin from the rest of Western Europe may appear to be a desperate move in response to Russian fears about the integration of Germany into the West and the threats to Soviet influence posed by the Marshall Plan. However, at the time, American policymakers viewed the blockade as a challenge to American interests and prestige, and they determined to take a strong stand. When they did so, in the form of the ongoing airlift, Stalin once again backed down in the face of Western resistance and a display of American military power. I often ask students, either as an exam question or during a classroom conversation, to discuss the lessons that American policymakers drew from Stalin's behavior and decisions during the late 1940s.

Just as the start of the Cold War is difficult to pinpoint, the timing of the transition from the early period to the later years of full-fledged hostilities is somewhat ambiguous. I usually conclude my discussions of the "origins" of the Cold War by focusing on two pivotal developments: the end of the Chinese Civil War and the release of an influential American policy report, known as National Security Council Paper No. 68 or NSC-68. The victory of the Chinese communists in late 1949 not only marked the culmination of more than twenty years of intermittent fighting but also seemed to threaten vital US interests throughout Asia. Partially in response to fears about potential Soviet-Chinese cooperation, the National Security Council issued its policy report in April 1950. I assign a portion of NSC-68 to demonstrate how American policymakers intended to wage the Cold War going forward—through a massive military buildup and redoubled effort at containing the spread of communism throughout the world.[16]

As this essay suggests, teaching about the origins of the Cold War is hardly a straightforward exercise in assigning blame or explaining causality. Questions about when, how, and why the United States and the Soviet Union became archenemies and how the superpower conflict affected the rest of the world produce a range of answers, depending on one's perspective. Fortunately, educators can rely on a host of revealing primary sources to help their students grapple with these important issues and to think more deeply about this central aspect of twentieth-century world history.

NOTES

1. Dennis Merrill and Thomas Paterson, eds., *Major Problems in American Foreign Relations*, Vol. II: *Since 1914* (Boston: Wadsworth Cenage, 2005).

2. For more on the Soviet agricultural development program, see Deborah Fitzgerald's *Every Farm a Factory: The Industrial Ideal in American Agriculture* (New Haven: Yale University Press, 2010).

3. Roosevelt's "Quarantine Speech" can be found in US Department of State, *Papers Relating to the Foreign Relations of the United States*, Vol. 1: *Japan: 1931–1941* (Washington, DC: Government Printing Office, 1943), 379–83.

4. Frank Costigliola, "'Unceasing Pressure for Penetration': Gender, Pathology, and Emotion in George Kennan's Formation of the Cold War," *Journal of American History* 83, no. 4 (March 1997): 1309–39.

5. The UN charter can be found online at http://www.un.org/en /documents/charter/.

6. Historical photographs from the various World War II conferences can be found online, either by searching Google Images or by visiting a specific website such as the *Life* magazine photo archive, http://images.google.com /hosted/life.

7. An excerpt of the Franck Committee report appears in Merrill and Paterson, *Major Problems in American Foreign Relations*, Vol. II. The original document can be found in "Political and Social Problems," June 11, 1945, Manhattan Engineering District Papers, National Archives, Washington, DC.

8. Merrill and Paterson's *Major Problems in American Foreign Relations* contains an excerpt from Kennan's "Long Telegram," 2:192–95.

9. George Kennan's "Sources of Soviet Conduct" can be found at http:// www.foreignaffairs.com/articles/23331/x/the-sources-of-soviet-conduct.

10. A portion of Novikov's memo can be found in Merrill and Paterson, *Major Problems in American Foreign Relations*, 2:197–200.

11. Merrill and Paterson, *Major Problems in American Foreign Relations*, contains the text of Churchill's "Iron Curtain" speech, 2:195–97.

12. See Thomas McCormick, *America's Half-Century* (Baltimore: Johns Hopkins University Press, 1995), for a compelling discussion about the connections between decolonization in the Mediterranean and the Truman Doctrine.

13. The text of Marshall's speech at Harvard University can be found at http://www.oecd.org/general/themarshallplanspeechatharvarduniversity june1947.htm.

14. The text of Truman's Inaugural Address can be found, among other places, on the Truman Library's website, http://www.trumanlibrary.org /whistlestop/50yr_archive/inagural20jan1949.htm.

15. See for example, John Lewis Gaddis, *The United States and the Origins of the Cold War* (New York: Columbia University Press, 1972), and Gaddis, *We Now Know: Rethinking Cold War History* (Oxford: Oxford University Press, 1997). For a counterpoint to Gaddis's depiction of Stalin, see Vladislav Zubok and Constantine Pleshakov, *Inside the Kremlin's Cold War: From Stalin to Khrushchev* (Cambridge, MA: Harvard University Press, 1997). Zubok and Pleshakov rely on declassified material from the archives in Moscow to shed light on Stalin's thinking and to reconstruct Soviet decision making.

16. A portion of NSC-68 can be found in Merrill and Paterson, *Major Problems in American Foreign Relations*, Vol. II, and the full document can be found in US Department of State, *Foreign Relations of the United States, 1950, National Security Affairs; Foreign Economic Policy* (Washington, DC: Government Printings Office, 1977).

KEY RESOURCES

Appy, Christian, ed. *Cold War Constructions: The Political Culture of United States Imperialism, 1945–1966*. Amherst: University of Massachusetts Press, 2000.

Chen, Jian. *Mao's China and the Cold War*. Chapel Hill: University of North Carolina Press, 2001.

Craig, Campbell, and Sergey Radchenko. *The Atomic Bomb and the Origins of the Cold War*. New Haven: Yale University Press, 2008.

Gaddis, John Lewis. *The United States and the Origins of the Cold War, 1941–1947*. New York: Columbia University Press, 2000.

Hasegawa, Tsuyoshi. *Racing the Enemy: Stalin, Truman, and the Surrender of Japan*. Cambridge, MA: Belknap Press of Harvard University Press, 2006.

Leffler, Melvyn. *A Preponderance of Power: National Security, the Truman Administration, and the Cold War*. Stanford: Stanford University Press, 1993.

Leffler, Melvyn, and David Painter, eds. *Origins of the Cold War: An International History*. New York: Routledge, 2005.

Levering, Ralph, et al. *Debating the Origins of the Cold War: American and Russian Perspectives*. Lanham, MD: Rowman & Littlefield, 2002.

McKenzie, Brian Angus. *Remaking France: Americanization, Public Diplomacy, and the Marshall Plan*. New York: Berghahn Books, 2005.

Offner, Arnold. *Another Such Victory: President Truman and the Cold War, 1945–1953*. Stanford: Stanford University Press, 2002.

Raack, R. C. *Stalin's Drive to the West, 1938–1945*. Stanford: Stanford University Press, 1995.

Schrecker, Ellen. *The Age of McCarthyism: A Brief History with Documents*. Boston: Bedford/St. Martin's, 2001.

Westad, Odd Arne. *Decisive Encounters: The Chinese Civil War, 1946–1950*. Stanford: Stanford University Press, 2003.

Two Scorpions in a Bottle

Nuclear Weapons and the Cold War

SHANE J. MADDOCK

In 1953, the famed atomic scientist J. Robert Oppenheimer warned that the United States and the Soviet Union could become like "two scorpions in a bottle, each capable of killing the other, but only at the risk of his own life."[1] As the scientific chief of the Manhattan Project created to produce the first nuclear weapons, Oppenheimer had been exultant at the first successful test of atomic bomb in July 1945. But, eight years later, Oppenheimer had grave doubts about the development of thermonuclear weapons, bombs that were thousands of times more powerful than the weapons used against Hiroshima and Nagasaki. His "scorpions in a bottle" metaphor captured quite vividly the dynamics of the nuclear arms race, which became a central and defining feature of the Cold War between the two postwar superpowers. The atom bombs he helped develop destroyed the Japanese cities of Hiroshima and Nagasaki in August 1945 and signaled an end to World War II, but they kindled the flame of a new international conflict. The fact that the United States and Great Britain had kept their collaboration on atomic weapons secret stirred deep suspicions in Soviet premier Joseph Stalin, and before the year ended he ordered a previously modest Soviet bomb project to proceed "on a Russian scale."[2] With those words, the Cold War–era nuclear arms race had begun.

Because the Cold War, the nuclear arms race, and the end of World War II are so deeply intertwined, when teaching about the nuclear arms race one often has to begin with the origins of the American bomb project in the late 1930s. US efforts to produce an atomic bomb had their roots in fears that Nazi Germany might acquire one. The US-British effort to beat Adolf Hitler to the punch thus constituted the first nuclear arms race. Although its impact has been exaggerated in popular accounts, an effective primary source for teaching students about this phase of the nuclear arms race is the letter that Albert Einstein and Leo Szilard sent to President Franklin Roosevelt in August 1939 warning him that German scientists had taken the lead in nuclear physics and might have already made progress toward producing atomic weapons. It is readily available on multiple Web sites. The letter highlights that the discovery of nuclear fission—the process of inducing certain elements to split their atoms, thereby releasing enormous energy—coincided with the outbreak of World War II. Einstein and Szilard also illustrate the European brain drain that contributed to the American and British bomb projects. Both men fled Central Europe to escape Nazi Germany's anti-Jewish policies. Other scientists, such as Enrico Fermi, did the same and made important contributions to the Manhattan Project.

Films are valuable classroom tools for teaching about this period, and the fiftieth anniversary of the atomic bombings produced a number of important documentaries. *Hiroshima: Why the Bomb Was Dropped* (1995) has won plaudits from many nuclear history specialists for its treatment of the Manhattan Project, the decision to use the bomb against Japanese cities, and the way in which policymakers tried to preempt debate about the bomb decision after the war ended. The film started as an ABC News special reacting to the successful efforts by veterans' organizations to quash the National Air and Space Museum's exhibit on the decision to use the bomb, but the contemporary issues take up only a small fragment of the film and one not need include them if you fear that they could prove distracting to students. Conversely, the sections on the debate surrounding the exhibit and its willingness to consider arguments that the bomb might not have been the only way to end World War II could be useful in sparking classroom discussion about the atomic bombs, their role in World War II, and the impact their use had on the postwar world.

An overlooked resource for discussing the atomic bombs in the context of the larger US strategic bombing campaign against Japan is the film *Fog of War* (2003). In this film, which covers Robert McNamara's life, Errol Morris draws him into a discussion of his service in the US Army Air Corps during World War II. McNamara served under General Curtis LeMay in the Japanese theater and advised him as an operations officer. McNamara vividly describes the strategic bombing techniques used against Japanese cities and the massive destruction of Japanese cities by conventional bombs, concluding that he and LeMay would have been prosecuted as war criminals if Japan had won the war. US victory led most of the public to ignore what had been done to Japanese cities.

Americans greeted news of the Japanese surrender in August 1945 with relief and jubilation. The atomic bombs seemed to be guarantors of world peace, and President Harry S. Truman and his national-security advisers initially harbored few fears about Soviet acquisition of the bomb. Despite warning from US scientists to the contrary, the president believed that the United States could maintain a monopoly on nuclear weapons for at least twenty years. For Truman, the US nuclear arsenal would counterbalance a perceived Soviet advantage in manpower if tensions between the two former allies led to war. Given this confidence in US nuclear strength, the bomb stockpile grew at a very moderate rate from 1945 to 1949. The nuclear arms race intensified in September 1949 when the United States detected evidence of the first Soviet atomic test. Truman quickly authorized a rapid expansion of nuclear bomb production and initiated a study of whether the United States should develop an even more powerful weapon. The bombs used against Japan had relied on explosive cores of uranium-235 and plutonium, both relatively rare elements that were naturally radioactive and unstable enough to create a fission reaction (splitting them into smaller elements) that released tremendous heat, light, and explosive force in addition to radiation. Scientists believed they could create an even more powerful weapon by reversing the process. They would take the lightest and simplest element, hydrogen, and use the heat, pressure, and force of a fission explosion to fuse its atoms to create a massive release of energy, heat, and light. Given that hydrogen is one of the most common elements in the world, in theory there would be no limit to the destructive capacity of these new thermonuclear weapons. Some policymakers and scientists blanched at building such powerful bombs, claiming they were genocidal and "an evil thing considered in any light."[3] Truman's number one concern, however, was whether the Soviets could produce hydrogen weapons, and, when told they could, he ordered a crash effort to produce thermonuclear weapons. The nuclear arms race then advanced on two tracks— a contest to have numerical superiority and another quest to have the most advanced technology.

The disturbing and humorous film *Atomic Cafe* (1982) conveys both the tension and the absurdity of the period from the end of World War to the end of the 1950s and gives students vivid illustrations of the impact that atomic weapons and the Cold War had on American society. The film is a collage of official government films, period songs with atomic themes, newsreel footage, advertisements, and radio and television clips from the era with no outside commentary from the film's creators. Sections of the film depict the aftermath of the atomic bombings in Hiroshima and Nagasaki, US bomb tests, reactions to Soviet acquisition of the atomic bomb, debates about whether the hydrogen bomb should be produced, atomic training exercises using American troops, and civil defense films. Few other documentaries are as rich and effective. Students see what the government told the public, along with footage that contradicts government pronouncements. In one example, soldiers are assured that they have nothing to fear from the nuclear tests in which they are participating because irradiated material would need to get into breaks in the skin to harm them. The film then shifts to soldiers telling a reporter that their mouths and noses were filled with dirt and sand stirred up by the nuclear explosion. Other teaching aids also exist for this period. Conelrad (conelrad.com) contains additional material that can be used to highlight the cultural impact of nuclear weapons, including music, films, and personal reminiscences about nuclear weapons and civil defense. One can also access unedited government civil defense films in collections produced by the Educational Archives. One DVD collection, *Patriotism* (2003), includes the classic *Duck and Cover* film from 1951 that sought to teach schoolchildren how to react in case of nuclear attack.

After both superpowers acquired thermonuclear weapons, they raced to be the first to deploy more powerful and accurate means of delivering nuclear weapons, including both intercontinental and submarine-launched ballistic missiles (ICBMs and SLBMs) and cruise missiles (which could be ground, air, or sea launched). ICBMs and SLBMs also acquired the ability to deliver multiple warheads to many different targets when fitted with devices called MIRVs (multiple independently targetable reentry vehicles). Arguments for increased stockpiles and new delivery vehicles hinged on justifications rooted in strategic thinking.

Most strategic thinking used nuclear deterrence as its first principle. At its root, deterrence simply sought to dissuade an enemy from threatening war out of fear that the other power could respond with a devastating nuclear strike. Building on this basic goal, numerous varieties of strategic thought emerged during the Cold War. Minimal deterrence sought only enough nuclear weapons to make one's foe uncertain whether a nuclear strike could be avoided if war broke out. Counterforce doctrine weakened the appeal of minimal deterrence. This strategic concept called for targeting a rival's nuclear delivery vehicles with the hope of destroying them before they could be launched. Some variants of counterforce called for a second-strike reserve that would allow one power to threaten the other with another salvo of nuclear weapons if its leadership refused to surrender after a first strike. Because counterforce necessitated having more nuclear weapons than one's enemy, the United States would have to produce more warheads every time the Soviet Union increased its deployments. To guard against Soviet counterforce targeting, the United States adopted the nuclear triad, under which nuclear weapons could be delivered by ICBMs, bomber aircraft, and submarines. By basing nuclear warheads on mobile platforms (submarines and aircraft) that could not be easily targeted, the triad sought to ensure that even if the Soviets struck first, the United States would have enough nuclear weapons to retaliate.

Fearing the escalating costs and risks of counterforce, Secretary of Defense Robert McNamara advocated the strategy of mutual assured destruction (MAD) in the hope of placing some limits on the growth of nuclear stockpiles. This doctrine called for both powers to build up their nuclear arms to a level where each would have a second-strike capability if the other side attacked first. For the strategy to be fully implemented, both sides had to accept transparency with regard to their stockpile levels and their basing decisions and conclude nuclear arms control agreements that would establish clear limits on the numbers and types of weapons deployed. McNamara's primary strategic goal was to foster stability in the nuclear competition with the Soviet Union.

The Bulletin of the Atomic Scientists (thebulletin.org), the National Security Archive (ww2.gwu.edu/~nsarchiv/), and the Nuclear Weapons Archive (nuclearweaponsarchive.org) all have numerous resources that help students grasp the often esoteric topic of nuclear strategy. *The Bulletin* website contains both historical and contemporary information on nuclear stockpiles and nuclear strategy. Clearly designed charts document the growth of both nuclear stockpiles and deployed delivery vehicles during the Cold War. All issues of *The Bulletin* dating back to the first issue in December 1945 are available in the archive section. Because it was a forum for debates on new technology and strategic doctrines, it offers numerous primary sources that one can utilize when discussing the arms race and strategic concepts. The National Security Archive offers electronic briefing books that collect primary sources on numerous nuclear topics, including nuclear strategy and government policies on nuclear targeting. The Nuclear Weapons Archive offers quick access to the stockpile numbers and the types of nuclear weapons deployed during each phase of the Cold War.

The film *Dr. Strangelove, or: How I Stopped Worrying and Learned to Love the Bomb* (1964) also engages the strategic debates of the 1950s and 1960s in a blackly comic and provocative fashion. Stanley Kubrick originally sought to create a dramatic film depicting nuclear war and read deeply in the writings of a number of prominent nuclear strategists, including Herman Kahn, Henry Kissinger, and Thomas Schelling. He subsequently concluded that the scenarios were so disturbing and absurd that only a satirical treatment could truly capture their essence. When students confront the film, they often don't know whether to laugh or be appalled as a crazed general takes matters into his own hands and orders a nuclear attack on the Soviet Union. The film's power comes from its exposure of many aspects of nuclear doctrine that the government had hidden from the public, including that military commanders had been predelegated authority to launch nuclear attacks if they lost communication with the Pentagon. The *New York Times* film critic Bosley Crowther chided Kubrick for prominently displaying the slogan "Peace Is Our Profession" throughout the US Air Force base depicted in the film, claiming it was an absurd and unbelievable touch, when in fact it was the Strategic Air Command's motto. Beyond its cutting depiction of military thinking, *Dr. Strangelove* also captured the deepening fear of nuclear annihilation that emerged in the late 1950s and continued into the early 1960s, especially after crises in Germany and Cuba seemed to take the superpowers to the brink of nuclear war.

Despite the fact that deterrence theory predicted that countries would take fewer risks in international politics to avoid nuclear war, nuclear crises came to define the period from 1955 to 1962. In both 1955 and 1958, Washington threatened nuclear retaliation against the People's Republic of China for its artillery attacks on the Taiwanese island of Kinmen and Matsu. Beijing backed down in each instance, but US actions helped energize Chinese efforts to acquire their own nuclear weapons. Also in 1958, Premier Nikita Khrushchev of the Soviet Union prompted a crisis when he demanded that the Western powers withdraw their militaries from the divided German city of Berlin in six months' time. He retreated from this stance in 1959 but reignited the crisis in 1961 when he repeated his threat. The second wave of threats and counterthreats led to heightened fears of nuclear war and calls from President John F. Kennedy to expand US civil defense efforts to protect the American public from nuclear attack. In August 1961, the Berlin Crisis ended with the erection of the Berlin Wall, physically dividing the eastern and western sections of the city. The retreat from the nuclear brink did not last long. Fourteen months later, in October 1962, the world faced the most serious nuclear confrontation of the Cold War when Khrushchev clandestinely deployed short-range nuclear missiles on the Caribbean island of Cuba. Kennedy demanded their removal and established a naval quarantine to prevent more weapons from reaching the island. Khrushchev ultimately agreed to remove the weapons in exchange for a US pledge not to invade Cuba. Kennedy also secretly promised to remove American missiles from Turkey, which threatened targets in the Soviet Union.

The Cuban Missile Crisis captures students' imagination like few other events in the Cold War. John F. Kennedy recorded many of his meetings and telephone conversations related to the crisis, and they can be accessed on the Miller Center for Public Affairs website (millercenter.org/presidentialrecordings). *The Fog of War* (2003) also contains segments in which Robert McNamara discusses the lessons he believes can be learned from the crisis, and these segments include excerpts from the tapes. The only caveat is that McNamara is not always a reliable source on the crisis and the tapes are used quite selectively in the film.[4] One can also access the tapes through printed transcripts, and several different versions are available. The first collection published and the most widely accessible is *The Kennedy Tapes*.[5] But Stanford University Press and the Miller Center produced later versions that are more accurate and more complete.[6] Other primary sources for teaching can be found on the National Security Archive website and at the Cold War International History Project (http://www.wilsoncenter.org/program/cold-war-international-history-project). The CWIHP site is invaluable because it includes Soviet documents from the crisis, translated into English.

The tenets of MAD, fears of future nuclear crises, and a burgeoning antinuclear movement helped pave the way for nuclear arms control agreements. A global antinuclear movement emerged in 1954 after a US hydrogen bomb test in the Pacific Ocean irradiated the crew of a Japanese fishing trawler. One of the fishermen died after his exposure to the radioactive material that rained down on the ship's deck. Opponents of nuclear testing emerged throughout the world and put pressure on all nuclear powers to ban testing. The US-based antinuclear movement included both established and new organizations, including Fellowship of Reconciliation, the War Resisters League, SANE: The Committee for a Sane Nuclear Policy, the Women's International League for Peace and Freedom, and Women Strike for Peace.

While men dominated government policymaking on nuclear issues during the Cold War, women have played prominent roles in antinuclear activism from Hiroshima to the present. After the bombing of Hiroshima, two leaders of the Women's International League for Peace and Freedom, Emily Balch and Dorothy Detzer, as well as Dorothy Day, founder of the Catholic Worker movement, condemned the attack. Detzer drafted a statement claiming that "a civilization which has spawned a Buchenwald, a Pearl Harbor and a Hiroshima is morally diseased."[7] Although the emerging Cold War pushed these initial antinuclear fears into the background, women retained prominent roles in peace and antinuclear organizations and were poised to take a large role when antinuclear activism became more robust in 1954. Women Strike for Peace emerged in 1961 as one of the most important antinuclear organizations of the early 1960s, rivaled only by SANE. The organization used dominant social conceptions of women's proper roles to its advantage, framing its critiques of nuclear testing and nuclear weapons in terms of mothers protecting their children. Its middle-class white membership and its emphasis on traditional female images and roles allowed WSP to avoid the taint of radicalism that afflicted other antinuclear organizations, but this strategy also led some leaders to dismiss the antitesting movement as rooted solely in maternal worries. As late as 1964, President Lyndon B. Johnson told his speechwriters to include some "peace demagoguery" for mothers "worried over children drinking contaminated milk" or fearful of birthing "a baby with two heads."[8]

The tendency to dismiss antinuclear warnings as rooted in feminine attributes and as fundamentally antimasculine also led to the dismissal and ridicule of male nuclear disarmament and arms control advocates. During his 1952 and 1956 presidential campaigns, critics labeled the Democratic presidential nominee Adlai Stevenson as "soft" and an "egghead," equating his call for a nuclear testing moratorium with proposals to ban the bomb, when it more accurately fell into the arms control category. In the wake of the 1952 campaign, one political commentator contended that the previously neutral term "egghead" had been redefined to refer to "a person of spurious intellectual pretensions, often a professor or the protégé of a professor. Fundamentally superficial. Overemotional and feminine in reactions to any problem. Supercilious and surfeited with conceit and contempt for the experience of more sound and able men. Essentially confused in thought and immersed in mixture of sentimentality and violent evangelism. . . . An anemic bleeding heart." The *New York Daily News* took its attacks on Stevenson further. Calling him Adelaide and mocking his voice as "fruity," the paper dismissed Stevenson's supporters as "typical Harvard lace-cuff liberals," "lace-panty diplomats," and "pompadoured lap dogs" who wailed "in perfumed anguish" at the accusations involving alleged communist infiltration of the government launched by Senator Joseph McCarthy (R-WI) and on occasion "'giggled' about their own anti-Communism."[9]

Despite the disparaging attitudes toward nuclear peace advocates exhibited by the mass media and political leaders, the American public heeded the movement's warnings and put pressure on policymakers to take action to limit the nuclear arms race. From 1958 to 1961, the United States, Great Britain, and the Soviet Union observed a voluntary test moratorium while they negotiated a formal test ban treaty. The moratorium broke down in 1961 in the midst of the Berlin Crisis, but after the Cuban Missile Crisis Kennedy and Khrushchev rekindled serious negotiations and signed the first nuclear arms control agreement, the Limited Test Ban Treaty, in 1963. That agreement banned all but underground testing. Efforts to limit nuclear weapons continued and produced the Nuclear Nonproliferation Treaty in 1968, which called for all states except the United States, Soviet Union, Great Britain, France, and the People's Republic of China to abstain from acquiring nuclear weapons. In 1969, the Strategic Arms Limitation Talks (SALT) began and produced three agreements—the Anti-Ballistic Missile Treaty, SALT I, and SALT II. These agreements placed caps on specific types of weapons but did not call for actual reductions in stockpiles. President Jimmy Carter and Soviet premier Leonid Brezhnev signed SALT II, but neither country ratified the agreement after the Cold War intensified when the Soviet Union invaded Afghanistan in 1979.

The failure of SALT II and the election of Ronald Reagan in 1980 helped reinvigorate the antinuclear movement. A powerful nuclear freeze movement emerged in the United States and Western Europe.

Reagan opposed the movement and accused it of playing into Soviet hands, but its popularity could not be ignored. In response, he called for the United States to abandon MAD and embrace defensive systems that would protect American lives rather than simply avenge them. Critics scoffed that a defensive shield would never offer complete protection against a nuclear attack and warned that even a partially effective shield would merely encourage the Soviet Union to add to its nuclear arsenal in an attempt to overwhelm it. A quest for national ballistic missile defense also threatened to undercut the Anti-Ballistic Missile Treaty, which limited each power to protecting one site with a ballistic missile defense battery. As the prospects for nuclear disarmament seemed their dimmest, however, Mikhail Gorbachev became the Soviet premier in 1985. Gorbachev wanted to limit military spending to concentrate on reviving a struggling domestic economy. To mute protests from the military about reduced budgets, he needed to conclude nuclear arms agreements with the United States. After some false starts, he found Reagan to be a willing partner. Despite his disdain for the nuclear freeze movement, the president had long believed nuclear weapons should be abolished. In 1987, Reagan and Gorbachev concluded the Intermediate Nuclear Forces Treaty, which eliminated an entire class of nuclear weapons. The two leaders also initiated the Strategic Arms Reduction process. The first START agreement, concluded in 1991, limited each power to a stockpile of six thousand warheads, and it remained in effect until 2009. After numerous failures to ratify and implement a substantive successor to the first START agreement, President Barack Obama and President Dmitry Medvedev of the Soviet Union concluded the New START agreement in 2010. This agreement promised to reduce stockpiles to 1,550 warheads by 2018. After the treaty is fully implemented, the superpowers will have decommissioned and destroyed 95 percent of the Cold War nuclear stockpile. These arms control agreements helped ease tensions between the two superpowers, and, in the end, nuclear weapons proved as central to the end of the Cold War as they had to its beginning.

The National Security Archive, the Cold War International History Project, and *The Bulletin of the Atomic Scientist* all offer primary sources for teaching about arms control and the end of the Cold War. The Swarthmore College Peace Collection (http://www.swarthmore.edu /library/peace/) also offers resources and serves as clearinghouse for anyone wishing to access more information on the antinuclear and peace movements during the Cold War. Of particular importance are resources concerning SANE: The Committee for a Sane Nuclear Policy, the Committee for Non-Violent Action, and Women Strike for Peace. The antinuclear movement of the 1980s inspired a number of films that illustrate its strength and mainstream appeal. When ABC broadcast *The Day After* in November 1983, it became the highest-rated made-for-television movie in history, with more than 100 million viewers. The film depicted families in Kansas and Missouri before, during, and after a nuclear war between the United States and the Soviet Union. Anticipation for the film built for months, and special screenings were held for military and government officials, including President Reagan. On the night of its original broadcast, ABC aired a live debate featuring the scientist Carl Sagan, former secretary of state Henry Kissinger, former national-security adviser Brent Scowcroft, the conservative commentator William F. Buckley, the political activist Elie Wiesel, and former secretary of defense Robert McNamara. The film often seems dated to modern audiences, but it is still a powerful cultural artifact from the period. Other items from the period that depict nuclear war and its aftermath are the British television drama *Threads* (1984) and the movie *Testament* (1983). Like *The Day After*, these films use the experiences of ordinary citizens to dramatize the effects of nuclear weapons. The release dates for all three films are also significant because the nuclear freeze movement peaked in 1984 and declined quite rapidly from that point.

The end of the Cold War also allows students to reflect on the overall impact of nuclear weapons on the US-Soviet confrontation. Some scholars have argued that nuclear weapons produced a long peace that prevented another general war from breaking out between the two Cold War alliance systems, NATO and the Warsaw Pact. An opposing viewpoint argues that nuclear weapons actually prolonged the Cold War by making it easier to sustain military spending and defense mobilization for decades. Conventional militaries would have required the conscription of numerous citizens, and such policies risked fomenting widespread disaffection, both in the United States and within the larger NATO group. Other commentators point to the numerous nuclear crises and argue that nuclear weapons actually destabilized the international environment and did not contribute to peace.

One can also ask students to ponder how these broader debates carry implications for contemporary world politics where preventing other countries from acquiring nuclear weapons has become a key aim of US national-security policy. Such an exercise also makes nuclear weapons more relevant to the students' daily lives. What happened in Cuba more than fifty years ago may seem like ancient history to contemporary students, but the implications of new powers, such as Iran, producing nuclear weapons or regional powers, such as Pakistan or North Korea, using nuclear weapons may have dire consequences for the students and their families and friends. One can begin discussing the roots of US opposition to nuclear proliferation. From the beginning of the nuclear age, US policymakers attempted to prevent nuclear weapons from spreading to other powers. Once the Soviets acquired nuclear weapons, Washington's emphasis changed and its commitment to preventing nuclear proliferation wavered. The promise of nuclear energy also led Dwight Eisenhower to offer peaceful nuclear aid to newly emerging nations during the 1950s, seemingly oblivious to the fact that nuclear reactors were the first step to acquiring nuclear weapons. The list of countries that the United States and other Western countries aided in constructing research and power reactors closely parallels the list of nuclear rogues that have worried the United States since the end of the Cold War, including Iraq, Pakistan, and Iran. Other states that have refused to sign the Nuclear Nonproliferation Treaty, such as Israel and India, have also benefited from Western nuclear aid. By the 1960s, John F. Kennedy and Lyndon Johnson placed greater emphasis on stopping proliferation, but every time the Cold War intensified, Washington tended to place more emphasis on maintaining superiority in the arms race than it did on capping the number of states that had access to nuclear weaponry. The National Security Archive and the Nuclear Proliferation International History Project (https://www.wilsoncenter.org/program /nuclear-proliferation-international-history-project) both have primary sources that one can utilize to introduce students to this complex subject.

Nuclear weapons and the arms race can seem daunting subjects, but the best results often come from centering on the human effects and consequences of their potential use and giving less attention to the sometimes overly abstract technical details of strategy and technology. When strategists discussed survivability and winning a nuclear confrontation, they focused on which power ended the conflict with more nuclear weapons intact and largely ignored human fatalities. Instructors will likely have much better results if they flip the script and ignore the weapons and concentrate on human beings.

NOTES

1. J. Robert Oppenheimer, "Atomic Weapons and American Policy," *Foreign Affairs* (July 1953): 529.

2. "Stalin's Secret Order: Build the Bomb 'on Russian Scale,'" *Cold War International History Project Bulletin* 4 (Fall 1994): 5.

3. Statement Appended to the Report of the General Advisory Committee, October 30, 1949, *Foreign Relations of the United States: National Security Affairs, Foreign Economic Policy* (Washington, DC: Government Printing Office, 1976), 1:572–73.

4. For more detail on the distortions in the film, consult Sheldon M. Stern, *The Cuban Missile Crisis in American Memory: Myths versus Reality* (Stanford: Stanford University Press, 2012).

5. Ernest R. May and Philip Zelikow, eds., *The Kennedy Tapes: Inside the Kennedy White House during the Cuban Missile Crisis* (New York: W.W. Norton, 1998).

6. Sheldon M. Stern, *"Averting the Final Failure": John F. Kennedy and the Secret Cuban Missile Crisis Meetings* (Stanford: Stanford University Press, 2003), and Timothy Naftali, Ernest R. May, and Philip Zelikow, eds., *The Presidential Recordings: John F. Kennedy*, Vols. 1–3: *The Great Crises* (New York: W. W. Norton, 2001).

7. Lawrence S. Wittner, *One World or None: A History of the World Nuclear Disarmament Movement through 1953* (Stanford: Stanford University Press, 1993), 56–57; Tentative Statement on the Atomic Bomb Prepared by Dorothy Detzer, "Atomic Bomb (1945–1946)" folder, Papers of Dorothy Detzer, Box 3, Swarthmore College Peace Collection, Swarthmore College, Swarthmore, PA.

8. Quoted in Lawrence S. Wittner, *Resisting the Bomb: A History of the World Nuclear Disarmament Movement, 1954–1970* (Stanford: Stanford University Press, 1997), 431.

9. Quoted in Michael Kimmel, *Manhood in America* (New York: Oxford University Press, 1998), 237; quoted in Richard Hofstadter, *Anti-Intellectualism in American Life* (New York: Vintage, 1963), 9–10, 227.

KEY RESOURCES

Boyer, Paul. *By the Bomb's Early Light: American Thought and Culture at the Dawn of the Atomic Age.* Chapel Hill: University of North Carolina Press, 1985.

The Bulletin of the Atomic Scientists (thebulletin.org).

Cold War International History Project. www.wilsoncenter.org/programs /cold-war-international-history-project.

Heefner, Gretchen. *The Missile Next Door: The Minuteman in the American Heartland.* Cambridge, MA: Harvard University Press, 2012.

Kaplan, Fred. *The Wizards of Armageddon*. Stanford: Stanford University Press, 1991.

Maddock, Shane J. *Nuclear Apartheid: The Quest for American Atomic Supremacy from World War II to the Present*. Chapel Hill: University of North Carolina Press, 2010.

May, Ernest R., and Philip D. Zelikow, eds. *The Kennedy Tapes: Inside the White House during the Cuban Missile Crisis*. Cambridge, MA: Harvard University Press, 1997.

National Security Archive. nsarchive.gwu.edu.

Newhouse, John. *War and Peace in the Nuclear Age*. New York: Knopf, 1988.

Nuclear Nonproliferation International History Project. www.wilsoncenter .org/programs/nuclear-nonproliferation-international-history-project.

Nuclear Weapon Archive. nuclearweaponarchive.org.

Rose, Kenneth D. *One Nation Underground: The Fallout Shelter in American Culture*. New York: New York University Press, 2001.

Schwartz, Stephen I., ed. *Atomic Audit: The Costs and Consequences of US Nuclear Weapons since 1940*. Washington, DC: Brookings Institution Press, 1998.

Walker, J. Samuel. *Prompt and Utter Destruction: Truman and the Use of the Atomic Bombs against Japan*. Chapel Hill: University of North Carolina Press, 2004.

Wittner, Lawrence S. *Confronting the Bomb: A Short History of the World Nuclear Disarmament Movement*. Stanford: Stanford University Press, 2009.

The Soviets' Cold War

Notes of a Diplomatic Historian

ANTHONY D'AGOSTINO

It should be no more difficult than teaching a survey of any other half-century—1789-1848, 1848-1918, or 1900-49. But teaching the Cold War as a period in the history of world politics, especially one with the Russian Revolution and Communism at its core, presents many more difficult hurdles. The first and perhaps the worst is that you are up against George Orwell. One of the most intelligent and artful political writers of his or any other time, Orwell has already had his most powerful works, *Animal Farm* and *1984*, read and studied in high school by almost all of your students, who have probably also got from him most of their ideas on how to write and, in fact, how to think. Now he confronts you, through them, with the stunning metaphor of pigs leading a revolt of the animals in the name of the bizarre idea of running the farm themselves and finally with the moral that, while all animals might think they are born equal, the pigs will inevitably come to consider themselves "more equal than others." These are overwhelming images. And the worst part is that they are not entirely misbegotten, if you think about Orwell's political writings, as your students have not, against the background of his experience in Spain, in a POUM brigade on the Aragon front, being fired upon by his presumed communist allies. Perhaps you already know that the communism that writers like George Orwell and John Dos Passos came up against might indeed prompt thoughts such as those expressed in *1984*. Of course, all our general reflexes against tyranny, to which Orwell appeals, cannot be regarded as unwholesome or naive. And the story of communism is, to a very great extent, a story with tyranny in it.

Setting the Stage

Even so, there must be more to the course than a one-sided morality play about the Russian revolution. A history course should have some history, which Orwell cannot provide. Lacking this, many of the students who do not rely on *Animal Farm* may instead already be won to a received political theory, the theory of totalitarianism, inspired and first explicated in Hannah Arendt in *Origins of Totalitarianism*, a book that is still read and admired in political science courses.[1] For me, totalitarianism is another impediment to thought. Most of those who invoke the term do not take into account that Arendt found its origins in nineteenth-century European imperialism and in racist and social Darwinist theories current among the expansionist powers. While she based her totalitarian ideal type on the similarity of the police regimes of Hitler and Stalin in the 1930s, she did not count Mussolini's fascism as totalitarian, despite Mussolini's having coined the term as a kind of boast about fascism. In fact, she saw the post-Stalin Soviet leadership of the 1950s as carrying out a process of "de-totalitarization." For Soviet history, she depended on the works of Isaac Deutscher, although he was always regarded by Cold Warriors as a pariah for his too even-handed and perhaps too knowledgeable writings about communism.[2] Today one hardly comes across serious attempts to equate fascism and communism, although many students still treat Hitler and Stalin as having a kind of kinship. The idea can be abused. The theory of totalitarianism has been explicated at length by Ernst Nolte and has become for him a way of arguing that fear of communism inspired and even legitimated Nazism.[3] Nolte thus took a first timid step toward a political rehabilitation of Hitler. Still, there is no great rush to take the theory much beyond the rather limited comparison made by Arendt. And yet it still moves. Despite the best efforts of my generation of Sovietologists and Soviet historians to deemphasize totalitarianism as an interpretation, it remains a staple of pundit and Beltway discourse and, to a lesser extent, of political theory.

Discussing the idea of totalitarianism in the early stages of the class usually brings forward a number of philosophical presuppositions among new students about things in general. They often suggest that "history only shows one tyranny replacing another," that "wars are hard-wired into human nature," or that "nothing ever changes." The course is not going to service inquiries of this sort. "'Twas ever thus!" is not a maxim for historians. But I think it is bad for me to be too assertive in the beginning about historical specificity. So I usually philosophize with the class for one session about these things with the hope of presenting my own biases in the best light. In the process I admit my chastened enthusiasm for Western civilization, warts and all, and for the spirit of the Enlightenment, in much the same mood as the Russian intellectuals of the nineteenth century. Down with religious obscurantism and barriers to science! Can we assume together that history indicates some kind of progress? I have to confess my own doubts about this fundamental proposition along with my perhaps sentimental attachment to it.

Yet all these reflexive ruminations give us not a real history but a substitute for it, a rather simplistic and even occasionally pernicious civics lesson that has to be criticized in pursuit of a more nuanced one. The terms have to be sorted out. But they cannot be dictated by the instructor, despite the fact that this is precisely what the students want most. As I see it, you have to realize that the course is itself the history and the civics lesson and all you are doing in an introduction to it is clarifying some of the discourse so that the students can express their own thoughts more eloquently. On one side, the Cold War is said to be about the struggle between democracy and totalitarianism (assuming the Soviet Union as a kind of continuation of Nazism). On the other, it is said to be a struggle between socialism and imperialism (assuming the Soviets and other communist regimes are truly socialist and not state capitalist, degenerate workers' states or examples of bureaucratic collectivism). This also assumes that the United States is an imperialist power. When pressed, those who maintain this add that the imperialism we are talking about is actually the "informal" kind described by Ronald Robinson and John Gallagher.[4] To my mind this does not say much more than that the United States has a relationship to many states that is similar to the one the British had with Argentina in the nineteenth century.

More than half of my brightest students entertain some notion of informal imperialism to describe US foreign policy, partly because of the overhang of the debates of the Vietnam War era. The civics lesson thus starts out from a thicket of passionate ideological assertions. All that can be done, I have concluded, is to clarify the political and economic terms: to try to understand democracy in terms of a contrast with dictatorship, not with socialism; to try to understand capitalism as contrasted with socialism, rather than with dictatorship. Whether a certain political term goes naturally with a certain economic term is a larger discussion that cannot detain us. Suffice it to say that we will be seeing cases of dictatorship that may be capitalist or socialist.

The Path to Cold War from the Soviet Perspective

One could say that the Cold War was the last chapter of the Russian Revolution. To speak therefore about the Soviet side of the Cold War is not just to render another perspective but to get to the heart of the matter. Well, then, should we say that the Cold War, that is, the struggle with communism, had its real origins in the Russian Revolution and the Allied intervention against it in 1917–21? That was the perspective of much of the Vietnam-era Cold War revisionism. D. F. Fleming wrote two effective volumes based on newspaper accounts to make this point.[5] Most of the brightest and most alert of my students, the ones who sit in the first rows, pretty much come into the course with this view. I think it is quite wrong. To be sure, there was an Allied intervention in the Russian civil war in 1919 and a kind of "cold war" in Anglo-Soviet relations in 1924–27. Yet, had the foreign policies of the great powers and of the United States in particular been consistently based on anti-communism, they would surely have taken the side of the fascist powers. Appeasement does, I admit, show this drift. In the end, however, appeasement was abandoned and fascism was fought to the end in league with the Soviet Union. Franklin Roosevelt's role in opposing appeasement was a radical break with the inertial line of the British and the French. To insist that FDR was only trying to save capitalism or that his antifascism was reducible to a free-trader reflex hostile to Nazi mercantilism indicates a certain blindness about the fundamentals of US national interest.[6] Many of my best students persist in this reduction of FDR's policy, often because they think it the ABC of Marxism, but in this case I think the civics lesson has distorted historical perspective.

As if this were not enough, there is the additional problem that a course that deals with a global struggle against communism after World War II cannot devote proper attention to the history of communism in Russia in the period 1917–45. But some way has to be found to let the student know that the communists were our allies in the war against fascism. The interwar period saw a lively debate on the left about the nature of the Soviet Union and whether it fulfilled the expectations of nineteenth-century socialism and social democracy. One cannot allow this important topic to devour the course, and it must be dealt with in one week or two at the maximum. I have found it best to assign some general readings about the Soviet experience, perhaps having the students read something by Richard Pipes on one side and someone like Isaac Deutscher on the other. A class discussion can clarify the large issues and give all the students a chance to air their perspectives. It must be borne in mind that this discussion, since it must deal primarily with presuppositions, cannot really accomplish much more than to give pointers for issues to be addressed later in the course.

On the contrary, I begin the course with a discussion of Roosevelt's ideas about "open spheres" governed by the Four Policemen, an alternative to the Cold War that the Soviets embraced unequivocally. Three of the policemen, China, the United States, and the Soviet Union, would no doubt have voted in a bloc against the fourth, Britain, for example on Indian independence. So the British could not be enthusiastic about the Four Policemen. Nor could British (and American) interests in the Middle East have easily got used to allotting the Soviets a share in Middle Eastern oil. There was bound to be pressure on the United States to accommodate the British view, as it was the British who were expected to keep order in Europe. This was a contradiction in the conception of the Roosevelt foreign policy that might have caused a turn toward the Cold War, even had FDR finished his fourth term.

Under President Harry Truman, the turn toward Cold War was taken quickly. It brought down the policy of French president Charles de Gaulle, the Franco-Soviet alliance, the Franco-Czech alliance, and the Soviet policy of reining in Mao Zedong to the advantage of the Guomindang and the United States. Truman's turn reached the point in May 1947 where communists were expelled from French and Italian governments and noncommunists from those in what was becoming the Eastern bloc. Mao reversed course and issued the slogan "Down with Chiang Kai-shek!" The line taken by the economist and *institutchik* Eugen Varga had failed, and he was subjected to withering criticism that really showed for the first time a Soviet turn to the Cold War as an ideological imperative. The Soviet Cold War in its first phase (1948 to 1953) was a defensive closing off of the bloc in the west and the opening up of struggle against the United States in the east. It followed that the Soviets must break with the too-militant Yugoslavian president Josip Tito, subject the East Central European regimes to sovietization, and supply Mao with the arms that were to take him to victory. "Who lost

China?" was the question William Knowland's *Oakland Tribune* asked in the name of the China Lobby. Most who teach the Cold War today would probably answer that China was never ours to lose. But they might also answer more sharply that China may have been lost by Truman and the Cold War. I cannot determine if this is a right-wing thought or a left-wing thought. At any rate, it is a thought.[7]

Not all of Cold War revisionism has been "discredited." Some of its assumptions about erroneous perceptions of the Soviet threat and the bureaucratization of Stalinism have pretty much stuck. If students see the origins of the Cold War in this light, we need no longer stress the central role of Soviet aggression—that is, presumably overt military threats against the Allied forces or their zones of influence—in the postwar order. We are speaking instead about the Soviet world analysis of 1944–47 and its forward policy at a time when Stalin wrongly insisted that the imperialists could not overcome their divisions and combine against the Soviet Union. That, after all, had been his experience, at least since the Soviet civil war. His outlook was articulated best by Varga, for whom Yalta had demonstrated that the United States and the British would fall out. The United States and the Soviet Union would agree broadly not only about war strategy but also about the fate of the European empires. Accordingly, the Soviets should restrain the revolution in Eastern Europe within a framework of all-party coalitions led not by communists but by peasant parties and an economic policy closer to the NEP (the Soviet economic policy of the 1920s that permitted free trade in foodstuffs) than to the era of the five-year plans. Moreover, in the Western governments where they had electoral strength communists would join in tripartite regimes of a reformist type with Social Democrats and Christian Democrats. All-party regimes in the East would in a sense be held hostage to the fate of tripartite regimes in the west. Czechoslovakia, with its elected communist regime, would be a neutral middle ground. Tito's Yugoslavia would be the model People's Democracy. Borders would be redrawn to the liking of the French prewar allies, Poland, Czechoslovakia, Yugoslavia, and Romania and at the expense of the prewar revisionist powers Germany and Hungary.[8] Communists in China would appease the United States and the Guomindang and join with them in sharing power if possible. Good relations with France would be promoted (but not at the expense of good relations with the United States) and rather less warm relations with Britain. De Gaulle saw things the same way and wanted to rebuild France in this environment.

The British were less enthusiastic.[9] But the Soviets would assist in the postcolonial adjustment that would be undertaken by the Labour Party.

So, students should gather, the Soviets were not really unleashing a campaign of aggression, nor were they merely defending their war gains in a bureaucratic manner. They had a multifaceted forward strategy. Even the staunchest Western defender of the status quo had to realize that the war itself had undermined the prewar "order." Like World War I, World War II had moved the political spectrum to the left. The Soviets hoped for new gains alongside the widespread liberal and social democratic postwar trends. Among the Tory former supporters of appeasement in the House of Commons, who were already threatened by a Labour victory, the idea quickly took hold that the Soviets were now the biggest threat of all. When one considers that these gentlemen felt the same way about the threat of socialized medicine and the Beveridge Report (the British blueprint for a welfare state), one can understand the hue and cry about Soviet aggression and the need of Churchill, defeated in 1945, to reverse course, a need that produced the Fulton, Missouri, speech proclaiming the need for a turn to the Cold War.

The Height of the Cold War

After the origins of the Cold War, there comes the hardening of the Cold War and the armed division of Europe into armed hostile blocs, a story that used to be told as a kind of Greek tragedy, fatally ordained by the Cold War itself. Yet the Kremlin hoped to avoid it by breaking with Tito, closing off the bloc in Europe, and turning to Asia to encourage Mao, Kim Il-sung, and Ho Chi Minh. However, Dean Acheson, Truman's secretary of state, told the Senate Armed Services Committee that war in Asia could only be prelude to war in Europe, which must be met with German rearmament. After the crisis of the European Defense Community, a project designed to make Germany's new military role more palatable to the French, he was to get it. Thus the Warsaw Pact (1955) was a response not to NATO (1949) but to the arming of West Germany. So it was the war in Asia that brought about the final division of Europe. And the division of Europe with German rearmament moved the French to devote more resources to building nuclear weapons.

This story provides another opportunity for students to look at the Cold War from a different perspective. While students might be accustomed to seeing the Cold War as either inevitable or, perhaps, the fault of the Soviet Union, events in the late 1940s and early 1950s can be used to argue that the Soviet Union was more politically ambitious than militarily aggressive. Additionally, asking students to reflect on the "inevitability" of the Cold War can lead to instructive conversations about contingency in history.

The hardening of the Cold War in the end failed. It would never prove possible for the United States to subsume all the antagonisms of world politics into a single-minded struggle of the free world against communism. This became evident when the Bandung Conference of 1955 grouped most of the rising nations of what came to be called the third world under the banner of neutralism and nonalignment. Gamal Abel Nasser of Egypt, Jawaharlal Nehru of India , Sukarno of Indonesia, and U Nu of Burma all joined with Zhou Enlai (Chou En-Lai) and Tito to raise the issue of the revolt of non-Westerners and non-Soviet communists against the Cold War. The 1960s were to see the success of a Western revolt against the Cold War. This gave rise to a vision of the world as divided north-south rather than east-west.

Students should be encouraged to consider the relationship between the Cold War and decolonization. Western leaders who clung to the Cold War, who structured containment into NATO, SEATO, and the Baghdad Pact (later CENTO), continued to accept that the Cold War had changed the discourse of world politics from the Roosevelt era, from postcolonial adjustment to anticommunism. Defense of a given European imperial position might therefore be made in the name of the free world pitted against the communist threat. But the defense of the West outside Europe never took hold. In the Suez crisis, it was shown that the United States would not in the end support all British and French interests in the Middle East against Nasser. The United States proved unwilling to present itself to the third world as a supporter of colonialism. After Suez there was a jail break of revolt in Africa. African American students in the United States talked excitedly about the emergence of Kwame Nkrumah's Ghana, Sekou Toure's Guinea, Modibo Keita's Mali, and Patrice Lumumba's Congo and set their own course in a fight against Jim Crow. The apparent hardening of the blocs in Europe had been accompanied by a world revolt against the Cold War itself.

Soviet *institutchiki* instinctively sensed an epic opportunity. Nikita Khrushchev had emerged at the head of the collective leadership by 1957, after the struggle against the "Anti-Party Group." He had already moved to reconcile with Tito, the better to use his influence among the neutralist nations, at the price of criticizing the personality cult of Stalin at the Nineteenth Party Congress, in 1956. This did not cause the break with Mao's China. At the Moscow Conference of Communist Parties in 1957, Mao still defended Khrushchev's line. But Khrushchev's subsequent decision to deny Mao further help with nuclear weapons was too much for Mao to tolerate. At the very moment that Soviet launching of Sputnik showed an ICBM capability, at a time when, as Mao liked to say, the east wind would prevail over the west wind, China and the Soviets began to quarrel. When a victory has been achieved or, as in this case, is in sight, the victors fall out. Khrushchev's effort to stay ahead of Mao as leader of the fight against imperialism brought him to the Berlin Crisis of 1961 and the Cuban Missile Crisis a year later.

The retreat of the Soviet missiles from Cuba and the fall of Khrushchev in 1964 marked the end of a period of forward policy on the part of the Soviets. During the 1960s they left the center stage in world politics. As de Gaulle said, they stopped acting like a first-rate power. They quietly built the next generation of ICBMs preparatory to the achievement of missile parity with the United States in 1969. Their apparent weakness made them more attractive to de Gaulle's France, which, having accepted the loss of Algeria, turned to the project of Europeanizing the Soviet Union under the slogan "Europe from the Atlantic to the Urals." This was a revival of de Gaulle's pro-Soviet pre–Cold War line of 1944–46. The way the balance of power worked, defeat won you friends, that is, it fostered realignment against the victor. After John Kennedy's victories in Berlin and Cuba, the United States found that it faced a Gaullist challenge on several fronts: French criticism of US efforts in Vietnam, French withdrawal from NATO war planning, even French pressure on the dollar. This was accompanied by a rising antiwar movement at home and the post-Watts radicalization of Black Power. This was all very heady for the Chinese. Maoism seemed to be at the forefront of world revolution and a mortal threat to the West, with radical supporters and adherents all over the globe. The Cold War, at least in the form of a Soviet-American military and ideological clash as the centerpiece of world politics, seemed to have disappeared.

Late Cold War

The historian might be tempted to treat the 1960s as a lull between two Cold Wars, the first having ended with the settlement on

Cuba in 1963 and the second to follow with the election of Ronald Reagan. That is the way it seemed to some contemporaries.[10] But, looking back, the 1960s seem more like part of a continuation of the long process of the waning of the Cold War, with the defeat of European imperialism presaged at Suez in 1956, the rise of the third world, the neo-Bandung with Maoism at its extreme left, and Gaullism challenging the whole idea of a united West. American policy was at loose ends. During the Tet Offensive in 1968, there was a seemingly fatal run on the dollar, and three years later the entire Bretton Woods system collapsed. It is hard to minimize the depth of the crisis facing the United States.

Out of this came the leaps and forward escapes of Richard Nixon and Henry Kissinger. China, noting the distress of the United States in its various aspects but especially in its losing cause in Vietnam, alongside the success of the Soviets in punishing Czechoslovakia, decided to make a turn to the weaker party. The opening to China thus provided Nixon and Kissinger with the possibility to refocus world politics back to the Soviet-American relationship, albeit in a new phase of détente. And, more than that, OPEC came to the rescue of the dollar. Quadrupling and then doubling again the price of oil during the Mideast war of 1973, OPEC solved the problem of the overhang of dollars in Europe, the economic basis, one could say, of the Gaullist challenge. Eurodollars paid for the more costly oil became petrodollars recycled into the US financial system, ultimately to pave the way for sovereign loans to Latin America, Africa, and Eastern Europe, with conditionality that we would later call neoliberalism.

Dashed against the rocks of despair, the United States found new "friends" in China and OPEC. This was eventually to lead to an escape forward to neoliberalism, financialization, and globalization, but it did not prevent a series of geopolitical losses to communism through the 1970s: Vietnam, Cambodia, Angola, Mozambique, Guinea-Bissau, and finally Nicaragua and possibly El Salvador—an impressive array of enemies, if you include OPEC radicals such as Algeria and Libya, along with all the others who might be smugly neutral about American decline. Détente was not enough to prevent the geopolitical decline of US power. No wonder the Cowboys rose up against the Yankees, as Carl Oglesby liked to put it. The struggle against détente in the United States, centered on the figure of Ronald Reagan, made its bid for power in the 1976 primaries and won it in 1980. At the same time, the balance of power was aiding the rise of the right in the United States. After the unsuccessful

Angolan (and presumably Cuban) attempt to seize Zaire's Shaba province in 1978, Jimmy Carter and his national-security adviser, Zbigniew Brzezinski, decided to "play the China card." China was encouraged to attack Vietnam, which it did to dramatize, as at Damansky Island in 1969, its availability for joint action against the Soviets. A string of geopolitical defeats for the United States had prompted an even more demonstrative realignment of China against the Soviet Union. It was also in 1978 that the Chinese leaders made their first careful steps in the direction of a market economy, all part of the process initiated by "playing the China card."

This is roughly the place in the narrative where Mikhail Gorbachev appears with his reforms and the subject turns to the fall of the Soviet Union and the end of the Cold War. The action up to this time has not been leading in the direction of these themes. The United States had been losing the Cold War, certainly in terms of any reasonable calculation of the balance of power, as the Chinese tilt toward the weaker power, the United States, readily attests. On the other side, Brezhnev was boasting of the list of countries that could be newly counted in the column of workers states pursuing noncapitalist development. If we recall George Kennan's 1946 prescriptions for containment, we have to note that containment had been broken on three continents.

The Reagan arms buildup, designed to impress the Soviets with the idea that, despite everything, the United States still had more cards to play, was not greeted by the Soviets with the sudden perception that they were all trapped rats and had better partition their country and drop communism as soon as possible. On the contrary, to the Soviets Reagan's foreign and defense policy had the aspect of a kind of alibi: they (the Soviets) take some countries, we (the West) fume and build some weapons to compensate. Gorbachev viewed "Grandfather Reagan," as he referred to him in 1988, as quite desperate and at the same time rather quaint. He thought it droll that Reagan had been forced by the circumstances of their meeting to say that he no longer considered the Soviet Union an "evil empire." The new Soviet leader and his first team thus began to consolidate their power in a mood of supreme confidence, not to say arrogance.

Much of this will be counterintuitive for many students, who will be accustomed to think that the Soviet Union, in order to have collapsed so abjectly in 1991, must already have been on the ropes in 1981. To prepare a contrary thought, it is useful to assign some excerpts from works that demonstrate Soviet confidence at the end of the Brezhnev era and Western forebodings about the Soviet threat. These might include those of the British intelligence historian Christopher Andrew and Reagan's leading Soviet expert, Richard Pipes.[11] In the end, however, I am forced to rely on my own account in *Gorbachev's Revolution, 1985–1991*.

Gorbachev's immediate task was to rise above the collective leadership and the restraints of the Brezhnev era that had been put in place mainly by Mikhail Suslov, the second secretary for ideology and architect of the Brezhnev era collective leadership, who died the same year as Brezhnev, in 1982. But Gorbachev, as it turned out, did not completely throw off the fetters and vanquish his opponents until he had in effect liquidated the entire Soviet experiment. He came into office defending Stalin's record and by turns changed into a radical de-Stalinizer as his struggles against those who would have limited him became more intense. Opening the Soviet bloc to democracy was his weapon of last resort. The fight to get to the top and vanquish opposition was thus at the same time a quest to reconcile socialism and democracy. The *glasnost* campaign, despite its best intentions, led to an ideological critique of Stalinism that turned into an exit from Marxism. Two other political measures hastened the collapse. The economist Abel Agenbagyan convinced Gorbachev of the need to get the party out of the economy, and Boris Kurashvili won him for the idea of "national fronts" in the Union Republics to support *perestroika*. The first ruined the economy; the second mobilized the Republics against Moscow.[12]

Despite the "exhaustion strategy" that Moscow perceived in the Reagan arms buildup, the United States was otherwise largely a passive observer of *perestroika* in the Soviet Union. In fact US experts feared that a trick was being played on them. Ronald Reagan had to insist against his hard-line advisers that the Soviets were getting back to Lenin and that this must be encouraged. Oddly enough, the collapse of the Soviet bloc and Soviet communism made him right. Reagan's "second Cold War," as Fred Halliday called it, might otherwise have been taken as a fit of hysteria at the Soviet successes of the 1970s. But the collapse of communism and the partition of the Soviet Union seemed to vindicate Reaganism and neoliberalism before history.

Is this right? Did Reagan and Margaret Thatcher, the British prime minister, defeat Soviet communism? Students should be encouraged to explore these questions. Certainly no one can claim that they "negotiated an end to Communism," as George Bush the Elder boasted in his presidential campaign in 1992. The Western soldiers of the Cold War had certainly not won at the front. Quite the reverse. The enemy, after seeming to win the day, had simply decided to go home and have a good cry. There is no precedent in modern history for the spiritual implosion of a great power in this way. It has resulted in the most dramatic shift in the world balance of power ever effected without war. Indeed, one cannot comprehend the present situation of world politics without recognizing this fundamental oddity. It has set the stage for all sorts of post–Cold War menaces and mischief. In the 1990s the United States naturally tried to rationalize the end of the Cold War as having had more of an inexorable logic than it really did. Worse, it got used to seeing post-Soviet Russia caving in everywhere. After the Soviet collapse in 1991, any sign of Russia acting like a great power, even a regional power, seemed to the United States like unsupportable imperialism. In fact, if the Cold War's civics lessons were as the triumphalists claimed, Russia's only permissible course would have been to recede further into the territory of the old Duchy of Muscovy. Russia delenda est!

Thus the Cold War, which years ago I use to teach as something that was ongoing and which led us historians directly into the present, continues oddly to reverberate in our current geopolitical dilemmas. Inevitably, volumes will continue to appear in order to show how the United States accomplished the destruction of Soviet power. But the historian and the teacher of the history of the Cold War will want to ask whether this was in fact a homicide or a suicide. Did the Soviet intellectuals and their struggle against Stalinism cause the Soviet Union to, in effect, think itself to death? From the viewpoint of world politics, the Cold War is an exceptionally curious story.

NOTES

1. Hannah Arendt, *Origins of Totalitarianism* (New York: Harcourt Brace, 1951); Abbot Gleason, *Totalitarianism: The Inner History of the Cold War* (New York: Oxford University Press, 1995).

2. David Caute, *Isaac and Isaiah: The Covert Punishment of a Cold War Heretic* (New Haven: Yale University Press, 2013).

3. Ernst Nolte, "The Past That Will Not Pass," in James Knowlton and Truett Cates, eds., *Forever in the Shadow of Hitler?* (Atlantic Highlands, NJ: Humanities Press, 1993).

4. Ronald Robinson and John Gallagher, *Africa and the Victorians: The Official Mind of Imperialism* (New York: St. Martins, 1961). See William Roger Louis, ed., *The Robinson and Gallagher Controversy* (New York: New Viewpoints, 1976).

5. D. F. Fleming, *The Cold War and Its Origins*, 2 vols. (Garden City, NY: Doubleday, 1961).

6. I say this despite my admiration for the sharp analysis in, for example, Patrick Hearden, *Roosevelt Confronts Hitler: America's Entry into World War Two* (DeKalb: Northern Illinois University Press, 1987).

7. Speech of Stalin to the Politburo, 14 March 1948, text in Brian Murray, "Stalin, the Cold War, and the Division of China," Cold War International History Project Working Paper no. 12 (June 1995). Stalin had turned by 1947–48, but not in his speech of February 1946, sometimes called a "declaration of Cold War." In 1946 he still maintained the impossibility of a united imperialist bloc against the Soviet Union.

8. E. S. Varga, "Demokratiia novogo tipa" (Democracy of a new type), in *Mirovoe khoziaistvo i mirovaia politika* (World Economy and World Politics) (March 1947). A fuller account appears in Anthony D'Agostino, *Soviet Succession Struggles: Kremlinology and the Russian Question from Lenin to Gorbachev* (Boston: Routledge, 1988).

9. William Roger Louis and Ronald Robinson, "Empire Preserv'd: How the Americans Put Anti-communism before Anti-imperialism," in Prasenjit Duara, ed., *Decolonization: Perspectives from Now and Then* (New York: Routledge, 2004).

10. Fred Halliday, *The Making of the Second Cold War* (London: Verso, 1983).

11. Christopher Andrew, *The World Was Going Our Way: The KGB and the Battle for the Third World* (New York: Basic Books, 2006) for rosy Soviet expectations. Niall Ferguson, *High Financier: The Lives and Time of Siegmund Warburg* (New York: Penguin, 2010), records the lament of a leading banker and participant in the Eurodollar market about the seemingly inexorable path of Soviet policy from victory to victory. Richard Pipes, *Survival Is Not Enough* (New York: Simon and Shuster, 1984), reports the Soviet threat at its most menacing in Reagan's first term.

12. My account of this is in *Gorbachev's Revolution, 1985–1991* (London: Macmillan, 1998).

KEY RESOURCES

Andrew, Christopher. *The World Was Going Our Way: The KGB and the Battle for the Third World*. New York: Basic Books, 2006.

Caute, David. *Isaac and Isaiah: The Covert Punishment of a Cold War Heretic*. New Haven: Yale University Press, 2013.

Claudin, Fernando. *The Communist Movement from Comintern to Cominform*. 2 vols. New York: Penguin Books, 1975.

D'Agostino, Anthony. *Gorbachev's Revolution, 1985–1991*. London: Macmillan, 1998.

———. *Soviet Succession Struggles: Kremlinology and the Russian Question from Lenin to Gorbachev*. Boston: Routledge, 1988.

Fink, Carole. *The Cold War: An International History*. Boulder, CO: Westview Press, 2014.

Gaddis, John Lewis. *We Now Know*. Oxford: Oxford University Press, 1997.

Gleason, Abbot. *Totalitarianism: The Inner History of the Cold War*. Oxford: Oxford University Press, 1995.

Halliday, Fred. *The Making of the Second Cold War*. London: Verso, 1983.

Walker, Martin. *The Cold War: A History*. New York: Henry Holt, 1993.

Westad, Odd Arne. *The Global Cold War: Third World Interventions and the Making of Our Times*. Cambridge: Cambridge University Press, 2007.

The End of the Cold War in the Classroom

MARIO DEL PERO

This essay on the end of the Cold War is divided in five different parts. The first discusses the different interpretations of what the Cold War was and their influence on the way we periodize it and its end (the *when* did the Cold War take place inevitably depending on the *what* the Cold War was). The second part examines the return of the Cold War—the so-called Second Cold War—in the late 1970s and early 1980s, after the long seasons of bipolar détente, which led many to believe that the Cold War had terminated or was about to terminate. The third part is on the new détente of the second half of the 1980s, which led to the final end of the Cold War. Particular attention is paid here to the implosion of the socialist regimes in Central-Eastern Europe and then of the Soviet Union itself and to the German question. The collapse of the Soviet Union and the reunification of Germany are considered the two key events that marked the real and final end of the Cold War. The fourth part is on historiography and illustrates the main interpretations advanced by historians to explain why and how the Cold War ended. Finally, in the fifth and last session I suggest documents, audiovisual materials, movies, books, and art artifacts that can be effectively used when lecturing on the end of the Cold War.

How Many Ends of the Cold War?

Lecturing on the end of the Cold War means going back to the first class of a Cold War course, where its origins, nature, and possible periodizations are introduced and discussed. In this first class, the lecturer explains that the Cold War can be interpreted and has been interpreted by historians in a variety of ways: as an ideological contest between different forms of modernity and views of the historical process; as a clash between alternative and intrinsically antagonistic socioeconomic systems; as a geopolitical rivalry for the global balance of power that had in Europe, and in Germany in particular, its most prized stake; as a cultural competition between two universalisms; as an arms race that endowed the two sides with the capability to annihilate each other (and the planet along with them) n+1 times; as a conflict waged through multiple and highly deadly proxy wars in the periphery. Depending on interpretations that are often shaped by our point of observation—the *where* of our location tending to define the *how* we interpret the Cold War—we have multiple and not always overlapping Cold Wars: the cultural Cold War, the ideological Cold War, the geopolitical Cold War, the economic Cold War, the military Cold War, and so forth and so on.

Accordingly, we have different ends of the Cold War. Clearly, the ideological dimension of the Cold reached its zenith in an early phase (ca. 1947–63), which was marked by a reciprocal refusal of legitimacy between the superpowers.[1] Consequently, and aside from its brief as much as intense revival in the late 1970s and early 1980s, that specific ideological Cold War came to an end at the beginning of the 1960s, when the United States and the Soviet Union finally decided to engage each other in a fruitful discussion that opened the long phase of détente. This was matched also by the partial solution of some of the most vexing geopolitical dilemmas that had triggered the Cold War in the first place, such as the (temporary) stabilization of the German question. In the early 1960s, even that piece of the puzzle came into place. The possibility of a nuclearization of the Federal Republic of Germany (FRG) was finally abandoned; the erection of the Berlin Wall, as brutal and obnoxious a symbol of the partition of Europe and Germany as it was, offered a partial answer to a key driver of many early Cold War crises; NATO and the Atlantic security framework continued to represent the tool of a dual containment of both the Soviet Union and Germany, the division and limited sovereignty of the latter constituting a sort of insurance against its possible reemergence as a great power.

But the end of *that Cold War*, undisputable as it is, was the end of *one Cold War among many*. Other Cold Wars continued, modified or partially disciplined as they were. And their true common denominator—a bipolar distribution of power and of the ensuing configuration of international relations—did not vanish. To really end, the Cold War needed to lose this structural feature. Losing its ideological nature was certainly a lot, but not enough. The end of the Cold War had to be the end of post-1945 bipolarism, which could be overcome peacefully or not, with a bang or with a whimper. And a bang, dramatic and mostly unforeseen, it finally was. Bipolarism—and the Cold War with it—ended with the ultimate implosion of one of its two poles, the Soviet Union and the empire (or bloc) it had built in Central-Eastern Europe.

The Return of the Cold War

Different factors contributed to the return of the Cold War in the late 1970s. This new Cold War followed the long season of détente, which had produced multiple accords between the United States and the Soviet Union, particularly but not exclusively on arms control. Détente had served to institutionalize the nuclear balance of terror: to guarantee that deterrence—the certainty of reciprocal total destruction in case of war—would preempt the two countries from risking a conflict.

This *strategic interdependence*—which went by the appropriate acronym MAD (Mutual Assured Destruction)—was hard to swallow for many in the United States. According to its critics, negotiating with Moscow was ethically reprehensible and constituted a way to cede the moral high ground that the United States had allegedly occupied throughout the Cold War. The new right of the Republican Party, which had found in Ronald Reagan its prophet, and the neoconservatives in the Democratic camp converged in arguing that détente did not make sense even in strategic terms. The Soviet Union—it was claimed—did not adhere to the basic logic of MAD, still hoped to be able to wage and win a nuclear war, and was intent in achieving a condition of nuclear superiority that it could use to pressure and blackmail the United States and its allies.[2]

Strategy and morality thus infused the new Cold War rhetoric in the United States. They were complemented by the economic neoliberal turn of the late 1970s. Free trade, floating exchange rates and financial speculation, removal of controls on capital flows, primacy of the individual consumer and of the struggle against inflation: they all converged in shaping a new economic model wrapped in the rhetoric of *liberty* and in the juxtaposition between individual-centered capitalism and state-directed planned economies. After years of discussions about possible and sometimes inevitable convergences between the two models, we had a return—and a strengthening—of the idea that there was an irreducible, binary antagonism between the capitalist and socialist economies.

The Muscovite leadership did its part in exacerbating tensions and providing ammunition to the anti-Soviet camp in the United States. Irritated by what they perceived to be interference in their domestic affairs, Soviet leaders stepped up their action against political dissenters at home. In Europe, they decided to update—and potentiate—their missile delivery systems, without fully considering the consequences of this. The decision to intervene militarily in Afghanistan in December 1979 was meant to be short term and was driven primarily by defensive concerns. In the political climate of the time, and following the many crises of the previous years, it was interpreted as another step of a global Soviet offensive.[3] The Carter administration (1977–81) reacted harshly, but the real winners were Ronald Reagan and the Republican Right: those "Cold Warriors" who would only benefit politically and electorally from a new Cold War.

During the Second Cold War (ca. 1979–84), US-Soviet relations sank to 1950s-like lows. On strategic issues, the United States closed ranks with its European allies, deciding to balance the Soviet deployment of a new generation of missiles with the counterinstallation of new tactical weapons (the so-called Euro-missiles). The language used by both sides turned very ideological, with Ronald Reagan denouncing the Soviet "evil empire" and communism as a "bizarre chapter in human history whose last pages are even now being written."[4] A new arms race took place, with significant increases in the defense budgets of the two superpowers. The Reagan administration even embarked on a chimerical attempt to develop a new antiballistic defense system, the so-called Strategic Defense Initiative (SDI), launched by Reagan in 1983. The United States and the Soviet Union confronted each other in various peripheral theaters of the Cold War—from Central America to Afghanistan—and through different proxies. Washington launched ambitious and costly covert operations, the most important being in Afghanistan, where it supported the mujahidin's struggle against the Soviet invader and its local allies. The Reagan doctrine, as it came to be known, proclaimed the necessity of globally supporting anticommunist and anti-Soviet groups.

Ending the Cold War

But, despite its ideological fervor, this new Cold War did not last long. By nourishing and intensifying preexisting fears of a possible nuclear holocaust, it produced a backlash from pacifist and antinuclear movements. Polls taken in the United States revealed that a majority of the public, while appreciating Reagan's nationalist posture and general sanguinity on the strength and vigor of the United States, wanted him to return to the negotiating table. The risk of an accidental escalation was too high to be even contemplated, as revealed by several crises in 1983, when the two sides came perilously as well as unwarily close to war. The ties built in the previous two decades were simply too profound to be reversed: the Soviet Union needed access to Western credits and technology, whereas Soviet resources, particularly natural gas, were increasingly important for many energy-hungry European countries, West Germany above all. Finally, dramatic political changes in the Soviet Union and the access to power of a new generation of leaders were bound to insert a quasi-revolutionary variable into the Cold War equation.

The short Second Cold War was thus followed by a new and definitive détente and the final breakdown of the Cold War order. As in the previous decades, this new diplomatic engagement between the United States and the Soviet Union focused primarily on arms and their control.

Through arms control, the new Soviet leader, the reformist Mikhail Gorbachev, hoped to achieve several interrelated objectives. Reducing unbearable military expenditures would liberate resources for the domestic reforms Gorbachev intended to undertake. Through diplomatic engagement and détente, Gorbachev hoped to consolidate his power, further weakening the many conservative opponents of his policy. Finally, the new Soviet leadership adopted a new strategic paradigm that emphasized promoting collective security and minimizing the risk of war rather than controlling Central and Eastern Europe and maintaining a massive nuclear arsenal.[5]

Similar motivations acted on the American side. The rearmament launched by Reagan after his election increased both the domestic deficit and the public debt, and Americans worried that this new arms race was draining resources from more productive investments and making the United States and its economy less competitive. Reagan was himself terrified by the prospect of a possible nuclear war and tended to reject, on moral more than strategic grounds, the very logic behind deterrence and MAD. Both domestically and internationally, Reagan faced calls for a less confrontational approach to the Soviet Union, and the imminent 1984 presidential elections provided a clear political incentive for a rapprochement with Moscow.

Nuclear weapons provided Reagan and Gorbachev with a key common denominator: a bridge that the two leaders effectively used to launch new forms of diplomatic interaction. The first summits between Gorbachev and Reagan in Geneva (November 1985) and Reykjavik (October 1986) did not produce tangible results, mainly because of the unwillingness of the US president to drop his beloved SDI. But they paved the way for future agreements, most importantly the Intermediate Range Nuclear Forces Treaty (INF) signed in December 1987. While it affected only a small percentage of the total nuclear arsenals of the two superpowers, the INF treaty had a high political and symbolic value, given that for the first time the two superpowers were actually agreeing to reduce nuclear arms.[6]

Superpower tension persisted, but they were progressively subordinated to other processes and, in the case of Gorbachev and the Soviet Union, to the attempt to reform a decrepit system without causing its final collapse. Gorbachev succeeded in pulling out of the Afghan war. But the pro-Soviet socialist regimes of Central-Eastern Europe could not survive the partial liberalization undertaken by the Soviet Union. The contrast with the wealth and affluence of the Western European capitalist societies was all too visible and contributed to the erosion of the consensus of the socialist regimes in the East. Like a house of cards, each Central-Eastern European country—beginning with Hungary and Poland—saw the fall of its socialist government, the end of a single-party system, and the beginning of a transition to capitalism and democracy.[7]

The collapse of the Soviet bloc in Europe marked the end of Cold War geopolitics, but it wasn't yet the end of the Cold War. The return of the German question loomed large over the future of Europe and the international system; so did the fate of Gorbachev and his reformist project. A reunified Germany was bound to transform the geopolitical landscape of Europe and to radically alter power equilibrium within the European Community (soon to become European Union, or EU). Many Western European leaders—beginning with the British prime minister, Margaret Thatcher—were uneasy about this prospect, but it was nevertheless understood that the question was not *whether* German reunification would happen but how and when. Gorbachev hoped to influence the process, creating a militarily neutral, reunified Germany. His wasn't, however, a realistic goal: for Germans, neutrality meant a violation of sovereignty, while the United States wanted Germany incorporated into the US-led Atlantic security system. Negotiations between the 4+2 powers (the two Germanys and the four post–World War II occupying powers) led to the inclusion of Germany in NATO and the reunification of the country in October 1990.[8]

The last piece of the puzzle was the Soviet Union itself. Gorbachev's political and economic reforms had unleashed forces that were about to destroy that country. Among them were the nationalist elites of the composite and multinational Soviet federation, particularly in the three Baltic republics (Lithuania, Latvia, and Estonia). Gorbachev had hoped to enlist (and use) them in his reformist crusade, only to find them challenging and in the end helping to tear down the Soviet state. In 1990 and 1991, Gorbachev oscillated incoherently in a vain attempt to contain these different pressures and even authorized the use of military force in Lithuania. In the summer of 1991, conservative forces within the Soviet Union tried to promote a coup d'état to regain control of the Soviet state. It was a poorly planned *putsch* that went nowhere. But the real winner was not Gorbachev. Led by the Russian president (and Gorbachev's rival) Boris Yeltsin, the presidents of the different republics and the nationalist leaders accelerated the process that led to the collapse of the Soviet Union and the birth of a group of independent states loosely connected in a new Union, initially renamed the Commonwealth of Independent States (CIS). In December 1991 the Soviet Union ceased to exist, and the Cold War finally ended along with it.

The topics discussed here can serve as the basis for classroom discussions or assignments. For example, if students have already discussed the role of Germany in the origins of the Cold War (which presumably they have), they can now analyze the renewed centrality of the German question in the last phase of the Cold War. It might also be fruitful to ask students to write a paper arguing for either 1989 or 1991 as marking the end of the Cold War. The purpose of the exercise would be not so much to see which year the students pick but rather to assess their ability to marshal evidence for their argument. Student could then present and defend their decisions in class.

Interpretations of the End of the Cold War

As of today, it's possible to divide the historiography of (and on) the end of the Cold War in six basic categories. They are not necessarily mutually exclusive, and overlaps are sometimes significant and unavoidable. But they have distinctive traits, which allow for the taxonomy (and the convenient definitions of different interpretative paradigms) I am about to propose.

The first interpretation is that of the *triumphalist* school. It claims that the United States, and more precisely Ronald Reagan, defeated the Soviet Union and won the Cold War. The intense rearmament of the early 1980s, a nationalist discourse that boldly asserted the uniqueness (and inner superiority) of the United States, the emphasis on individual freedom, the celebration of the consumerist model—it is claimed—put the Soviet Union in a corner, further eroded its appeal and legitimacy, and accelerated its final, inevitable collapse.[9] This interpretation possibly dominates the public and political narrative of the Cold War in the United States. Few historians would, however, fully subscribe to it, and many have stressed how Reagan's policies made the task of Gorbachev and the reformers more complicated, by playing to the advantage of the Soviet hard-liners who denounced the inner aggressiveness of US policy vis-à-vis the Soviet Union.[10]

The second interpretation is the *structuralist* one. Here the emphasis is on the action of long-term historical forces—of structures, indeed—more than specific policies, contingencies, or individual deeds. There are many possible "structuralisms," ranging from Marxism to neoliberalism, but the common assumption is that deep systemic transformations, particularly in the economic realm, rendered the Soviet model of planned economy increasingly inefficient and unable to adapt to a changing world marked by technological innovations, transnational finance, capital mobility, and radical transformations in the field of communication and information.[11] An emphasis on structures and, often, on unintended (and even unwanted) consequences tends to downplay the agency of individuals and overlook the resilient power of politics and policies.

This is what a third and fourth cluster of interpretations of the end of the Cold War—*the top-down* and *the bottom-up* schools—emphasize. A top-down reading stresses the central role played by political leaders: their visions, actions, choices and sometimes mistakes. Concerning the end of the Cold War, these interpretations focus in particular on figures like Reagan and Gorbachev (to whom from time to time are added the French president François Mitterrand, the German chancellor Helmut Kohl, the British prime minister Margaret Thatcher, and even Pope John Paul II). These leaders are praised or lambasted for their courage or for their errors, for their readiness to engage each other in fruitful diplomatic exchanges or for their inability to understand the strength of underlying historical forces. But the key variable in explaining the end of the Cold War is indeed their actions: what they did and were capable of doing or what they didn't do or proved incapable of doing.[12]

The bottom-up school moves from a similar logic but highlights the importance not of leaders but of groups, people, NGOs, and the like. When it comes to the end of the Cold War, what is emphasized is the importance of a variety of social and political actors: human rights groups, dissidents, peace activists, antinuclear organizations, churches, and so on. They all mobilized in challenging a Cold War order they considered unjust, dangerous, and oppressive. And through their actions they helped tear this order down, either by pressuring leaders to make decisions they would otherwise have not made or by being at the forefront of those revolutionary processes that in Central-Eastern Europe led to the collapse of the pro-Soviet socialist regimes.[13]

A fifth interpretation is a *Euro-centric* one. According to this viewpoint, it is not on the US-Soviet relationship that historians must concentrate to understand the end of the Cold War but on intra-European dynamics. The Cold War and its end are read here as a primarily European story whose end was marked by the conclusion of the European geopolitical divide and the reunification not just of Germany but also of the European continent, whose most important and tangible example was the enlargement of the European Union. The stress on the centrality of Europe's geopolitics usually combines with an emphasis on the agency of European actors. A German-led Western Europe—it is argued—ably exploited the allure of its social and economic model and on the increasing financial and technological dependence of the Soviet Union to drive and control the process that led to the peaceful demise of the Soviet bloc.[14]

Finally, there is the *"Cold War Has Not Ended"* interpretation, which seems to have gained new traction as a consequence of the 2014 Ukrainian crisis and of the renewed tensions between Russia and the United States. The political, economic, and even environmental costs of the Cold War—it is argued—are still very much with us, as quintessentially revealed by the fact that we continue to live in a nuclear world: in a situation where the nuclear balance of terror and MAD still represent the main deterrent against new major wars and where Cold War debris and remains are everywhere, from deeply contaminated lakes to nuclear waste destined to be stocked for n+1 years, from unsolved (and Cold War–exacerbated) local conflicts to Cold War institutions (beginning with NATO) capable of surviving the end of the US-Soviet bipolar competition even when struggling to define a rationale for their continuing existence.[15]

Once students are familiar with the general contours of Cold War historiography, they can be asked to analyze and discuss these different approaches. Students can be divided into two groups to debate the "bottom-up" versus the "top-down" approach to Cold War historiography. Another idea is simply to ask students to choose the interpretation of the Cold War that they find most convincing and explain the basis for their choice. Teachers can also distribute a primary source from the course (or ask students to find a primary source related to the Cold War) and write a brief response paper explaining how the document could be used to support different Cold War interpretations.

Materials for the Classroom

Teachers of the history of the Cold War have now three excellent primers at their disposal: the three-volume *Cambridge History of the Cold War*, the *Routledge Handbook of the Cold War*, and the *Oxford Handbook of the Cold War*.[16] Combined, they offer an immensely rich collection of essays—general and introductory, analytical and thematic, interpretative and historiographical. We can choose several of these essays for our session on the Cold War and construct a reader that combines them with the best histories of the Cold War now available and with those studies that correctly highlight the transformational impact of the 1970s.[17]

When it comes to primary sources, historians of the Cold War and of international relations broadly have to follow the rules (and times) of the archives. As of today, many documents on the 1980s and the end of the Cold War are still classified, although a body of new materials is slowly being made available to researchers. In preparation for their finals and to write their papers, students can, however, access several collections of documents that have been collected, edited, and published by research institutes and groups. Among them, I'd like to mention here the National Security Archive (NSA) and the Cold War International History Project (CWIHP), two Washingtonian institutions that in the past two decades have immensely contributed to the study of post-1945 international relations by offering primary-source documentation, US and international, which now extends also to the last years of the Cold War.[18] Both the NSA and the CWIHP have published excellent anthologies of documents on the last phase of the Cold War, which contain documents on the superpowers and their interaction. These anthologies include CIA estimates, memoranda of conversation between Gorbachev and Reagan, and a broad array of materials on the relationship between the Soviet Union and its lesser allies in Central-Eastern Europe.[19] Two excellent collections of US documents that also offer highly revealing audiovisual materials are the American Presidency Project at the University of California Santa Barbara and the Presidential Speech Archive at the Miller Center of the University of Virginia. Finally, important primary sources can be accessed at the Zurich-based Parallel History on Cooperative Security (PHP), formerly the Parallel History Project on NATO and the Warsaw Pact, which has assembled many document on security issues concerning also the Cold War and its last phase.[20]

Among these rich materials, which historians now have an increasingly hard time consulting and digesting, teachers have an embarrassment of choice. In my class on the end of the Cold War, I assign four primary sources for discussion: (1) a transcript of a summit conversation between Gorbachev and Reagan (usually from the 1986 Reykjavik meeting); (2) speeches by the two, such as Reagan's 1983 "Evil Empire Speech" and Gorbachev's 1989 discourse on the "Common Home in Europe"; and (3) an analysis of the economic and social troubles of socialist regimes in Central-Eastern Europe (an intelligence estimate or an internal document of one of these regimes). These three kinds of sources well complement one another and allow students to engage both with the different meanings of the Cold War and with the main drivers of its final implosion.

Audiovisual materials are nowadays extremely useful, if not indispensable, teaching tools. Iconic pictures and emblematic videos help keep the attention of students and leave them with a vivid image of the events studied and discussed in class. For my lecture on the end of the Cold War I typically use illustrative pictures and video clips, all of which can be found through Google searches. The first picture shows the strikes of the workers of the Solidarity (Solidarność) movement in Poland, in 1980: the beginning of a new wave of protests against the socialist systems of the Soviet bloc that would decisively contribute to its downfall. A second picture I use, showing the massive antinuclear demonstration in New York City in 1982, reveals the popularity and the global dimension of the protest against MAD and the very logic behind nuclear deterrence. I also show the famous photo of Reagan and Gorbachev at the 1985 Geneva summit. The summit fell short of expectations, as we have seen, but contributed to the development of a solid, warm, and amicable personal relationship between the two leaders, which the image—with the reassuring background presence of a fireplace—plastically conveys. A final effective image captures the lonely Chinese student facing a tank during the dramatic crackdown of the students' protests in Tiananmen Square in Beijing in June 1989. It's an image that communicates multiple and somehow contradictory messages: the persistence of repressive practices and limitations on political dissent in many parts of the world, new détentes and ends of the Cold War notwithstanding; the transnational, if not global, flow of ideas and models that has marked the contemporary age; the responsibility of the individual; the overestimation of the power of such individual in an increasingly fragmented and atomized society.[21]

The images are to be complemented by three brief video clips. The first is from the "evil empire" speech given by Reagan in 1983, mentioned earlier, which highlights the kind of bombastic and jingoistic language deployed by the US president during the short and intense phase of the so-called Second Cold War.[22] The second clip provides a sort of anticlimax to the first one: it's Reagan's 1988 speech at Moscow State University, which symbolized the zenith of the second, final détente of the late 1980s.[23] Finally, the last clip cannot but be about the fall of the Berlin wall, the ultimate, quintessential symbol of the Cold War and the division of Europe.[24]

Finally, I like to conclude each of my class with a suggestion for a book, a movie, and an artist related to the period and issues we have just discussed. The end of the Cold War and the 1980s offer a huge variety of possibilities, and mine are just proposals that I hope help teachers approach the subjects with different toolboxes from that of the historian. The movie I propose is *Good Bye Lenin*, a 2003 German film directed by Wolfgang Becker, which describes in effective, tragicomic terms the collapse of socialist rule in East Berlin. The book is Tom Clancy's debut novel *The Hunt for Red October* (1984), which portrays the defection of a Soviet submarine commander (not accidentally of Lithuanian nationality) and the successful effort of the CIA to take possession of the Soviet Union's new, experimental submarine.[25] The book is significant not so much for its (limited) literary value but for its symbolic relevance and for what it reveals about images and stereotypes of the Soviet Union in 1980s America. Finally, the artist I recommend is Keith Haring. The inner social and political content of Haring's work was somehow balanced by its symbolizing the consumerism and even the hedonism of the United States in the 1980s, which was so central in the cultural dimension of the last phase of the Cold War.

Images are to be used to highlight specific points made in class: to visualize facts, events, people, and interpretations described during the lecture. In this specific case, the images offer useful reminders of the structural weaknesses of the Soviet regime, the persistence of some of the achievements of détente, particularly the centrality of arms control, and the pervasive and politically influential fear of a nuclear holocaust. The familiar and somehow reassuring image of Reagan and Gorbachev exemplifies the role played by individuals—and by the two superpowers' leaders—in this last phase of the Cold War. Videos provide sounds and voices for the history we discuss in class (as well as a useful break in a two-hour class). The two Reagan speeches serve to underline the transformations in the foreign-policy discourse of the United States during the 1980s, from the bombastic and aggressive nationalism of the "Second Cold War" to the accommodating rhetoric of the new détente. Finally, the images of the enthusiastic crowds celebrating the fall of the Berlin Wall offer a vivid example of what the Cold War was for (and how it was lived by) people on the ground and helps to balance and integrate the inevitable emphasis placed by a Cold War course on grand strategies, alternative modernization projects, and global geopolitical visions—because the Cold War was many things—indeed, we began this essay by showing that there were many Cold Wars—and its end had multiple meanings, implications and consequences.

NOTES

1. Anders Stephanson, "The Cold War as US Project," in Federico Romero and Silvio Pons, eds., *Reinterpreting the Cold War: Issues, Interpretations, Periodizations* (London: Frank Cass, 2005), 52–69.

2. Justin Vaïsse, *Neoconservatism: The Biography of a Movement* (Cambridge, MA: Harvard University Press, 2011).

3. Odd Arne Westad, *The Global Cold War: Third World Interventions and the Making of Our Time* (Cambridge: Cambridge University Press, 2005), 288–331; Leopoldo Nuti, ed., *The Crisis of Detente in Europe: From Helsinki to Gorbachev, 1975–1985* (London: Routledge, 2009).

4. Ronald Reagan, *Commencement Address at Notre Dame University*, May 17, 1981, http://www.reagan.utexas.edu/archives/speeches/1981/51781a.htm; Ronald Reagan, *Remarks at the Annual Convention of the National Association of Evangelicals in Orlando, Florida,* March 8, 1983, http://www.reagan.utexas.edu /archives/speeches/1983/30883b.htm.

5. Archie Brown, *The Gorbachev Factor* (Oxford: Oxford University Press, 1996); James Graham Wilson, *The Triumph of Improvisation: Gorbachev's Adaptability, Reagan's Engagement, and the End of the Cold War* (Ithaca, NY: Cornell University Press, 2014).

6. The text of the INF Treaty is available at http://www.state.gov/t/avc /trty/102360.htm.

7. Jacques Lévesque, "The East European Revolutions of 1989," in Melvin Leffler and Odd Arne Westad, eds., *The Cambridge History of the Cold War*, Vol. III: *Endings* (Cambridge: Cambridge University Press, 2012), 311–32.

8. Mary Elise Sarotte, *1989: The Struggle to Create Post-Cold War Europe* (Princeton: Princeton University Press, 2009).

9. The historian who possibly comes closest to offering an interpretation of this kind is John L. Gaddis. Among his many works, see in particular *We Now Know: Re-thinking Cold War History* (Oxford: Oxford University Press, 1997) and *The Cold War: A New History* (New York: Penguin, 2005).

10. Beth A. Fisher, "US Foreign Policy under Reagan and Bush," in Leffler and Westad, eds., *Cambridge History of the Cold War*, 3:267–88.

11. Two different but excellent examples of interpretations that adopt, at least in part, a structuralist approach are Giovanni Arrighi, *The Long Twentieth Century: Money, Power and the Origins of Our Times* (London: Verso, 1994), and Daniel J. Sargent, *A Superpower Transformed: The Remaking of American Foreign Relations in the 1970s* (Oxford: Oxford University Press, 2015).

12. For two good examples see Melvin P. Leffler, *For the Soul of the Mankind: The United States, the Soviet Union and the Cold War* (New York: Hill & Wang, 2007), and Vladislav M. Zubok, *A Failed Empire: The Soviet Union in the Cold War from Stalin to Gorbachev* (Chapel Hill: University of North Carolina Press, 2007).

13. Matthew Evangelista, *Unarmed Forces* (Ithaca, NY: Cornell University Press, 2002); Daniel C. Thomas, *The Helsinki Effect: International Norms, Human Rights, and the Demise of Communism* (Princeton: Princeton University Press, 2001); Sarah B. Snyder, *Human Rights Activism and the End of the Cold War: A*

Transnational History of the Helsinki Network (Cambridge: Cambridge University Press, 2013).

14. Federico Romero, *Storia della Guerra Fredda: L'ultimo conflitto per l'Europa* (Torino: Einaudi, 2010); Michael Cox, "Another Transatlantic Split: American and European Narratives and the End of the Cold War," *Cold War History* 1 (2007): 121–46.

15. Richard Ned Lebow and Janice Gross Stein, *We All Lost the Cold War* (Princeton: Princeton University Press, 1995); J. R. McNeill, "The Biosphere and the Cold War," in Leffler and Westad, eds., *Cambridge History of the Cold War*, 3:422–44; Heonik Kwon, *The Other Cold War* (New York: Columbia University Press, 2010).

16. Leffler and Westad, eds., *Cambridge History of the Cold War*; Artemy M. Kalinovksy and Craig Daigle, eds., *The Routledge Handbook of the Cold War* (London: Routledge, 2014); Richard H. Immerman and Petra Goedde, eds., *The Oxford Handbook of the Cold War* (Oxford: Oxford University Press, 2013).

17. Westad, *The Global Cold War*; Zubok, *A Failed Empire*; John Lamberton Harper, *The Cold War* (Oxford: Oxford University Press, 2011); Sargent, *Superpower Transformed*; Niall Ferguson, Charles Maier, Erez Manela, and Daniel Sargent, eds., *The Shock of the Global: The 1970s in Perspective* (Oxford: Oxford University Press, 2011).

18. See the National Security Archive, http://nsarchive.gwu.edu, and the Cold War International History Project, http://www.wilsoncenter.org/program/cold-war-international-history-project. In addition, one can use sources published by the historians Jussi M. Hanhimäki and Odd Arne Westad in *The Cold War: A History in Documents and Eyewitness Accounts* (Oxford: Oxford University Press, 2003).

19. For two, illustrative examples see the Woodrow Wilson Center Digital Archive, *End of the Cold War*, http://digitalarchive.wilsoncenter.org/collection/37/end-of-the-cold-war, and the National Security Archive, *The Shevardnadze File: Late Soviet Foreign Minister Helped End the Cold War*, http://nsarchive.gwu.edu/NSAEBB/NSAEBB481/.

20. The American Presidency Project, University of California, Santa Barbara, http://www.presidency.ucsb.edu; Presidential Speech Archive, University of Virginia, http://millercenter.org/president/speeches; the Parallel History on Cooperative Security, http://www.php.isn.ethz.ch/.

21. On this, see the excellent reflection of Daniel T. Rodgers, *The Age of Fracture* (Cambridge, MA: Harvard University Press, 2011).

22. Ronald Reagan, *Remarks at the Annual Convention of the National Associations of Evangelicals*, Orlando, FL, March 8 1983, http://www.reaganfoundation.org/bw_detail.aspx?p=LMBYGHF2&lm=berlinwall&args_a=cms&args_b=74&argsb=N&tx=1770.

23. Ronald Reagan, *Address at Moscow State University*, May 31 1988, http://millercenter.org/president/reagan/speeches/speech-3416.

24. Among the many videos available on the fall of the Berlin wall, see this clip from the NBC coverage: https://www.youtube.com/watch?v=fKMwhEDjHg.

25. Tom Clancy, *The Hunt for Red October* (Annapolis, MD: Naval Institute Press, 1984).

KEY RESOURCES

Borstelmann, Thomas. *The 1970s: A New Global History from Civil Rights to Economic. Inequality.* Princeton: Princeton University Press, 2011.

Evangelista, Matthew. *Unarmed Forces: The Transnational Movement to End the Cold War.* Ithaca, NY: Cornell University Press, 2002.

Immerman, Richard H., and Petra Goedde, eds. *The Oxford Handbook of the Cold War.* Oxford: Oxford University Press, 2013.

Kalinovksy, Artemy M., and Craig Daigle, eds. *The Routledge Handbook of the Cold War.* London: Routledge, 2014.

Romero, Federico. "Cold War Historiography at the Crossroads." *Cold War History* 4 (2014): 685–703.

Rossinow, Doug. *The Reagan Era: A History of the 1980s.* New York: Columbia University Press, 2015.

Sargent, Daniel J. *A Superpower Transformed: The Remaking of American Foreign Relations in the 1970s.* Oxford: Oxford University Press, 2015.

Stephanson, Anders. "Fourteen Notes on the Very Concept of the Cold War." http://h-diplo.org/essays/PDF/stephanson-14notes.pdf.

Teaching the Cold War to the Post-9/11 Generation

DAVID BOSSO

One of the more sobering realizations many history teachers have come to over the past few years is that their students have little, if any, recollection of the tragic events of September 11, 2001. Their lives have been influenced as much by heightened national security, global terrorism, natural disasters of epic proportions, and the aggrandizement of fundamentalist movements as it has been by the growing influence of social media, instant access to information, economic shifts, and more intricate global interactions. Whether singular and seminal or emergent and evolving over time, the events, ideas, and movements that shaped the zeitgeist of an era leave lasting impressions both individually and collectively. They shape our identities and influence our perspectives, values, memories, and experiences. Those of an earlier generation have vivid recollections of the moment they heard President Kennedy was shot and when we landed on the moon. It is likely that the Challenger shuttle disaster and the Iranian hostage crisis are seared into the memories of those who were children in the 1970s and 1980s. Students born since that horrific day in September 2001, however, have experienced too many events—hurricanes, tsunamis, war, terror attacks—and such saturated media coverage that it is understandable if they are often confused, mistaken, or otherwise overwhelmed when they try to make sense of it all. It is no wonder that students often feel that historical events are vastly distant in both time and space.

This disconnect need not exist. Although the Cold War ended more than two decades ago, many current global events are themselves consequences of Cold War policies and actions. Moreover, numerous situations contain elements of Cold War circumstances and can be used as vehicles to help today's students of the post-9/11 era to better understand what has transpired over the past decade or so. In many ways, teaching the Cold War offers a wide variety of opportunities for teachers to effectively utilize inquiry as a pedagogical foundation, to illuminate historical trends over time, to demonstrate local connections to global events, to highlight the significance of current events in evocative and powerful ways, and to better equip students to communicate conclusions and take informed action. Teaching the Cold War, then, is an excellent avenue by which students can make better sense of the world in which we live, connect current events to a larger historical context, and examine cultural and political issues in meaningful ways. Such efforts will indeed foster the skills and dispositions that we continue to claim are vital to our work as teachers: to cultivate lifelong learning, empathy and tolerance, a global orientation, and knowledgeable and active citizenship.

Introducing Post-9/11 Students to the Cold War

Teachers must remember that the Cold War is a topic with little immediacy for today's students. Thus, teachers should not expect students to have much general knowledge about what the Cold War entailed. Teachers may want to begin their coverage of the Cold War by using an introductory visual of a map showing the American and Soviet spheres of influence at the height of the Cold War. Students should be able to use this image to situate themselves geographically in the Cold War but also to understand the fundamental concept of bipolarity in the Cold War. Teachers should also introduce students to the larger context, and concepts of international relations, war, national security, and other factors related to a conceptual framework must be kept in mind when designing and preparing lessons to teach about the Cold War. To highlight such topics and ideas when teaching the Cold War, teachers can choose from numerous events, many of which are expounded upon in this book. Regardless of which events and concepts are utilized to illuminate the critical features of the Cold War and its enduring impact, the following key elements of the era ought to be considered for deeper student understanding:

- The Cold War, derived from ideological differences between the United States and the Soviet Union, was a long-term standoff between the two superpowers in the decades following the Second World War. Consequently, the era was characterized by political tensions, strategic gamesmanship, attempts to expand political and economic influence, and the involvement of other global players.
- Although the superpowers did not engage with each other militarily, they used other entities in an effort to gain military, political, and economic superiority. Such relationships and ensuing events involved complex causes and effects, influenced the lives of millions of people across the globe, and continue to impact the world today.
- Technological advances and cultural factors, particularly as related to nuclear expansion and space exploration and corresponding propaganda efforts, heightened the degree of competition between the two superpowers.
- The legacy of the Cold War continues to shape international events today. Such events and their potential outcomes can be better understood if we use the Cold War as a cultural, political, and economic backdrop.

Today's students are familiar with the global conflict between religious fundamentalism and secularism that has influenced many international events of the post-9/11 era. They are less likely to understand the ideological divisions between communism and capitalism that served as the basis for the Cold War. Students should be introduced to these terms, not only the ideals of each as put forth in, say, the US Constitution and the *Communist Manifesto* but also the ways by which such values and visions became manifest in reality. Using events such as China's Great Leap Forward and the Cultural Revolution—in particular, primary sources such as images and personal narratives—can highlight the shortcomings of communist policies. Similarly, analyzing the civil rights movement in the United States presents a unique window into the challenges of democratic societies. Whatever historical events, examples, and resources they use, effective teachers create conditions for students to analyze, critique, and generate conclusions about the advantages and disadvantages of different ideologies, as well as the impact such beliefs have had on the ways in which historical events have transpired and cultural norms have developed.

Political science concepts such as the containment policy, superpower, spheres of influence, balance of power, power vacuum, geopolitics, national security, mutual assured destruction, brinkmanship, détente, and proxy war are also essential for students to know and be prepared to apply. For instance, the ways by which ideological differences play out in real terms can be better understood if students realize that US foreign policy following the conclusion of the Second World War was dictated by the containment policy. Additionally, while students may have basic knowledge about the Korean and Vietnam Wars, they might have difficulty understanding the larger political context without knowing the reasons for containment strategies.

Because of the scope and complexity of the Cold War, a regional or chronological approach, while effective in many history courses, may limit the connections students make among the various themes and concepts that weave their way throughout the duration of the course. Such approaches may seem disjointed and overwhelming for students as they jump from one region or time period to another in an effort to keep everything within a particular historical context. Thus, not only does a thematic approach create greater coherence and fosters deeper understanding, but also framing the Cold War era in such a manner provides an excellent opportunity for inquiry to take place. While a world history course that covers various countries might initially lend itself toward a regional approach, such a course might be better served by finding common themes that exist among the regions and histories. A thematic unit centering on human rights and social justice might include discussion of Mao-era policies, the decision to use the atomic bomb, the Berlin Airlift, and US sanctions against Cuba. A unit centered on the theme of power, authority, and governance might analyze Stalin's tactics against political opponents, the impact of McCarthyism, *glasnost* and *perestroika*, the right to privacy versus national security, and a host of other engaging or controversial issues.

Multiple perspectives and resources from one or more of the regions and time periods can inform students' understanding of each of the themes. Furthermore, examples from recent and current events might supplement various themes—again, whether directly or indirectly associated with the Cold War. For instance, protesters in Tiananmen Square in 1989, the Patriot Act, the Miracle on Ice, North Korea's new leadership, and Putin's assertiveness can be used to highlight any number of themes of the Cold War. Framing a course this way allows teachers and students

103

to examine historical issues and events as well as contemporary ones, perhaps even in conjunction with one another.

Certainly, utilizing a thematic approach allows a wide continuum of inquiry opportunities to exist, from a single activity within a lesson, to an entire lesson in and of itself, to experiences that might be more long-term, such as a project-based learning. By keeping inquiry at the center, this approach helps students to develop the skills and mind-set required to effectively answer such questions in a manner that facilitates their investigation and generates new questions for further inquiry. With the understanding that inquiry can take a variety of forms, vary in intensity and time, and require different types and amounts of resources, the important thing to keep in mind is that inquiry puts the student at the center and focuses on students' active engagement rather than their passive interaction with course concepts and materials. An inquiry experience, however applied, will spark student interest and lead students to new learning in a way that is meaningful, engaging, and memorable.

At the center of any meaningful inquiry are student- and teacher-generated questions that put the student at the heart of the learning process. The questions that students ask about Cold War issues and circumstances (as well as other topics throughout the curriculum) tend to be about larger issues and ideals, as well as those that are reflective of historical themes, cultural universals, and enduring understandings, particularly when they can relate them to current events and their own lives. *Compelling questions* (similar to overarching or essential questions) can be fashioned by students and teachers alike and guide the conveyance of the curriculum, and the class can return to them again and again even as they generate new questions and new understandings. Importantly, effective compelling questions may never be answered commonly or fully as students interact with various resources and construct their understandings in novel and personally meaningful ways. *Supporting questions* focus on specific knowledge and evidence in support of compelling questions. As students are encouraged and guided appropriately in the development of supporting and compelling questions, they will be better positioned to construct their own meaning of larger issues. They will also become more skilled at posing additional questions as the inquiry process evolves. Beginning any inquiry with the active construction of compelling and supporting questions is a valuable instructional approach to facilitate student learning.

Making the Cold War Relevant
to Post-9/11 Students

Students who have grown up since the 9/11 attacks have a strong sense of the intersection between the global and the local. Indeed, the attacks themselves provided a vivid example of both the process of globalization and the way that global trends have affected Americans in their daily lives. The Cold War is an ideal topic for helping students to see historical evidence of both increasing global integration and the ways that globalism touches Americans in a variety of ways. Doing so not only will engage students in the history of the Cold War but may give them a greater appreciation of history in general.

By considering local and even personal connections to global events, the teacher of the Cold War can underscore the relevance of course materials and concepts, increase the degree of authenticity, take advantage of local and state resources, and shed light on larger global issues. For instance, a building once used as a bomb shelter in one's community might stimulate meaningful discussion of the Cold War, moral issues related to use of weapons and proportional response, the use of propaganda, and the value of strategic and political decision making. Similarly, students' parents, grandparents, or other relatives might be an excellent resource for insights into local perspectives and recollections of the space race or the Cuban Missile Crisis, and the interview experience will be memorable for all parties involved.

Numerous additional examples abound, and museums and historical organizations, both online and in person, stand at the ready to provide an abundance of resources to assist teachers in their efforts to use a local lens to examine global issues. By infusing local and state examples into a modern world history course and using an inquiry focus, teachers can better enable students to understand their place in a larger historical, political, economic, and cultural context. Furthermore, student understanding of the relevance and magnitude of historical events and enduring issues increases when they are equipped with the skills, knowledge, and dispositions needed to comprehend complex issues through the lens of local and even personal connections to global experiences.

Just as the Cold War can help students to understand the background of a broad concept such as globalization, it can also illuminate

the genesis of specific current events that interest the post-9/11 generation. An analysis of current events in the Middle East, the role of the
United States vis-à-vis its Middle Eastern counterparts, and predictions
of possible outcomes can be enhanced with a thorough examination of
Cold War–related events in the region. Recent Russian aggrandizement
in Crimea and corresponding Western reactions can be better explored
if students have a sound understanding of Cold War tensions and the
concept of spheres of influence and power vacuums. Political rhetoric
and national policies in China and North Korea become clearer when
students have a nuanced understanding of the causes, effects, and
characteristics of the Cold War.

To better enable students to understand the world today, it is often
valuable to provide them with the tools, insights, resources, skills, and
knowledge to examine the past. Online and/or hardcopy resources
such as *The Week* and *Upfront* offer teachers and students intriguing
overviews on current events in historical contexts. *World Press Review*
and *Kidon Media Link* provide access to world headlines, media articles,
quotes, political cartoons, and the like so that multiple perspectives can
be examined. The Avalon Project at the Yale School of Law is an excellent
reservoir of numerous primary-source documents categorized by topic
and subtopic (e.g., clicking on the Cuban Missile Crisis provides hundreds of resources related to the event). The *New York Times* has a site
dedicated to the teaching of the Cold War, with lesson plans and additional resources. The History Channel's Cold War page includes numerous useful articles, videos, pictures, and speeches. The National Archives
Library Information Center contains an extensive collection of resources
related to significant Cold War events, and the Gilder Lehrman Institute
of American History provides expert commentary and analysis on Cold
War and post–Cold War policy and events. With such resources readily
available, the opportunities for inquiry, analysis, discussion, and the
communication of conclusions are wide-ranging—and collaborating
with science, math, art, music, and teachers from other disciplines ex-
pands the possibilities even more so.

The current generation of students is increasingly exposed to interdisciplinary courses, at both the high school and the college levels.
Therefore, an interdisciplinary approach to the Cold War may engage
students' interest and build on their academic experiences. While it
seems that the most appropriate and natural vehicle by which to teach
the Cold War is through a social studies curriculum, this should not

preclude one from looking for interdisciplinary connections. The sheer magnitude of the Cold War offers a variety of opportunities and resources to address associated events, issues, and concepts across the disciplines. Music, movies, memoirs, primary sources, and a number of other resources are readily available online.

A short Huffington Post article, "Cold War, Hot Songs: The Best Music to Emerge from the Fear of Nuclear War," identifies several songs (with accompanying video) that address concerns of nuclear war. CNNfyi.com provides an overview of the role of music during the Cold War, including specific analysis of various songs. Simple online searches will lead to any number of collections of Cold War music, often replete with insightful analysis and interpretation of lyrics. A similar search for Cold War films will result in a number of sites suggesting top-ten or must-watch movies, ranging from *The Manchurian Candidate* to *Thirteen Days* to *The Hunt for Red October*. Goodreads.com provides a solid list of Cold War literature for young adults, such as spy novels and other fiction. Unfortunately, it does not appear that there are many Cold War–related memoirs suitable for high school students. An image search on Google for Cold War propaganda generates hundreds of thumbnail pictures of posters, and one can similarly search for Cold War political cartoons. Singular images or a series of visual resources can provide the foundation for engaging and stimulating lessons.

A student born in 2001 will not have any first-hand memories of the 9/11 attacks, but she will have grown up in a world characterized by military conflict, human rights abuses, and natural disasters. As a result, today's students tend to have a keen interest in social justice. A knowledge of the Cold War can help these students understand the root causes of some examples of social injustice in the world as well as the way that earlier generations have tried to address the social injustices that they witnessed.

At first glance, it might seem difficult to find opportunities for students to take informed action related to the material and concepts of a modern world history course. It is important to bear in mind that taking informed action does not necessarily mean that students are actively agitating for change in the community or in a larger context. Students interested in global human rights violations may trace the concept of "human rights" to the Cold War era. Many students will be able to see how the superpower rivalry between the United States and the Soviet Union contributed to past human rights abuses and how the lingering effects of the Cold War still influence current human rights violations. But students should be pressed to understand that the very concept of "human rights" is historically contingent. In other words, what might appear to students as an objective truth is actually a concept that has varied over time and location. During the Cold War there was no single definition of "human rights" that all parties agreed upon. Students can consider whether that is still true today and can expand their discussion to address current events topics such as human trafficking, religious extremism and terrorism, environmental degradation, and global labor conditions.

Students who want a more "experiential" approach can research their local community to determine how it was affected by the Cold War. One exercise would be to have students find a local building that is representative of the Cold War, perhaps in its use or in its architectural style. Students can study the history of the building and submit their findings to a local newspaper. Similarly, students can conduct oral history interviews with individuals to explore the wide range of Cold War experiences. Students might be particularly interested in how underrepresented groups fared during the Cold War and how the Cold War in some ways may have improved their status in society while in other ways continue to limit their opportunities. Students who take part in these exercises will feel empowered to find solutions to a variety of social injustices that they perceive in their community.

Engaging the Post-9/11 Student

Social media, nonstop news cycles, and the rapid pace of global interaction mean that students are bombarded with and often overwhelmed by information and ideas. It is no surprise that students often focus more on *answers* than on *questions*. Teachers, however, will be the first to recognize and appreciate that the questions that students ask and the discussion that these questions generate are crucial components of historical thinking. A topic as broad and multifaceted as the Cold War allows numerous opportunities to teachers to ask open-ended questions to students. It also gives students the opportunity to ask their own questions and to probe, reflect, deduce, and debate. For students who may be accustomed to finding an answer by typing a question into Google or opening Wikipedia, study of the Cold War is a way to develop useful critical thinking skills.

An opening activity for a Cold War class can involve asking students to react to a photo of the dismantling of the Berlin Wall. Students can use the image to explore questions related to the proper role of authority and when and to what extent intervention by a foreign power is appropriate. Similarly, Cold War propaganda posters can be used to set the stage for a deeper inquiry into the psychological aspects of political rivalries and the persuasive techniques used by different governments. A short video about Sputnik can be used to encourage further analysis of economic, scientific, and educational issues stemming from political tensions. In any case, the prompts that spur inquiry are rooted firmly in the curriculum and directly guide the inquiry process. They may be images, quotes, controversial statements, primary-source excerpts, audio or video clips, artifacts, or any other "hook" that generates interest, stimulates questions and discussion, and sustains inquiry. Such compelling questions might include but certainly are not limited to the following:

- Was the Cold War an inevitable outcome of the Second World War?
- Is a "cold" war better than a "hot" war?
- How do the actions of government leaders influence the daily lives of individuals?
- In what ways did the Cold War influence various nations' priorities and goals?
- To what extent did the United States achieves its goals during the Cold War?
- What is the relationship between geopolitics and national security?
- To what extent did leaders and events shape the Cold War, and to what extent did the Cold War shape leaders and events?
- In what ways does the Cold War continue to influence global events today?

Supporting questions typically have more direct answers. Examples of supporting questions about the Cold War might include the following:

- What were the primary causes of the Cold War?
- How did the Cold War shape US foreign and domestic policy?
- Who were the significant leaders during the Cold War era?
- What major events took place during the Cold War era, and how did such events reflect Cold War strategies?

- In what ways was the Cold War beneficial and detrimental for the superpowers and other nations?
- How and why did the Cold War end?
- Are there recent or current examples of cold wars?
- What are the advantages and disadvantages of "cold" and "hot" wars?
- What is MAD, and why does it prevent nuclear warfare?

It is wise for teachers to be prepared with core compelling questions that are embedded throughout a unit or the course itself, with the intention of guiding students in the direction of such questions. These are intimately tied to the underlying themes of the course. As the academic year progresses, however, the gradual release of responsibility to students as they become more comfortable and able to ask and answer their own questions will certainly occur, and it should not be surprising when students' questions parallel the very questions developed by the teacher to guide the progression of the course curriculum. A compelling question such as "Are the benefits of war worth the costs?" might not be created by students word for word. The questions they generate before, during, and after lessons on the Cold War, however, may help shape compelling questions that closely mirror the overarching themes present throughout the course.

The Cold War and the War on Terror

Members of the post-9/11 generation have lived their lives facing the specter of terrorism, which in some ways is reminiscent of the Cold War–era gloom of seemingly imminent nuclear annihilation. Moreover, the political rhetoric that typically follows a terrorist event—whether the Paris attacks in November 2015, kidnappings and killings by Boko Haram, the Boston Marathon bombings, the Fort Hood shooting in 2009, or any other of the numerous domestic and foreign terrorist activities—has been ratcheted up, sensationalized, and politicized in ways that exacerbate the polarization that seems to have emerged in the past two decades.

Numerous additional examples that have occurred recently bear this out. Debates over the plight of Syrian refugees are redolent of fears of a fifth column during the Cold War. Bombast from presidential candidates and pundits parallels the grandstanding and intimidation tactics of Joseph McCarthy and others during the Red Scare. As with events of the past, including the Cold War, nationalism, ethnocentrism, and xenophobia have become manifest in the hyperbole found as much on mainstream media as on social media. Our daily lives are saturated with videos, images, and sound bites, often accompanied by the word "viral" as an ironic adjective.

Although threats of terrorist activities have regrettably colored the zeitgeist of the post-9/11 generation, such fears also provide fertile ground for teachers to develop lesson plans that will allow their students to better understand the complexities and nuances of the world in which they live. Compelling questions such as "Is fear an effective political tactic?" and "Can terrorism be defeated?" might guide students' research as they look for ways to better understand the deeper issues that connect various historical and current events. An inquiry centering on the tension between personal liberties and national security in recent times might very well generate impressive compelling and supporting questions, as well as plenty of opportunity for students to communicate their conclusions. Students should be encouraged to explore these connections—but should also be cautioned that historical comparisons have their limits.

Designing lessons that encourage students to compare and contrast various terrorist actions and the ensuing reactions with Cold War events and their accompanying dialogue is an excellent way to facilitate inquiry. While the events themselves are worthy of analysis, the contemporaneous cultural and political context, along with subsequent media coverage and social commentary, are important facets to consider as well. For example, various aspects of terrorist events have been appropriated by a range of political and special interest groups to advance their agendas, further intensifying the national discourse—often in irrational and histrionic ways. Comparing speeches, letters to the editor, media punditry, and other sources from the Cold War period and the post-9/11 era is a valuable way to helps students analyze the diverse perspectives associated with certain historical events. Students may need guidance to critically examine such sources as they look for bias, embellishment, logical fallacies, loaded words, glittering generalities, and the like.

Likewise, scrutinizing America's intervention and presence in the Middle East and the ways by which its actions may have contributed to the rise of terrorism, while potentially controversial, nevertheless will prompt students to critically examine foreign-policy decisions and their intended and potential outcomes. Tracing the causes and effects of modern terrorism to Cold War events is an intriguing exercise for students as they seek to make better sense of current global events. For example, as students learn more about the US invasions of Afghanistan and Iraq, US tensions with Iran, the rise of al-Qaeda and ISIS, and the like, an investigation will reveal that such developments did not occur in a vacuum following 9/11. As students discover their strong connections to Cold War policies and decisions, they will be better positioned to understand the historical trajectory that stretches back to the second half of the twentieth century and the long-term effects of American and Soviet maneuverings. Questions such as "To what extent should American foreign-policy and national interests take into account the human rights stance of its allies?" and "In what ways does international consensus building today mirror similar efforts during the Cold War?" will, at the very least, encourage students to analyze the rationale and challenges of certain foreign-policy choices. If done properly and with an emphasis on objectivity, such activities will mitigate against irrational and misinformed perspectives that serve only to further fuel the relative hysteria that has been infused into the national conversation.

The subject of terrorism is a lens through which the concepts of national interests, geopolitics, asymmetrical warfare, ideology, balance of power, and similar terms can be examined. Providing opportunities for students to analyze global affairs, the causes and effects of military intervention, international tensions, and political posturing not only will likely prompt students to ask questions that will guide further inquiry but will cultivate a broader appreciation of pressing issues that have an impact on their lives.

Sample Inquiry: The Berlin Wall

Framing the Inquiry

A lesson about the Berlin Wall might begin with an image prompt, such as civilians attempting to climb through the barbed wire fence atop the Berlin Wall. Under the expert guidance of the teacher, students will begin to ask questions about the image and what it represents. Initially, students might construct questions that have specific, factual answers, and they may be simple yes/no questions. Supporting questions, such as "Who are the people in the image? Are they running away from, or running toward, something? Are they scared? If so, why? When was the image taken? Why is there a barrier?" can provide the foundation for a deeper examination into the topic of the Berlin Wall, its place in history, and its larger symbolic significance. During this stage of inquiry, students are connecting the novel learning situation with prior knowledge, course content, and the broader curricular and topical context. Students are also formulating predictions and hypotheses related to the impending investigation. In this sense, with help from one another and from the teacher, students can use their initial questions to begin thinking in a more holistic manner in order to develop larger, more essential questions that will guide their inquiry. Compelling questions such as "Why is freedom so important to people?" and "Why might people risk injury or death (to themselves or others) for an idea?" can be explored in a variety of ways using a multitude of resources, and they can frame future inquiry because they are thematic in their essence and applicable across topics, eras, and regions.

Evaluating the Evidence

A logical next step in the lesson might include the critical examination of primary sources related to the Berlin Wall. Images (for example, a photo essay from *Time*, "The Rise and Fall of the Berlin Wall" [http://content.time.com/time/photogallery/0,29307,1631993,00.html]), videos clips, political cartoons, and documents (such as those from "A City Divided: Life and Death in the Shadow of the Wall" from the National Archives [http://www.archives.gov/research/foreign-policy/cold-war/berlin-wall-1962-1987/]) can be used to give students an opportunity to consider the purpose of the Wall from the Soviet perspective and the challenges associated with the Wall from the Western point of view. This phase of the inquiry process involves gathering and evaluating information related to the posed questions. Furthermore, the scope of the inquiry is further delineated as hypotheses and predictions are reconsidered and revised. All the while, students ought to pose additional questions based on the new evidence that is gleaned from the resources, further guiding their inquiry and provoking other ideas, trends, connections, considerations, realizations, and thoughts. In some cases, it may valuable for students to analyze evidence from the perspective of a particular role that has been assigned to them—for example, US diplomat,

Soviet policymaker, or resident of East Berlin—and then sharing their findings with their peers while attempting to come to a consensus about an issue. For instance, having students consider the question "Was the Wall necessary?" in a group setting by incorporating the viewpoints of the assigned roles is sure to provoke enhanced engagement and interaction.

Communicating Conclusions

Throughout the inquiry process, students must continue to review and synthesize their findings, reflecting on their learning and thinking of ways to communicate their new understandings. To demonstrate their learning, students might construct pro and con arguments related to escape or resistance from the point of view of someone living in East Germany. Perhaps students are interested in interviewing relatives who lived during the era in order to capture their recollections, perceptions, and insights. Another idea is to have students write and deliver speeches about what freedom means to them in a TED-style event. Students might also use their accumulated evidence to inform an argument about the need to dismantle or reinforce the Wall from opposing points of view. From a current-events perspective, students might take into account recent statements related to the US-Mexico border or similar situations elsewhere in the world, examining why such issues exist and remain controversial. However students communicate their findings and conclusions, their inquiry will have provided a basis for an ensuing investigation.

Conclusion

Whether or not they articulate this idea, students yearn to grow—to learn more about the world, to care deeply and passionately about something, and to make a difference. Teachers, as lifelong learners, also want to grow as professionals—to continuously improve their craft, to become experts in their respective disciplines, and to better themselves for their profession and their students. Inquiry lessons that are relevant, authentic, and focused on enduring understandings encourage students and teachers to embark on a paradigm shift together that leads to new ways to engage with content and skills. If participating in a lesson simply means acquiring knowledge for a test or a grade, we are responsible for perpetuating an educational culture that inadvertently encourages expediency and superficiality on a regular basis. Inquiry lessons—designed with relevance and connections, authenticity and in-depth analysis, and enduring understandings and engagement in mind—offer a robust and valuable alternative.

With a sound content basis about the Cold War, informed by prior knowledge and augmented by the material in this book, teachers can reconsider instructional strategies in a manner that incorporates the era and its associated events in new and engaging ways. Studying the Cold War allows students born after the pivotal events of September 11, 2001, to develop a firmer understanding of the broader factors of international dynamics and a more profound appreciation for the complex events since that tragic day. Providing opportunities for further investigation into the incredibly multifarious historical, political, economic, geographic, and cultural variables of the Cold War and the post–Cold War era will increase the likelihood that students will have a more profound and enduring understanding of and connection to course content, enhance their global orientation, and foster active and knowledgeable citizenship—the very ideals we seek to nurture in our students.

KEY RESOURCES

A&E Television Networks. "Cold War." 2015. http://www.history.com/topics/cold-war.

"The Avalon Project." Lillian Goldman Law Library, Yale Law School. 2008. http://avalon.law.yale.edu/subject_menus/coldwar.asp.

"Cold War International History Project." Woodrow Wilson International Center for Scholars. Washington, DC. 2015. http://www.wilsoncenter.org/program/cold-war-international-history-project.

The Cold War Museum. Vint Hill, VA. http://www.coldwar.org/.

Corera, G. "The New Cold War: How Russia and China Are Hacking British Companies and Spying on Their Employees." *The Telegraph.* June 25, 2015. http://www.telegraph.co.uk/technology/internet-security/11699833/The-new-Cold-War-how-Russia-and-China-are-hacking-British-companies-and-spying-on-their-employees.html.

Legvold, R. "Managing the New Cold War: What Moscow and Washington Can Learn from the Last One." *Foreign Affairs.* July/August 2014. https://www.foreignaffairs.com/articles/united-states/2014-06-16/managing-new-cold-war.

National Council for the Social Studies. *The College, Career, and Civic Life (C3)*

Framework for Social Studies State Standards: Guidance for Enhancing the Rigor of K-12 Civics, Economics, Geography, and History. Silver Spring, MD. 2013.

Rothstein, D., and L. Santana. *Make Just One Change: Teach Students to Ask Their Own Questions.* Cambridge, MA: Harvard Education Press, 2011.

Suri, Jeremi. "Postwar Politics and the Origins of the Cold War." The Gilder Lehrman Institute of American History. New York. 2015. http://www.gilder lehrman.org/history-by-era/1945-present/postwar-politics-and-cold-war.

US National Archives and Records Administration. "Military Resources: The Cold War." Washington, DC. N.d. http://www.archives.gov/research/alic /reference/military/cold-war-and-marshall-plan.html.

Wineburg, Sam. *Historical Thinking and Other Unnatural Acts: Charting the Future of Teaching the Past (Critical Perspectives on the Past).* Philadelphia: Temple University Press, 2001.

PART THREE

The Cold War and American Society

Teaching Propaganda and Ideology in Cold War History

KENNETH OSGOOD

Propaganda and ideology were integral to the waging of the Cold War. From the earliest beginnings to the end of the conflict, the United States and the Soviet Union put a premium on influencing the behavior, politics, and cultures of peoples and nations. They employed every medium and manner of communication to do so. Few Americans today realize that for nearly fifty years, the US government had an official propaganda agency—the US Information Agency, or USIA—focused on influencing the perceptions and politics of countries around the world.[1] So, too, did the Soviet Union maintain an elaborate propaganda apparatus, spending an astonishing sum on global information campaigns. Both sides used radio and TV broadcasts, films, concerts, cultural initiatives of all kinds, every conceivable form of publication, and elaborate public relations stunts for ideological warfare. These were not peripheral activities, marginal to the foreign policies of the superpowers. Rather, they were extensive, often secret, and backed up by the financial, technological, and cultural power of the Cold War's major protagonists. The impact was significant—not just on the Cold War but also on the very nature of international relations. Indeed, the goal of influencing foreign publics transformed the very nature of world politics over the course of the twentieth century. Known today as "public diplomacy," activities to influence the perceptions and politics of others became indispensable components of statecraft, practiced by weak and strong states alike.

This essay argues that teachers at all levels not only *should* integrate propaganda into their lessons and courses on Cold War history but that they *can* easily do so. Many excellent studies exist to provide context for the exploration of these topics. Online documents, images, and videos make propaganda history more accessible than ever. This essay uses readily available sources to provide ideas, examples, and inspiration for teachers. It focuses primarily on films, as they are the most accessible form of propaganda for classroom use, yet it should be noted that propaganda takes many forms, many of them less obvious and harder to identify as propaganda per se. Although I include a few examples from the Soviet side of the story, I focus primarily on US activities because sources are more plentiful and because of my belief that it is essential for Americans to develop their basic knowledge about the role of propaganda in US foreign policy in order to function as informed citizens in their democracy.

Living in an information age with all news filtered through a highly polarized media environment—in which powerful interests seek to sway public perceptions to advance often hidden agendas—today's students have much to learn about basic media literacy by looking at how propaganda has been used in the past. Integrating propaganda into the teaching of Cold War history thus carries with it an additional bonus: it can help students develop the ability to navigate competing claims of truth in the information age, an important skill not just for the study of history majors but also for informed citizenship. What's more, it's tremendously fun and exciting for instructor and student alike.

Introducing Propaganda and Ideology

Few subjects are better able to awaken student interest in the Cold War than propaganda. Propaganda history can provide a shared frame of reference around which teachers can invite students into the strangely ideological world of Cold War history. Moreover, because much propaganda crosses over to the multimedia universe and adopts an "entertainment" ethos, propaganda is an accessible medium. Students know something about it. Bombarded by commercial propaganda in the form of advertising, they have an acute, maybe even over-developed, sense of cynicism surrounding the art and practice of spin. Yet students rarely have many tools with which to analyze and assess the myriad ways in which others seek to manipulate their emotions, opinions, and actions.

Accordingly, my approach to teaching about propaganda always includes a general discussion of the meaning and methods of propaganda. I first begin with definitions. I ask students what they think of when they hear the word "propaganda." Invariably they mention lies, deception, trickery, and the Nazis. I then try to expand their thinking by discussing other types of propaganda, such as electioneering or advertising. "How do you know if something is propaganda?" I ask. This question elicits a range of contradictory responses, illustrating the ways in which propaganda is in the eye of the beholder; most people typically describe their own activities as "education" or "information," while deriding messages from opponents as "propaganda." Then I ask them to think about these types of questions: Does something have to be a lie to be considered propaganda? Is propaganda different from education? Does something have to "work" to be considered propaganda? Does it have to be planned or premeditated? Don't we all use "spin" and propaganda in our everyday lives when we project images of ourselves to get what we want—when we are presenting ourselves to a romantic interest, or on a job interview, or even in an essay for school where we write what we think the teacher wants to hear? I ask them these kinds of questions to prod students to consider the role of persuasion in everyday human activity. We "spin" all kinds of things about ourselves to get what we want or to project an image we want others to maintain about us.[2]

Having thoroughly confused them and having led them to believe that "everything" is propaganda, I then direct them to my preferred definition: "any technique or action that attempts to influence the emotions, attitudes, or behavior of a group, usually to benefit the sponsor. . . . The purpose of propaganda is to persuade—to change or to reinforce existing attitudes and opinions."[3] I highlight three notable features of this definition. First, it emphasizes influence and persuasion, the key purposes of propaganda. Second, propaganda is more than mere words. It includes "any technique," including actions, that is employed to influence others. Words *and* deeds can be propagandistic. Emotive symbols are also key features. Flags, currency, music, parades, and all manner of spectacles and contrived happenings are used by those seeking influence and power. Third, this definition emphasizes the role of the sponsor. It may be useful to think of propaganda as something that *benefits the sponsor*. A comparison with education rein-forces the point: educators typically seek to open up students' minds, not to close them. Even if they do present a point of view to students, it is rarely to benefit the teacher. Propaganda, by contrast, typically serves a secret agenda that benefits its sponsor in some fashion. Advertising, most obviously, seeks not to uplift the viewer but to sell products to the benefit of another.

I also seek to dispel popular misconceptions. Many equate propa-ganda with "lies," but propaganda is not necessarily untruthful. Indeed, it is often based on facts, because propaganda that rings true to the intended audience is more likely to be persuasive than elaborate false-hoods. The United States claimed during the Cold War that it pursued a "strategy of truth" to gain credibility with audiences. But factual infor-mation is not the same as truth. Propaganda often uses carefully selected, factually "correct" information to influence attitudes. The manipulation of information is often more effective as propaganda than outright lies. Moreover, propaganda often uses symbols, exaggerated images, empty slogans, glittering generalities, and other techniques to activate a desired emotional response. While perhaps not relying on deception, these tech-niques are inherently manipulative.

Having introduced students to the intractable question of "what is propaganda," I then help them understand common propaganda tech-niques. Again, this is valuable for multiple reasons: it gives students tools to use when analyzing specific case studies from the Cold War and it develops skills at critical reading that will help them navigate the information flood around them. Most students find that once they are able to identify propaganda in one area, they can readily apply that insight to another.

Perhaps the most accessible introduction to basic propaganda tech-niques was written in the 1930s by the Institute of Propaganda Analysis, which sought to publicize the insidious effects of Nazi and communist propaganda. The short article "How to Detect Propaganda" summarizes the most common rhetorical techniques. A similar but more comprehen-sive source of propaganda techniques that sparks students' curiosity is a US Army manual from the Vietnam era, Psychological Operations Field Manual No. 33–1. When discussing these texts, I point out that these documents focus almost exclusively on words and rhetorical devices. I then ask students to consider the role of symbols, images, and sounds in effective propaganda. I usually augment the discussion with an exercise that directs students to find examples from the contemporary world that use one or more of the techniques described in the documents. Alternatively, I direct small groups of students to "teach" the class about a given technique using an example from current events they identify themselves.[4]

Having provided students with some analytical tools to help them recognize and understand the layered meanings of propaganda, I then turn to specific cases that engage key facets of Cold War history. I typically structure my selection of cases around competing claims of truth. I give students two or more different sources that take different points of view and that use different evidence to build their cases. This allows students to see the range of debates on a given topic. More important, being exposed to a contrasting message helps them to see what a given piece of propaganda is leaving out or "spinning" in a particular fashion.

Civil Defense and the Nuclear Danger in Cold War Propaganda

Of all the symbols of the Cold War, none resonates more powerfully than the mushroom cloud, its billowing plume evoking the ever-looming danger of cataclysmic destruction. American policymakers recognized that the threat of nuclear war provided a ready-made explanation for the Cold War—we are defending ourselves against an enemy that could destroy us—and thus helped "sell" the Cold War to the American public. On the other hand, officials saw nuclear fear as dangerous. If unchecked, runaway fears of "the bomb" would be demoralizing and would fuel a "peace at any price" attitude. In short: a little fear was good; too much was dangerous.

Thus, the government used civil defense—the program to prepare civilians for nuclear war—to manage public perceptions. Civil defense officials sought to alert Americans to the nuclear danger by dramatizing the likelihood of an attack, while at the same time easing public anxieties by suggesting survival was possible. Pamphlets and posters conveyed this seemingly contradictory message unmistakably. One pamphlet, "Six Steps to Survival," depicted a menacing mushroom cloud as a family of four (the nuclear family!) looked on. The cover image itself reinforced the terror and likelihood of a nuclear strike, with a heading that asked simply "If an enemy attacked today would you know what to do?" Yet, while inspiring fear, the pamphlet also suggested a way out: preparedness.

The family depicted on the cover was poised, confident, and self-assured as it looked out at the nuclear devastation. Inside the pamphlet, readers learned that if they prepared themselves—by stocking up on food, turning basements into fallout shelters, and taking steps to minimize the effects of radioactive fallout—they could indeed survive an attack. This seemingly contradictory message in fact represents a communication strategy I call the "Goldilocks" approach. Officials wanted to stimulate just enough fear to mobilize American support for the Cold War and the armaments race but not too much fear, which could induce a hopeless paralysis.[5]

In the classroom, civil defense films are great ways to explore this type of perception management.[6] *Duck and Cover* remains the most effective for classroom use because the very absurdity of Bert the Turtle diving into his shell as a lesson in nuclear survival effortlessly stimulates student interest. Students immediately recoil at the naiveté of the message that ducking under a school desk would protect children from nuclear war. This primes them to explore questions such as: What did the government think it would accomplish through this film? What message was the government sending to children? Was it meant to assuage childhood fears or stimulate them? Did the film try to promote a climate of fear or reassurance? With some direction from the teacher, students easily see the Goldilocks approach in this film: it at once emphasizes that "the flash" of an atomic bomb could come at any moment, while reassuring children that they could survive by simply ducking and covering. Another useful film to use is *Survival under Atomic Attack*, which was part of a very large-scale information campaign targeting adult audiences.

The challenge in teaching this material is to get students to move past the absurdity of these films and consider what they tell us about America in the nuclear age. One exercise is to ask students about the depiction of America and Americans in these films. They might notice that the figures in the films are overwhelmingly white, middle-class suburbanites. Gendered imagery also emerges strongly in civil defense films. Many project a prototypical "nuclear family" (itself a concept worth discussing), with the wife and mother serving distinct functions stemming from her presumed role as homemaker and caregiver. Analyzing this dimension not only opens a window into the cultural universe of postwar America but also allows students to see how propaganda and media are rooted in a specific historical context. Like much of postwar media, civil defense materials depicted only a segment of the population and projected an idealized vision not just of nuclear war but of American life itself.[7]

Civil defense propaganda also provides a way to ask students questions about how policies are "sold" to the American public. *Frontlines of Freedom,* prepared jointly by the United States and Canada, provides a provocative means for exploring this issue. Perhaps the most overtly "ideological" of any civil defense film, it opens with a short history lesson that sums up all of US history as a defense against tyranny (grotesquely linking the Indian wars and the fight against Nazi Germany as similar endeavors, transitioning seamlessly from one to the other in a matter of seconds). The film ridicules American scientists who had recommended global control of atomic energy and then tells the story of how the "United States, Canada, and other free nations" valiantly resisted the Soviet threat. The film thus provides excellent material for assessing how the Cold War was sold by evoking longer themes in American history, by demonizing the enemy, and by framing Western actions as benign and defensive. It also accentuates a simple but oft-forgotten fact: civil defense propaganda was employed by many countries, including most NATO members, not just the United States.

Contrasting government propaganda messages with a more critical message is another approach. Teachers can present an opposing view by using the British filmmaker Peter Watkins's chilling docudrama *The War Game* (not to be confused with *War Games* from 1983). The film was made for the BBC in 1965, but British officials withheld the film from broadcast until 1985, deeming it too horrifying for the general public. For classroom use, excerpts of the film (even only the first ten minutes) make for an excellent exercise when juxtaposed with civil defense propaganda, as *The War Game* more realistically conveys the panic, pandemonium, and physical devastation that people would encounter following a nuclear war. Images of dead bodies and radiation burns on children drive home the hideous reality of what survival after atomic attack would really look like. Moreover, the film rather self-consciously mocked civil defense propaganda and thus served as a form of "counter-propaganda" that challenged reassuring messages of government programs. In this respect, the film highlights the ways in which people came to resist and recoil against civil defense programs. For students today, the film is not particularly gruesome (though it is not likely suitable for elementary school children), but the projection of the horrifying consequences of a nuclear attack would have been frightening indeed to viewers in its day. Thus, the censorship of the film invites questions worthy of discussion. Why would such a film be withheld? Was it a matter of the more sensitive media climate of its day—or might the political impact of the film have posed greater concerns to government officials?

Other examples of how the government's reassuring message came to be resisted in popular culture include the novel and film *On the Beach* (1957 and 1959), Stanley Kubrick's *Dr. Strangelove* (1964), Bob Dylan's "Let Me Die in My Footsteps" (1962) and "A Hard Rain's A-Gonna Fall" (1962), and Tom Lehrer's uproariously funny parody "We Will All Go Together When We Go" (1959). All are excellent for classroom discussion about the ways in which popular culture and generational change provoked a competing narrative about the Cold War going into the 1960s. Cynicism about nuclear war was crucial to the erosion of the Cold War consensus, the rise of the New Left, and the student, antiwar, and environmental movements. Civil defense may have tried to ease anxieties about nuclear war, but over time it contributed to enduring cynicism and doubt.

The Rhetoric of War and Peace

The centrality of nuclear fear to the Cold War experience meant that matters of war and peace figured prominently in propaganda. The ever-looming menace of human destruction and a desire to prevent the unthinkable gave rise to a seemingly contradictory message in the public protestations of leaders on both sides. Time and again, in ways both brazen and subtle, American and Soviet leaders reminded audiences around the world that they possessed astonishing power to make war while also proclaiming their commitment to peace. When Dwight Eisenhower spoke of "waging peace" and Ronald Reagan touted "peace through strength," they were following a Cold War pattern of blurring the language of peace and the language of war. This was no accident. Leaders on both sides understood that waging the Cold War demanded the moral legitimacy of a pursuit of peace.

Pushing students to see this interplay between war and peace in Cold War propaganda yields many insights into the nature of the conflict. It can also help students understand the myriad rhetorical purposes of political language itself. After all, language and rhetoric are forms of propaganda, intended to influence the thoughts and perceptions of others at home and abroad. Recognizing this fact, Soviet and American leaders carefully crafted messages to send discrete signals to distinct audiences, addressing not just their own populations and followers but also the world community. To amplify the desired messages, government propaganda agencies disseminated key speeches and quotations around the world through leaflets, books, posters, radio broadcasts, films, and briefing kits for the press.

When leaders on both sides spoke, they used both bellicose and pacific language to frame their nation's purpose in international affairs. A simple statistic illustrates the point. During the Cold War, an astonishing 96 percent of all presidential addresses mentioned the word "war," and 85 percent of those simultaneously referred to peace.[8] Speeches by Soviets leaders followed a similar pattern. Thus, when Soviet premier Nikita Khrushchev toured the United States in 1959, for example, he repeatedly pledged his country's commitment to "peaceful coexistence" while also boasting that the Soviet Union was churning out missiles "like sausages." Even Eisenhower's celebrated farewell address, which famously warned of the dangers of the military-industrial complex, professed America's timeless commitment to peace while also stressing the importance of maintaining "mighty" armed forces "ready for instant action."

Cold War rhetoric highlights a consistent feature of modern war propaganda. Selling war and international conflict virtually requires a parallel effort at promoting peace. In an age where peace is regarded as the preferred state of society, populations must be convinced that every possible opportunity for peace has been thwarted and that war has been thrust upon an otherwise peace-loving people by a treacherous foe. Similarly, positive, hopeful ideas—especially the hope for a better and more peaceful world to come—are core themes of war propaganda. One need look no further than Woodrow Wilson's plea for a "war to end all wars" for an example. If he could sell America's entry into what was then the bloodiest, most destructive, and most futile war in human history as a quest for peace, surely there is something about the idea of peace that is central to the waging of modern war. Indeed, during the Cold War, few concepts figured more prominently in presidential rhetoric. Between 1946 and 1991, American presidents used the word "peace" in every State of the Union address, every address to the United Nations, every address to foreign legislative bodies, and all but one inaugural address. All told, Cold War presidents evoked the theme of peace in 81 percent of their speeches and 69 percent of their press conferences. This rhetoric consistently portrayed Americans as peace-loving individuals who had been thrust into perilous conflict by evil and aggressive communist opponents.[9]

Yet, the hope for peace and the threat of war were almost always linked, hitched like Siamese twins. The reasons are more logical than one might think. Two major forces were at play. On one hand, there was the logic of deterrence, which virtually demanded a threatening message. Deterrence was a psychological game and perceptions were key. To prevent a conflict from escalating to nuclear war, each side had to believe that an attack would be greeted with unacceptable retaliation. This was the logic of the strategic doctrines "massive retaliation" and "mutual assured destruction," or MAD: if you attack my interests, my allies, or me, you will be utterly devastated. This delicate balance of terror hinged not just on having a powerful military force with which to retaliate against an enemy attack. It also relied on the credibility of that threat, which, in turn, called for a steady stream of direct and implied threats to convey to the enemy that certain actions would result in calamitous counteractions.

On the other hand, there was the appeal of peace to a world gripped by nuclear fear. The constant threats of nuclear war were deeply unsettling to people everywhere and carried political costs. Nuclear bravado stoked public fears about being embroiled in a nuclear holocaust and stimulated a lively and occasionally powerful international peace movement. Within Western democracies, especially, the worldwide anti-nuclear movement took aim at a cornerstone of the US defense posture, which rested on having a preponderance of nuclear power to counterbalance the Soviet advantage in conventional armed forces. American leaders fretted that runaway fears of nuclear war would jeopardize their ability to gain public support for the nuclear weapons buildup they viewed as vital to US security. Soviet leaders capitalized on this vulnerability. They pushed a propaganda line that called for a ban on all nuclear weapons—an attractive proposition that also served their interests, since for the first few decades of the Cold War the Soviet Union lagged far behind the US in this area. American leaders, in turn, sought to discredit the Soviet position by framing their calls for a nuclear ban as insincere. The communists talked peace, American propaganda claimed, merely to mask their preparations for war. This was not just a matter of counterpropaganda, for both sides went to great lengths to stress their own peaceful intentions, while situating their opponent as the warmonger, the threat to peace.

Teachers can get students to explore this dynamic in many ways, for speeches are perhaps the most easy-to-find primary sources. The American Presidency Project, an Internet database hosted by the University of California, Santa Barbara, is the most comprehensive source.[10] It is a fully searchable archive of every presidential speech and public statement. Teachers can readily construct an assignment that sends students searching for a presidential speech to analyze messages of threat and reassurance or of war and peace in the text. The themes are so commonplace, in fact, that a lesson on virtually any major Cold War crisis can integrate an analysis of this kind of rhetoric, as a quick glance at John F. Kennedy's speech during the Cuban Missile Crisis or Ronald Reagan's "Star Wars" speech reveals. In framing the discussion, teachers should emphasize the persuasive purposes of public speeches; this is language carefully crafted to influence the thoughts and perceptions of multiple audiences, foreign and domestic. As such, rhetoric functions as propaganda and plays a key role in the in the projection of the American image abroad.

For a distinct lesson with some contemporary relevance, few case studies are more rich for classroom discussion than a look at Eisenhower's Atoms for Peace campaign. In December 1953, Eisenhower spoke before the United Nations—itself a key forum for waging the war of words—and delivered one of the most important speeches of his presidency, one that kicked off one of the most sustained propaganda campaigns in US history.

The speech exemplified the war-and-peace dichotomy in Cold War rhetoric. Eisenhower's opening words focused on illustrating the awesome power of the US nuclear arsenal. The American stockpile "exceeds by many times the explosive equivalent of the total of all bombs and all shells that came from every plane and every gun in every theatre of war in all of the years of World War II," he announced. The message sought to inform Americans of new nuclear-age realities, especially in the wake of the development of hydrogen bombs, thermonuclear weapons that far exceeded the power of the atomic bombs used against Japan. It also served as a veiled threat to the Soviets, reminding them of America's preponderant power. But then Eisenhower turned his message around by appealing eloquently to the need for peace. Four times he spoke of freeing the world from the grip of atomic fear, of hastening "the day when fear of the atom will begin to disappear from the minds of the people." Speaking eloquently of the need to "solve the fearful atomic dilemma," Eisenhower stressed that atomic materials should be used to serve the needs rather than the fears of humanity. "My country wants to be constructive, not destructive," he emphasized. Then came the key passage: a proposal for turning atoms for war into atoms for peace. He suggested that the United States and the Soviet Union donate some of the nuclear materials from their stockpiles to an international agency that would use them for peaceful purposes in agriculture, medicine, and electric power production. He claimed this would bring benefits to the entire world community and could open the door to a disarmament agreement that might lead eventually to an end to the strategic arms race.

The speech and the attendant Atoms for Peace proposal kicked off a massive global propaganda campaign that lasted through the entirety of Eisenhower's presidency. The US Information Agency, which disseminated propaganda in nearly every country in the world, made Atoms for Peace its number one propaganda theme for nearly eight years. It churned out news story after news story hyping US discoveries and accomplishments in peaceful atomic research; it sent traveling Atoms for Peace exhibits to dozens of countries; it produced scores of films highlighting peaceful atomic research; and its radio broadcasts included regular features on the subject. The extraordinary public relations campaign utilized every arm of the executive branch—from the Department of Labor to the Post Office—to hype the proposal in statements and press releases.[11]

To help students see the ways in which Atoms for Peace propaganda sought to convey distinct messages to the world community, teachers can begin with a careful analysis of the rhetorical purposes of Eisenhower's speech. Many of these messages appear contradictory, but they begin to make sense as the multiple audiences and purposes are considered. Two excellent articles by the communication specialist Martin Medhurst diagram Eisenhower's strategic uses of language and are excellent resources for teachers seeking to develop a lesson.[12] To simplify matters, teachers can look at how the speech spoke to different audiences. First, the speech sought to convey the strength and power of US military forces to inspire caution in Soviet behavior and to reassure Americans allies that the United States possessed the strength to deter communist aggression. Second, it sought to awaken the American people to the dreadful power of the thermonuclear age to stimulate their acceptance of the nuclear arms race, in part by subtly implying that the destructive power Americans possessed was shared by the Soviet Union. The Soviets had just recently detonated their first hydrogen bomb, and Eisenhower carefully alluded to this threat to stimulate public acceptance for his own nuclear weapons buildup. Third, to US allies, Eisenhower's speech served as a reminder that US nuclear power still remained preeminent and that the United States could protect them, while at the same time easing their fears of a possible war by stressing the peaceful intentions of the United States. Fourth, to the developing world, Eisenhower's proposal for cultivating the peaceful uses of atomic energy sought to demonstrate the US commitment to the economic development of impoverished nations. Fifth, to allies, neutrals, and domestic audiences, Eisenhower sought to claim the moral high ground in the Cold War. By making a seemingly attractive proposal that the Soviets would likely reject (since they then lagged far behind the United States in the nuclear arms race), Eisenhower could discredit the Soviet "ban the bomb" and "peaceful coexistence" lines as mere propaganda.

Finally, in a theme that ran through the speech and the attendant propaganda campaign, Atoms for Peace actually sought to facilitate the buildup of US nuclear forces by easing public anxieties about the nuclear danger. As a secret government report explained, the Atoms for Peace campaign would cause people "to no longer think of mushroom clouds and mass destruction when hear[ing] the words *atom, atomic,* or *atomic energy,* but rather of the peaceful uses of atomic energy in the fields of industry, agriculture, and medicine." Cleverly, by flooding the global media with talk of the peaceful applications of atomic energy, Eisenhower hoped to divert attention from the ongoing nuclear buildup, thus preparing the way for public acceptance of US efforts to develop a weapons stockpile capable of destroying the world many times over.[13]

There are other ways to explore the meaning and purpose of Atoms for Peace. The Eisenhower library website contains an accessible collection of documents, including a summary of how Soviet propaganda responded to the proposal, illustrating the propaganda war that ensued.[14] Teachers can also use Atoms for Peace films, accessible via YouTube, to help students see how the United States promoted the many beneficial uses of atomic energy in its campaign to sell the friendly atom. The two most accessible and easily found such films are "A Is for Atom," an animated film produced by General Electric, and "Our Friend the Atom," a Disney documentary that also promoted an exhibit on the atomic age at Disneyland. Both films reveal how Americans sought to educate viewers on basic nuclear science, promote the many peaceful applications of nuclear research and technology, and thereby tame the fears of the atomic age. Students could also be tasked with researching the long-term implications of Atoms for Peace. The proposal was more than propaganda: it included a tangible proposal for spreading the technology for nuclear power around the world. It has thus been credited with hastening nuclear proliferation and even with giving nuclear aspirants like Iran core aspects of the technology that laid the foundation for its current nuclear program. Such research could lead students to see the interplay between propaganda and policy, as well as the contemporary relevance of Cold War decisions.

Ideology in Cold War Propaganda

Propaganda also opens a window into the ideological nature of the Cold War. The ideological divide that separated the capitalist and the communist systems contributed to superpower antagonism. Ideology also functioned as a key weapon of political combat. The United States and the Soviet Union saw themselves as locked in a titanic struggle for global influence. Ideological propaganda—in the form of a codified set of ideals, aspirations, and beliefs—provided a mechanism for gaining political leverage abroad. The power of ideas and symbols to move people was useful for mobilizing allies and winning over neutrals; just as important, propaganda could weaken enemies by exploiting vulnerabilities and sowing discord, insecurity, and dissent. Accordingly, both superpowers devoted enormous resources to influencing the perceptions and politics of foreign societies. They likewise toiled to mobilize their own populations to support the sacrifices in blood and treasure required to fund the arms race, militarize economies, and consent to waging real and proxy wars across the globe.

The superpowers utilized propaganda about everyday matters to sell the superiority of their ways of life while demonizing those of the other. Communist propaganda depicted capitalism, with its relentless quest for profits and resources, as the root cause of working-class struggles, racial strife, war, imperialism, and the cultural shallowness

132

of consumer-driven popular culture. Conversely, American propaganda suggested that communism led naturally to the kind of oppressive totalitarianism that characterized the Soviet system, with its dictatorial one-party rule, censored press, secret police, and forced-labor camps. Holding out the false promise of the liberation of the global working class, communism masked the secret Soviet intention of worldwide domination.

The superpowers harped on these themes relentlessly in propaganda campaigns that reached the world over. They also used these themes to mobilize their own populations. Films intended for domestic audiences provide an accessible way to introduce students to how both sides placed economic issues at the center of the ideological divide—and how both sides attached all good and evil to their respective economic practices. On the US side, *Make Mine Freedom* is an excellent example. One of a series of propaganda films made and disseminated by the conservative Harding College, it represented a common thread in American propaganda: it emphasized the insidious character of communist ideology itself, with the dangerous appeal of communism's utopian promises masking a subversive intent that would lead invariably to conflict, war, and enslavement. Other readily available films suitable for classroom use that emphasize these themes include *How to Spot a Communist*, a campy and unintentionally comical film (students love it!) that conveys the message that communists can be anywhere and are best identified by their ideas and associations, and *The Big Lie*, an Army indoctrination film that stresses the link between communist ideology and Nazi totalitarianism.

The Soviet Union, too, emphasized the false promises of its ideological opponent. Soviet propaganda relentlessly dramatized the hypocrisy of the American commitment to freedom and equality, presenting "monopolistic capitalism" as an inherently exploitive force that trampled on the rights and liberties of workers and minorities. It likewise situated greedy machinations of capitalism as the root of war and imperialism. *American Imperialist: Mr. Wolf* offers an accessible introduction to this message. It works especially well when juxtaposed with *Make Mine Freedom,* as the two films adopt a similarly simplistic style to convey polar opposite messages. Made by the Soviet Union in 1949, the film follows the story of Mr. Wolf, a fabulously wealthy businessman who sells off his enterprises to move his family to their own private "island of peace." Waxing poetic about his eternal commitment to peace, he banishes all weapons from his island. Soon, however, his idyllic life is interrupted by the discovery of oil, which tears his family apart and provokes an armed invasion by Wolf's industrialist competitors. Not to be outdone, Wolf then reveals that he has a large secret stash of weapons on his island and summons a warship to defend his interests, thus giving the lie to his pacific protestations. Thus the core message: capitalists make phony peace promises that mask a hostile and exploitive reality. This film, like *Make Mine Freedom*, emphasizes hypocrisy and the ideological nature of the Cold War competition. Each side situated itself as the standard bearer of peace, prosperity, and freedom—while framing the other as a deceitful imposter.[15]

While these films were intended for domestic audiences, their content accurately reflects recurring themes projected by both superpowers to the world community. The propaganda war was a global ideological contest to win hearts and minds—and both superpowers presented an idealized self-image and a demonized image of their opponent in their quest to win support from peoples around the world. As much as the propaganda war was rooted in the economic dimension of the communist-capitalist competition, its cultural dimensions were unmistakable. Superpower propaganda devoted enormous energy to demonstrating the superiority of each side's way of life. Idealized images of family life, gender relationships, working conditions, scientific accomplishments, athletic prowess, and cultural and artistic creations were all central to the ideological contest.[16]

Race and Civil Rights in Cold War Propaganda

Another key question emerges naturally from the discussion of Cold War propaganda: How wide was the gap between rhetoric and reality? The problem is more complex than it first appears. One can simultaneously discern truth, exaggeration, and falsehood in the films just discussed. The question is even messier when framed with respect to civil rights, itself one of the most important themes in the Cold War's propaganda battles.[17] During the early Cold War, racial segregation was perhaps the greatest liability facing the United States, for it called into question the nation's commitment to freedom and equality. Soviet propaganda exploited this vulnerability for all it was worth. In radio broadcasts, newspaper articles, magazine features, and films, Soviet propaganda publicized the brutality and wickedness of the Jim Crow system. As the nonwhite populations of Latin America, Africa, and Asia struggled to free themselves from the yoke of foreign domination, many could not help seeing parallels between their own situations and those of African Americans. It was a message that resonated. Racial discrimination and segregation naturally undermined the US argument that the American system offered a model for nonwhite nations to follow.

American officials were deeply disturbed by the possibility that the Soviet Union would use racial inequality in the United Sates to undermine America's appeal in the developing world. Students can explore this topic on the John F. Kennedy Presidential Library's website, which has digitized a collection of documents related to JFK's civil rights policies. Of special note is a memorandum dated June 14, 1963, from the State Department's Bureau of Intelligence and Research, with the subject "Soviet Media Coverage of Current US Racial Crisis."[18] The memo summarizes Soviet propaganda during the latter part of the 1963 Birmingham campaign, which made headlines in the United States and elsewhere for the brutal suppression of demonstrators old and young with fire hoses, police dogs, and mass arrests.

History teachers often note that the gruesome images from Birmingham had a powerful effect on the civil rights struggle in the United States. Yet the Birmingham episode also had a global impact, garnering extensive worldwide press coverage and triggering an international outcry. The State Department's memorandum blamed much of this global attention on Soviet propaganda, noting that "Soviet broadcasting on the current US racial crisis has been enormous," with 1,420 Soviet commentaries on the topic beamed worldwide in just twelve days. According to the memo, Soviet propaganda emphasized key recurring themes: "that racism is inevitable in the capitalist system and can only be eradicated along with capitalism itself; that the Federal Government is actually supporting the racists by its general inertia and because of unwillingness to antagonize Southern Democrats; that the hypocrisy of US claims to leadership of the free world is laid bare; and that US racism is clearly indicative of its policies toward colored peoples throughout the world." Each of these points, all of which are discussed in detail in the memo, offers provocative fodder for discussion. Of special note is the last point—that the government's inaction in the South was "indicative" of policies toward other nonwhite peoples, an allegation often made by Soviet propaganda suggesting that Americans would do little to support the independence movements in emerging African, Asian, and Latin American nations. Indeed, the US record on this score is bleak, a topic also worth discussing.[19]

Teachers can also explore how the United States tried to tamp down the impact of Soviet propaganda on these matters. This was a major project of the US Information Agency, the government propaganda agency that blanketed the globe with Americans news and views from 1953 to 1999. The USIA tried to put racial conflict "in perspective" by placing civil rights in a narrative of progress. To blunt international criticism of segregation, it presented the quest for racial equality as "unfinished business": a problem, but one that was being addressed. It frankly admitted the existence of discrimination but downplayed its impact by suggesting that progress was being made. This message emerges clearly from a USIA film released after the Birmingham conflict, *Nine from Little Rock* (1964), and thus offers a nice complement to the memorandum from the JFK library.[20] The film was translated into seventeen languages, distributed to ninety-seven countries, and released to the American public, even receiving an Academy Award in 1965. Like other USIA propaganda, the film conveyed the message that the federal government was "the hero of the civil rights movement."[21] It also offered a tranquil narrative of the crisis. While admitting the race hatred of a small "minority," the film downplayed the severity, duration, and violence of the incident at Central High School in Little Rock, Arkansas, devoting little more than a minute of visual footage to the riotous resistance to integration there and instead prioritizing images of blacks and whites living side by side, the noble efforts of US troops to enforce the law, and the positive growth of the nine students in the seven years following the incident. Thus it conveyed the message that the crisis, as difficult as it was, had a happy ending: the nine students who integrated Central High School went on to happy marriages and successful careers. Their past was troubled, but their future was bright. The narrator— Jefferson Thomas, one of the nine—conveys this message at film's end, repackaging the Little Rock incident as "an American success story." The USIA was thus using recent history to soften the more explosive situation that followed the Birmingham campaign of 1963.[22]

Juxtaposing the USIA's film with the State Department's summary of Soviet propaganda provides an opportunity for students to assess competing narratives about the struggle for civil rights. In addition, it opens up a broader conversation about the meaning of truth. Americans maintained that the Soviets employed a "big lie" strategy but that the United States pursued a "strategy of truth." Do these sources support that interpretation? In *Nine from Little Rock*, the USIA did tell a story that was factually accurate. It admitted that the 1957 incident in Little Rock happened and that racism in America was real. But it whitewashed the story, manipulating the facts to serve its own purposes. Was this deceitful or truthful or something else? Likewise, Soviet propaganda presented racial discrimination in the United States as evidence of the hollowness of the American promise of freedom and equality. Was this a "lie"? Did inequality and the lack of political freedoms in the Soviet Union undermine the credibility of Soviet claims? In the Cold War, did the two sides tell *the* truth or *a* truth—or untruths?

Conclusion

The exercises described in this chapter provide some examples of ways to introduce propaganda into the study of Cold War history. It is equally valuable, however, to create unstructured or semi-structured exercises that give students the freedom to find and analyze their own examples of Cold War propaganda. Many websites and You-Tube videos can be found through simple online searches. I typically give purposely vague assignments such as "Find an example of Cold War propaganda to share with the class. Give a five-minute presentation explaining the propaganda techniques and purposes in the material." I like to send students on these kinds of "fishing trips" because the very freedom of the exercise awakens their interest and curiosity and puts them in the role of co-instructors of the course. Students invariably listen more attentively to their peers than to me, and when I interject with questions or comments, the students are more receptive to my input. This kind of active learning is invaluable.

However one approaches it, Cold War propaganda provides a way not just to understand the superpower conflict but to explore deeper questions about the meaning of truth, the interpretations of American history, and the role of ideology in shaping human behavior. There is great pedagogical value in developing student skills at assessing competing narratives and competing claims of truth. This not only gives them historical insights into the nature of debates on a given topic in history but also develops their critical reading and thinking skills. To analyze these sources, students need to identify hidden assumptions, weigh competing evidence, examine the meaning of evidence that is either consciously used or deliberately omitted, and familiarize themselves with the use of rhetorical techniques in persuasion. Such valuable skills transcend Cold War history and equip students to be thoughtful analysts in the information age.

NOTES

1. The definitive history of the USIA is Nicholas J. Cull, *The Cold War and the United States Information Agency: American Propaganda and Public Diplomacy, 1945–1989* (Cambridge: Cambridge University Press, 2008).

2. A fun book that makes this point is Bill Press, *Spin This!: All the Ways We Don't Tell the Truth* (New York: Atria Press, 2014).

3. Kenneth Osgood, *Total Cold War: Eisenhower's Secret Propaganda Battle at Home and Abroad* (Lawrence: University Press of Kansas, 2006), 7–9.

4. The complete Field Manual can be found at https://fas.org/irp/doddir/army/fm33-.pdf. Other websites publish an abbreviated version of this long document. The key section is Appendix I, which summarizes propaganda techniques. Other useful sources for discussing the intersection of propaganda techniques and the political use of language include George Orwell's short but timeless essay "Politics and the English Language" and a memorandum by former Speaker of the House Newt Gingrich, "Language: A Key Mechanism of Control," both easily found online.

5. Guy Oakes calls this a strategy of "emotion management" in his excellent analysis of civil defense propaganda that argues that "civil defense was inevitably based on deceit, mythmaking, and illusion." See Oakes, *The Imaginary War: Civil Defense and American Culture* (New York: Oxford University Press, 1994), 166. Many civil defense posters and artifacts can be found at http://www.civildefensemuseum.com, which includes virtual tours of fallout shelters, posters, documents, and films.

6. Dozens of civil defense films, including those discussed here, can be found at http://www.atomictheater.com. Helpfully, the site includes synopses of each film and some historical context.

7. The best resource for this type of analysis (including the gendered and racial dimensions of civil defense) is Laura McEnaney, *Civil Defense Begins at Home: Militarization Meets Everyday Life in the Fifties* (Princeton: Princeton University Press, 2000).

8. Kenneth Osgood, "Eisenhower's Dilemma: Talking Peace and Waging Cold War," in Osgood and Andrew K. Frank, eds., *Selling War in a Media Age: The Presidency and Public Opinion in the American Century* (Gainesville: University Press of Florida, 2010), 140–69. This article also summarizes the Atoms for Peace proposal and other peace initiatives of Eisenhower's presidency.

9. Ibid.

10. The American Presidency Project is at http://www.presidency.ucsb.edu.

11. Osgood, *Total Cold War*, 153–80.

12. Martin J. Medhurst, "Eisenhower's 'Atoms for Peace' Speech: A Case Study in the Strategic Use of Language," in Medhurst, ed., *Cold War Rhetoric: Strategy, Metaphor, and Ideology* (East Lansing: Michigan State University Press, 1990), 29–50; and Medhurst, "Atoms for Peace and Nuclear Hegemony: The Rhetorical Structure of a Cold War Campaign," *Armed Forces and Society* 24, no. 4 (Summer 1997): 571–93.

13. Osgood, "Eisenhower's Dilemma," 156.

14. Key documents from the Atoms for Peace campaign are on the Eisenhower library webpage at https://www.eisenhower.archives.gov/research/online_documents/atoms_for_peace.html.

15. Teachers can find useful references to other films from the US and Soviet sides, as well as helpful analysis, in Tony Shaw and Denise J. Youngblood, *Cinematic Cold War: The American and Soviet Struggle for Hearts and Minds* (Lawrence: University Press of Kansas, 2010).

16. For propaganda about everyday life, including its race, class, and gender dimensions, see Laura A. Belmonte, *Selling the American Way: US Propaganda and the Cold War* (Philadelphia: University of Pennsylvania Press, 2008), and Osgood, *Total Cold War*, 214–88.

17. See Brenda Gayle Plummer's chapter in this volume for more on the intersection of civil rights and the Cold War.

18. The memorandum was compiled by Thomas Hughes, assistant secretary of state for intelligence and research, and is reproduced in full on the JFK Library website: http://www.jfklibrary.org/Asset-Viewer/Archives/JFKNSF-295-016.aspx. For brief context and analysis, as well as a digitized reproduction of the memo, see Rebecca Onion, "How the Soviets Used Our Civil Rights Conflicts against Us," *Slate: The Vault*, July 9, 2013, http://www.slate.com/blogs/the_vault/2013/07/09/civil_rights_coverage_how_the_soviets_used_evidence_of_racial_strife_against.html.

19. See especially Thomas Borstelmann, *The Cold War and the Color Line: American Race Relations in the Global Arena* (Cambridge, MA: Harvard University Press, 2001).

20. The film can be found on YouTube and on the National Archives website, http://unwritten-record.blogs.archives.gov/2015/03/16/restoring-nine-from-little-rock/.

21. Cull, *The Cold War and the United States Information Agency*, 211–13; Tony Shaw, *Hollywood's Cold War* (Amherst: University of Massachusetts Press, 2007), 167–98; Borstelmann, *Cold War and the Color Line*, 102–4.

22. Dudziak, *Cold War Civil Rights: Race and the Image of American Democracy* (Princeton: Princeton University Press, 2000), 218–19.

KEY RESOURCES

Belmonte, Laura. *Selling the American War: US Propaganda and the Cold War*. Philadelphia: University of Pennsylvania Press, 2008.

Cull, Nicholas J. *The Cold War and the United States Information Agency: American Propaganda and Public Diplomacy, 1945–1989*. Cambridge: Cambridge University Press, 2008.

Hixson, Walter L. *Parting the Curtain: Propaganda, Culture, and the Cold War, 1945–1961*. New York: St. Martin's Press, 1997.

McEnaney, Laura. *Civil Defense Begins at Home: Militarization Meets Everyday Life in the Fifties*. Princeton: Princeton University Press, 2000.

Oakes, Guy. *The Imaginary War: Civil Defense and American Culture*. New York: Oxford University Press, 1994.

Osgood, Kenneth. *Total Cold War: Eisenhower's Secret Propaganda Battle at Home and Abroad*. Lawrence: University Press of Kansas, 2006.

Shaw, Tony, and Denise J. Youngblood. *Cinematic Cold War: The American and Soviet Struggle for Hearts and Minds*. Lawrence: University Press of Kansas, 2010.

Tudda, Chris. *Truth Is Our Weapon: The Rhetorical Diplomacy of Dwight D. Eisenhower and John Foster Dulles*. Baton Rouge: Louisiana State University Press, 2006.

Teaching "Fear" and "Anxiety" in the Cold War

MOLLY M. WOOD

Two men enter the living room of a small house and immediately walk over to a mirror on the wall, stand in front of it, and hold up identification cards. The camera switches to the perspective "behind" the two-way mirror, where a man in uniform announces, "Replacement team is here, sir," and buzzes the two men into an outer office, where they sign in. Then each picks up a sidearm from a small safe. "See you in twenty-four," one of them says to the desk officer, as they head into an elevator. When the elevator doors open again, far underground, they exit and punch a wall code, which slowly opens a thick steel door. The previous two-man shift leaves and the door closes behind the new team. Each takes a chair in front of a bank of computer monitors. They chat amiably as they punch buttons and work through their protocol. Suddenly an alarm sounds, followed by an anonymous voice giving them a code, which they each copy down, along with additional instructions. The men know exactly what to do. Their movements are confident and business-like. This exact scenario has been practiced hundreds of times. They both reach for identical red locked boxes. From each box they remove separate envelopes, which they open. The launch codes match. They then each enter the launch codes into their separate computers. The message comes back over the computer: "Launch order confirmed." They realize that this is not a drill and the younger officer says, quietly, "Holy shit."

Countdown begins. "T minus sixty," the disembodied voice says. The officer in charge says, "Okay, let's do it." They each insert a launch key into separate locks and turn them to "set." At this point, we see the first slight hesitation from the senior officer. His junior prompts him: "Sir?" And they both proceed with manual enabling of missiles by flipping a series of switches. But while the younger officer, Phelps, continues flipping switches, the senior officer, Larsen, starts mumbling, "This has got to be a mistake" and reaches for his phone. Meanwhile, the other officer has proceeded to enable all ten missiles. No one answers the phone. Larsen shouts at Phelps, "Get me wing command post." "That's not the correct procedure, captain," Phelps replies. "Try SAC headquarters," Larsen responds, sounding increasingly desperate. "That's not the correct procedure" comes the same response. "Screw the procedure," Larsen yells. "I want someone on the goddamn phone before I kill twenty million people!"

Finally Phelps grabs his phone. Again, no one answers. "I got nothing here," he says. "They might've been knocked out already." "All right," Larson replies, "on my mark to launch." And the countdown resumes at T minus twelve. At T minus five, Larson removes his hand from the key that he must turn in order to launch the missiles. "Sir, we have a launch order," Phelps says. "Put your hand on the key, sir!" The countdown reaches zero. Larson stares at the key, murmuring unintelligibly. Meanwhile, Phelps has taken out his sidearm and is pointing it at Larson's head. "Sir, we are at launch. Turn your key," Phelps commands. Larson continues to murmur, saying, "I'm sorry. I'm so sorry." And one more time, Phelps says, as he clicks the safety off his weapon, "Turn your key, sir." The scene ends abruptly.[1]

This fictional scenario occurs at the beginning of the 1983 film *War Games*. It was, of course, an elaborate drill, intended to push the team to the very brink and make sure that they would follow through with their orders even if they *really believed* they would be launching the missiles. The clip effectively and seemingly plausibly illustrates the human resistance to "killing twenty million people." The scene also provides the context for the premise of the film, the misguided belief that tasking a supercomputer, instead of a human being, with the "decision" to launch missiles would result in a "foolproof" system. The scene also serves as one way of opening a discussion about Cold War fears and anxieties, in this case the heightened fears of nuclear war with the Soviet Union in the early 1980s. While we in the classroom are accustomed to teaching about "what happened" during the Cold War from a variety of perspectives, using an ever-growing array of imaginative resources, it remains a challenge to help students to understand, analyze, and interpret the very real *emotions*, namely fear and anxiety, associated with the duration of the Cold War. Students should understand that these fears were heightened and lessened at various times, depending on external events or the decisions of policymakers, but they never disappeared. As long as the United States and the Soviet Union remained ideological enemies and as long as both maintained the seemingly endless arms race, the possibility of nuclear war hung over American society from the late 1940s to the late 1980s. This chapter outlines some general suggestions for planning and leading classroom discussions about fears, anxieties, and other emotional responses to selected Cold War "moments" or "snapshots" over time, in this case from the 1950s, 1960s, and early 1980s, using documents, film, and fiction, with a focus on popular culture sources. I utilize some central questions to focus classroom discussions on this topic: What exactly were people afraid of or anxious about at different times during the Cold War? How do we know? Who exactly felt these fears and anxieties and why? How do we know? What was the historical impact of "fear and anxiety" on the Cold War era? What can historians learn about the American past from studying "fear and anxiety" in the Cold War era?[2]

In my classes we begin to address these issues first during the era of the "Great Fear[s]" associated with the early Cold War years.[3] We first work through a number of traditional primary sources, including portions of the Long Telegram, the Truman Doctrine, and the following excerpt from President Harry S. Truman's memoirs, reflecting his reaction to news about North Korea's 1950 attack on South Korea:

> In my generation, this was not the first occasion when the strong had attacked the weak. . . . I remembered how each time the democracies failed to act it had encouraged the aggressors to keep going ahead. Communism was acting in Korea just as Hitler, Mussolini, and the Japanese had acted ten, fifteen, and twenty years earlier. I felt certain that if South Korea was allowed to fall Communist leaders would be emboldened to override nations closer to our own shores. . . . If this was allowed to go unchallenged it would mean a third world war, just as similar incidents had brought on the second world war.[4]

I ask students to think about the ways Truman compares the North Korean aggression to the outbreak of World War II and what that might imply for the US reaction to the attack. I also ask them to analyze the fears Truman articulates here about what "Communist leaders" would do if South Korea "was allowed to fall." I urge them to think about the language Truman uses, especially in reference to the 1949 "fall" of China, and why Truman refers to a possible "third world war," in addition to the possible emotional implications of such evocative language.

I also want students to think about the reality of living with the "the bomb" in the 1950s. I often use clips from the 1982 film *The Atomic Café*, which relies entirely on archival footage from the late 1940s and 1950s, evocatively edited and arranged, including footage from civil defense and US military films, television commercials, as well as "on the street interviews" with "regular people."[5] Intended both as a satire to mock the attitudes of the early atomic age and as a cautionary reminder of the hubris widely associated with the Reagan administration's confrontational stance toward the Soviet Union early in his first term, the film can be useful for critiquing both the 1950s and the early 1980s. For the 1950s, however, I ask students to consider the ways in which historians look back and interpret the actions and attitudes of people who had serious discussions about "how to survive a nuclear attack" and built bomb shelters in their back yards. A classic example, of course, is to show "duck and cover" exercises from elementary school classrooms and to show short clips of the cartoon character Bert the Turtle from the 1951 civil defense film created to teach children what to do in case of a nuclear attack.[6] Another favorite clip from *Atomic Café* shows reactions to the 1949 announcement of the successful Soviet atomic bomb test. As a catchy upbeat jingle plays in the background ("Everybody's worried 'bout the 'tomic bomb"), a boy of about ten is being zipped into his "fallout suit" (which looks like a snow suit). Then his father completes the outfitting by placing a helmet that looks a little like a gas mask over his head, covering his head and face completely with special shields for his eyes and a vent for breathing. Then a voiceover by the father: "Well, this suit is made of this material," he explains, " . . . inside this layer is shredded lead for resistance against atomic rays." He then sends his son on his way. Dressed as he is, the boy needs help getting on the bike, which he does awkwardly, and you can hear him give a little exclamation of surprise in the background as he almost tips over before pedaling away. While students inevitably giggle at the scene, I ask them to consider seriously the lengths to which parents would go to protect their children if they really believed an atomic attack was possible or likely.

In addition, I ask them to think about the impact of these kinds of preventive measures on children. As Lisle Rose has noted, "the bomb instilled a quiet panic, especially among the young, who would come to maturity in the sixties and early seventies."[7]

Rose provides some useful examples for exploring many of those fears and anxieties in her book *The Cold War Comes to Main Street: America in 1950*. For example, in response to debates in 1950 about the development of a new, more powerful hydrogen bomb, he cites the appearance of several scientists on a weekly radio show from the University of Chicago that was broadcast on NBC. The panelists explained to the American public the vast range and destructive power of such a new "hell bomb." While a blast the size and power of the one at Hiroshima would destroy Manhattan, they explained, a new thermonuclear blast would extend throughout the whole of southern New York and parts of New Jersey. Four separate blasts could destroy almost everything from Boston to Washington, DC, on the eastern seaboard.[8]

The climate of Cold War fears in the 1950s has also been connected quite persuasively to historical analysis of gender roles. Elaine Tyler May's groundbreaking 1988 book *Homeward Bound: American Families in the Cold War Era* is still useful for mining anecdotes for use in lecture and discussion about the ways in which suburban domesticity and virulent anticommunism were intertwined. Print advertisements serve as ideal primary sources for illustrating the connections between fears of communism and nuclear war and the defense and preservation of the traditional "nuclear" family.[9] The focus on consumerism in the 1950s also reveals the connections between the Cold War mentality and gender ideologies. Suburban women were identified as the primary consumers for the family and thus the primary target for advertising of household goods and items targeted at the family. But the message from advertisers and from the government was unequivocal: in the competition with the Soviet Union, the United States is the clear winner as long as we continue to exhibit and buy our transformational consumer products. The American "way of life" and living standard were used as evidence of our superiority. The political value of domestic consumerism made worldwide headlines when American television broadcast a series of exchanges between Soviet premier Nikita Khrushchev and Vice President Richard Nixon at the American National Exhibition in Moscow in 1959. The dialog between the two politicians, known as the "kitchen debate," featured discussions about the benefits of American capitalism as demonstrated in the model of an American suburban home, complete with useful labor-saving kitchen devices.[10]

Of course, other fears and anxieties, beyond "the bomb" and "fall-out fears," were pervasive during this era, too. After a general discussion of the Red Scare, including mention of Senator Joseph McCarthy, the Korean War, the Alger Hiss case, and the 1953 execution of Julius and Ethel Rosenberg, I ask the students to read the telegram McCarthy sent to President Truman in the wake of the infamous Wheeling, West Virginia, speech, in which he made his first public claim about "known communists" in the US State Department in order to emphasize the climate of fear and mistrust.[11] There are two films I use to illustrate two different facets of the relentless message that "communists are everywhere." The first is the 1962 film *The Manchurian Candidate*, based on Richard Condon's 1959 novel of the same name.[12] I often use a clip from this film in class, after providing students with an overview of the film's plot. The main characters, Captain Bennett Marco and Sergeant Raymond Shaw, along with the rest of their infantry platoon, had been captured during the Korean War and brainwashed. The communists planted false memories about Shaw's wartime heroism and conditioned him to act as an assassin when put into a hypnotic state. When the prisoners are released and return to the United States, Shaw receives the Medal of Honor and is greeted by his mother, Eleanor Iselin, and his stepfather, Senator John Iselin. Senator Iselin is portrayed as a Joseph McCarthy-esque figure, making accusations of communist infiltration in the Defense Department to enhance his political career. At first it appears that it is the ultra-ambitious Eleanor Iselin who is the real anticommunist crusader. She says, "We are at war. It's a cold war. But it will get worse and worse until every man, woman, and child in this country will have to stand up and be counted to say whether they are on the side of right and freedom or on the side of the traitors of this country." In reality, however, it is the Iselins who are the communist operatives, and Eleanor Iselin is Raymond Shaw's Soviet controller, the one who will trigger her brainwashed son's hypnotic state, causing him to attempt to assassinate the president of the United States.

By making Shaw's mother the ultimate defector, the film pandered to common and long-standing stereotypical fears of traitorous women spies, a fear that reemerged strongly during the Cold War, coinciding with significant challenges to traditional gender roles after World War II. In 1948, the American public had learned the story of Elizabeth Bentley, a Soviet case officer who defected to the FBI. As Kathryn Olmsted has shown in her research on Bentley and other American women spies, popular culture, especially film, reflected increasing fears of strong women. The "femme fatale," or the female communist operative, was "cold, ruthless and above all humorless."[13] Ethel Rosenberg, convicted of conspiracy to commit espionage in 1951 and executed, along with her husband, Julius, in 1953, was portrayed in this way by the media and by Federal Bureau of Investigation officials. According to Olmsted and others, both government officials and the American public considered her a "bad mother" who both dominated her weaker husband and abandoned her children to "ideology." Rosenberg's "emotionless mask in public made her seem more unnatural, more evil even than Julius."[14] President Dwight D. Eisenhower embraced this interpretation as well. He argued in a private letter that "in this instance it is the woman who is [the] strong and recalcitrant character, the man is the weak one. She has obviously been the leader in everything they did in the spy ring." He acknowledged, in passing, the possible aversion to the execution of women that some might feel but concluded that to "interfere" in the planned execution would only encourage the Soviet Union to "simply recruit their spies from among women."[15] Actor Angela Lansbury's portrayal of the "ruthless" and "domineering" wife and mother Eleanor Iselin in *The Manchurian Candidate* made her the "prototypical evil Communist Woman."[16] By making Eleanor Iselin a middle-aged mother of an adult child, the film reinforces Red Scare anxieties about the possibility of subversive threats to traditional gender roles and therefore to the American family and home.

One of the clips from *The Manchurian Candidate* that I often use in class is the so-called Garden Party scene from the film, which vividly demonstrates the power of the brainwashing that has been inflicted on the American prisoners by a cadre of evil communists. The scene opens in Major Bennett Marco's bedroom. An ominous-sounding narrator explains: "The war in Korea was over. Captain, now Major, Bennett Marco had been reassigned to Army intelligence in Washington. It was by and large a pleasant assignment except for one thing. Night after night, the major was plagued by the same reoccurring nightmare." Meanwhile, the camera pans to a clock by the bed, which reads 3:10 A.M., and finally to Marco, played by Frank Sinatra, fully dressed, sweating, and falling into fitful sleep and then into a nightmare. The scene changes abruptly. Eight GIs are seated, in uniform, yawning and completely uninterested, as a well-dressed middle-aged woman in a flowered hat stands among them on a stage, giving a lecture about hydrangeas. The camera pans to the audience, full of other well-dressed women, drinking tea and examining various flower bouquets. When the camera has moved full circle around the room and focuses again on the stage where the men are still sitting, the scene has changed and the speaker is now a bald, mustached man with Asian features, speaking in accented English about the "American visitors" on the stage, while large photographs of Stalin and Mao are prominently featured behind the stage. The speaker explains to his audience that he has indeed brainwashed the Americans so that they believe they are waiting out a storm in the lobby of a hotel while the Ladies Garden Club holds its meeting.

In other words, the brainwashed soldiers "see" a room full of harmless coiffed mothers and grandmothers, but in reality the audience consists of uniformed men flanked by armed guards, representative of the communist powers of the world.

As the scene progresses, various members of the audience, crude stereotypes of "evil communists" of every persuasion as distinguished by their clothes, accents, and features, question the speaker about his brainwashing techniques, and finally one asks for further "proof" that the brainwashing has been successful. The speaker then instructs Raymond Shaw to strangle one of the other Americans "to death." Which he does, quietly and methodically and horrifyingly as the other men continue to sit and yawn, hearing and seeing only what they have been conditioned to see and hear: a boring lecture about the best soil drainage for hydrangeas. When the solider is strangled, Bennett Marco wakes screaming from his nightmare.

I like the shock value of the scene. It is so bizarre, so compelling, I believe, for a discussion about the extent to which audiences were willing to believe that communists had harnessed the nefarious power of mind control and that they had in fact infiltrated the highest levels of American politics. If you cannot trust a Medal of Honor winner, a veteran of our armed forces, whom can you trust? An additional topic of conversation involves challenging students to compare these American fears of Soviet infiltration and mind control to the Central Intelligence Agency's own Project MKULTRA, started in the early 1950s to explore— on human subjects, often without their consent—the possibilities of behavioral control and mind manipulation on multiple levels.[17] In other words, I challenge students to analyze this fact: for the most part, whether applied to the nuclear arms race, the space race, mind-control experiments, or any other aspect of the Cold War, whatever *they* were doing, *we* were probably doing it, too.

After the super-creepy *Manchurian Candidate*, I move to a completely different kind of film to illustrate another side of Cold War fear and anxiety in the early 1950s. The film *Good Night and Good Luck* (2005) is set in 1953 and focuses on the CBS television journalist Edward R. Murrow's on-air condemnation of Senator McCarthy's attacks against a member of the US Air Force who faced discharge because of charges of communist influence in his family.[18] All of this takes place in the context of McCarthy's ongoing congressional investigations of alleged communist activity in the US government as CBS News, in the early days of television, struggles with deciding how to respond and proceed. One of the reasons I like this film is that it artfully mixes in archival newsreel footage from the 1950s and is shot entirely in black and white. I work with students to make sure they can distinguish the archival footage from the actors' portrayals; I want to make sure they understand that there is no actor who portrays McCarthy in the film, that every time he appears, it is in original footage.[19] Noting this also provides an additional opportunity to discuss, in class, the use of film for understanding history—documentary versus "Hollywood film," for instance—and, in this case, to discuss the differences between portrayals of events of the past on film and actual film footage from the past.

With this film I also ask students to consider what it means to live in a "climate of fear" in the early 1950s. What was it exactly that there was there to be scared of? What exactly were McCarthy's claims? How did Murrow and CBS respond to those claims and to McCarthy's political influence? I urge them to think about the risks CBS News took by allowing Murrow to engage with McCarthy, during these early days of television and television news in particular, and to attack him on the air. I ask them to consider why William Paley, head of CBS News, explained that "We don't make the news, we report the news." And especially I want them to struggle with the sense of fear, professional and personal, that pervades the film. In terms of Murrow's challenge to McCarthy, I ask them to consider two statements made by the Murrow character in the film: "I cannot accept that there are two equal and logical sides to every story" and "We must not confuse dissent with disloyalty."

Moving forward chronologically into the early 1960s, I want students to consider the country's mood, post–Cuban Missile Crisis. I often assign the 1962 book *Fail-Safe* (made into a movie in 1964). To prepare for an hour-long class discussion, students consider a list of discussion questions. Specifically, I want students to think about the book as a source of historical information, as a *primary source* reflective of American society in 1962. I make sure students read the book's brief preface, where the authors explain that while their book is a work of fiction, they want to emphasize that "the people in this novel are our contemporaries and they deal with a problem that is already upon us."[20] I also want students to be able to explain why the authors claim that "Men, machines and mathematics being what they are, this is, unfortunately, a 'true' story."[21] I ask students to consider why, if the authors were so concerned about the possibility of "accidental war," they chose to write a work of fiction rather than a scholarly work. This question usually provokes some thoughtful insights about the ways in which fiction, a compelling story with interesting individual characters, might have reached a popular audience in 1962 and, indeed, why that same book might be particularly useful to historians fifty years later.

The plot of *Fail-Safe* starts with the same basic premise, accidental nuclear war, as the better known (and hilariously brilliant) *Dr. Strangelove*. In *Fail-Safe* (emphatically not hilarious), a group of American bombers is headed straight toward Moscow, and there is no way to recall them or even to shoot them down. It's all a horrifying mistake, of course, the result of a shattering combination of human and mechanical error. In order to emphasize the overall theme of fear and anxiety about possible "accidental" nuclear war, I turn to some of the dialogue from the book. I instruct students (usually in small groups of three to five students) to first read the dialogue I have picked out and then to explain the context of the scene. What is happening at this point in the story? Why did the authors choose to put those particular words down on paper, and, explicitly, what does the dialogue tell us about fear, about the workings of various parts of the government in times of crisis, or about nuclear strategy? For instance, Brigadier General Warren A. Black says, as part of a heated dinner party discussion about the possibility of nuclear war and whether or not it can be avoided, "I have the awful feeling that we are reconciled, both we and the Soviets, to mutual destruction."[22] In considering this quote students usually talk about the concept of "mutual destruction" and what it might have been like to believe, as this character seems to, that it could be inevitable. This can lead directly to a more extended discussion of the ways in which

Americans learned to "live with fear" during the nuclear age. Another theme to be explored, related directly to the overall anxieties and fears of the era, is the hubris of believing that a truly "fail-safe" mechanism could be put in place, one that would make an accident "impossible." As one colonel explains to a visiting congressional representative who is touring the Strategic Air Command War Room, "What all of this machinery assures is that if we do go to war it is not by accident or because of the act of some madman. This system is infallible."[23] But of course the system is not infallible. In another exchange about the possible American responses to an accidental missile launch against the United States, a chief academic theoretician asks, "How could we really know it was an accident? How could they prove it?" He argues that even if it were an accident we would have to retaliate "with everything we had."[24]

We explore again the possibility of accidental—or purposeful—nuclear war during the tense years of the early 1980s. *War Games*, as noted already, was released in June 1983. I ask students to watch and discuss the opening sequence, described at the beginning of this chapter, in order to discuss again the "accidental war" premise of the film in the context of renewed fears of nuclear war during the early years of the Ronald Reagan presidency. In *War Games*, a teenage computer hacker thinks he is playing a wild new computer strategy game called "Global Thermonuclear War," but instead he has initiated a *real* "war game" that will result in a nuclear first strike. In addition to the *War Games* sequence, I also show in class the "attack segment" (approximately six minutes) of the made-for-television movie *The Day After*, which first aired on November 20, 1983.[25] The clip begins with a control room sequence showing military personnel on the phone confirming a "massive attack against the US," consisting of "over three hundred missiles inbound." As the scene switches to a downtown scene (Kansas City, Missouri, is destroyed by the blast, and the survivors featured in the film are located in Lawrence, Kansas), air raid sirens blast as people run, panicked, through the streets to take shelter. There is then a long-distance shot of Kansas City and a blast of blinding light, followed by a shot of the iconic mushroom cloud in the distance. From there, scenes of horror and mayhem flash quickly and seemingly endlessly for the next three minutes or so. Another mushroom cloud. People stampeding. Buildings being blown apart. Roaring fires. And snapshots of individuals and groups of people in a split second transformed into the eerie image of a skeleton and then nothing, to effectively illustrate the instantaneous obliteration, with no trace, of all of those within a certain radius of each blast. The only sounds are of wind, explosions, roaring fire, and screams. Even given the dated production values of a made-for-television film from 1983, the students usually are fairly shocked by the graphic depiction of nuclear holocaust.

The majority of the film, as the title suggests, explores the aftermath of a nuclear explosion—what the survivors endure. I explain to the students that that film, especially the sequence that they viewed, relied partly on declassified government film footage of early nuclear tests. I provide students with additional context to encourage them to understand the heightened level of fear and anxiety about possible nuclear war with the Soviet Union, in 1983. We discuss increased US-Soviet tensions, from the December 1979 Soviet invasion of Afghanistan through President Reagan's infamous 1983 speech condemning the Soviet Union as an "evil empire."[26] The same month he gave that speech, in March, Reagan announced his Strategic Defense Initiative (SDI), a far-fetched proposal to eventually build a defensive shield that would protect the United States from incoming Soviet missiles.

Two primary sources, the first volume of Reagan's published diary and his 1990 memoir, *An American Life,* are also very useful for supplementing our discussions about these years, particularly for a focus on 1983.[27] For example, Reagan wrote about his preparation for the speech announcing the Strategic Defense Initiative in his diary entry for March 7, 1983: "I'm going to take our case to the people only this time we are declassifying some of our reports on the Soviets and can tell the people a few frightening facts."[28] I ask students why Reagan would be so intent on providing "frightening facts" to the American public and what impact this might have had. Later in March, as he made further preparations for the speech, he described in his diary working on a draft of the speech. "I did a lot of re-writing," he explained, "much of it was to change bureaucratic talk into people talk."[29] I want to know how the students interpret this statement. What do they believe that Reagan meant by contrasting "people talk" and "bureaucratic talk," and what might this reveal to us about Reagan's reputation as "the Great Communicator"?

Reagan also wrote, in his diary and memoirs, about his reaction to the news that, on September 1, 1983, the Soviet Union shot down a Korean passenger plane. Echoing the words from his speech earlier in 1983, Reagan wrote, "If the Free World needed any more evidence in the

summer of 1983 that it was facing an *evil empire* [my italics], we got it
the night of August 31 when a Russian military plane cold-bloodedly
shot down a Korean airliner, Flight 007, murdering 269 innocent pas-
sengers, including a U.S. congressman and sixty other Americans."[30]
He also wrote, linking the incident directly to his SDI proposal:

> If, as some people had speculated, the Soviet pilots simply mistook
> the airliner for a military plane, what kind of imagination did it take
> to think of a Soviet military man with his finger close to a nuclear push
> button making an even more tragic mistake? If mistakes could be made
> by a fighter pilot, what about a similar miscalculation by the commander
> of a military launch crew? Yet, if somebody made that kind of mistake—
> or a madman got possession of a nuclear missile—we were defenseless
> against it. Once a nuclear missile was launched, no one could recall it,
> and until we got something like the Strategic Defense Initiative system
> in operation, the world was helpless against nuclear missiles.[31]

Then Reagan drew further connections between the KAL incident and
his private screening of *The Day After*. He watched the film at Camp
David on October 10, more than a month before the scheduled November 20 air date. In his memoir, he excerpted part of his diary entry from
that same night: October 10: "It is powerfully done. . . . It's very effective and left me greatly depressed. . . . My own reaction: we have to do
all we can to have a deterrent and to see there is never a nuclear war."[32]

The KAL flight apparently drifted off course, into Soviet airspace.
However, the Soviets had been earlier tracking an American spy plane,
and, while that plane had already returned to its base on one of the
Aleutian Islands, there was some understandable confusion about what
plane was now in Soviet airspace and considerable hesitation on the
ground to give an order to shoot down the plane. As Hoffman observes,
the "[Soviet] command post duty officer wondered if the Americans
would really fly a spy plan directly into Soviet airspace." Finally, the
order to "destroy target" was given.[33] Because Hoffman's account so
vividly describes the confusion and hesitation on the part of the Soviets
before the plane was destroyed, it provides further insight into the
ways in which incidents could escalate wildly during the Cold War,
contributing to the very real fear of accidental nuclear catastrophe.
Naturally, American leaders, starting with Reagan, reacted with intense
anger to the KAL tragedy and had an initial urge to react strongly, on

the basis of only the "raw" and spotty intelligence that was available in the immediate aftermath of the incident. As Hoffman concludes, American leadership "launched what became a major U.S. rhetorical offensive against the Soviets, accusing them of deliberately killing the people on the airliner."[34] In the meantime, however, clearer heads prevailed among the US intelligence agencies, which concluded that the incident *was* surely a terrible mistake. Later that same month, the CIA concluded in a report for the White House that the relationship between the United States and the Soviet Union was "pervasively bleak."[35]

David Hoffman describes "a wave of fear about nuclear war" in the fall of 1983 that "gripped both the Soviet Union and the United States." The Soviets in particular were increasingly convinced that a long-planned NATO military exercise, scheduled for November 2–11, 1983, in Europe, could instead be cover for a real nuclear attack. Able Archer was a standard operation in many ways, but it increased Soviet suspicions because it included the simulation of Pershing II missile participation for the first time and because of the number of high-level American officials scheduled to take part in the exercise. As both David Hoffman and Peter Vincent Pry show, the Soviets were still reeling in many ways from the response to the KAL incident and were fearful enough in November 1983 to be excavating new underground bunkers in the Ural Mountains, to the puzzlement of US intelligence analysts. Given the Soviet fears, the Americans removed many of the highest-ranking American officials from participation in Able Archer, including President Reagan, but the operation continued otherwise as scheduled, without incident.[36] After the completion of the exercise, Reagan admitted to his diary that perhaps the Soviet leaders really were more frightened of attack than he had previously thought: "I feel the Soviets are so defense minded, so paranoid about being attacked that without being in any way soft on them, we ought to tell them no here has any intention of doing anything like that."[37] Twelve days about the completion of Able Archer, the real Pershing II missiles arrived in Europe, and it would take several more years, after the arrival of Mikhail Gorbachev, for the Cold War to finally thaw.

By talking with students about the ubiquitous nature of popular culture, we can begin to see the popular culture of the American past as rich primary source material, reflecting the *mood* of the times. We understand why, in the second episode of the first season (set in 1960) of the popular television series *Mad Men*, a nervous Betty Draper, the bored suburban wife of successful advertising executive Don Draper, attempts to open a dialogue with her taciturn psychiatrist by saying, "I guess a lot of people must come here worried about the bomb. Is that true? It's a common nightmare people say." Or the cult-like popularity of the 1984 film *Red Dawn*, which graphically portrays a sudden Soviet attack on the United States and the small band of high school students who wage a guerrilla war against the invaders. Or the critical interest generated by the recently developed television drama *The Americans*, created by a former CIA agent, which explores the lives of two Soviet spies posing as a married couple living in suburban Virginia in the 1980s.[38] Pop culture in a variety of forms has pervaded the lives of most Americans, especially since the 1950s, which makes it an effective tool for gaining a greater understanding of the emotional content of the Cold War era. Understanding what fears and anxieties people felt and how they attempted to reflect those feelings through cultural expression is not only part of the historian's task but also part of the work of classroom teaching.

NOTES

1. *War Games*, theatrical, dir. John Badham (1983; MGM/UA Entertainment Co.).

2. My comments in this chapter are focused on stimulating classroom discussion, but I have also used some of these same ideas to create a variety of writing assignments, group presentations, or other projects, both in and outside the classroom.

3. "The Great Fear" comes from the title of David Caute's 1978 book, *The Great Fear: The Anticommunist Purge under Truman and Eisenhower* (New York: Simon & Schuster, 1978). However the term can be appropriated to refer explicitly to fears of the atomic bomb during the same period.

4. All three sources are available online from a number of sites. For the full text of George Kennan's "Long Telegram," see for instance the National Security Archive at the George Washington University, http://www2.gwu.edu /~nsarchiv/. The Truman Doctrine and selections from Truman's memoirs are available at the Harry S. Truman Presidential Library and Museum website at http://www.trumanlibrary.org/. For the excerpt on Truman's reaction to the North Korean invasion see Harry S. Truman, *Memoirs*, Vol. II: *Years of Trial and Hope* (New York: Doubleday, 1955), 332–33. The full text of the memoir is also available online at a number of sites including the Internet archive at http:// archive.org/stream/yearsoftrialandho00234mbp/yearsoftrialandho00234mbp _djvu.txt.

5. *The Atomic Café*, theatrical, dir. Jayne Loader, Kevin Rafferty, and Pierce Rafferty (1982; Libra Films).

6. "Bert the Turtle" video clips are in the public domain and are widely available on YouTube. I use the "duck and cover" classroom clips from *Atomic Café* to show children taking cover under their desks with their hands clasped behind their necks as they assumed the position they were taught, to "duck" and "cover" their heads.

7. Lisle A. Rose, *The Cold War Comes to Main Street: America in 1950* (Lawrence: University Press of Kansas, 1999), 311.

8. Ibid., 106. Rose also provides some useful examples, in her epilogue, of the impact of Cold War fears on children.

9. I have found the website "Vintage Ad Browser" to be an excellent source for advertisements: www.vintageadbrowser.com.

10. Elaine Tyler May, *Homeward Bound: American Families in the Cold War Era* (20th rev. and updated ed., New York: Basic Books, 2008); see also Lizabeth Cohen, *A Consumer's Republic: The Politics of Mass Consumption in Postwar America* (New York: Vintage Books, 2003).

11. Scans of the telegrams are available on the "Teaching with Documents" section of the National Archives website at http://www.archives.gov/education/lessons/mccarthy-telegram/#documents.

12. *The Manchurian Candidate,* theatrical, dir. John Frankenheimer (1962; United Artists Pictures); Richard Condon, *The Manchurian Candidate* (1959; reprint ed., New York: Pocket Star, 2004).

13. Kathryn Olmsted, "Blond Queens, Red Spiders, and Neurotic Old Maids: Gender and Espionage in the Early Cold War," *Intelligence and National Security* 19, no. 1 (Spring 2004): 80.

14. Olmsted, "Blond Queens, Red Spiders, and Neurotic Old Maids," 88.

15. I am grateful to Lori Clune for an e-mail exchange about Ethel Rosenberg and for the suggestion that I might want to use the Eisenhower quote. See her *Executing the Rosenbergs: Death and Diplomacy in a Cold War World* (New York: Oxford University Press, 2016), 114. For the original quote, see Dwight D. Eisenhower to Major John S. D. Eisenhower, June 16, 1953, Box 3, File: December 1952–July 1953 (1), Ann Whitman File, 1953–1961, DDE Diary Series, Dwight D. Eisenhower Papers, Dwight D. Eisenhower Library, Abilene, KS.

16. Kathryn Olmsted, *Red Spy Queen: A Biography of Elizabeth Bentley* (Chapel Hill: University of North Carolina Press, 2002); see also Michael Rogin, *Ronald Reagan, the Movie: And Other Episodes in Political Demonology* (Berkeley: University of California Press, 1987).

17. John Marks, *The Search for the Manchurian Candidate* (New York: W. W. Norton, 1991).

18. *Goodnight and Good Luck*, theatrical, dir. George Clooney (2005; Warner Independent Pictures).

19. I might also show them additional short clips of McCarthy in action from the House Un-American Activities Committee Hearings. Film clips are widely available, for instance on www.history.com.

20. Eugene Burdick and Harvey Wheeler, *Fail-Safe* (New York: Harper-Collins, 1962), 7.

21. Ibid., 8.

22. Ibid., 99.

23. Ibid., 43.

24. Ibid., 161.

25. *The Day After*, television, dir. Nicolas Meyer (1983; American Broadcasting Co.). The attack segment and the entire movie are both available on YouTube.

26. Ronald Reagan, Address to the National Association of Evangelicals, March 8, 1983, available at the "Voices of Democracy" website: http://voicesof democracy.umd.edu/reagan-evil-empire-speech-text/.

27. An excellent secondary source for providing an overview and context for the tense months of autumn 1983 is chapter 3, "War Scare," in David E. Hoffman's Pulitzer Prize–winning book, *The Dead Hand: The Untold Story of the Cold War Arms Race and Its Dangerous Legacy* (New York: Anchor Books, 2009), 73–100; Douglas Brinkley, ed., *The Reagan Diaries*, Vol. I: *January 1981–October 1985* (New York: HarperCollins, 2009); Ronald Reagan, *An American Life* (New York: Simon & Schuster, 1990), 582.

28. Brinkley, *The Reagan Diaries*, 203.

29. Ibid., 209.

30. Ibid., 273, and Reagan, *An American Life*, 582.

31. Reagan, *An American Life*, 584.

32. Ibid., 585.

33. Hoffman, *The Dead Hand*, 73–78.

34. Ibid., 80.

35. Ibid., 89.

36. Peter Vincent Pry, *War Scare: Russia and America on the Nuclear Brink* (Westport, CT: Praeger, 1999), 36–37, and Hoffman, *The Dead Hand*, 94.

37. Hoffman, *The Dead Hand*, 95.

38. *Mad Men*, episode 2, "Ladies Room" (originally aired July 26, 2007); *Red Dawn*, theatrical, dir. John Milius (1984; MGM/UA Entertainment Co.); Laura Holson, "The Dark Stuff, Distilled," *New York Times*, March 29, 2013.

KEY RESOURCES

American Historical Review. AHR has had a regular "film reviews" section since 1988.

Brinkley, Douglas, ed. *The Reagan Diaries*, Vol. I: *January 1981–October 1985*. New York: HarperCollins, 2009.

Carnes, Mark C., ed. *Past Imperfect: History according to the Movies*. New York: Henry Holt, 1995.

Caute, David. *The Great Fear: The Anticommunist Purge under Truman and Eisenhower*. New York: Simon & Schuster, 1978.

Film & History: An Interdisciplinary Journal.

Gaddis, John Lewis. *The Cold War: A New History*. New York: Penguin Books, 2006.

Hanhimaki, Jussi M., and Odd Arne Westad, eds. *The Cold War: A History in Documents and Eyewitness Accounts*. Oxford: Oxford University Press, 2004.

Hoffman, David E. *The Dead Hand: The Untold Story of the Cold War Arms Race and Its Dangerous Legacy*. New York: Anchor Books, 2009.

Journal of American History. Since 1986 the *JAH* has published a collection of movie reviews in each December issue.

Mintz, Steven, and Randy Roberts, eds. *Hollywood's America: United States History through Its Films*. St. James, NY: Brandywine Press, 1993. [Revised as *Hollywood's America: Twentieth-Century America through Film*. Malden, MA: Wiley-Blackwell, 2010.]

O'Connor, John E., and Martin A. Jackson, eds. *American History/American Film: Interpreting the Hollywood Image*. New York: Ungar, 1979.

Reagan, Ronald. *An American Life*. New York: Simon & Schuster, 1990.

Rose, Lisle A. *The Cold War Comes to Main Street: America in 1950*. Lawrence: University Press of Kansas, 1999.

Toplin, Robert Brent. *History by Hollywood: The Use and Abuse of the American Past*. Urbana: University of Illinois Press, 1996.

Truman, Harry S. *Memoirs*, Vol. II: *Years of Trial and Hope*. New York: Doubleday, 1955.

Using Popular Culture to Teach the Cold War

LAURA A. BELMONTE

Teaching the history of the Cold War to undergraduates is one of the greatest joys of my academic career. I began teaching the Cold War when the Berlin Wall first fell, when my students and I were first adjusting to a world no longer divided into capitalist and communist blocs. That world is completely alien to my students today. Few of them were alive when the Cold War shaped our daily lives. Their views of global politics are filtered through a post-9/11 lens, but that same perspective makes them quite eager to learn about the decades of Cold War that preceded the War on Terror and help to explain the fraught international landscape of the early twenty-first century.

Popular culture provides a great pathway for achieving some of these aims. Thanks to Netflix, Hulu, YouTube, iTunes, asynchronous learning platforms like Blackboard and DL, and advances in instructional technologies, it is easier than ever to access a huge array of cultural reflections of the Cold War from multinational perspectives and to integrate them into the classroom. Movies, television shows, comic books, novels, and music used alongside other primary sources such as memoirs and government documents engage a wide variety of learners. It can also be useful to expose students to forms of culture that can be used as secondary sources—for example, movies that depict an earlier historical period. These cultural products can also be used to explore issues of historical memory, or how historic events are perceived and understood in subsequent periods. There is great pedagogical value in helping students develop analytical skills that make them savvier consumers of culture in an age when they are constantly bombarded by information.[1]

My Cold War course starts with primary sources and a lecture that explain the origins of communism and anticommunism. I find that many students have a shaky grasp of concepts such as the political left and right and accordingly provide them an extensive glossary in which terms including "socialism," "totalitarianism," and "dictatorship" are defined. Students are expected to arrive the first day of class having read Karl Marx and Frederick Engels's *The Communist Manifesto*. The text is readily available online and always sparks a great discussion. Students consider the ideals of communism and begin assessing how and why Marxism drew such impassioned supporters and detractors. They are also encouraged to start considering how the theory of communism differed from its implementation in nations such as the Soviet Union, China, and Cambodia.

Popular culture is an integral element of all of the lectures and readings of this course.[2] Each lecture is accompanied by PowerPoint presentations that are replete with photographs, video clips, and music. Groupings of primary and secondary sources and films correlate with each lecture. To help students understand how and why watching film for historical purposes differs from viewing them for entertainment, I recommend including a short workshop explaining different film genres, contexts, and objectives.[3]

Possible options for the origins of the Cold War lecture are *Red Flag* (1999), an episode from the PBS documentary series *People's Century*.[4] Depending on the length of the course period, all or parts of Warren Beatty's Oscar-winning opus *Reds* (1981) perfectly complement this course module. At nearly three and half hours, the film requires a significant investment of time, but it pays real dividends. Hollywood simply does not make films like this anymore, and there are few that can rival its serious treatment of political ideas. While a few students grouse about the sappy romance between John Reed (played by Warren Beatty) and Louise Bryant (played by Diane Keaton), most gain a richer understanding of the radical left in the United States, the progression of the Russian Revolution, and the first Red Scare. Two particularly powerful scenes can easily be shown as snippets. In the first, Louise Bryant testifies to a congressional committee about the camaraderie and social justice she has witnessed in Russia but asserts that she does not think a similar system would work in the United States. The second features Emma

Goldman (played by Maureen Stapleton) expressing to John Reed her horror at the violence and suffering that have consumed Russia, shattering her Bolshevik ideals.[5]

While examining the roots of the Cold War planted during World War II, students read several primary documents describing tensions among the Big Three.[6] To illustrate the ways that Americans were encouraged to embrace their Soviet allies, I show excerpts of *Mission to Moscow* (1943), paired with Todd Bennett's fine article on the film's role in Franklin Roosevelt's diplomacy.[7] I also show NOVA's excellent episode on wartime atomic espionage and the Venona Project, *Secrets, Lies, and Atomic Spies* (2002). The companion website offers examples of decoded intercepts, portions of interviews, resources on espionage and cryptography, and a teacher's guide.[8]

As the course shifts moves from the late 1940s and into the 1960s, the possibilities for cultural materials to use in the classroom expand exponentially. One exceedingly valuable source for contextual clips is CNN's 24-part series on the Cold War originally released in 1998. A long-awaited and reasonably priced DVD version was issued in 2012, and the series offers a breathtaking sweep of firsthand testimonies from both high-level policymakers and ordinary citizens representing more than thirty nations.[9] Instructors can use the series to provide background and color for lectures and can also address some of the controversies the series triggered when released, especially for its comparative treatment of McCarthyism and Stalinism. These discussions can be framed in ways that compel students to grapple with the role of the television industry in promoting and challenging US Cold War policies and in shaping popular perceptions of the conflict.[10]

It is hard to imagine teaching McCarthyism without drawing on its myriad reflections in popular culture. From Arthur Miller's 1953 play *The Crucible* to George Clooney's *Good Night and Good Luck* (2005), there is a trove of fiction and film that can be paired with hearing transcripts, memoir excerpts, and government reports. *Salt of the Earth* (1954) recounts a true story of Mexican American workers and their families striking at a zinc mine. Students are engaged by the story of how and why a union expelled by the Congress of Industrial Organizations (CIO) and filmmakers and actors listed on the Hollywood blacklist joined forces with local residents of Grant County, New Mexico, to make the pro-union, feminist film.[11] Woody Allen's *The Front* (1976) uses humor to convey serious messages about McCarthyism and features Zero

Mostel, an American actor who was blacklisted in 1952 after being accused of joining the Communist Party of the United States. When Mostel appeared before the House Un-American Activities Committee (HUAC) three years later, he refused to name names, invoked the Fifth Amendment, and challenged the committee's right to investigate his political beliefs. His stance won him many admirers on the political left, but Mostel struggled professionally until the blacklist system began to crumble in the late 1950s. The drama *Guilty by Suspicion* (1991) offers a more formulaic dramatization of the blacklist's effect on the film industry. *The Red Menace* (1949), *I Was a Communist for the FBI* (1951), and *Big Jim McClain* (1952) provide examples of the staunchly anticommunist films some Hollywood studios made to prove their patriotism and to protect their industry in the aftermath of the Hollywood Ten hearings.[12]

The Way We Were (1973) might be best known for its somewhat cloying romance between Hubbell Gardiner (played by Robert Redford) and Katie Morosky (played by Barbra Streisand), but there is a thoughtful story about the American radical left and the rise of McCarthyism at the film's core. The script was written by Arthur Laurents, who modeled the Morosky character on a fiery young Marxist Jew he met in 1937 during his undergraduate years at Cornell University. Laurents was disgusted by the producers' decision to give the Gardiner character equal prominence and to omit critical scenes that better explained how Katie's refusal to abandon her political ideals, not Hubbell's infidelity, ultimately drove the couple apart. The DVD includes a fascinating short documentary on the making of the film that features one of these excisions.[13]

Invasion of the Body Snatchers (1956) takes a metaphorical approach to McCarthyism.[14] A science fiction thriller depicting an extraterrestrial invasion of a small town in California, the film can be read as either an indictment of mindless conformity or an anticommunist warning about the threat of internal subversion. Selected scenes can be paired with testimonies from government investigations of suspected communists and excerpted secondary sources such as Ellen Schrecker's *Many Are the Crimes: McCarthyism in America* and John Earl Haynes and Harvey Klehr's *Early Cold War Spies: The Espionage Trials That Shaped American Politics*. The multiplicity of perspectives encourages students to grapple with the implications of contemporary revelations about Soviet espionage in the United States and to contemplate the challenges of ensuring national security while preserving civil liberties.[15]

Civil defense programs and early nuclear testing have also inspired marvelous cultural resources.[16] Documentaries like *The Atomic Café* (1982), *Race for the Superbomb* (1999), and *The Fog of War* (2003) can be mined for clips that inspire both laughter (the "Bert the Turtle" civil defense cartoon aimed at children never fails to trigger guffaws) and horror (the Atomic Energy Commission film on "Operation Cue" includes footage of the "mannequin families" used on Nevada test sites that is truly chilling).[17] There is a cornucopia of Hollywood feature films with nuclear themes, including *Godzilla!* (1954), *Them!* (1954), *The Day the Earth Caught Fire* (1961), and *Fail-Safe* (1964).[18] Survival after nuclear war is depicted in *Five* (1951) and *On the Beach* (1959). *Hiroshima, Mon Amour* (1959), a highly influential Japanese film,[19] uses flashbacks to dramatize the real-life effects of the Hiroshima atomic bombing.[20]

There are rich cinematic sources to supplement readings on gender and the Cold War.[21] *My Son John* (1952) and *The Manchurian Candidate* delve into associations of communism with emasculation and loss of individualism.[22] *Ninotchka* (1939) and its musical remake, *Silk Stockings* (1957), are fun films that reflect prevailing Western claims that communism masculinized women, crushed human emotions, and deprived people of the wonders of consumerism.[23]

No Cold War class is complete without a screening of *Dr. Strangelove or: How I Learned to Stop Worrying and Love the Bomb* (1964). The Stanley Kubrick film not only remains hilariously funny but brilliantly satirizes the language of nuclear deterrence and tropes of gender and sexuality in the early Cold War era. I preface the film with assigned readings on nuclear strategy from Herman Kahn and Henry Kissinger and a bloc of pieces from Elaine Tyler May, Robert Dean, and David Johnson.[24] I also have students watch the short documentary *Inside the Making of Dr. Strangelove* (2000).[25] These contextual readings help students understand Kubrick and screenwriter Terry Southern's parodies of Cold War–era militarism, paranoia, and masculinity. If time does not permit a full showing, isolated scenes such as President Merkin Muffley (played by Peter Sellers) admonishing General Buck Turgidson (played by George C. Scott) and the Russian ambassador in the War Room or the mad ravings of General Jack D. Ripper (played by Sterling Hayden) about the perils of fluoridated water encapsulate the film's key themes.[26] More subtle scenes such as the eroticized midair refueling of the B-52 in the film's opening credits or the quick pan on the real-life motto of the

Strategic Air Command—"Peace Is Our Profession"—also provide good starting points for discussion.[27]

The James Bond novels and films contain a wealth of cultural material spanning most of the Cold War. A short explanation of how Ian Fleming's background as a British naval intelligence officer and journalist informed his approach to the character of James Bond, an officer in the British Secret Intelligence Service better known as MI6, helps set the stage for clips from several of the Bond films. One could choose any number of characters from *Dr. No* (1962), *From Russia with Love* (1963), *The Spy Who Loved Me* (1977), *Moonraker* (1979), *Octopussy* (1983), and *The Living Daylights* (1987) to show how cinematic depictions of the Soviets, empire, and the threat of nuclear war evolved over the course of the Cold War.[28]

There are dozens of songs with Cold War themes that can be interwoven throughout coverage of the early Cold War years. I often begin class by having students listen to one or two songs that they are asked to link to larger course themes. Conelrad's six-disc anthology *Atomic Platters: Cold War Music from the Golden Age of Homeland Security* is a fantastic source of music of varied genres and themes. The collection also includes public service announcements and a DVD of Cold War–era educational films produced by the Federal Civil Defense Administration. An extensive companion website includes contextual information on the songs and artists featured as well as complete lyrics for every selection. The combination makes it very easy to teach gems like Carson Robison's "I'm No Communist" (1952), Ray Anderson and the Homefolks's "Sputniks and Mutniks" (1958), and Sheldon Allman's "Crawl Out through the Fallout" (1960).[29]

The uses of music as a means of popular resistance to communism also merit attention. From the immense international popularity of Willis Conover's "Music USA" broadcasts on Voice of America to contraband rock and jazz albums smuggled behind the Iron Curtain, there are numerous ways to convey the cultural importance that people living under communism accorded Western music and musicians.[30] The Finnish-Estonian documentary *Disco & Atomic War* (2009), recently released in English on DVD, deftly and cleverly shows the role of Western radio and television in undermining communism.

Political cartoons and animated cartoons are also available in abundance. The editorial cartoons of artists like Herblock are easily accessed via Google Images and provide some of our most vivid cultural reflections of key events like the Cuban Missile Crisis. One can change the default Google search and find cartoons from the Soviet Union, Eastern Europe, and elsewhere to show opposing viewpoints. For a bit of levity, instructors can present snippets of *The Rocky and Bullwinkle Show* (1959–64) highlighting the comically inept Russian spies Boris Badinov and Natasha Fatale. Badinov and Fatale's homeland, Pottsylvania, is an obvious spoof of either East Germany or the Soviet Union. The Soviets, incidentally, failed to see the humor and banned the show for promoting anticommunist propaganda.[31]

Comic books are another valuable tool for teaching culture during the Cold War. With the onset of the Soviet-American rivalry, comic book writers and artists tackled nuclear anxieties, communist subversion, and the ideological battle between communism and capitalism using both over-the-top and subtle approaches. Well-known comic book heroes like Spiderman, the Fantastic Four, and the Incredible Hulk had Cold War origins and battled communist villains. Reflecting the era's emphasis on the traditional family as a bastion of peace and security, a 1954 congressional investigation targeted the violence and sexual content of the genre. US propagandists, eager to capitalize on the medium's broad accessibility, distributed hundreds of thousands of comics with anticommunist themes to foreign audiences.[32]

Comic books were only a small facet of the global cultural skirmishes of the Cold War. Instructors can draw on a great variety of primary and secondary sources to illuminate how the capitalist and communist blocs vied for hearts and minds. "Brave New World," an episode of the PBS series *People's Century* (1999), has terrific excerpts of Soviet propaganda films about the United States as well as footage of the 1959 American National Exhibition in Moscow, site of the famous "Kitchen Debate." An emerging literature on cultural diplomacy addresses how museums, theaters, sports stadiums, trade fairs, and libraries became Cold War battlegrounds.[33] Cultural diplomacy also provides a great pathway for examining how and why the United States often fumbled in its attempts to refute communist exploitation of the propaganda vulnerabilities created by American racism and segregation in the 1950s and early 1960s. Excerpted secondary readings segue wonderfully into selections from Dave Brubeck's superb musical *The Real Ambassadors* (1962).[34]

A unit on the Berlin Wall draws on a deep historiography[35] and offers the chance to incorporate foreign film and public history. *One, Two,*

Three (1961) is a satire featuring C. C. McNamara, a Coca Cola executive stationed in West Berlin (James Cagney) who hopes to promote his product across the continent. When the daughter of his boss falls in love with an East German communist who wants to take her to Moscow, McNamara attempts to refashion him into a European gentleman while simultaneously trying to outmaneuver Soviet bureaucrats. Wilder, an Austrian Jew who emigrated to the United States in 1933, was filming in Berlin when the Wall was constructed and had to relocate the production to Munich. When the film was released, some critics found it politically tone-deaf, but it now stands as a fitting satire of Cold War consumerism, the US–West German alliance, and the ideological clash between communism and capitalism. *The Spy Who Came in from the Cold* (1965), the British film adaptation of John Le Carré's 1963 spy novel, starts and ends at the Berlin Wall and provides a stark contrast to the campiness of the James Bond films. Wim Wenders's *Wings of Desire* (1987) is a plaintive German film in which two angels eavesdrop on the residents of a divided Berlin, capturing the angst of the city a mere two years before the Wall came down. *The Wall Jumper* (1998), Peter Schneider's 1998 German novel, touches on a similar themes.

Der Tunnel (2001), a German film available with English subtitles, is based on the true story of the East German swimming champion Hasso Herschel, who was imprisoned for participating in the 1953 East Berlin protests and who later defected, leaving his beloved sister behind. In the film, he and an engineer friend begin to dig a tunnel from West Berlin to East Berlin. They eventually enlist the help of about thirty other West Germans seeking to help those trapped behind the Wall. To finance their venture, they allow an American television crew to film the tunnel construction. The film captures the terror of the East German police state and shows the human toll the Wall exacted. The dangers of the tunnel project itself are particularly well realized.

A Web-based tour of the Berlin Wall Memorial is a moving capstone for this module. The site includes a short film, a mobile tour guide, and a collection of audio oral histories.[36] Students are able to gain a sense of the physical magnitude and imposing nature of the Wall and to see why escape attempts rarely succeeded. The site is a great starting point for a discussion of Cold War tourism and the ways that the Cold War is commemorated.[37]

As the course moves into the final phase of the Cold War, there are a plethora of memoirs, films, novels, and songs that can augment lectures. The 1994 Chinese epic *Huozhe* (To Live) follows one family's tumultuous experiences with Maoism from the triumph of the communist revolution in the 1940s to the aftermath of the Cultural Revolution in the 1970s. The Chinese government banned the film and prohibited the director, Zhang Yimou, from making films for two years. Excerpts of novels, oral histories, and memoirs can be used in conjunction with the movie.[38] *The Killing Fields* (1984) is a potent and moving way to expose students to the proxy wars that swept millions of people in the developing world into wars and political upheavals triggered by the larger Cold War. The film and an emerging memoir literature on the Cambodian genocide shatter John Lewis Gaddis's depiction of the Cold War as a so-called Long Peace.[39]

The resurgence of Cold War tensions in the early 1980s is reflected in numerous films and songs. The escalation of the nuclear arms race drew an especially impassioned cinematic response ranging from the earnest *War Games* (1983) to the somber *Testament* (1983) to the bleak *Threads* (1984), a British television film that is unstinting in its depiction of the long-range effects of radiation exposure. Aired in November 1983, the television movie *The Day After* drew more than 100 million viewers and played a role in Ronald Reagan's move toward more conciliatory rhetoric about the Soviets. Nonetheless, during the 1980s Hollywood released a stream of features that capitalized on popular antagonism toward the Russians, including *Red Dawn* (1984), *Rocky IV* (1985), and *White Nights* (1985). Musicians generally were much more critical of the era's renewed militarism. Punk Rock performers like The Clash, Government Issue, Suicidal Tendencies, and The Dead Kennedys lambasted Cold War authoritarianism across the political spectrum. The German artist Nena's "99 Luftballons" (1984) pairs a deceptively upbeat melody with somber lyrics about a nuclear holocaust triggered by two children releasing red balloons into the sky. Frankie Goes to Hollywood's "Two Tribes" (1984) links subtle anti–Cold War lyrics with a bombastic music video (easily found on YouTube) showing Ronald Reagan and Yuri Andropov in a wrestling match. Sting's "Russians" (1985) blends Russian-inspired music with lyrics in which a father conveys his fears of nuclear annihilation, declaring "I hope the Russians love their children too"—as if that were in question. Billy Joel tackles the Cold War in two particularly vacuous songs, "We Didn't Start the Fire" (1989) and "Leningrad" (1989).

In addition to *Dr. Strangelove*, another film I never fail to teach is *The Lives of Others* (2006). Winner of the Oscar for Best Foreign Language Film, this German film is set in East Germany in 1984 and is deeply affecting. It tells the story of a Stasi captain named Gerd Wiesler (played by Ulrich Mühe, a former East German stage actor who lived under Stasi surveillance and who later discovered his actress wife had been a state informer), who becomes infatuated with a playwright and his actress girlfriend, whom he's secretly observing. The superbly written and acted drama rivets students and always sparks a terrific discussion. The Stasi's surveillance techniques and the extraordinary depth of their internal spying network to the very end of the Cold War illuminate the fear and repression that undergirded communism at its worst.[40]

The end of the Cold War is captured with humor and poignancy in *Good Bye, Lenin* (2003). To protect his mother's fragile health after she emerges from a coma, a young man tries to prevent her from learning that her beloved communist state is no more. Although Berlin has been swept by Western consumerism, he recreates East Germany using everything from food items found in abandoned East bloc apartments to lovingly recreated East German newscasts filmed by him and his friends. Near its end, the film takes a serious turn when it tackles the long-range impact of his father's decision to flee to the West years earlier.

The current popularity of the FX Soviet spy drama *The Americans* shows that the Cold War has ongoing cultural relevance. By blending primary sources, secondary accounts, novels, music, films, and other cultural materials, professors can integrate popular culture and enliven an already exciting period. The biggest challenge is narrowing down the extraordinary array of options available for teaching the Cold War's cultural dimensions.

NOTES

1. For an approachable introduction to studying popular culture, see Stacy Takacs, *Interrogating Popular Culture: Key Questions* (London: Routledge, 2014).

2. There is a substantial body of literature of popular culture and the Cold War in many different regions. Some excellent examples include Richard Stites, *Russian Popular Culture: Entertainment and Society since 1900* (New York: Cambridge University Press, 1992); David Caute, *The Dancer Defects: The Struggle for Cultural Supremacy during the Cold War* (New York: Oxford University Press, 2003); Stephen J. Whitfield, *The Culture of the Cold War*, 2nd ed. (Baltimore: Johns Hopkins University Press, 1996); and Tony Shaw, *Hollywood's Cold War* (Amherst: University of Massachusetts Press, 2007).

3. For an especially good resource on using films as historical evidence, see

Tom Gunning, "Making Sense of Films," History Matters, http://historymatters .gmu.edu/mse/film/.

4. Much of the *People's Century* series is posted on YouTube.

5. *Reds*, DVD, dir. Warren Beatty (1981; Paramount Pictures, 2006). Louise Bryant's congressional testimony can be found at timestamp 00:3:31, chapter 1, disc 2. Emma Goldman expresses her disillusionment with the Soviet Union at timestamp 01:03:00, chapter 6, disc 2.

6. There are numerous excellent primary source collections on the Cold War. The most international in scope and content remains Jussi Hanhimaki and Odd Arne Westad, eds., *The Cold War: A History in Documents and Eyewitness Accounts* (Oxford: Oxford University Press, 2004). For those seeking to highlight a few key events in more depth, the Bedford Series in History and Culture offers several short, inexpensive volumes on Cold War–related topics such as the Kitchen Debate, decolonization, Maoism, NSC-68, and the democratic revolutions of 1989.

7. Todd Bennett, "Culture, Power, and *Mission to Moscow*: Film and Soviet-American Relations during World War II," *Journal of American History* 88, no. 2 (September 2001): 489–518.

8. See http://www.pbs.org/wgbh/nova/venona/. Unfortunately, the film itself is hard to find. It is not included in NOVA's digital archive and is available only in VHS format.

9. The companion volume is a helpful guide. See Jeremy Isaacs, *Cold War: An Illustrated History, 1945–1989* (Boston: Little Brown, 1998).

10. Arnold Beichman, *CNN's Cold War Documentary: Issues and Controversies* (Palo Alto: Hoover Institute Press, 2000). On the role of the television industry in the early Cold War, see Thomas Doherty, *Cold War, Cool Medium: Television, McCarthyism, and American Culture* (New York: Columbia University Press, 2003), and Nancy Bernhard, *US Television News and Cold War Propaganda, 1947–1960* (New York: Cambridge University Press, 2003).

11. James J. Lorence, *The Suppression of Salt of the Earth: How Hollywood, Big Labor, and Politicians Blacklisted a Movie in the American Cold War* (Albuquerque: University of Mexico Press, 1999).

12. As of May 2016, full versions of *The Red Menace* and *I Was a Communist for the FBI* were posted on YouTube. *Big Jim McClain* can be rented inexpensively through YouTube or Amazon Video.

13. *The Way We Were*, DVD, dir. Sydney Pollack (1973; Columbia Pictures Industries, 1999).

14. The film is available for inexpensive rental on iTunes, YouTube, and Amazon Video.

15. Inexpensive primary source collections on McCarthyism are readily available. See, for example, Albert Fried, *McCarthyism: The Great American Red Scare* (New York: Oxford University Press, 1996); Ellen Schrecker, *Many Are the*

Crimes: McCarthyism in America (New York: Little, Brown, 1998); John Earl Haynes and Harvey Klehr, *Early Cold War Spies: The Espionage Trials That Shaped American Politics* (New York: Cambridge University Press, 2006).

16. For historic context, see Paul S. Boyer, *By the Bomb's Early Light: American Thought and Culture at the Dawn of the Atomic Age* (Chapel Hill: University of North Carolina Press, 1994); Kate Brown, *Plutopia: Nuclear Families, Atomic Cities, and the Great Soviet and American Plutonium Disasters* (New York: Oxford University Press, 2013); Kenneth Rose, *One Nation Underground: The Fallout Shelter in American Culture* (New York: New York University Press, 2004); and Laura McEnaney, *Civil Defense Begins at Home* (Princeton: Princeton University Press, 2000).

17. *The Atomic Café* is posted by Vimeo at https://vimeo.com/25154726. *Race for the Superbomb* is posted on YouTube. The PBS series *American Experience* originally aired the film and has a website with valuable primary sources, the transcript, and participant interviews at http://www.pbs.org/wgbh/amex/bomb/filmmore/index.html. The "Operation Cue" clip including the "mannequin families" is found at timestamp 01:05:00. "Duck and Cover" (the civil defense film featuring Bert the Turtle) and the full-length version of *The Fog of War* are posted on YouTube.

18. *Godzilla* and *Fail-Safe* can be rented on Amazon Video or YouTube. *Them!* and *The Day the Earth Caught Fire* are available for rental on iTunes or Amazon Video.

19. *Five* and *Hiroshima, Mon Amour* can be rented on iTunes, Amazon Video, or YouTube. There are several clips from *On the Beach* posted on YouTube, but the full version of the film is not currently available online or on DVD.

20. American, British, Japanese, and French filmmakers critique these films and many other shorts and documentaries in Jack G. Shaheen, ed., *Nuclear War Films* (Edwardsville: Southern Illinois University Press, 1978).

21. The classic text is Elaine Tyler May, *Homeward Bound: American Families in the Cold War Era* (1988; rev. and updated ed., New York: Basic Books, 1999). For countervailing views, see Joanne Meyerowitz, ed., *Not June Cleaver: Women and Gender in Postwar America, 1945–1960* (Philadelphia: Temple University Press, 1994). For an excellent recent overview, see Helen Laville, "Gender and Women's Rights in the Cold War," in Richard H. Immerman and Petra Goedde, eds., *The Oxford Handbook of the Cold War* (New York: Oxford University Press, 2013), 523–39.

22. While one can occasionally find excerpts from *My Son John* on YouTube, I have never been able to find the entire film in more than twenty years of searching. By contrast, the original version of *The Manchurian Candidate* has been issued on DVD multiple times.

23. *Ninotchka* and *Silk Stockings* are both available for rental on YouTube and Amazon Video. Two terrific choices for accompanying articles are Helen

Laville, "'Our Country Endangered by Underwear': Fashion, Femininity, and the Seduction Narrative in *Ninotchka* and *Silk Stockings*," *Diplomatic History* 30, no. 4 (September 2006): 623–44, and Susan E. Reid, "Cold War in the Kitchen: Gender and the De-Stalinization of Consumer Taste in the Soviet Union under Khrushchev," *Slavic Review* 61, no. 2 (Summer 2002): 211–52.

24. Herman Kahn, *On Thermonuclear War* (Princeton: Princeton University Press, 1961); Henry Kissinger, *Nuclear Weapons and Foreign Policy* (New York: Harper, 1957); Elaine Tyler May, "Explosive Issues: Sex, Women, and The Bomb," in Lary May, ed., *Recasting America: Culture and Politics in the Age of Cold War* (Chicago: University of Chicago Press, 1989), 154–69; Robert D. Dean, "Masculinity as Ideology: John F. Kennedy and the Domestic Politics of Foreign Policy," *Diplomatic History* 22, no. 1 (2002): 29–62; and David K. Johnson, *The Lavender Scare: The Cold War Persecution of Gays and Lesbians in the Federal Government* (Chicago: University of Chicago Press, 2004).

25. *Inside the Making of Dr. Strangelove* is posted on YouTube. For a DVD reissue that includes it, see *Dr. Strangelove: Or How I Learned to Stop Worrying and Love the Bomb*, DVD, dir. Stanley Kubrick (film, 1964; DVD, 2001; Columbia Tristar Home Entertainment).

26. President Muffley confronts General Ripper and the Russian ambassador in the War Room at timestamp 00:37:40. General Ripper's recitation on fluoridation is found at timestamp 00:45:44.

27. The timestamp for the SAC motto is 00:14:56.

28. For useful cultural and political analyses, see James Chapman, *License to Thrill: A Cultural History of the James Bond Films*, rev. ed. (London: I. B. Tauris, 2008), and Jeremy Black, *The Politics of James Bond: From Fleming's Novels to the Big Screen* (Winnipeg: Bison Books, 2005).

29. Conelrad, *Atomic Platters: Cold War Music from the Golden Age of Homeland Security* © 2005 by Bear Music, ASIN: B000A5HJ86, Compact discs/DVD. The companion website is found at http://www.atomicplatters.com/index.php.

30. Uta Poiger, *Jazz, Rock and Rebels: Cold War Politics and American Culture in a Divided Germany* (Berkeley: University of California Press, 2000); Timothy W. Ryback, *Rock Around the Bloc: A History of Rock Music in Eastern Europe and the Soviet Union, 1954–1988* (New York: Oxford University Press, 1990); Leslie Woodhead, *How the Beatles Rocked the Kremlin: The Untold Story of a Noisy Revolution* (New York: Bloomsbury USA, 2013).

31. Cyndy Hendershot, *Anti-Communism and Popular Culture in Mid-Century America* (Jefferson, NC: McFarland, 2002), 85–87.

32. Examples of actual comic books might be hard to find, but one can easily find blogs, museum exhibits, and databases that address the connections between the Cold War and comics online. There are many examples of comic books produced by the US Department of State and the United States Information Agency in Record Group 306 at the National Archives II in College Park,

Maryland. For scholarly appraisals of popular comics, see Matthew J. Costello, *Secret Identity Crisis: Comic Books and the Unmasking of Cold War America* (London: Bloomsbury Academic, 2009), and Rafiel York and Chris York, eds., *Comic Books and the Cold War, 1946–1962* (Jefferson, NC: McFarland, 2012). I refer to several comics used in US international information campaigns in my *Selling the American Way: US Propaganda and the Cold War* (Philadelphia: University of Pennsylvania Press, 2008).

33. In a rapidly growing body of work, see Michael Krenn, *Fallout Shelters for the Human Spirit: American Art and the Cold War* (Chapel Hill: University of North Carolina Press, 2005); Naima Prevots, *Dance for Export: Cultural Diplomacy and the Cold War* (Middletown, CT: Wesleyan University Press, 1999); Stephen Wagg and David Andrews, *East Plays West: Sports and The Cold War* (New York: Routledge, 2006); Robert Haddow, *Pavilions of Plenty: Exhibiting American Culture Abroad in the 1950s* (Washington, DC: Smithsonian Institution Press, 1997); and Reinhold Wagnleitner, *Coca-Colonization and the Cold War: The Cultural Mission of the United States in Austria after the Second World War* (Chapel Hill: University of North Carolina Press, 1988).

34. Highlights of a robust literature include Mary Dudziak, *Cold War Civil Rights: Race and the Image of American Democracy* (Princeton: Princeton University Press, 2000), and Penny Von Eschen, *Satchmo Blows Up the World: Jazz Ambassadors Play the Cold War* (Cambridge, MA: Harvard University Press, 2004).

35. See, for example, Frederick Taylor, *The Berlin Wall: A World Divided, 1961–1989* (New York: Harper, 2007).

36. For an English-language version of the Berlin Wall Memorial site, see http://www.berliner-mauer-gedenkstaette.de/en/.

37. Resources on Cold War tourism abound. Good examples include Cold War Tourist, http://coldwartourist.com/; 10 Cold War Tourism Sites You Can Visit, http://o.canada.com/news/10-cold-war-tourism-sites-you-can-visit; Frank Burres, "Spring Travel Issue: Cold War-Era Tourist Sites Feature Weapons of Mass Attraction," *Washington Post*, March 21, 2013; and Cold War Sites, http://www.historvius.com/cold-war-sites/pe125. For a smart, often humorous appraisal with a US focus, see Jon Wiener, *How We Forgot the Cold War: A Historical Journey across America* (Berkeley: University of California Press, 2012).

38. See, for example, Jung Chang, *Wild Swans: Three Daughters of China* (New York: Simon & Schuster, 1991); Fens Jicai, *Ten Years of Madness: Oral Histories of China's Cultural Revolution* (San Francisco: China Books and Periodicals, 2007); and Gao Yuan, *Born Red: A Chronicle of the Cultural Revolution* (Palo Alto: Stanford University Press, 1987).

39. Loung Ung, *First They Killed My Father: A Daughter of Cambodia Remembers* (New York: Harper Perennial, 2006), and Haing S. Ngor, *Survival in the Killing Fields* (New York: Basic Books, 2003).

40. Germany's ongoing efforts to grapple with the legacies of the Stasi are brilliantly examined in Anna Funder, *Stasiland: Stories from behind the Berlin Wall* (New York: Harper Perennial, 2011).

KEY RESOURCES

Bennett, Todd. "Culture, Power, and *Mission to Moscow*: Film and Soviet-American Relations during World War II." *Journal of American History* 88, no. 2 (September 2001): 489–518.

Conelrad. *Atomic Platters: Cold War Music from the Golden Age of Homeland Security.* © 2005 by Bear Music. ASIN: B000A5HJ86. Compact discs/DVD.

Costello, Matthew J. *Secret Identity Crisis: Comic Books and the Unmasking of Cold War America.* London: Bloomsbury Academic, 2009.

Haddow, Robert. *Pavilions of Plenty: Exhibiting American Culture Abroad in the 1950s.* Washington, DC: Smithsonian Institution Press, 1997.

Krenn, Michael. *Fallout Shelters for the Human Spirit: American Art and the Cold War.* Chapel Hill: University of North Carolina Press, 2005.

Prevots, Naima. *Dance for Export: Cultural Diplomacy and the Cold War.* Middletown, CT: Wesleyan University Press, 1999.

Ryback, Timothy W. *Rock around the Bloc: A History of Rock Music in Eastern Europe and the Soviet Union, 1954–1988.* New York: Oxford University Press, 1990.

Shaw, Tony. *Hollywood's Cold War.* Amherst: University of Massachusetts Press, 2007.

Von Eschen, Penny. *Satchmo Blows Up the World: Jazz Ambassadors Play the Cold War.* Cambridge, MA: Harvard University Press, 2004.

Wagg, Stephen, and David Andrews. *East Plays West: Sports and the Cold War.* New York: Routledge, 2006.

Whitfield, Stephen J. *The Culture of the Cold War.* 2nd ed. Baltimore: Johns Hopkins University Press, 1996.

Civil Rights and
the Cold War Era

BRENDA GAYLE PLUMMER

When presidential candidate Mitt Romney campaigned before an audience at the West Hills Elementary School in Knoxville, Tennessee, in March 2012, he sought a theme connected to Tennessee's heritage. Romney chose to recite the lyrics to "Davy Crockett," a popular hit from the early 1950s. Film footage shows that the assemblage behind him consisted largely of people who were born more than a half-century after the song made the charts. In similar fashion, those seeking to connect to today's school population may find that the events of the Cold War do not resonate personally with students. The words "Marx" and "Lenin," for example, might evoke a classic comedian and a member of the Beatles, respectively. Ironically, even those associations are in the remote past for undergraduates who were born well after the collapse of the Soviet Union and the deaths of Groucho Marx and John Lennon.

An instructor teaching the Cold War thus has to contend with students' lack of a readymade mental frame of memories and references into which information can be tidily dropped. On a planet now characterized by the diversity and complexity of international issues, it may be difficult to communicate the reality of a past world perceived as divided between two irreconcilable powers engaged in lethal struggle. The task becomes even more complicated when the issue of civil rights enters the picture. Here a teacher might have a slight advantage, since the civil rights movement has been enshrined in national history, if only as the obligatory salute to Martin Luther King Day. Yet many students will not connect civil rights, most often thought of in the domestic context only, with world affairs. In part, the connection has been made opaque by the long-standing view that civil rights in the United States are a "family affair." After all, racial minorities have sought citizenship rights and not independence. If we look at the behavior of US ethnic minorities more closely, however, we see that, while pursuing full citizenship rights, they also interest themselves in issues that affect their places of origin. African Americans have concerned themselves with decolonization in Africa, and Jewish American and Irish Americans have been active on behalf of Israel and Ireland, respectively.

Things become even more problematic when we consider that discussion of race and minority rights has been uncomfortable for many people, as these issues are associated with the ideological polarization characteristic of the present moment. In some instances, a teacher will have to "give permission" to talk about subjects that are often treated with reticence. This has much to do with establishing a climate of trust in the classroom, which includes not framing dialogue in terms of "right" and "wrong" answers and insisting on mutual civility. Additionally, while science has established that race is a sociocultural rather than a biological entity, barriers remain to freeing discourse from the old familiar boxes and categories.

One pathway through these thickets is to help students examine in detail particular events that may not be major components of the Cold War story but that, in shedding light on the decisions of policymakers and the mindset of the period, also help explain its connection to civil rights. It is important to remember that the East-West contest was not only about the threat of military confrontation. It was also about how each side wished to demonstrate the cultural superiority of its society. A prime example of this rivalry, one in which civil rights concerns play a part, is reflected in the Brussels World's Fair of 1958, which provided an opportunity to showcase the cultural values of the United States and its progress since World War II.[1] Less than a year after the Little Rock, Arkansas, school desegregation crisis made world headlines, the US State Department saw the Fair as a chance to put a better spin on American race relations for global consumption. Planners for the US venue at the Fair signed up the African American opera singers Leontyne Price and William Warfield to sing in Brussels. They recruited twelve African American docents, ages nineteen to twenty-five, and a group of college-age Hawaiians and Puerto Ricans, a selection intended to represent America's diverse people of color and to suggest that they were allowed to participate fully in American life. During training for their stint in Brussels, all of these young people were instructed to acknowledge, if asked, that racism existed in American society but to say that the situation was improving. This take on race relations was consonant with another US initiative for the Fair, an exhibit to be called "Unfinished Business." The exhibit would attempt to explain slum conditions in American cities and environmental degradation. Calling it "Unfinished Business" would help viewers understand that the United States meant to remedy these problems and not hide them. A display on segregation featured newspaper headlines collages about racial disturbances, followed by photographs and charts that detailed improvements in black education, wealth holding, and the like. This was meant to silence non-aligned and Eastern bloc critics who routinely pointed to Jim Crow to discredit the United States. The culmination was a photomural showing black and white children playing together. It had a caption that said, in part: "The goal that draws us together is not utopia, but larger freedom with more justice. Democracy is our method. Slowly but surely it works."[2]

The exhibit at Brussels was mounted in a small building spatially removed from the main US pavilion, and few Fair visitors ever saw it. "Unfinished Business" had another problem: four powerful southern congressmen opposed it and made such a fuss that the State Department agreed to take certain pictures down, such as one showing a black teenage boy dancing with a white girl. Foggy Bottom also bowed to the legislators' argument that the exhibit did not give a balanced picture of the United States because it didn't take segregationist views into account. When Eisenhower agreed, the exhibit was closed. The story of the United States at the Brussels World Fair demonstrates that as late as 1958 American leaders could not agree about how to represent the country's identity as a multiracial nation. It also reveals the reform narrative that the State Department used to exculpate the country from accusations of racism. This incident in Cold War history helps students see the connection between the domestic and the global. Additionally, YouTube has become a primary source of film documentation. Several clips are available that illustrate the Fair and convey a visual sense of the period.[3]

A teacher might ask students to watch these clips and write descriptions of their contents. What messages are the filmmakers trying to convey? How are they conveyed? What production values help to get the message across? Are there conspicuous absences in the narratives?

A follow-up to such an assignment might be to have students track down references to the Brussels Fair in newspapers and government documents, such as the series *Foreign Relations of the United States*, and write detailed descriptions of what they observe. What did the press say about US objectives at the fair? What can be learned from photographs? Did government documents, meant for perusal by government officials, have a different slant on the event and its meaning?

Cultural diplomacy further underscores the unsettled position of African Americans in its portrayal of ideal American home life. Notions about domesticity in the Cold War context have fascinated historians, and a significant body of scholarship has developed concerning the Cold War's "home front." As Elaine Tyler May has noted, the home was a key weapon in the psychological war against nuclear annihilation. It offered "the promise of security in an insecure world." American leaders touted the home, and especially suburban life, as the way to insulate the nation from class conflict. "The American dream" was ostensibly available to all groups. In 1959, as part of a cultural exchange, the American National Exposition opened in Moscow. Vice President Richard M. Nixon was on hand to tour with Soviet premier Nikita Khrushchev a display of the latest US kitchen appliances. In the famous "kitchen debate" between the two men, Nixon argued that the United States would have the upper hand in the Cold War so long as the nation ensured and nurtured "abundant family life available in modern suburban homes within the price range of the average US worker."[4]

America's racial-ethnic minorities had considerable difficulty qualifying as the "average workers" of Nixon's consumerist projection. His model was predicated on a division of gender labor that rested on the family wage, the ability of a single breadwinner to support a family. The glamorous housewives who peopled the ads for washers and ovens during this era did not include African American women, who could not afford to retire from the workforce. Indeed, discrimination in employment was a major impetus for the civil rights insurgency. As the historian William Jones reminds us, the famous march on Washington in 1963 was titled the March on Washington for Jobs and Freedom.[5]

Earlier in the Cold War, progress for women had been defined differently. Rather than making the kitchen easier to use, feminists like Mary McLeod Bethune, president of the National Council of Negro Women, wanted to free women from the kitchen altogether. The Council of American Women, an organization that fell victim to the postwar purges, did not prescribe a privatized life for stay-at-home wives. Instead, it advocated public programs of government-sponsored childcare, daycare facilities in factories, and communal kitchens to relieve working women of the strains of the "double shift." As a result of enduring patterns of housing and job discrimination, fewer African American women would be among the ranks of homeowners in any case. Their bondage to the kitchen rested on the bias that had long confined so many to domestic employment.[6]

US relations with South Africa during the apartheid era constitute another entry point into the connection between civil rights and the Cold War. Washington was unwilling to challenge apartheid because of its desire for strategic minerals deemed essential to national security, its perception of South Africa as a Cold War ally, and its conflation of nationalism and communism in emerging countries. How would the United States square its reliance on a racist South African regime with its desire to entice African states into the Cold War camp? By 1964 the federal government had aligned itself rhetorically with the American civil rights leadership. What would it mean, then, to support racial justice at home and to deny it abroad? This is an issue that could prompt lively class discussion. In general, the "Cold War imperative," Mary L. Dudziak's claim that Cold War competition triggered federal commitment to desegregation, provides a springboard for students to consider the relationship between domestic reform and foreign-policy initiatives.[7] The simultaneity of decolonization in Africa and the US civil rights movement made Jim Crow an embarrassment when African diplomats were refused service at public accommodations in the United States. The US State Department's *Foreign Relations* series provides primary source documentation about US policy with regard to Africa during the Cold War.[8]

The illustrative episodes described—among others—have both domestic and international implications, but students might also be engaged by looking at the impact of the Cold War on specific persons. Too often teachers' efforts to paint a broad picture for students of sweeping historical processes leaves them bewildered rather than informed as individual subjectivity gets lost in the drama of global events. Insofar as the personal is political, many students might respond more deeply to narratives about specific people. The film *Scandalize My Name: Stories from the Blacklist*[9] features interviews with Harry Belafonte, Ossie Davis, and other black entertainment-industry figures who were blacklisted during the McCarthy period. They describe the loss of work and the psychological stress that they and others endured in the early 1950s. The career of the leftist singer and actor Paul Robeson is relevant in this regard, and his music and YouTube clips of his performances are available for study. Mary L. Dudziak's work on the blacklisting of the African American entertainer Josephine Baker details officials' particularly vindictive treatment of an international star.[10] African Americans who were investigated, blacklisted, or punished for dissidence included a number of women such as Charlotta Bass, the publisher of the *California Eagle*; Theresa Robinson, an official with the fraternal Elks organization; the singer Lena Horne; the actress Fredi Washington; and the pianist Hazel Scott. Even the conventional liberal Mary McLeod Bethune drew the suspicious gaze of authorities, whose reach suggested that it was the civil rights advocacy of these women rather than any allegiance to Moscow that troubled anticommunist crusaders.[11] The experience of African Americans who were adversely affected by the second Red Scare could be the basis of an assignment that teachers would vet for accuracy and competent writing. Students would prepare a one-to-three-paragraph, well-researched submission to Wikipedia on a single individual's exposure to censure or proscription.

Periodization is just as significant with regard to civil rights as it is in general studies of the Cold War. The content of lectures and discussion will vary depending on whether a given course will treat the entire Cold War period. If it does, and if civil rights are to be a theme throughout, a teacher might want to track the differences over time in the way that civil rights issues appear and are engaged. In the late 1940s civil rights organizations were greatly influenced by the lessons of World War II. Nazism as the logical extension of racist ideology, the impact of the Holocaust, and the wartime sacrifices of African Americans and other minorities lent energy to the effort to effect change. As hostilities between the United States and its erstwhile ally the Soviet Union deepened, mainstream civil rights organizations purged leftist members and swore allegiance to a new formulation of liberalism. Cold War liberalism was anticommunist but reformist in accepting the necessity for the democratic inclusion of all citizens in the political and civic life of the nation. Assigning students to develop a chronological chart of what they consider key Cold War developments and having them defend those choices is a way to assist them in developing a sense of the temporal changes that occur during the period and the significance of those changes.

The creation of the United Nations was another legacy of World War II. The UN is unpopular with many Americans today, but students might be surprised to learn about the enthusiasm with which the organization was received in the late 1940s and the efforts made by the federal government to interest and involve US citizens in creating its charter. Civil rights leaders quickly recognized the UN as a forum where racial injustice could be aired. In 1946 the National Negro Congress filed a petition that protested conditions in the United States. The National Association for the Advancement of Colored People followed suit in 1947. In 1951 the Civil Rights Congress sent a petition called "We Charge Genocide" to the international body. These primary-source documents, which have been published,[12] shed light on the way that civil rights groups sought to marshal international opinion at a time when global sensitivity to racism, colonial unrest, and the growing conflict with the Soviet Union made the United States particularly vulnerable to reproach.

Teachers might use these documents as the basis for a discussion about why civil rights groups felt compelled to address an international forum. Why didn't they bring these concerns to Congress instead? What did they expect the UN to do? What was the reaction of US officialdom? Was the UN a more influential body then than today? What would be the consequences for the United States of incurring negative international opinion? These questions could be the basis of a writing assignment or, equally, an essay exam.[13] The Library of Congress and the National Archives provide on their respective websites useful information about using government records to teach history.[14]

The Cold War intensified in the early 1950s as the Korean War and both superpowers' development of the hydrogen bomb brought a militant phase to the conflict. During this period, the gap between democratic aspiration and the actual performance of the US government and American civil society was stark. McCarthyism, described earlier, curtailed the reach of reform but did not succeed in destroying an incubating movement for change that insistently used a Cold War argument to justify its call for change. Activists reasoned that the United States could prove the superiority of its society over that of the communist bloc by extending freedom to all of its citizens.

The period between the death of Stalin and the Cuban Missile Crisis, 1953–62, is also the classic period of the civil rights era. It encompasses events ranging from the *Brown* decision through the Montgomery bus boycott, the sit-ins and James Meredith's integration of the University of Mississippi. These years are generally considered to encompass a thaw in the Cold War, but they were punctuated by crises such as the Hungarian revolt and the beginning of the Vietnam War. The civil rights movement continued to make use of the Cold War logic of reform: the pursuit of democracy would enable the United States to assume the moral leadership of the world. Decolonization in sub-Saharan Africa from 1957 on lent support to the argument. If the United States wanted dominant influence in the emerging nonaligned countries, it had to disavow racism.[15]

The mid-1960s to 1980 was a period of relative economic prosperity in both the West and the Soviet Union. The civil rights movement consolidated its legislative gains but receded with the resurgence of radicalism. Radical organizations disdained Cold War liberalism. The Student Nonviolent Coordinating Committee (SNCC), for example, claimed it did not care whether its supporters had once belonged to the Communist Party as long as their objective was liberation. While growing opposition to the Vietnam War abetted the radical turn, not every antiwar protester was a radical. The heavyweight boxing champion Muhammad Ali refused the draft and was labeled a traitor. His conflicts with the authorities over the meaning of his championship and civic responsibility, along with his legal difficulties, are recorded in Bill Siegel's 2013 documentary *The Trials of Muhammad Ali.*[16] Civil rights advocates who increasingly opposed the war and defined themselves as Black Power proponents compared the military service that conscription demanded of black and brown men with the lack of justice and opportunity available to them in civilian life. These activists often identified with Cuba, with other leftist governments in the Middle East and Asia, and with national liberation fronts in Africa. This in turn placed them in the sights of the FBI, local police agencies, and the national intelligence community, inaugurating a new era of repression. Counterintelligence programs (COINTELPRO) sought during this time to neutralize groups such as the Black Panther Party and the Revolutionary Action Movement. Whether or not government officials genuinely believed in the potential of radical organizations to endanger national security, they explained their repressive responses as anticommunist initiatives.[17]

By the time of Ronald Reagan's accession to the presidency and the renewal of an arms race that contributed to the collapse of the Soviet Union in 1989, the focus of civil rights insurgency had shifted from people of color specifically to a larger public constituency. Women as a class and people with disabilities began to intensify their claim to civil rights entitlements. While the states failed to ratify the Equal Rights Amendment to the Constitution, the Americans with Disabilities Act was on its way to final passage in 1990. The relationship of these developments to the waning Cold War was negligible. For all intents and purposes, the Cold War–civil rights nexus ended with the collapse during the Nixon-Ford era of black radical organizations and those originated by other racial-ethnic minorities.

The periodization used here is only a suggested one. Just as historians have not arrived at a universally agreed-upon periodization for the Cold War generally, the subtopic of civil rights is open to debate and interpretation. Depending on the chronological scope of a given course, teachers may want to structure events differently. Some may not agree that Black Power and its engagements with Third World radicalism form part of the Cold War experience, while others see them as central. A discussion about this provides a way to introduce students to a conscious understanding of historiography. Encourage them to think about the distinction between history and the writing of history. How have historians divided up chunks of time and given these names? What is included and excluded in the way that historians label epochs? Do they all agree?

Just as personal narrative can make the Cold War legible to those born years afterward, so can film help to visualize the ethos of the era. Choices include both documentary and feature film. Entire movies will likely not be practical, but carefully chosen segments can work. Interested students might be motivated to seek out engaging films in their entirety and view them on their own time. A caveat is that African Americans were not well represented in commercial cinema for most of the Cold War period. The conventions of segregation all too often relegated black actors to roles as buffoonish servants. The enterprising searcher can nevertheless tease out pertinence from some contemporaneous Hollywood pictures. For example, the spate of race relations movies that appeared at the turn of the 1940s decade was the film industry's efforts to grapple with race at the time. These movies include *Home of the Brave* (1949), *Intruder in the Dust* (1949), *Lost Boundaries* (1949), *Pinky* (1949), *The Jackie Robinson Story* (1950), and *The Well* (1951). Collectively, they provide a window on Cold War liberalism's construction of the issue.

182

Documentaries will likely be more useful, and some clips of original footage are also primary sources. YouTube has an extract from Jackie Robinson's testimony before the House Un-American Activities Committee, during which he slammed Paul Robeson. Paul Robeson's life is explored in the 1999 PBS documentary *Here I Stand*, named for Robeson's eponymous book. The film, directed by S. Clair Bourne, includes interviews with persons who knew Robeson, such as Harry Belafonte and Ossie Davis; contemporaneous footage; and excerpts from Robeson's films and concert performances. Footage of the pianist and early television personality Hazel Scott's appearance before the Un-American Activities Committee appears in *Scandalize My Name*, cited earlier. Scott, once married to the well-known Harlem congressman Adam Clayton Powell Jr., was an outspoken civil rights advocate who refused to knuckle under to demands by the entertainment industry that she play stereotyped roles. YouTube also hosts a series of video recordings by David Du Bois, the stepson of W.E.B. Du Bois, who describes his memories of Du Bois and of the circles that Du Bois and his second wife, Shirley Graham Du Bois (David's mother), frequented during the Cold War, including the American Communist Party.

For visually oriented student cohorts, pictures are indispensable. PowerPoint is a far better tool as a slide projector than as a medium for conveying other forms of information. The fair use doctrine for education makes it possible to pull visuals from any number of sources. While we often see movies and pictures as sources of entertainment only and become passive watchers, students should be taught to approach film and graphics as analyzable data. Have them ask questions such as: What is depicted here? Who took this picture or drew this illustration? What was it meant to convey and how? What does it represent to you?

Newspapers and magazines usefully convey the ambiance of the Cold War years. The mainstream (i.e., white) press was slow to pick up on civil rights, but African American papers and journals are replete with information, including insights about the linkage between US goals abroad and dilemmas at home. The best newspapers for this purpose are the *Amsterdam News*, the Baltimore *Afro-American*, the *Chicago Defender*, and the *Pittsburgh Courier*. Students should be encouraged to peruse broadly: they will be amazed at the prices of gasoline and steak dinners in days of yore. In addition to the databases available through university library subscriptions, Google has digitized and made available online a prodigious amount of content from *Ebony* and *Jet* magazines. Students

"Race Mixing is Communism." Little Rock, 1959.

might use these sources as a way of understanding the black press's perspective on the Cold War and how—and why—it differed from that of mainstream serials like the *New York Times*, the *Wall Street Journal*, *Life*, and so on. Their observations could form the basis of discussions, papers, and/or exams.

Some of the primary sources that students will examine are in digital form. More conventional items include federal records, which are increasingly digitized. Records of the House Un-American Activities Committee, the Senate Internal Security Committee, and the Committee on Government Operations Permanent Subcommittee on Investigations (Senator Joseph McCarthy's committee) constitute important sources on the inquisitorial aspect of the Cold War. University and state libraries that are federal repositories usually have print copies of the hearing sets. The Federal Bureau of Investigation's extensive website is a massive trove of information about individuals, groups, and events investigated and reported on by the FBI that are salient to the history of the Cold War and its intersection with civil rights.[18] Court records also provide valuable information and can be accessed online. One of these is the amicus curiae brief that the Justice Department filed in the 1954 *Brown v. Board of Education* case.[19] The brief claimed that "it is in the context of the present world struggle between freedom and tyranny that the problem of racial discrimination must be viewed." It thus made school desegregation a priority in the anticommunist struggle. The Justice Department had also filed briefs in earlier cases, notably *Shelley v. Kraemer*, 334 US 1 (1948), that made racially restrictive covenants in real estate transactions unenforceable.

This chapter thus far has dealt largely with sources and interpretations. Methods of delivery, aside from the conventional lecture, should rely heavily on discussion and teacher-student interaction. It is important to defeat the widespread perception that history is something that happens "out there" somewhere to other people rather than engaging all of us as active agents in its flow. As a research and writing assignment, the teacher might instruct students to ask their parents, grandparents, or other relatives what they recall of the Cold War period. Do they remember duck-and-cover drills in elementary school? Did they arrive in the United States as refugees from Hungary or Poland? Did they see Senator McCarthy on television or footage of Khrushchev banging his shoe on the table at the UN? What were their feelings at the time of the US-Soviet showdown over missiles in Cuba? Are there Vietnam veterans in the family? How did family perceptions of China change from the Korean War era to Nixon's opening to China in 1972? What did parents think when the Berlin Wall came down in 1989? Students might also reflect on how the experiences of their families helped to construct their own identities in the present.

One of the ironic legacies of the Cold War has been its impact on education. When in 1959 the Soviets launched Sputnik, the United States was still in the throes of the Little Rock, Arkansas, school desegregation crisis. Radio Moscow made a point of announcing to the world exactly when the satellite was over Little Rock.[20] In the ensuing angst about the unpreparedness of Americans to compete with Soviet accomplishments in science, Congress passed the National Defense Education Act (NDEA). NDEA provided major funding for higher education, with emphasis on the sciences, mathematics, engineering, and area studies. It also provided federal loans for the greatly enlarging population of US college graduates.

With no communist enemy to fear, post–Cold War policymakers and the general public are less apt to see creation of an educated citizenry as an intrinsic part of national security or as ensuring national competitiveness in the global market. The view that higher education is a luxury has become increasingly common, even in the face of general unanimity that it deeply influences not only income but also individuals' other life chances. As a result, today's students often struggle to stay in school, amassing substantial debt and working more hours than was customary during the Cold War years. The task for teachers is to work around the handicaps to learning caused by this situation.

Doing more activities in class and assigning less homework is one option for addressing the problem. Primary sources can be incorporated into lectures or distributed to students to read and discuss in small in-class groups. Given a certain disinclination to read complex material among some cohorts, having documents read in class may ensure that the material will be absorbed. Documents from a variety of sources might stimulate interest. Diplomatic correspondence, personal letters, court decisions, contemporaneous posters and film footage, and transcripts of congressional hearings should all prompt students to ask and answer "how and why" questions. Students might also be encouraged to keep journals in which they record their responses to the intersection of civil rights and the Cold War. Another assignment, which could be done in a small group, is to prepare a PowerPoint presentation based on the analysis of a particular document within its social and political context. For example, the 1947 Report of the President's Committee on Civil Rights, "To Secure These Rights,"[21] was the Truman administration's definitive statement of its civil rights policy. Students might use parts of that to test Dudziak's "Cold War imperative" against the concerns expressed in the document.

Many colleges and universities provide space on their servers for professors and teaching assistants to upload class content and communicate electronically with students. Additionally—or in the absence of such provision—teachers can make use of media such as Facebook and Twitter to engage their classes in course material. This might work best with students who already have an interest in history, political science, or American studies and are majoring in these or related fields.

NOTES

1. An excellent and accessible source of information about this that can work in the classroom is Michael L. Krenn's "'Unfinished Business': Segregation and US Diplomacy and the 1958 World's Fair," *Diplomatic History* 20 (Fall 1996): 591–612.

2. Quoted in Michael L. Krenn, *Black Diplomacy: African Americans and the State Department, 1945–1969* (Armonk, NY: M. E. Sharpe, 1999), 107.

3. For other ways in which the US government sought to use race to for the purposes of cultural diplomacy, see Penny Von Eschen, "Who's the Real Ambassador? Exploding Cold War Racial Ideology," in Christian G. Appy, ed., *Cold War Constructions: The Political Culture of United States Imperialism, 1945–1966* (Amherst: University of Massachusetts Press, 2000), 110–31.

4. Elaine Tyler May, *Homeward Bound: American Families in the Cold War Era*, rev. ed. (New York: Basic Books, 2008), 1, 19–23, 155.

5. William P. Jones, *The March on Washington: Jobs, Freedom, and the Forgotten History of Civil Rights* (New York: W. W. Norton, 2013).

6. "Mrs. Bethune Sees Hope for Colonial People," *California Eagle*, May 24, 1945, 1; Jacqueline Ann Castledine, "Gendering the Cold War: Race, Class, and Women's Peace Politics, 1945–1975," PhD diss., Rutgers University, 2006, 72–73.

7. Dudziak's law journal article "Desegregation as a Cold War Imperative," *Stanford Law Review* 41 (November 1988): 61–120, might be too legalistic for undergraduates. An alternative is her broader and more culturally oriented treatment, *Cold War Civil Rights: Race and the Image of American Democracy* (Princeton: Princeton University Press, 2000). See also Thomas Borstelmann, *Apartheid's Reluctant Uncle* (New York: Oxford University Press, 1993).

8. Some of the pertinent *Foreign Relations* series have been made available online. See, for example, *Africa*, Vol. XIV, *Foreign Relations of the United States, 1958–1960*, https://history.state.gov/historicaldocuments/frus1958-60v14; *Congo, 1960–1968*, Vol. XXIII, *Foreign Relations of the United States, 1964–1968*, https://history.state.gov/historicaldocuments/frus1964-68v23/index; and *Documents on Africa, 1973–1976*, Vol. E-6, *Foreign Relations of the United States, 1969–1976*, https://history.state.gov/historicaldocuments/frus1969-76ve06.

9. ©1999, Starz Encore Entertainment.

10. Mary L. Dudziak, "Josephine Baker, Racial Protest, and the Cold War," *Journal of American History* 81 (1994): 543–70.

11. William Barlow, "Commercial and Noncommercial Radio," in Jannette L. Dates and William Barlow, eds., *Split Image: African Americans in the Mass Media*, 2nd ed. (Washington, DC: Howard University Press, 1993), 189–264; Mame Hoffman to Mary McLeod Bethune, March 31, 1947, Records of the National Council of Negro Women, Mary McLeod Bethune Memorial Museum, Washington, DC.

12. The text of the National Negro Congress petition is online at http://fau .digital.flvc.org/islandora/object/fau%3A5359. Excerpts from the NAACP petition are online on the Library of Congress site at http://www.loc.gov/exhibits /naacp/world-war-ii-and-the-post-war-years.html#obj11. The Civil Rights Congress petition is available at http://babel.hathitrust.org/cgi/pt?id=mdp.39015 074197859;view=1up;seq=26. While Library of Congress, National Archives,

and presidential library URLs can be assumed to be fairly stable, addresses and content can change on nongovernmental sites. That is why I have added a "date accessed" to this note. A useful tool for tracking down information that a site no longer displays but that may be in the ether somewhere is the Internet Archive, also known as the Wayback Machine, https://archive.org/web/.

13. A valuable source for the use of the UN as a forum is Carol Anderson, *Eyes Off the Prize: The United Nations and the African American Struggle or Human Rights, 1944–1955* (Cambridge: Cambridge University Press, 2003).

14. Library of Congress, http://www.loc.gov/teachers/usingprimary sources/; National Archives, http://docsteach.org/.

15. Thomas Borstelmann's *Cold War and the Color Line: American Race Relations in the Global Arena* (Cambridge, MA: Harvard University Press, 2001) provides a useful overview of this issue.

16. © Kartenquim Films.

17. A brief and accessible study for students is Peniel E. Joseph, "Waiting till the Midnight Hour: Reconceptualizing the Heroic Period of the Civil Rights Movement," *Souls* 2, no. 2 (2000): 6–17.

18. The FBI's publicly available online records can be accessed at http://vault.fbi.gov/.

19. The text of *Brown v. Board of Education* (347 US 483) can be found on a number of Internet sites, including FindLaw: http://caselaw.lp.findlaw.com/scripts/getcase.pl?court=US&vol=347&invol=483.

20. Gerard Degroot, *Dark Side of the Moon: The Magnificent Madness of the American Lunar Quest* (New York: New York University Press, 2006), 66.

21. Available online from the Harry S. Truman Library at http://www.trumanlibrary.org/civilrights/srights2.htm#48.

KEY RESOURCES

Anderson, Carol. *Eyes Off the Prize: The United Nations and the African American Struggle or Human Rights, 1944–1955.* Cambridge: Cambridge University Press, 2003.

Borstelmann, Thomas. *Apartheid's Reluctant Uncle.* New York: Oxford University Press, 1993.

Degroot, Gerard. *Dark Side of the Moon: The Magnificent Madness of the American Lunar Quest.* New York: New York University Press, 2006.

Dudziak, Mary. *Cold War Civil Rights: Race and the Image of American Democracy.* Princeton: Princeton University Press, 2000.

Horne, Gerald. *Black and Red: W.E.B. Du Bois and the Afro-American Response to the Cold War.* Albany: SUNY Press, 1986.

Joseph, Peniel E. "Waiting till the Midnight Hour: Reconceptualizing the Heroic Period of the Civil Rights Movement." *Souls* 2, no. 2 (2000): 6–17.

Krenn, Michael L. "'Unfinished Business': Segregation and US Diplomacy and the 1958 World's Fair." *Diplomatic History* 20 (Fall 1996): 591–612.

———. *Black Diplomacy: African Americans and the State Department, 1945–1969.* Armonk, NY: M. E. Sharpe, 1999.

Von Eschen, Penny. "Who's the Real Ambassador? Exploding Cold War Racial Ideology." In *Cold War Constructions: The Political Culture of United States Imperialism, 1945–1966,* edited by Christian G. Appy, 110–131. Amherst: University of Massachusetts Press, 2000.

Woods, Jeff. *Black Struggle, Red Scare: Segregation and Anti-Communism in the South, 1948–1968.* Baton Rouge: Louisiana State University Press, 2004.

National Security and the National Pastime

THOMAS W. ZEILER

W e were known as the Reds before the Communists.
Let them change their name," protested the vet-
eran Cincinnati sportswriter Tom Swope, as McCarthyism rampaged
through the country in the early 1950s. In response to the pressures from
the second Red Scare, and much to his disgust, Swope's Cincinnati Reds
baseball club changed its nickname to "Redlegs" from 1953 through
1958.[1] This was not the national pastime's only brush with the Cold War.

That is because sports like baseball intersect with the stuff of history
and thus prove to be fertile ground for classroom instruction. For a few
decades, historians have embedded athletics in national and global
culture, society, politics, diplomacy, and economy. Sport is no longer
studied for its own sake or solely for the poetry behind the act of athleti-
cism, although the art and physicality of sports figures attract us to
games in the first place, and the body of literature that addresses its
feats and failures reflects this interest.[2] To be sure, bringing sports into
the classroom is appealing because sports are fun. Students by and
large have participated in them, and so there is a built-in, natural means
of relating games, events, and sports figures to historical issues. To be
sure, athletics reaches deeply into national cultures and transcends international boundaries, and thus, by gauging the interaction of sports in
domestic society as well as global affairs, historians may illuminate
trends, patterns, and change over time. Sports help students, many of
whom have trouble understanding the import of the Cold War (or even
liking history), relate to this monumental half-century of conflict.

One need only consider the Olympic Games to recognize the intersection of sports and world politics—Nazi nationalism in Berlin, terrorism in Munich, civil rights in Mexico, and human rights in Beijing, to name just a handful. The Olympic movement amply shows that sports addresses even bigger themes of international politics, economics, and culture. Thus, it provides a good framework for classroom discussion and exercises.[3] One obvious exercise is to assign a research paper on an Olympics, a political event in an Olympics, or a figure. Another is to debate the use of the Games as a venue for politics—the Nazi showcase in 1936, Black Power in 1968, and the 1980 US boycott resulting from the Soviet invasion of Afghanistan are just three examples. And events beyond the Olympics were also tied to the East-West conflict. Think of ping-pong diplomacy with China, the heated Canada-Soviet hockey match in the midst of détente in 1972, or the campaign against South African apartheid in international games.

While the Olympics provide an obvious example of the intersection between sports and international affairs (including issues of gender and equality, such as the inclusion of women on Middle Eastern teams or whether marketing and support for women are at the same level that men enjoy), baseball can be a rewarding topic for exploring the Cold War and American culture. The background to the two episodes that this chapter focuses on—the 1949 appearance before Congress by Jackie Robinson (which links race to the Cold War) and the 1951 playoff games (which address technology, the military, and patriotism in wartime)—is important to keep in mind. This is especially so for acknowledging the transformative effects of the Second World War on American society. That conflict taught Americans that national security trumped recreation; by the time of the Cold War, they were somewhat accustomed to the notion that baseball served a larger purpose of victory, national unity, safety from threats, and preservation of values and the American way of life.[4] High-profile players—Ted Williams, Joe DiMaggio, Bob Feller, Hank Greenberg, Warren Spahn—served in the military, and, along with bond drives and other campaigns for the war effort at ballparks, they brought the war home to fans. Spectators were also enlisted for the war effort and asked to return foul balls for collection and shipment to bases. Servicemen were permitted free entry into games. Students might be asked to compare these actions and sacrifices to the current War on Terrorism but also to inquire into the prominent status of baseball as it exited the world war, having helped to defeat fascism, and was now called upon to prosecute communism.

An appealing way to approach World War II is by asking students to write a biography of the military service of a baseball figure—including a female player in the All-American Girls Professional Baseball League, which was established in 1943 and ended in 1954. Possible subjects include the New York Yankees catcher and multilinguist Moe Berg, who enlisted in the Office of Strategic Services (OSS) during the war. Berg's photographs of Tokyo from the rooftop of a hospital during an exhibition tour to Japan in 1934 of All-Star baseball players, including Babe Ruth and Lou Gehrig, were later used by the American military to bomb targets in the city during the Second World War. During the war, he worked with US intelligence services to contact resistance groups in Yugoslavia and also purportedly engaged in espionage to determine whether Nazi Germany possessed the atomic bomb. His is a colorful story of fact mixed with fiction about his undercover exploits, though his baseball card has been displayed at CIA headquarters—thereby tying him to the Cold War as well.[5] The transition from world war to Cold War was also apparent in the greatest moment in baseball history: the integration of the sport by Jackie Robinson in 1947. The superpower conflict had created a defensive, uneasy mindset in general in the country, however, and even Robinson and the national pastime were affected.

The Robinson-Robeson Standoff

Robinson, already a famed college and amateur athlete, had served in the US Army in World War II, but when race joined with politics and foreign policy to shape the postwar era of baseball, itself steeped in the Cold War, he took on iconic status.[6] One of the interconnections was his appearance before the House Committee on Un-American Activities (HUAC) to counter the testimony of the famous black singer and left-wing activist Paul Robeson. It is a revealing episode about race and the Cold War, a teachable moment in which a baseball figure is a means of showing the dangers of rigid anticommunism.

In July 1949, the famous Robeson questioned whether blacks would participate in a war against the Soviet Union. HUAC called upon the pillar of the black community, Jackie Robinson, to respond. He had broken the color barrier in the national pastime with dignity (thus he was acceptable to white America) and was a relatively conservative, religious, married black man with a military record (and thus a perfect representative of the American way of life and the success of democracy). Beyond his fame in the sport, the sheer stature of a baseball player in American society was remarkable and attests to the importance of Robinson's achievements both on and off the playing field. The context grows even more broad if instructors consider that the year before the Robinson-Robeson standoff, President Harry S. Truman established a Committee on Civil Rights to report on the violence blacks faced throughout the South and to issue recommendations. As well, another institution of American life—the United States Army—was compelled to integrate (though, notably, a year after the institution of baseball did so; the process of desegregating the military took until 1950). Students should be drawn to using the historic event of Robinson's breaking into Major League Baseball to examine other issues in Cold War America, including integration in other walks of life and his apparent rebuttal to Robeson's seemingly anti-American, communist-infused charges.[7]

There was no doubt of Cold War prominence when, before HUAC, Robinson refuted Robeson's charges that African Americans would never take up arms against the Soviet Union, which, unlike the United States, lent support for equal rights for minorities.[8] Robinson's appearance came during a critical period in the emerging Cold War. Just weeks before his testimony, the Berlin airlift had succeeded in ending a crisis over that hot spot of the Cold War (and ultimately over the divided Germany). Three months before, the treaty creating the North Atlantic Treaty Organization (NATO) had been signed by the United States, Canada, and Western European allies to confront aggressors (i.e., the communist bloc). Communists were marching toward victory in China, which would establish the People's Republic in October 1949. Unbeknownst to HUAC members, the Soviets would stun the world by exploding their first atomic bomb a month after Robinson's appearance before them, but they had long investigated the possibility that spies and subversives were operating in America to steal nuclear secrets.

The Cold War was an ideological as much as a security battle, and baseball played its part in fascinating ways that might surprise students who delve into the periodicals of the time. The Soviets, for instance, claimed that American players had no rights and could be bought and sold like slaves in the capitalist marketplace of the Major Leagues. Americans countered that baseball helped combat socialistic ideology and indoctrinated young men in the American way of life. That went for watching baseball, as well as playing it, especially in Little League (which, with its pledge to trust in God and country, displayed the ideals of Americanism for the world to see). Why not ask students to explore the values of communism and capitalism through the processes and lessons of baseball and ask too whether any of them played Little League and picked up on these themes of American values.

Thus, the politically fraught HUAC episode is ripe for debate by students. One means of doing so is for students to role-play debate across a host of issues that touch on the incident. Black opinion was complicated by the Left's support for black economic and civil rights throughout the 1930s and beyond. Students can be assigned to either side of the communist-anticommunist debate. As well, they can consider the pros and cons of baseball integration (also pushed by communists) and the baseball establishment's resistance to it. Students can be assigned to play the role of African American historical figures to reveal the complexities of Cold War life. For instance, while some African Americans welcomed efforts by the American Communist Party on civil rights and economic aid, the same people were also not necessarily opposed to capitalism or patriotism. By the time of Robinson's HUAC appearance, the Cold War had magnified the supposed heresies of the Left, thus compelling blacks, like other citizens, to take sides in the ideological struggle between capitalism and Marxism. Anticommunist "Red Scare" hysteria and Red-baiting had polarized Americans but also marginalized those who seemed to undermine Americanism.

Radicalism was suppressed, and Robinson made it clear in carefully scripted remarks that appeared on the front page of the *New York Times* (easily accessible online through the newspaper's archive) on July 19, 1949, that he favored moderation in politics and loyalty to American principles of democracy but that communism had little to do with discrimination in race relations. As he noted to Congress, "The white public should start toward real understanding by appreciating that every single Negro who is worth his salt is going to resent any kind of slurs and discrimination because of his race, and he's going to use every bit of intelligence, such as he has, to stop it. This has got absolutely nothing to do with what Communists may or may not be trying to do."[9]

For this issue, a series of questions that relate to the Cold War is appropriate for students to consider once they have read the entire testimony. Why was a baseball player called upon to refute communism?

Why did he describe Robeson's views as "silly"? What did Robinson think of pacifism? How did Robinson connect race and ideology not only into a direct indictment of communism but also into an indirect critique of using communism as an excuse to ignore racism? That is, what did he think of the implicit fear that blacks were prone to radicalism? How did he define progress on race in America, in contrast to Robeson's views on progress in the Soviet Union (and Jim Crow backwardness in the United States)?

Students might also engage in research to gauge the response of the black community, white America, and Congress to Robinson's remarks. They will find a range of opinions—from applause by whites to support, disappointment, and anger on the part of African Americans.[10] Asking students to move beyond just listing the various responses and instead setting them in the context of the Cold War would be especially fruitful. In addition, the issue of race, baseball, and the Cold War after Robinson's HUAC appearance can be followed by his civil rights activities. After living through the civil rights movement and the Vietnam War in the 1960s, Robinson later regretted his opposition to Robeson, another black man, and his position as a representative of the Cold War establishment. In fact, the FBI—which had earlier tried to protect him from death threats—now opened a file on him (available online) to keep abreast of his affiliations with civil rights groups, most of which were deemed to be leftist.[11]

The Shot Heard 'Round the World

At exactly 3:38 P.M. on October 3, 1951, Bobby Thomson, the third baseman for the home team New York Giants, hit what in baseball lore is considered the most famous home run in history. The setting could not have been more dramatic. Two runners were on base in the bottom of the ninth inning, in the third and final game of a tied playoff series—a game that would determine which team would win the National League pennant and play in the World Series—between two archrivals, the Giants and the Brooklyn Dodgers, in New York City, the center of the baseball world. The Dodgers were leading 4–2, but Thomson drove the second pitch from Brooklyn's Ralph Branca into the left field stands for a 5–4 victory, thereby capping the most dramatic pennant race ever.[12] The event instantaneously became an American legend, a symbol to rival Pearl Harbor, the Kennedy assassination, and

9/11 for a generation. The following day's newspaper headlines trumpeted it as "the shot heard 'round the world," alluding to Ralph Waldo Emerson's nineteenth-century hymn.

Thomson's home run opens windows on many aspects of American life and baseball during the Cold War. For instance, there was the waning intimacy that fans had with players—both Branca and Thomson were local heroes who lived in immigrant neighborhoods—as the game moved out of cities and into the suburbs. Suburbs themselves were critical to the game (and, in part, Cold War creations). There was also culture, which encouraged conformity—evidenced by the Organization Man and the Man in the Grey Flannel Suit and reinforced by the identical housing that dominated the suburbs; the team-playing and lack of independence; and the service work that characterized the American Century. Baseball, too, had its "Chairman of the Board," the great but colorless pitcher Whitey Ford (absent from the Yankees in 1951–52 because he was serving in the Korean War) but also "company men" of broadcasting and management (Vin Scully and Walter Alston) who fit a standardized mold. Cold War America prioritized safety and conventionality, and baseball reflected that trend. Relatedly, women have been characterized as being "contained" in the home, as they retreated from the workforce at a time when American mainstream values cherished suburban families over the feminism and independence of the World War II era.

The development of television itself was tremendous; historians point to the "tube of plenty" as a defining element of Cold War America. While a debate was raging among broadcasters about whether television was a benefit or a bane to the game, the playoff series was the first sporting event in the country to be shown on coaxial cable nationwide. There had been no coast-to-coast transmissions before the 1951 series; games were filmed in New York and then the film was flown to California for distribution. ATT planned to install the cable for the 1951 World Series, but the playoffs so riveted the nation's attention that nationwide television came into being before the championship. It was so unexpected and so rushed that the transmission lacked a commercial sponsor. National audiences were eager to watch, and TV sales skyrocketed. Hotels put televisions in lobbies, and TV watchers clotted around dealer windows, department store fronts, and bars in several cities. It was hard to tell how many watched that first game because many areas of country still could not receive television transmissions, but the estimates are that some 70 million (out of a total US population of nearly 155 million people) watched the first game of the 1951 playoff, and smaller but still big number watched the pivotal game three. Television was transformative, leading to more night games, cities' loss of cultural events to the suburbs, and changes in recreational and living patterns to accommodate a turn inward to focusing on the nuclear family and the self-sufficient house, or, to use a Cold War metaphor, "containment in the home."

Then there was geography, abetted by Cold War economic trends. New York City was the center of the baseball world in 1951, and, although the New York Yankees in particular would dominate the sport, the pastime stood on the brink of the era in which franchises would shift westward and new ones would be created for the first time in a half-century. By itself, expansion into the Midwest, the Far West, and the South was a by-product of Cold War defense and energy dynamics (the suburbs, the interstate highway system, a boom in automobile sales, and a search for nonunionized labor were other results). Thus, baseball's moves are fodder for student projects such as presentations on the impact of new teams on urban and regional development, itself tied to Cold War service and manufacturing industries, from the first move (the Boston Braves to Milwaukee, in 1953, and then to Atlanta, in 1966), to the move of the two New York teams involved in the Thomson shot to California, to baseball outposts in Texas, Minnesota, and Seattle during the Cold War.

The Thomson shot also reflected the concerns of the Cold War. In 1945, *Time* magazine announced an "American Century" in which the United States had a responsibility to lead the world by spreading its influence. Americans hoped for peace, security, and prosperity after war, at least as World War II came to an end. But the Cold War, shortages of housing and other essentials faced by consumers, and nagging fears of a return of massive unemployment at Great Depression levels led to anxiety, anger, paranoia, and a backlash against government. The Thomson feat came right in the midst of this age of worry, a period best characterized as the second Red Scare fomented by real crises abroad (including the Korean War, which had resulted in a vicious stalemate by the time of the playoff games) and at home, by Cold War hysteria, and by the machinations of McCarthyism. At the same time, there was a certain ignorance, even arrogance, about America's centrality in world affairs. Did people around the globe really care about all things American, including its idiosyncratic national pastime and a shot supposedly heard around the world? Still, the event was so famous that, as one joke went in 1957, after the Soviets launched Sputnik, the first satellite to orbit the earth, they would follow by sending more dogs, then cats, and even cows in the "herd shot 'round the world."

Such notions of centrality surrounding a moment of baseball folklore were also accurate partly because of the Korean conflict and the larger Cold War. In reality, the shot heard around the world was literally listened to by thousands of American military personnel stationed in Europe and Asia, because it was carried in those distant locations by Armed Forces Radio. Again, the Korean War occupied headlines as well. The entire 1951 baseball season was played as the war had turned sour for the Americans. On opening day of the season, the hero of the Pacific War and the daring rollback of communist forces in Korea the year before, Commanding General Douglas MacArthur arrived in the United States after having been dramatically relieved of his duties by President Truman. It was a bold and justified but, at the time, unpopular act by the president, who threw out the first ball in Washington, DC, on April 20 to a chorus of boos. Meanwhile, New York City held a massive ticker tape parade for MacArthur, and the Giants delayed the start of their game to accommodate parade goers. The team also recruited a US Marine who had been wounded three times in the Korean War to throw out the first ball. Then MacArthur himself appeared the next day at the Giants' Polo Grounds stadium. He noted that, having been in Asia for two decades, he had dearly missed baseball. His presence at the ballpark, followed by appearances at Yankee Stadium and Ebbets Field, home of the Dodgers, throughout the season prompted frenzied outbursts of applause from fans. For example, in Brooklyn he debuted after a well-orchestrated ceremony featured his World War II heroics; MacArthur materialized in full-dress uniform out of a limousine driven through a gate in right field to speak to the crowd about how he cherished Ebbets Field.

The Cold War resonated throughout the 1951 season. For instance, Thomson's homer occurred on the same day as Truman's acknowledgment that the Soviets had detonated a second atom bomb, an event that emphasized that the United States was clearly no longer the sole owner of nuclear weaponry. That led newspapers to editorialize that the Giants had exploded their own bomb, too, by beating the Dodgers! Some wondered, though, why a mere baseball game competed for coverage with a real-world, and dangerous, event like the atomic bomb. (Students might be asked to put the sport in a proper perspective.) There were also more minor baseball-related asides. Sportswriters called the Giants' second baseman, Eddie Stanky, who in 1949 set a National League record for walks, the "Gromyko" of the sport, in reference to the Russian diplomat who had walked out of the United Nations over a dispute and thus allowed the Security Council to approve the American-led UN military mission to Korea. When the Dodgers' manager, Charlie Dressen, chastised a pitcher for lacking guts, the *New York Times* criticized the statement because the "public doesn't associate courage with a game children play when they turn newspaper pages and see the latest casualty lists from Korea." Some Dodgers watched the first playoff game on television while giving blood for American soldiers, and a few days later a group of antiwar protesters at the City College of New York voted to adjourn their meeting to listen to the third game on the radio. A research exercise for students might entail combing through newspapers to identify ways in which the Cold War was embedded in this event, or vice versa.[13] Students might also debate the issue of whether attention to sports distracts the public from more "important" social and political issues.

The Thomson home run might also provide an opportunity to examine technology, which was so instrumental to the Cold War (think weapons, Sputnik, the space race). In this case, television was important, but there was also the evolving technology (or lack thereof) of baseball, too. That is, the sport has long been the preserve of "gut instinct" thinking among managers and owners, but it has also been about statistics compilation. The two managers of the playoff teams, Leo Durocher of the Giants and Charlie Dressen of the Dodgers, personified the unwritten rules of strategies shaped by intuition. Yet in the Dodger front office worked a young Canadian named Allan Roth, who approached then-Dodger president Branch Rickey to discuss his childhood hobby of tracking each game pitch by pitch and keeping a record of each player's strengths and weaknesses. Rickey approved of this scientific approach, and he encouraged Roth to build a detailed record of the season by tallying hits, runs, the record of hitters against various pitchers, pitch counts, and other details. This presaged the use of computers in the 1970s, themselves products of Cold War technology. Unfortunately, Charlie Dressen managed by his gut that day; even though Roth revealed that Branca had surrendered most of his home runs to the Giants that year, including two to Thomson, Dressen called in his pitcher to face the Dodgers slugger. Roth reportedly slowly shook his head with worry, and the next few minutes bore out his statistical analysis. In our modern era of globalization fueled by technology—of laptops and hand-held devices so dear to students—it would be appealing to trace the contours of how this technological moment in baseball history related to other inventions and developments in Cold War America.

In the classroom, the Shot Heard 'Round the World, like the Robinson-Robeson debate, can be set squarely in the Cold War context. The national-security state lends itself to local research (a focus on how the Cold War played out in municipalities and counties has not grabbed the attention of scholars as much as how it affected events and policies at the regional, national, and international levels), and baseball teams and events allow students to examine easily accessible documents and data—newspapers, city and team archives, oral histories—to write histories of the interconnections between the sport and the larger national context. The Thomson shot itself can be found on the Internet; students could be asked to view it, listen to the Russ Hodges radio coverage, then build Cold War history around it. The issue of patriotism is also a possible avenue for discussion and research, as students could relate the Korean War to their own experiences in the post-9/11 era (such as the respect for the flag and military on display at games or the singing of "God Bless America" or "America the Beautiful" before or during the contests), and discover how their lives are affected by the larger national security and cultural histories of the Cold War.

NOTES

1. Jonathan Fraser Light, *The Cultural Encyclopedia of Baseball* (Jefferson, NC: McFarland, 1997), 160.

2. For sports surveys, start with Richard O. Davies, *Sports in American Life: A History*, 2nd ed. (Malden, MA: Wiley-Blackwell, 2012); Steven A. Riess, ed., *Major Problems in American Sport History* (Boston: Houghton Mifflin, 1997).

3. For the Cold War and sports, see Stephen Wagg and David L. Andrews, eds., *East Plays West: Sport and the Cold War* (London: Routledge, 2000), and Heather L. Dichter and Andrew L. Johns, eds., *Diplomatic Games: Essays on the International History of Sport and Foreign Relations since 1945* (Lexington: University of Kentucky Press, 2014). A quick overview of many topics can be found in Alan Bairner, John Kelly, and Jung Woo Lee, eds., *Routledge Handbook of Sport and Politics* (London: Routledge, forthcoming).

4. For an excellent survey of these issues, see Robert Elias, *The Empire*

Strikes Out: How Baseball Sold US Foreign Policy and Promoted the American Way Abroad (New York: New Press, 2010). See also Ron Briley, "Amity Is the Key to Success: Baseball and the Cold War," *Baseball History* 1 (Fall 1986): 4–19.

5. See Nicholas Dawidoff, *The Catcher Was a Spy: The Mysterious Life of Moe Berg* (New York: Vintage Books, 1995).

6. Damion L. Thomas, *Globetrotting: African American Athletes and Cold War Politics* (Urbana: University of Illinois Press, 2010); Charles K. Ross, ed., *Race and Sport: The Struggle for Equality On and Off the Field* (Jackson: University of Mississippi Press, 2004); Robbie Lieberman and Clarence Lang, eds., *Anticommunism and the African American Freedom Movement: "Another Side of the Story"* (New York: Palgrave Macmillan, 2009).

7. For the Robinson-Robeson episode (and the related civil rights–Cold War interaction through the eyes and actions of Jackie Robinson), see Thomas W. Zeiler, *Jackie Robinson and Race in America: A History with Documents* (Boston: Bedford/St. Martin's, 2014). For a full analysis, see Ronald A. Smith, "The Paul Robeson-Jackie Robinson Saga and a Political Collision," *Journal of Sport History* 6, no. 2 (Summer 1979): 5–27.

8. See Martin Duberman, *Paul Robeson: A Biography* (New York: New Press, 2005), for background on Robeson and his beliefs and especially 336–62 for the Paris speech and reaction to it.

9. For the full text, see Zeiler, *Jackie Robinson*, 111–15, or Jackie Robinson's Statement to House Unit, *New York Times*, July 19, 1949, 1, 14.

10. For the varied reactions of African Americans, see Smith, "The Paul Robeson-Jackie Robinson Saga," 18–21, and in primary sources, see, for example, coverage in the black *Pittsburgh Courier* and *Philadelphia Afro-American* in mid-July, after Robinson's testimony.

11. For the FBI files on Robinson (which include mentions of Robeson and the communist and socialist press), see https://vault.fbi.gov/Jack%20 Roosevelt%20(Jackie)%20Robinson. For primary sources on the civil rights–Cold War linkage, see Michael G. Long, *First Class Citizenship: The Civil Rights Letters of Jackie Robinson* (New York: Times Books, 2007); National Archives, *Teaching with Documents*, "Beyond the Playing Field—Jackie Robinson, Civil Rights Advocate," http://www.archives.gov/education/lessons/jackie-robinson/. It is also instructive to view the film biography of Jackie Robinson in which Robinson himself starred (*The Jackie Robinson Story*, Legend Films, DVD, 2006), particularly the patriotic closing scene that alludes to his HUAC testimony and views about freedom and democracy.

12. The discussion of the "shot heard 'round the world" episode and its ramifications is drawn from Jules Tygiel, *Past Time: Baseball as History* (New York: Oxford University Press, 2000), 144–64, and Elias, *The Empire Strikes Out*, 182–88.

13. See Tygiel, *Past Time*, 155–58.

KEY RESOURCES

The Library of Congress has numerous relevant sources in a variety of different collections containing Robinson correspondence, memorabilia, and miscellaneous materials. http://memory.loc.gov/ammem/collections/robinson/jraboutcol.html.

Russ Hodges's famous call of Bobby Thomson's "shot heard 'round the world": http://m.mlb.com/video/v4429233/bknnyg-bobby-thomsons-shot-heard-round-the-world.

The digitized National Archives, in its Teaching with Documents section, has an excellent collection, "Beyond the Playing Field—Jackie Robinson, Civil Rights Advocate," that focuses on Robinson's political activism. See http://www.archives.gov/education/lessons/jackie-robinson/.

The University of Massachusetts, The Jackie Robinson Educational Archives, provides a wealth of educational resources. http://www.umass.edu/pubaffs/jackie/.

See also Ken Burns, Sarah Burns, and David McMahon, *Jackie Robinson* (Florentine Films, 2016), which includes footage of Robinson's testimony to Congress.

Briley, Ron. "Baseball and the Cold War: An Examination of Values." *OAH Magazine of History* 2, no. 1 (Summer 1986): 24.

Elias, Robert. *The Empire Strikes Out: How Baseball Sold US Foreign Policy and Promoted the American Way Abroad.* New York: New Press, 2010.

Robinson, Ray. *The Home Run Heard 'Round the World: The Dramatic Story of the 1951 Giants-Dodgers Pennant Race.* Mineola, NY: Dover, 2011.

Smith, Ronald A. "The Paul Robeson-Jackie Robinson Saga and a Political Collision." *Journal of Sport History* 6, no. 2 (Summer 1979): 5–27. http://library.la84.org/SportsLibrary/JSH/JSH1979/JSH0602/jsh0602b.pdf.

Tygiel, Jules. *Past Time: Baseball as History.* New York: Oxford University Press, 2000.

Wisendale, Steven. "The Political Wars of Jackie Robinson." *Nine* 2, no. 1 (1993): 18–28.

Zeiler, Thomas W. *Jackie Robinson and Race in America: A Brief History with Documents.* Boston: Bedford/St. Martin's, 2014.

PART FOUR

The Global Cold War

Viewing Poland's Cold War through Literature and Film

PHILIP PAJAKOWSKI

I am for the first time since coming to Moscow gravely concerned by the attitude of the Soviet government."[1] Writing in the context of the Warsaw Uprising of 1944, US ambassador W. Averell Harriman identified the centrality of the Polish question to the deterioration of relations between the United States and the Soviet Union in the final months of World War II. The refusal of the Soviet authorities to allow the Americans to aid Polish insurgents fighting the Germans suggested to Harriman that Stalin preferred to see anticommunist Poles defeated by the Germans and thereby neutralized as future opponents of communist rule. Poland remained at the center of Cold War tensions for the coming years, and, although early assigned to the status of Soviet satellite, the country became a chronic source of discontent for the communist bloc leadership. Polish resistance to communist rule took the form of intellectual criticism, violent protest, and labor organization, culminating in the Solidarity movement of the 1980s. Poland thus stood at the center of the conflicts arising from the Soviet takeover of Eastern Europe in the late 1940s and played an outsized role in the eventual collapse of the Soviet bloc. As such, Poland is an important topic for courses covering the origins of the Cold War and the effects of the Cold War on Eastern bloc countries.

As important as Poland was to the development of the Cold War in Europe, the Cold War also clearly held enormous importance for the history of Poland. The establishment of communist rule and the corresponding severance of ties to the West entailed radical shifts in government, the economy, intellectual life, religion, and culture. These traumatic developments were reflected in artistic expression, both as a reflection on the country's status and as an object of Communist cultural policy. In the early years of communist rule, Polish artists found themselves caught between the moral imperatives of explicating the tensions arising from the new regime and the insistence of the new authorities on conformity to communist values. Study of artistic expression can thus reveal the severe stresses placed on Polish society, and an excellent source for such study is Jerzy Andrzejewski's postwar novel *Ashes and Diamonds* and the classic film of the same title directed by Andrzej Wajda and released in 1958. The novel and film insightfully portray the political and existential crisis of postwar Poland and also reveal the vicissitudes of communist cultural policy in the 1940s and 1950s.

Poland and the Origins of the Cold War

Poland's relationship with the Soviet Union before and during World War II can provide students with a window into the origins of the Cold War in Europe. The Polish case is particularly illuminating because it illustrates the regional tensions that predated the Cold War. Poland's experiences during World War II, moreover, can be used to help students to understand Stalin's growing ambitions in Europe and the tensions that eventually eroded the Big Three alliance.

Even students familiar with Poland's role in the early Cold War may not be aware of the earlier history of Polish-Soviet tensions. When the Polish state reemerged at the end of World War I after over a century of partition, the two countries could not find a diplomatic resolution to disputes over their border and went to war in 1920. The Treaty of Riga, which ended that conflict, awarded territories to Poland that the Soviet Union had claimed and placed substantial White Russian, Ukrainian, and Lithuanian minorities under Polish rule. Despite a nonaggression pact signed in 1932, the two countries remained mutually distrustful, full cooperation made difficult by the cultural and political differences that separated the predominantly Catholic and Western-oriented Poles from their communist eastern neighbors. The relationship collapsed with the signing of the Molotov-Ribbentrop Pact in 1939, which established political and economic cooperation between the Soviet Union and Nazi Germany and assigned the eastern third of Poland to the Soviets in the forthcoming partition of the country at the outbreak of World War II.

World War II marked a desperate period in Poland's history. Under a harsh German occupation and divided between hostile German and Soviet spheres, the Poles' situation appeared next to hopeless for the first years of the war. Following the military defeat of September 1939, a Polish government-in-exile, composed of politicians from various camps of the prewar state, claimed sovereignty over the country. Eventually based in London and recognized as the legitimate Polish government by the British, American, and, after the German attack in 1941, Soviet states, the government-in-exile sought to maintain Poland's interests in negotiations with the Allied powers. Though fractious and given to recriminations over who was to blame for the defeat of September 1939, the London Poles agreed on several concerns for the postwar future. They were determined to maintain the border with the Soviet Union established under the Treaty of Riga, and they sought to reestablish a sovereign state with no interference from their Soviet neighbor, a wish succinctly summarized in the Poles' insistence on free elections after the war.[2]

Despite conflicting interests, the Polish and Soviet governments maintained an uneasy alliance until May 1943. The prime minister of the London Polish government, Władysław Sikorski, sought cooperation with the Soviets on a number of issues, including the establishment of Polish military formations recruited from soldiers interned in the Soviet Union. This collaboration collapsed, though, when the Germans announced they had discovered the bodies of thousands of Polish officers who had been held in Soviet camps since the annexation of eastern Poland in 1939. Though long disputed by the Soviets, who admitted guilt only in 1990, the Katyń massacre poisoned relations between Poland and the Soviet Union and led to the severance of diplomatic relations between the London Poles and the Soviets.

Freed from commitments to the representatives of prewar Polish political leadership, Stalin could now seek to establish a new basis for Poland's government as he saw fit. The nucleus for the postwar Polish government comprised leftist Poles residing in the Soviet Union and communist activists working in occupied Poland. The resuscitated Polish communist movement, clearly associated with the Soviets and in command of resistance forces far inferior to those of the nationalists, appeared an alien and nearly traitorous group to many Poles. Nonetheless, as the Soviet military swept into Poland in 1944, the communists formed the basis for a new government in Lublin, the first large town to be liberated from German occupation within the projected boundaries of a new Polish state.[3]

Faced with the prospect of a Polish communist government installed with the support of the advancing Soviet military, the London Polish government took desperate measures. The London Poles held command over the underground Home Army (AK), the largest resistance force in occupied Europe. Under the code name Operation Tempest, soldiers of the Home Army rose up and attacked German units directly behind the advancing front. Rather than greet their Polish allies, however, Red Army troops disarmed and in some cases captured or even killed them.[4] As the final effort of Operation Tempest, the Polish commanders thus opted for a dramatic gamble, ordering the concentration of AK forces in Warsaw to take control of the city before the Soviet army arrived.

The Warsaw Uprising, the most concerted and violent act of resistance in occupied Europe of World War II, set approximately thirty thousand Polish insurgents against the German forces controlling the city. The uprising began on August 1, 1944, and continued for two months. Although the Home Army seized control over most of Warsaw, the anticipated Soviet advance stalled, and no relief came from the Red Army. Whereas the Soviet command cited technical, military causes for the delay, the Poles suspected a deliberate strategy of allowing the Germans to destroy the AK. Students may have a vague understanding of the Warsaw Uprising, but they may not quite grasp its significance in the early Cold War. The military delay as well as Stalin's rejection of an American request to land supply planes on Soviet soil after relief missions over Warsaw led to Ambassador Harriman's skeptical evaluation of Soviet intentions. Students should be reminded of Harriman's words, who assigned the most cynical motives to Stalin's actions:

> I can only draw the conclusion that this action [was taken out of] ruthless political considerations in order that the underground may get no credit for the liberation of Warsaw and that its leaders be killed by the Germans or give an excuse for their arrest when the Red Army enters Warsaw. Under these circumstances it is difficult for me to see how a peaceful or acceptable solution can be found to the Polish problem.[5]

Thus, undersupplied and isolated, the Home Army maintained a heroic but futile effort to defend the city. Reinforced German units retook

Warsaw by the end of September and in the process engaged in brutal reprisals, including the execution of thousands of civilians. After the surrender of Home Army forces, the Germans expelled the remaining civilian population and destroyed much of the city. Although eventually commemorated as valiant resistance to Nazi oppression, the uprising exhausted the military resources of the London Poles and marked the end of hopes for the retention of full sovereignty and territorial integrity after the war.[6]

As the influence of the London Polish government declined, Stalin sought to shape the postwar state to suit Soviet interests and also to win British and American acceptance of these goals.[7] The major outline of an agreement on Poland was reached in February 1945 at Yalta. By this time, the Soviets had occupied most of Poland and had begun to establish the basis for the postwar political orientation of the country, giving Stalin a clear advantage at the conference. The great powers agreed that the communists of the Lublin organization would form the basis for the new Polish government, although noncommunists from within the country and in emigration would also participate. The borders of the country would shift to the west; the Soviet Union would reclaim the lands annexed in 1939 and Poland would be compensated by the annexation of not yet clearly specified German territory. Finally, the Yalta agreement called for free elections in Poland as soon as possible but stipulated that any government that emerged must be friendly to the Soviet Union.[8]

A bitter disappointment to the London Poles, the Yalta agreement remained a highly controversial document and the subject of serious criticism throughout the Cold War. Students of the subject may consider the apparent contrast between Harriman's pessimistic remarks cited earlier and the somewhat more hopeful evaluation of the state of Polish-Soviet relations made by Charles Bohlen, Franklin Roosevelt's interpreter at Yalta. Harriman's suggestion that the Soviets simply could not be trusted to deal with the Poles honorably may be contrasted with Bohlen's reminiscences of Yalta, in which he held out the possibility of genuine cooperation and maintained that the compromises made regarding Poland probably represented the greatest concession the Western allies could gain at this time in regard to accommodation of noncommunist interests in postwar Poland.[9] Further, the disputes regarding Poland's status raise questions regarding the interplay between regional conflicts and relations between the great powers as well as the specific tensions that led to the Cold War. As we have seen, disputes between Poles and Soviets predated the Yalta Conference or even World War II, but Poland's relationship to the Soviet Union contributed to the breakdown in the wartime alliance. Moreover, events in Poland also reflected the growing estrangement between the Western allies and the emerging Soviet bloc.

The developments in Poland during World War II can serve as the basis for in-class discussions or assignments analyzing American military and diplomatic policies during the war. Students may feel an instinctive sympathy toward Poland (much as many Americans did at the time), especially in light of the brutality that Poles experienced during the Warsaw Uprising and at Katyń. At the same time, some students may take the pragmatic position that the United States simply could not have done more for Poland without undermining the ultimate goal of working with the Soviet Union to defeat Germany with a minimum of loss of American life. Debating these issues in class will give students insight into the dilemma that Roosevelt and his advisers wrestled with throughout the war.

Students may also evaluate the Yalta agreements and the impact of great-power decisions on the affairs of a smaller country by examining the profound social and economic changes that Poland underwent in the immediate postwar years. In conjunction with the shift in borders, affirmed at Potsdam but later contested by the Western powers, an enormous transfer of populations shifted millions of people from east to west. The German inhabitants of Poland's new western territories were forcibly removed from their homes, and their property was confiscated for redistribution. Poles from the lost eastern lands replaced the Germans and received property under the auspices of the Ministry of Recovered Territories, headed by the communist leader Władysław Gomułka. The new western boundaries, not recognized by the United States and its allies, were guaranteed by the Soviet Union and so served to bind Poland to that country.[10] Alongside the distribution of formerly landed property, the new government instituted a massive land reform under which large estates, primarily in the hands of the aristocracy, were divided among peasant farmers without compensation to the former owners. Additionally, the confiscation and nationalization of large-scale manufacturing firms marked the foundation of a communist economy.

Students should also be aware of the repression of political opponents of the communist authorities. Despite the official dissolution of the Home Army and other resistance organizations in the closing months of the war, armed struggle against the new regime continued in the immediate postwar years. Nationalist fighters remained active in forested regions and engaged in assassination of communist officials. This armed conflict continued until 1947, when a concerted effort of government security forces backed by the Soviet military violently suppressed resistance forces loyal to the old Polish leadership.[11] By 1947, the Polish United Workers Party (PZPR) had effectively eliminated rival political groups. In a definitive break of connections with the West, the Polish government, under strong Soviet pressure, rejected American economic aid through the Marshall Plan. Polish communists, acting in concert with Soviet directives, were now free to reshape Polish society in a way that conformed to the Soviet experience and that contributed to the emerging Cold War division of Europe.

Andrzejewski's *Ashes and Diamonds*

Students are almost certainly aware that the goals of Poland's Stalinists, like those throughout the Soviet bloc, included political control and economic transformation. They may not realize that Polish Stalinists also demanded a new consciousness among the entire population and that such a consciousness had to be deliberately constructed. Artistic expression could contribute to the reshaping of cultural values, and therefore artists were to assume an important and carefully disciplined role in Stalinist society. A rechanneling of cultural content constituted an important aspect of the transformation that Soviet domination brought to Polish society and also provides a window into the beliefs of intellectuals and the communist authorities.

The complex and, for American students, surely obscure development of Poland's relationship to the Cold War may be examined through a variety of approaches. On the levels of ideology and high politics, historiographical controversy surrounds Stalin's decisions before the outbreak of World War II as well as his projections for postwar East Central Europe. The actions of the London Polish government, in particular the undertaking of the Warsaw Uprising, also lend themselves to discussion and debate, as do the position of Poland in relation to the United States and the Soviet Union. To make these issues less remote, examination of artistic interpretations of the period can be highly rewarding. The depiction of these events in fiction presents a personal dimension that reveals the experience of people who lived through the violence and uncertainty that marked Poland in the 1940s and after.

Jerzy Andrzejewski's novel *Ashes and Diamonds* and its subsequent film adaptation are particularly useful resources for exploring the early Cold War in Poland. The novel, first published in 1948, has been translated into English and is widely available for use in high school or college courses. The film adaptation from 1958 has been remastered and released on DVD as part of the Criterion Collection. Instructors interested in the Cold War in Eastern Europe or those who want to use a case study to explore the effect of the Cold War on a particular nation could assign the novel and screen the movie as well. The novel and the movie have subtle differences that can lead to fruitful discussions or paper assignments. Courses on cinema during the Cold War may want to use the movie as a counterpoint to the American films that often dominate these courses. But the book and the film can be incorporated into just about any course on the Cold War because they show the personal decisions that Poles faced in the early years of the Cold War.

Born in Warsaw in 1909, Jerzy Andrzejewski was among the most prominent young Polish authors of the 1930s. He wrote for conservative Catholic periodicals, and his work retained a moralist concern for ethical questions that also underlie *Ashes and Diamonds*. During the war, he participated in the nationalist resistance as the editor of an underground periodical. Despite his previous connections to Catholic nationalist circles, he joined in the reconstruction of his country under communist leadership and held governing positions in writers' associations as well as a seat in parliament.[12] Andrzejewski's association with both Catholic nationalist politics and the new communist authorities inform the ambiguities in and sources of debate surrounding his postwar novel.

Written in 1947 and published early in 1948, *Ashes and Diamonds* reflects the political and cultural values of the rising communist authorities yet also the lingering pluralism of the immediate postwar years before the onset of the full Stalinist monopoly of power. The story is set in the fictional town of Ostrowiec in the final days of World War II. The plot centers on an interrelated series of characters in this microcosm of Polish society. Among the main figures are the Kossecki family: Antoni, the father and a successful lawyer before the war, has recently returned from Gross-Rosen concentration camp, where, we learn in the course of the story, he survived by collaborating with the Germans as a sadistic trustee prisoner. The mother, Alicja, has spent the war in Ostrowiec and now struggles to maintain the alienated family by working as a seamstress. The older son, Andrzej, is a secretive, disillusioned lieutenant in the AK, and the younger son, Alek, is a high school student and member of a murderous, pseudo-patriotic gang of adolescent boys. Alongside the Kossecki family are two major characters, Szczuka, the newly appointed chief of the local Communist Party organization, and Maciek Chelmicki, Andrzej Kossecki's friend and subordinate in the AK, who has been assigned the task of assassinating Szczuka. The war has deeply scarred all these characters. Szczuka limps from wounds he suffered while detained in the same concentration camp as Antoni Kossecki. Beyond his political duties, Szczuka seeks news of his wife, a native of Ostrowiec, who has died in Ravensbrück concentration camp. Chelmicki and Andrzej Kossecki are veteran survivors of the Warsaw Uprising and lament their lost comrades and lost sense of purpose as the war draws to a close and the fighting over the fate of Poland continues. Alek and his friends represent a generation of young people who have learned little but violence and semifascist rhetoric in growing up. To complete the panorama of postwar Polish society, the novel includes lesser characters, including scheming aristocrats, opportunists who weigh the career perspectives opened by the new regime, poor laborers, an underground AK military commander, and Krystyna, a bartender of aristocratic heritage and the love interest of Maciek Chelmicki.[13]

As the plot develops, the novel presents readers with a number of moral and ethical questions generated by the introduction of communist rule over the Polish population. Much of the story takes place in the Hotel Monopole, where members of all political and social classes gather to celebrate the Germans' defeat, either at an official banquet organized by the communists or in general revelry in the hotel bar. Beyond its clearly symbolic name, the hotel setting allows representatives of all levels of Polish society to meet and interact. Amid the celebrations, however, unquiet thoughts are expressed regarding the nature of the new authority and its close association with Russia. In one notable conversation, Szczuka encounters an old friend, Kalicki, a member of the leftist but nationalist Polish Socialist Party. Despite their affection and mutual respect, the two find no common ground as Kalicki rejects Szczuka's defense of the connection of Poland to the Soviet Union. For Kalicki, "Russian imperialism and Russian aggression are the same . . . please spare me your propaganda. I know where I stand. The East will always be the East. Anyhow, you'll see in a year or two. Poland won't exist any longer. Our country, our culture will be lost, all of it."[14]

The binding duty to oppose the new regime emerges in a discussion between Andrzej Kossecki and his superior in the underground. The colonel, an obvious representative of the traditional Polish military caste, presents a bald appraisal of the current political landscape:

> In today's set-up, we Poles are divided into two categories: those who have betrayed the freedom of Poland and those who do not wish to do so. The first want to submit to Russia, we do not. They want communism, we do not. They want to destroy us, we must destroy them. . . . And what were you fighting for? Wasn't it for the freedom of Poland. But did you imagine a Poland ruled by blind agents carrying out orders from the Kremlin and established by Russian bayonets? What about your colleagues, your contemporaries? How many of them died? What for?[15]

The colonel justifies the murder of the idealistic, conscientious Szczuka as a necessary act that individual conscience requires and history will judge.

A sense of defeat in victory permeates the novel and presents the characters with the choice between participating in building a new society based on principles they dislike and struggling against hopeless odds to restore the old Poland. The character who reflects this dilemma most clearly is the would-be assassin, Maciek Chelmicki. In the course of stalking Szczuka in the streets of Ostrowiec and the halls of the Monopole, Maciek meets Krystyna, a bartender at the hotel. Like Maciek, Krystyna has lost her family in the war and displays a rather disillusioned, cynical outlook, but, as their chance encounter turns to love, both see the other as the chance to begin a new life. As Maciek considers moving to Warsaw with Krystyna and resuming his studies at the polytechnic, the prospect of killing Szczuka appears ever more sinister and disruptive to life. These doubts lead to a tense meeting with Andrzej, at which Maciek attempts to convince his superior to relieve him of the assignment. "Try to understand . . . I just don't want to go on killing, destroying, shooting and hiding. I want a simple, ordinary life, that's all."[16] When Andrzej reminds Maciek of his duty as a soldier and his wartime service, he remains reluctant. "What is it I'm supposed to sacrifice everything for? I knew, in those days. But now? You tell me! What do I have to kill that man for?"[17] Maciek nonetheless agrees to carry out this assignment as his last service to the AK, with fatal consequences for both himself and Szczuka. As the two friends part, Maciek asks Andrzej if he believes he is in the right, to which Andrzej responds, "No. But that isn't what matters."[18] The novel thus suggests the intersecting ideological commitment, personal loyalty, and moral judgment that the characters confront.

Less ambiguous but still open for discussion are issues that arise concerning Antoni Kossecki. This clear representative of the old order, a respected, if rather dour, attorney, has compromised himself by his bestial behavior during the occupation. Since his return from Gross-Rosen concentration camp, he has secluded himself in his study and avoided contact with his family, clearly in terror that his activities in the camp will be revealed. He finally, though, resolves to confront the authorities with an exculpatory explanation of his wartime crimes. Claiming that war represents a separate mode of existence from peace, he argues that his brutality in the camp is irrelevant to his normal life of law-abiding public service. In effect, he argues that he never would have harmed his fellow citizens if not for the extraordinary circumstances of life in a concentration camp. He thus offers himself as a potentially valuable contributor to the new order and is stunned when his communist interlocutor, a former junior associate in the law, is unreceptive to his arguments. Although Kossecki's ultimate fate is uncertain, his case presents arguments regarding the ultimate disposition of collaborators who betrayed their compatriots out of fear.

Amid the general ambivalence and sense of loss and disillusion in postwar Poland that Andrzejewski portrays, students may wonder whether any hope or faith in ultimate triumph can be found here. In this context readers may well consider the significance of the novel's epigraph, a quotation from the romantic poet Cyprian Norwid:

> From you, as from burning chips of resin,
> Fiery fragments circle far and near:
> Ablaze, you don't know if you are to be free,
> Or if all that is yours will disappear.
>
> Will only ashes and confusion remain,
> Leading into the abyss?—or will there be
> In the depth of the ash a star-like diamond,
> The dawning of eternal victory!

Did Andrzejewski regard the emerging dominance of the communists as a victory for the people of Poland? In his analysis of the book, Carl Tighe regards the reference to the poem as clear evidence that Andrzejewski considered the communist future as the diamond concealed in the country's current historical crisis. Tighe nonetheless also finds fundamental ambivalence in the unflattering portrayal of many of the communist characters as well the author's clear absorption in historic Polish cultural forms. Ambivalence, reflective of Andrzejewski's personal experience, is also the preeminent theme that Paul Coates identifies in a novel focused on a nation in transition and the potential for individuals to change their characters and circumstances. In his essay on the appeal of communist ideology to Polish intellectuals, on the other hand, Czesław Miłosz criticized the novel as unambiguously portraying the new authorities as the only hope for a progressive reconstruction of the country, to which only deluded madmen could offer violent resistance.[19]

Wajda's *Ashes and Diamonds*

After the immediate postwar years, in which artists had enjoyed a measure of freedom, the cultural policy of socialist realism was imposed in 1949. The new policy, the cultural expression of high Stalinism, entailed the severance of cultural ties to the West, thus restricting the translation of Western literary works or the import of West European or American films. More drastically, the authorities, who enjoyed a monopoly over outlets for artistic production, established strict standards for expression. Artistic works had to promote communist values through the portrayal of themes that glorified communist goals and the work of the party in promoting them. Socialist realism eschewed the examination of psychological intricacies or ambivalence in fictional characters. Instead, images and narratives depicted the straightforward achievement of goals in production and socialist construction by unambiguously dedicated heroes.[20] Under these policies, Andrzejewski's somewhat nuanced portrayal of the postwar political struggle could not have been published.

After Stalin's death, in 1953, and Khrushchev's address to the Twentieth Congress of the Communist Party of the Soviet Union in 1956, Polish communists and the general public called for a move away from Stalinist policies. After public demonstrations and the humiliating and painful necessity of ordering security forces to fire on working-class protesters in Poznan, the party leadership turned to Gomułka, who had lost office and Communist Party status for resisting some of Stalin's policies, as a potential reformer who could find a solution to the crisis facing communist authority. Despite Soviet opposition and the threat of military action, the Polish leadership prevailed on Khrushchev to accept Gomułka's promotion to party general secretary in October. Gomułka undertook a limited course of reform measures that, although they did not satisfy public demands, nonetheless achieved a peaceful resolution of the crisis. Among his concessions were the abandonment of forced collectivized farming, an accommodation with the hierarchy of the Catholic Church, and the revocation of socialist realism to make space for greater freedom of cultural expression and exploration of controversial historical and political topics. The Polish October thus established a compromise between state and society that marked the beginning of the dynamic among communist power, public protest, and mutual adaptation that marked Polish society into the 1980s.

Ten years after the publication of Andrzejewski's novel, Andrzej Wajda's film by the same title appeared in Poland's cinemas. The film, whose screenplay was prepared in part by Andrzejewski, may be seen as an interpellation both of the period depicted and of the attitudes purveyed by the novel. *Ashes and Diamonds* was the third film in which Poland's preeminent director addressed the wartime experience, one of the most prominent themes of his career. Wajda's three war films of the 1950s present a progression of artistic and official attitudes toward the recent past. In the first, *A Generation*, from 1955, Wajda portrayed the education of working-class Poles and their movement into communist resistance politics in a clearly socialist realist manner. The second, *Kanal*, from 1957, sympathetically addressed the hitherto taboo theme of the Warsaw Uprising and the heroics of the AK.[21] In *Ashes and Diamonds* Wajda reworked Andrzejewski's novel to explore the personal and political dynamics of the immediate postwar experience.

In presenting his story, Wajda altered the narrative and characterization in important ways. The Kossecki family, with the exception of Andrzej, disappears, so that the theme of the corruption of prewar values, especially seen in Antoni, is diluted. Central to the film are the characters of Szczuka and Maciek, played by the charismatic Zbygniew Cybulski. Maciek's character in fact dominates the film as Wajda introduces scenes of his courtship of Krystyna and a memorable portrayal of

Still from *Ashes and Diamonds*.

his mourning for his lost comrades by lighting vodka shots into vigil lamps. Szczuka, though, represented in rigid poses and through stilted dialogue, has been modified in ways that raise questions regarding Wajda's portrayal of the era's politics. Instead of having spent the war years in a concentration camp, Szczuka has been in the Soviet Union, where he has acquired some noticeably Russian habits. Further, rather than searching for news of his martyred wife, he seeks his son in a subplot not present in the novel. The son, as we discover, is a resistance fighter serving with the nationalists and has been arrested by the communist security forces. Viewers of the film may discuss why the director has altered the main communist character in this way and how this affects our evaluation of the political values of the major figures in the story.

The film, condensed into a portrayal of the day and night of the war's end, enacts central scenes from the novel, including the parties in the Hotel Monopole and Maciek's romance with Krystyna. The mode of portrayal combines images of a country shattered by war with surreal features reflecting religious motifs or themes from national mythology, including a crucifix hanging upside down and a white horse sauntering along a city street. As in the novel, the irony of Poland's victory in war in the midst of fratricidal politics and an uncertain future are evident,

Still from *Ashes and Diamonds*.

especially in the final sequences of the assassination of Szczuka and Maciek's subsequent death at the hands of Polish soldiers.[22] Having resolved to shoot Szczuka after much hesitation, Maciek kills the communist leader at the moment that fireworks explode in the sky in celebration of the Germans' surrender, and Szczuka dies in the assassin's arms. Shortly afterward, Maciek is shot by Polish soldiers in a misunderstanding. He staggers through a field of laundry hanging to dry, bleeds through one of the hanging sheets in a gory parody of the Polish flag, and dies on a garbage heap.

When juxtaposed with the novel, Wajda's film raises themes of artistic responsibility as well as political perspective. Do the novel and film differ in their portrayal of the contending political factions? Is the film more sympathetic to the nationalists than the book? What might explain the differing interpretation of events? How do the film and the novel relate to socialist realism, a policy that was imposed shortly after the publication of the novel and lifted shortly before the film was shot? Does the portrayal of Szczuka in the film reflect weariness with exhortatory communist rhetoric?

Moreover, for American readers, the relatively open discussion of dissent and resistance under the communist government may appear surprising and may invite consideration of the extent of repression and compliance in the Soviet bloc as part of a general discussion of the vicissitudes of communist cultural policy. To what degree did the communists rely on negotiation and accommodation with intellectuals? How did the communists seek to reshape public attitudes while maintaining some sense of continuity with national traditions?

Considered together, the novel and film versions of *Ashes and Diamonds* offer students a window into Polish politics of the early Cold War. The story of Szczuka, Maciek, Krystyna, and the Kosseckis graphically portrays the paradoxes facing the people of a small country placed for a time at the forefront of international political and ideological conflict. For Poles, that conflict assumed the direct, personal character of tension between the desire to maintain full cultural and political sovereignty and the longing for the resumption of normal, peaceful life. Was the requisite accommodation with their powerful neighbor merely a painful necessity, or did communism offer a potential for renewal of the national spirit? Given the failure of the prewar authorities to defend the country against German aggression, the new system and a fixed Soviet alliance held appeal to intellectuals critical of their country's past. *Ashes and Diamonds* presents the dilemma of artists torn between loyalty to their historical identity and the pressures applied by the new regime. Thus, the ambiguities found in Andrzejewski's novel reflect the author's attachment to his cultural traditions and sympathy for the plight of the nationalists but also his convictions about the decay of bourgeois society. Wajda's film adds an extra layer of critique of the postures assumed by Polish Stalinists. Throughout, two Polish artists dramatically construct the world of people caught within the tragedy and violence of East Central Europe of the 1940s.

NOTES

1. W. Averell Harriman and Elie Abel, *Special Envoy to Churchill and Stalin, 1941–1946* (New York: Random House, 1975), 340.

2. Andrzej Paczkowski, *The Spring Will Be Ours: Poland and the Poles from Occupation to Freedom*, trans. Jane Cave (University Park: Pennsylvania State University Press, 2003), 37–110.

3. Norman Davies, *God's Playground: A History of Poland*, Vol. 2 (New York: Columbia University Press, 1983), 542–47.

4. Paczkowski, *Spring*, 118–20.

5. Harriman and Abel, *Special Envoy*, 344; on the Warsaw Uprising in general, 335–49.

6. Paczkowski, *Spring*, 121–22.

7. Sergei Kudryashov, "Diplomatic Prelude: Stalin, the Allies, and Poland," in A. Kemp-Welch, ed., *Stalinism in Poland, 1944–1956: Selected Papers from the Fifth World Congress of Central and East European Studies, Warsaw, 1995* (New York: St. Martin's, 1999), 33.

8. Paczkowski, *Spring*, 139–41; Gale Stokes, ed., *From Stalinism to Pluralism* (New York: Oxford University Press, 1991), 16–17.

9. For excerpts from Bohlen's memoirs, see Stokes, *From Stalinism to Pluralism*, 19–27.

10. Paczkowski, *Spring*, 152–54.

11. Paczkowski, *Spring*, 138–39, 142–43, 233–34.

12. Carl Tighe, "Jerzy Andrzejewski: Life and Times," *Journal of European Studies* 25, no. 1 (1995): 341–42.

13. For plot summaries and analysis of the novel, see Tighe, "Andrzejewski," 343–53; and Paul Coates, "Forms of Polish Intellectual Self-Criticism: Revisiting *Ashes and Diamonds* with Andrzejewski and Wajda," *Canadian Slavonic Papers*, 38, nos. 3-4 (1996): 287–92.

14. Jerzy Andrzejewski, *Ashes and Diamonds*, trans. D. J. Welsh (Evanston, IL: Northwestern University Press, 1991), 149.

15. Ibid., 49–50.

16. Ibid., 212.

17. Ibid., 213.

18. Ibid., 216.

19. Tighe, "Andrzejewski," 349–53; Coates, "Forms," 288–92; Czesław Miłosz, *The Captive Mind*, trans. Jane Zielonko (New York: Vintage Books, 1981), 102–5.

20. Paczkowski, *Spring*, 255–61; Carl Tighe, "The Polish Writing Profession, 1944–56," *Contemporary European History*, 5, no. 1 (1996): 72–85.

21. On *A Generation* and *Kanal*, see Janina Falkowska, *Andrzej Wajda: History, Politics, and Nostalgia in Polish Cinema* (New York: Berghahn, 2007), 36–53.

22. Falkowska, *Wajda*, 53–64; Coats, "Forms," 292–96.

KEY RESOURCES

Andrzejewski, Jerzy. *Ashes and Diamonds*. Translated by D. J. Welsh. Evanston, IL: Northwestern University Press, 1991.

Coates, Paul. "Forms of Polish Intellectual Self-Criticism: Revisiting *Ashes and Diamonds* with Andrzejewski and Wajda." *Canadian Slavonic Papers* 38, nos. 3-4 (1996): 287–303.

Falkowska, Janina. *Andrzej Wajda: History, Politics, and Nostalgia in Polish Cinema*. New York: Berghahn, 2007.

Kemp-Welch, A. *Poland under Communism: A Cold War History*. New York: Cambridge University Press, 2008.

Kersten, Krystyna. *The Establishment of Communist in Poland, 1943–1948*. Translated by John Micgiel and Michael H. Bernard. Berkeley: University of California Press, 1991.

Kudryashov, Sergei. "Diplomatic Prelude: Stalin, the Allies, and Poland." In *Stalinism in Poland, 1944–1956: Selected Papers from the Fifth World Congress of Central and East European Studies, Warsaw, 1995*, edited by A. Kemp-Welch, 25–40. New York: St. Martin's, 1999.

Miłosz, Czesław. *The Captive Mind*, translated by Jane Zielonko. New York: Vintage Books, 1981.

Paczkowski, Andrzej. *The Spring Will Be Ours: Poland and the Poles from Occupation to Freedom*. Translated by Jane Cave. University Park: Pennsylvania State University Press, 2003.

Tighe, Carl. "Jerzy Andrzejewski: Life and Times." *Journal of European Studies* 25, no. 1 (1995): 341–80.

Toranska, Teresa. *Them: Stalin's Polish Puppets*. Translated by Agnieszka Kolakowska. New York: Harper & Row, 1987.

Wajda, Andrzej. *Three War Films (A Generation/Kanal/Ashes and Diamonds)*. The Criterion Collection. Polish with English subtitles. 2005.

The Cold War
in Western Europe

J. SIMON ROFE

From Stettin in the Baltic to Trieste in the Adriatic, an iron curtain has descended across the Continent."[1] When he uttered these words in March 1946, the then former British prime minister Winston Churchill was in the small college town of Fulton, Missouri, in the center of North America. The continent to which he was referring to was thousands of miles away across the Atlantic. Europe, the ancestral home of the majority of American citizens, was divided between East and West by the "Iron Curtain" for the next forty-five years. In fact, the distinction between "Eastern" and "Western" Europe became the dominant terminology to describe the continent, eliding the designation of "Central" Europe (or "mitteleuropa" in German), which both pre- and postdated the Cold War. The division of the continent's most powerful nation into East and West Germany, as the German Democratic Republic (GDR) and the Federal Republic of Germany (FRG) were colloquially known, reflected this new spatial reality in one nation.

This chapter addresses our goal of understanding and teaching the Cold War in Western Europe through two distinct approaches. First, the chapter considers the periodization of the Cold War, particular to Western Europe. Second, it looks to a number of key speeches that explain the relationship between Europe and the Cold War, suggesting ways that these speeches can be used in the classroom to teach the Cold War. One rationale for the use of speeches is that they can prompt "critical reflection" on the part of students; in other words, "it gets them thinking" which, as teachers in university, is our overarching goal.

Speeches also allow students to engage with a primary source through audio and video media. Finally, the speeches themselves can be supplemented with contemporaneous journalistic accounts to help students understand a variety of reactions to these key addresses.

Beginning and Ends: Periodizing the Cold War in Western Europe

In teaching a course on the Cold War, a particularly fruitful way to begin a class is to pose an open-ended question: "When did the Cold War begin and end?" The task provides for a series of clear learning objectives to be met across three facets of teaching in university:

- Benchmarking
- Critical reflection
- Active-learning opportunity

Importantly, this question and the exercise that unfolds can be utilized with first-year students through postgraduates; what alters is the application of greater levels of analysis facilitated by the teacher. Students will typically answer the question initially by saying "1945," the end of the Second World War, or "1989," when the Berlin Wall "fell." These two answers are not *wrong*, of course; however, this characterization overlooks the opportunity to meet the higher-level learning objectives to which higher education aspires. The goal is achieved by considering with our students a range of alternative start and end dates—in other words, listening to our students, and responding accordingly.

Benchmarking

Perhaps the most practical and certainly the most immediate benefit of the task for history teachers is that it allows them to benchmark the class. By "benchmarking" I am referring to the experiential practice of learning from one's students their relative levels of knowledge and their aptitude for the learning at hand.[2] Put colloquially, it is about gauging the level of a class. History teachers, even those without years of experience, do this as a matter of course almost subliminally on walking into a classroom, as they have a memory bank of being in classes with peers of varying levels of ability. Importantly, it also has a self-reflective quality that allows us to contemplate best practices from across the sector as we understand that a range of ability can influence the effectiveness of our teaching. In terms of the practicalities, benchmarking can be achieved in many ways: a pre-course survey, a pop quiz at the outset, some small group work, or, in this case, any of those to achieve answers to the overarching question of when the Cold War began and ended. It is also worth stating that benchmarking is an iterative process and should be revisited over the duration of a course as students (and teachers) progress at different rates at different times. The necessary function of any benchmarking exercise is in the teacher's observing and listening in order to provide tailored learning solutions during the rest of a course that can enhance the students' opportunity to succeed.

Critical Reflection

As well as being a key facet of the history teacher's own tool kit, the opportunity for students to critically reflect on their learning is a crucial part of their individual learning journey.[3] The task here of addressing "When did the Cold War begin and end?" immediately confronts students with the challenge of identifying what constitutes the "Cold War." As scholars, we know this is no simple task in itself, but it allows us as teachers to observe and orient our classes around students' abilities to reflect on their practice, even if they may not be versed in the terminology of critical reflection. A range of factors affects students' answers; there are those without any particular prior knowledge of the Cold War and those "strategic learners" who might simply be looking for a "passing grade." By demonstrating that the start of the Cold War is contested, we can show the value of critical analysis. It also serves to challenge a student's ontological position on what they may consider to be "facts," that is, why they think the way they do. The different factors that emerge will in turn influence the course of the class by posing a series of second-order questions: To what extent was the Cold War an ideological conflict between liberal internationalism and communism? Was it about "East" and "West"? Was it a "war" for the hearts and minds of the world's population, or was it an imperialist contest for territory and resources? To what extent was it a product of the international system or indigenous factors that acquired a global narrative? And to what extent was it "cold"? The people of Egypt, the Congo, Nicaragua, the Korean peninsula, and Vietnam might suggest it was "hot," as conflicts with connections to either Moscow or Washington served to bring the Cold War to their lives. As scholars, we know that it was a combination of factors, and, by posing a question such as what constitutes the Cold War, we can illustrate that students will need to make judgments of their own about their various merits.

It is important to give students a variety of approaches and options to prompt their investigation into the start of the Cold War. If they want to focus on the ideological differences, have them consider what role the 1848 publication of the *Communist Manifesto* or the 1917 revolution in Russia played in determining the beginning of the Cold War. Of course, students would then have to account for the cooperation between the Soviet Union and the West during World War II. Students should also be asked to investigate the role of individuals. Did the Cold War start when any reasonable and practical possibility to avoid it was gone? If so, was that when FDR died, when Truman started to take a tougher stance, when Stalin signaled his intentions to ensure a friendly government in Poland, or some other later decision? A teacher could also have students determine which event from 1945 until 1950 best serves as the Cold War's starting date. Was it the Yalta Conference, the end of World War II with Soviet troops throughout Eastern Europe, the Truman Doctrine, the Soviet Union's explosion of an atomic weapon, or something else? And of course classes can have similar discussions about the end of the Cold War. It is worth noting that discussions about the origins and endpoints of the Cold War almost invariably focus on events in Europe. Students can be asked to reflect on this phenomenon. Do questions about the *chronological* boundaries of the Cold War hinge on our understanding of the *spatial* boundaries? In any event, the process of exploring the chronological and geographic parameters of the Cold War prompts much deeper questions about its nature.

Depending upon the knowledge and abilities of the student body at any given level, a second tranche of critical reflection can follow on from the question of when the Cold War began. These activities might be reserved for a subsequent class at the discretion of the teacher, but knowing that there are follow-on activities assists in determining what to emphasize in the original task. For example, teachers can ask students to explore the value of periodizing in historical studies as a class-based question, a piece of homework, or an online exercise. Why is it important for historians to identify historical "periods," and what are the pitfalls of this exercise? Moreover, how are periods a reflection of the time period itself, and how are they a product of a historian's perspective? Historical "theory" invariably seems abstract to undergraduate students and is notoriously difficult to teach well. Nevertheless, if it is brought into students' learning experience in this fashion it is possible to engage them. "Theory does more than identify the ingredients of historical problems," wrote Professor William A. Green. He continued, "It explains the process which gives those ingredients meaning."[4] It is the intellectual quest for explanation and meaning that the task of contemplating when the Cold War begins and ends involves. By contemplating where the temporal margins of the Cold War lie, we can bring to our students the values and judgments that underpin their assessments. (Contemplating periodization with our students in this fashion also allows us to look forward in time consider the terminology of the "post–Cold War" period so that students appreciate how terms like "post," "orthodox," and "re-visionism" are used by historians.)

The historiography of the Cold War in Europe can also be reflected upon as a further learning opportunity in the questioning of how the Cold War began and ended. An effective way of undertaking this, I have found, is to chart the evolution of particular authors in the field. As an example, one can track the thinking of John Lewis Gaddis since the publication of *The United States and the Origins of the Cold War* in 1972 through to his Pulitzer Prize–winning biography *George F. Kennan: An American Life* in 2012. Whatever a teacher's own view of Gaddis's work, his work is likely to appear on any Cold War syllabus, and by assigning different readings from Gaddis's catalogue one can address studies in historiography with students who might normally turn away from the subject. Furthermore, and related to this point, the temporal dimension to studying the Cold War can be drawn out straightforwardly in Gaddis's "long peace" argument, which is based upon a transparent balance of power tied to nuclear weaponry.[5]

Finally, a second tranche of critical reflection engendered by the task of looking at the beginning and end of the Cold War makes explicit reference to the spatial dimensions of the Cold War and Western Europe. The Cold War can be understood as a phenomenon with Western European dimensions, but it must also be understood in its larger global context. Whether a course focuses on Western Europe or another region, providing the global dimension is a worthwhile exercise. The task serves to put the Cold War in Western Europe in its appropriate global context, be that in relation to Eastern Europe or Africa or Latin America. As Professor Sir Laurie Freedman noted in a review of Odd Arne Westad's *Global Cold War*, "The Cold War began and ended in Europe, but some of its most severe effects were felt in the Third World."[6] Freedman's review illustrates the relationship between Europe and the rest of the world, which is relevant to a student's learning whatever the focus of their course.

Active Learning Opportunity

Active learning entails involving students in their learning experience in a way that goes beyond passive, Pavlovian listening and instead engages them so that they are participants in the learning rather than simply recipients.[7] McCombs and Whistler point out "that learning is most meaningful when topics are relevant to the students' lives, needs, and interests and when the students themselves are actively engaged in creating, understanding, and connecting to knowledge."[8] As Paul Ramsden, chair of the Higher Education Academy in the United Kingdom in 2003, argued, higher education is "about changing the ways in which learners understand, or experience or conceptualize the world around them."[9] Active learning lends itself to the task of addressing the beginning and end of the Cold War in Western Europe in a number of ways. First, by addressing a question in class and eliciting a response from students, we move past a simple lecture format. Some students can be reluctant to speak in class, of course, especially something advertised as a "lecture," and so a further active-learning approach can be employed. An open-ended question such as the one suggested lends itself to discussion among peers, and so utilizing small groups to discuss the relative merits of various dates is a fruitful way to engage students with a variety of learning styles.[10] This opens up the possibility of collaborative and peer-to-peer learning or peer instruction in our classes. Corneli and Danoff go further in proposing "paragogy," where the prefix "para" means "alongside," in which teachers and students are co-creators of the learning experience.[11] This we recognize as teachers, as we know we learn in our classes. Corneli goes on to note that paragogical approaches may be "at odds with established educational systems in some respects," and particularly to the culture of certain institutions and student bodies, where a lecture "should" be a passive, monodirectional learning experience.[12]

In pursuing the higher-level learning outcomes that university teachers are tasked with providing, through the consideration of when the Cold War both began and ended, the opportunity exists for students to develop their abilities associated with working in small groups or teams. Perhaps either by simply speaking up or coming to the front of class and adding remarks to a white/blackboard or online wiki, students can demonstrate both their learning and associated presentation skills. Of course, other visual tools can be used, such as Wordle, described as a "toy for generating 'word clouds'" that emphasize the most recurrent words in any document, particular if the discussion becomes an out-of-class exercise.[13] Broader opportunities to use class time for discussion and exercises rather than the information transfer that characterizes a traditional lecture, known as "flipped classroom" concepts, exist as we address our task of finding the temporal parameters of the Cold War.[14]

In practice or praxis, that is, distinguishing between practice and theory in the abstract, the task of challenging students to think about the beginning and end of the Cold War in Western Europe or elsewhere is an immensely rewarding one. It has the capacity to impart knowledge and aid learning in a number of ways while taking into account the range of students' abilities, knowledge, and learning styles. It is just one task, of course; another is outlined in the next section.

Words and Pictures: Using Speeches to Understand the Cold War in Western Europe

A second approach to learning and teaching the Cold War in Western Europe that we might consider here is the use of a series of speeches. These speeches as historical artifacts have the capability to engage students on at least three levels: in terms of their content as documents; as audio; and as visual and symbolic sources. They have been chosen to represent a temporal dimension to the Cold War in Western Europe, and in exploring the context to each there is the opportunity to engage students in a range of learning experiences. A typical grouping might include these three speeches:

- "Sinews of Peace," Winston Churchill, March 6, 1947
- "Ich bin ein Berliner," President John F. Kennedy, June 26, 1963
- "Tear Down This Wall," President Ronald Reagan, June 12, 1987[15]

Collectively, the three speeches cover the onset of the Cold War, the centerpiece of Europe's physical division in Berlin at its height, and the dénouement to the "Second Cold War" as a precursor to its overall demise. Developing a series of overarching questions allows students to gain insight into the longue durée of the Cold War and to enhance their research skills among a range of primary and secondary sources. These questions can include: What is the significance of Berlin to the conflict? What opportunities do the speeches provide for reconciliation between the protagonists? Who were the audiences for the speech? In each case, students' answers will allow the class to consider Western Europe in the context of the Cold War in spatial and temporal terms.

In terms of the pedagogy involved, studying these speeches allows us to deploy a range of content or textual analysis tools that can assist students in their learning. We take textual analysis to be an appreciation of how individuals interpret their environment through their actions— put simply, how they fit into the world around them, in this case through a series of public pronouncements.[16] Content analysis has become something of an umbrella term, sometimes used interchangeably with "textual analysis" but also including the practice of analyzing any text or document (written or audio) through an interpretive lens.[17] Identifying to students that they are developing these skills has proven useful in increasing levels of engagement as they become mindful of the transferrable skills they need to illustrate to future employers.

The principles of the flipped classroom can again be used in providing access to the speeches as plain text, audio, or video. That all three of these speeches are available in each format is a blessing for historians of the Cold War, allowing them the range of source material denied to historians of the ancient world, for example. It allows the history teacher to deploy these resources at the appropriate moment during a course. Perhaps this is at the outset, or perhaps they are better deployed at particular points during the course. Equally, as there are a variety of formats, dividing class into thirds and asking each third to consider the speech in a different format, rotating groups over the course of a semester, has proved worthwhile as students enjoy the variety of learning experiences: reading, listening, and watching. The subsequent class time can be devoted to discussion and problem solving. It also allows for an element of role play as we can ask our students, while they are conducting their textual analysis, to consider what the protagonists were trying to achieve in their speeches. Jeff Woods's reflections on teaching a class on the White House tapes at Arkansas Tech University in 2002 illustrate the value of an audio source to his class: "Hearing the people rather than just reading about them seems to have made a difference. They empathized and thus found the key to a greater understanding of history."[18]

Importantly, also there is the opportunity for a second order of critical analysis with more advanced students with this approach; the teacher can ask about the antecedents and the context for the speeches. Students can explore the formation of each speech by studying drafts of the document in presidential or governmental papers. They can consider which individuals were involved in the process of crafting the speeches, examining their politics and the extent of their influence. Students can also discuss the immediate context for each speech. This particularly allows students to explore the domestic origins of foreign policy. With respect to Churchill's speech, this is particularly relevant given he was out of office but would return in October 1951; as for the Truman speech and his immediate US audience, the week after his remarks in Missouri he announced the Truman Doctrine, pledging the United States to overcome communism wherever it threatened "freedom." It is this sort of linkage that the history teacher can utilize to illustrate the significance of these speeches.

A further avenue of learning, particularly in emphasizing Western Europe within the global context of the Cold War, is to set our students the task of finding contemporaneous journalistic accounts of the speeches from different countries around the world. This has been particularly useful for a class of international students, whose language expertise can allow students to bring different global perspectives to bear. It also brings an alternate primary source to our students.

There is a great variety of primary documents that can be employed: in the case of Kennedy and Reagan the US presidential public papers, available and searchable on line at the American Presidency Project, as well as the *Foreign Relations of the United States* series provided by the US Department of State Office of the Historian, which students can readily access.[19] In the case of Churchill's speech, the Churchill Archive and the Churchill Archive Centre at the University of Cambridge both provide resources that students can engage with.[20] One of the prime rationales for choosing these three speeches over others is the availability of these resources in an accessible format for students at all levels. Exposing students to these primary documents, in their archival settings if not the physical archive, serves to facilitate not only greater levels of learning and knowledge retention but also comprehension and critical analysis. Matt Loayza shares this view, having used document-based assessments in his class: "Document-based assignments have contributed significantly to greater student enthusiasm, overall grasp of the course materials, and quality of class discussions in all of my courses."[21]

In recognizing the spatial dimension to the Cold War, one can ask, What was the significance of the venue? In the case of Reagan's speech, the venue within Berlin with the Brandenberg Gate as a clear backdrop meant that the message and the symbolism could not have been clearer to Reagan's Cold War counterpart in Moscow.

Furthermore, the stature of the three speakers provides the chance to explore the value of historical biography. All three of these figures have considerable biographical libraries for students to engage with. John Lewis Gaddis, in reflecting upon his thirty-year journey in compiling his opus on George F. Kennan, calls for a principle of fairness to be applied to viewing historical figures in the context in which they found themselves: "sensitivity to context."[22] Appreciating the context for any endeavor in historical study is an apt juncture to draw this chapter to a close.

NOTES

1. Winston S. Churchill, *Sinews of Peace*, Westminster College, Fulton, Missouri, March 5, 1946, http://www.winstonchurchill.org/resources/speeches/1946-1963-elder-statesman/the-sinews-of-peace.

2. This is a distinct understanding from the definition of benchmarking drawn from what might be termed the "quality movement" in education as a whole, which in turn is drawn from the private sector with a distinct set of targets to improve output, performance, and/or productivity.

3. See, for example, Jack Mezirow, ed., *Fostering Critical Reflection in Adulthood* (San Francisco: Jossey-Bass, 1990), and Steven D. Brookfield, *Becoming a Critically Reflective Teacher* (San Francisco: Jossey-Bass, 1995).

4. William A. Green, "Periodizing World History," *History and Theory* 34 (May 1995): 99–111.

5. John Lewis Gaddis, *The Long Peace* (Oxford: Oxford University Press, 1987); and Gaddis, "Great Illusions, the Long Peace, and the Future of the International System," in Charles Kegley, ed., *The Long Postwar Peace* (New York: HarperCollins, 2001).

6. Odd Arne Westad, *The Global Cold War: Third World Interventions and the Making of Our Times* (Cambridge: Cambridge University Press, 2006), reviewed by Lawrence Freedman, *Foreign Affairs*, May/June 2006.

7. See, for example, Kent Killie, "Active Learning and Teaching about the United Nations," United Nations Studies Association, http://unstudies.org /content/active-learning-teaching; Charles. Bonwell and Jason Eison, *Active Learning: Creating Excitement in the Classroom AEHE-ERIC Higher Education Report No. 1* (Washington, DC: National Academy for Academic Leadership, 1991).

8. B. L. McCombs and J. S. Whistler, *The Learner-Centered Classroom and School: Strategies for Increasing Student Motivation and Achievement* (San Francisco: Jossey-Bass, 1997).

9. Paul Ramsden, *Learning to Teach in Higher Education* (London: Routledge, 2003), 78.

10. The concept of "learning styles" has been the subject of considerable debate itself. A 2004 report by the Learning and Skills Research Centre in the United Kingdom found that the instrument that is used to assess learning styles is fundamental to their identification. Frank Coffield, David Moseley, Elaine Hall, and Kathryn Ecclestone, *Learning Styles and Pedagogy in Post-16 Learning: A Systematic and Critical Review* (London: Learning and Skill Research Centre, 2004).

11. Joseph Corneli and Charles Jeffrey Danoff, "Paragogy," in *Proceedings of the 6th Open Knowledge Conference* (Berlin, 2011). See also http://paragogy.net /images/1/1d/Paragogy-book.pdf.

12. Joseph Corneli, "Paragogical Praxis," *E-Learning and Digital Media* 9, no. 3 (2012): 267–72. Yenn Lee and J. Simon Rofe, "Paragogy and Flipped Assessment: Experience of Designing and Running a MOOC on Research Methods," *Open Learning: The Journal of Open, Distance and e-Learning* (2016): 1–14.

13. http://www.wordle.net/.

14. See http://www.uq.edu.au/teach/flipped-classroom/what-is-fc.html.

15. Each of these speeches is readily available on YouTube: https://youtu .be/jvaxVUvjWQ (Churchill); https://youtu.be/jvaxVUvjWQ (Kennedy); https://youtu.be/5MDFX-dNtsM (Reagan).

16. Alan Mckee, *Textual Analysis Sage Research Methods* (London: Sage, 2003).

17. Steve Stemler, "An Overview of Content Analysis," *Practical Assessment, Research & Evaluation* 7, no. 17 (2001).

18. Jeff Woods, *Teaching New Media: A Class on the White House Tapes*, 2002, http://shafr.org/si tes/default/files/Woods.pdf.

19. "The Public Papers of the Presidency" can be found at http://www .presidency.ucsb.edu/ws/. *Foreign Relations of the United States* can be found at https://history.state.gov/historicaldocuments.

20. The Churchill Archive can be found at http://www.churchillarchive .com/ and the Churchill Archives Centre at https://www.chu.cam.ac.uk /archives/. The two repositories contain the same base documents, but they are presented differently, which allows for an interesting question to be posed on the presentation of historical documents.

21. Matt Loayza, "Learning by Doing: Teaching the History of the US Foreign Relations with Original Documents," December 2006, 4–9, http://shafr .org/sites/default/files/Loayza.pdf.

22. John Lewis Gaddis, "Spiderman, Shakespeare, and Kennan: The Art of Teaching Biography," January 2013, 39–42, https://shafr.org/sites/default/files /Passport-January-2013.pdf.

KEY RESOURCES

Craig, Campbell, and Fredrik Logevall. *America's Cold War: The Politics of Insecurity*. Cambridge, MA: Harvard University Press, 2009.

Fink, Carole. *The Cold War: An International History*. Boulder, CO: Westview Press, 2014.

Gaddis, John Lewis. *The United States and the Origins of the Cold War*. New York: Columbia University Press, 1972.

———. *The Long Peace*. Oxford: Oxford University Press, 1987.

———. *George F. Kennan: An American Life*. New York: W.W. Norton, 2011.

Harper, John Lamberton. *The Cold War*. Oxford: Oxford University Press, 2011.

Leffler, Melvyn, and David Painter, eds. *Origins of the Cold War: An International History*. New York: Routledge, 2005.

Walker, Martin. *The Cold War: A History*. New York: Henry Holt, 1993.

Westad, Odd Arne. *The Global Cold War: Third World Interventions and the Making of Our Times*. Cambridge: Cambridge University Press, 2007.

Did the Cold War Really End?

Teaching the Cold War from East Asian Perspectives

HIROSHI KITAMURA

November 23, 2010, was a fateful day for the residents of Yeonpyeong Island in South Korea. For approximately an hour that afternoon, North Korea fired scores of shells at the normally quiet fishing community. As the attack turned the island into flames, local citizens fled to underground bunkers, while the South Korean military scrambled to hold its ground. Shortly after the cross-fire settled, then-President Lee Myung-bak vowed to conduct "a strenuous retaliation" against further provocations.[1] President Barack Obama immediately issued a "strong condemn[ation]," and other countries followed suit.[2] Tensions remained high in the months that followed. "If they attack, we are fully prepared," noted a South Korean air force member stationed in the area, more than two years later.[3]

This dangerous incident, occurring some two decades after the collapse of the Soviet Union, urges us to question a common assumption: Is the Cold War really over? For more than six decades, the Korean peninsula—a land artificially split along the thirty-eighth parallel—has remained in a state of war, as the north and the south never signed a formal peace treaty in the aftermath of the Korean War. While South Korea (the Republic of Korea) has gone on to thrive in the global capitalist economy, North Korea (the Democratic People's Republic of Korea) remains secluded behind its "Iron Curtain" and continues to run what one scholar has called a "mature" Stalinistic state in the second decade of the twenty-first century.[4] What, then, should we make of this ongoing conflict? Doesn't the divide between the "Cold War" and the "post–Cold War" vary by region and society? Is there a single Cold War experience that blankets the globe or rather a multitude of local experiences that resist coherent generalizations?

East Asia is rife with events and incidents that can yield provocative and creative insights about the Cold War. In this chapter, I explore how we might teach the history of this global confrontation from a regional angle.[5] In recent years, a growing number of studies have probed beyond the politics of Moscow and Washington, DC, by examining the Cold War in the "third world."[6] A focus on East Asia can further this endeavor by demonstrating the role of local leaders and publics in shaping the bipolar international struggle. Students will be able to grapple with a variety of agendas that challenged and diverged from US and Soviet intentions. The history of East Asia is a tense mixture of global and local initiatives. By studying the negotiations of individuals and institutions from both "above" and "below," we can pursue a deeper understanding of the Cold War itself.

My goal is not to deliver a comprehensive coverage of East Asian experiences. Rather, I divide the discussion into three broad chrono-logical blocs ("beginning," "middle," and "end") and explore a set of topics that will prove useful for discussion. Nor is my aim to provide definitive answers to memorize and record. I instead strive to raise questions from multiple viewpoints in the hope of provoking fruitful classroom conversations about this global conflict.

Rethinking the Beginning: From the Atomic Bomb to the Korean War

Students often come to class with a presumption that the Cold War began immediately after August 15, 1945—the day Emperor Hirohito famously went on the air to announce Japan's capitulation to the Allied forces. A course on the Cold War in East Asia can serve to complicate this simplistic delineation. A good way do this is to open the semester with the atomic bomb. President Harry Truman's decision to drop America's first nuclear bombs over Hiroshima and Nagasaki— on August 6 and 9, respectively—has provoked heated debates on the causes and motivations for unleashing this devastating weapon. The "orthodox" argument is that the bombs were dropped to end the war quickly and save American lives. In this line of argument, the bombs curtailed further deaths by preventing the US military from launching a land invasion on Japan's main islands and by sparing the Japanese population from full extinction.[7]

Cold War implications surface in the "revisionist" claim that the bombs were diplomatic tools to contest Soviet expansion. In this line of reasoning, Truman, a hard-liner unlike Franklin Roosevelt, was determined to curtail Stalin's postwar ambitions by boasting of America's first fission bombs at the Potsdam Conference and "presenting" them in Japan to prevent the Soviets from taking part in the postwar reconstruction of Asia.[8] The revisionist perspective has been reinforced by the revelation that Stalin knew of the US bomb program as early as 1942—three years sooner than Truman—thanks to the clandestine work of his spies and sympathizers.[9] To be sure, the bomb decision comes with other interpretations as well. Some, for instance, maintain that the weapons were used to "show the results" of the Manhattan Project, a two-billion-dollar, government-funded program. Others note that the mushroom clouds were used to teach a lesson to the Tojo-led "yellow race" after Japan's sneak attack on Pearl Harbor.[10]

Instructors could use the bomb decision to explore how and why the war ended, debate the strategic benefits and moral costs of atomic weapons, and rethink the origins of the Cold War. There is an abundance of policy documents, memoranda, petitions, polls, and letters that will serve well in the classroom. For example, one could draw primary sources from Cynthia Kelly, ed., *The Manhattan Project: The Birth of the Atomic Bomb in the Words of Its Creators, Eyewitnesses, and Historians* (2009), and from Philip Cantelon, Richard Hewlett, and Robert Williams, eds., *The American Atom: A Documentary History of Nuclear Policies from the Discovery of Fission to the Present* (2nd ed., 1992). An effective way to study the issue is to assemble a role-play by dividing the class into three groups: policymakers, military officials, and scientists. Students could each play a given role and advance their own perspectives. It might be productive to assign a role-play paper, in which students, taking one of the three occupational positions, convey their policy recommendations to the president of the United States regarding the use or nonuse of the bomb.

A discussion on Hiroshima and Nagasaki could be followed by a conversation on the "early Cold War" in East Asia. One might start with bomb-struck Japan, where General Douglas MacArthur administered a six-and-a-half-year occupation. While often touted as one of the most "successful" US occupations to date, the effort to "democratize" Japan was not without controversy, as it involved a forceful attempt to disseminate policies, ideas, and values. Students can come to understand the tense politics of this experience by studying the Americans' effort to create a new Japanese constitution, the military men's fraternization with Japanese women, and media censorship—all of which are discussed in John Dower's highly readable *Embracing Defeat: Japan in the Wake of World War II* (1999).[11] It would also be vital to study the rise of Cold War tendencies under the "reverse course," through which MacArthur began to prioritize the reconstruction of Japanese industries and purge left-wing activists from their job positions.[12] Visual resources can enrich these discussions particularly by offering a firsthand glimpse into everyday life. For this, one could turn to the John W. Bennett Digital Collection at Ohio State University (http://library.osu.edu/projects/bennett-in-japan/1a_intro.html) or view feature films made during the era, such as Akira Kurosawa's *Drunken Angel* (1948) and *Stray Dog* (1949)—both of which present the occupation era as marred by crime, poverty, sexual exploitation, and social misery.

In studying the early Cold War, one must also examine the tensions unfolding in China, which culminated in the birth of the People's Republic of China (PRC) in 1949. The rise of the PRC goes along with the so-called lost-chance debate, which asks whether the United States could have established a nonconfrontational if not friendly relationship with Mao's China.[13] Students may argue over this question by comparing Truman's "China White Paper" (1949), which offers an official explanation of America's policy approach, with the dispatches of US Foreign Service officers in China, who noted, time and again, that the communists were more popular and *democratic* than the Nationalist Party led by Jiang Jieshi (Chiang Kai-shek) and that US interests would be better served by allying with the former.[14] Students could also turn to the classic writings of Mao Zedong, such as "Guerrilla Warfare" (1937) or "On New Democracy" (1940).[15] Looking at these documents would help students acquire a *transwar* perspective that could present the origins of the Cold War as a blend of local and global initiatives.[16]

The climax of the early Cold War was the Korean War. Too often treated as a "forgotten war" buried in the cracks of the Second World

War and the Vietnam War, the three-year struggle across the thirty-eighth parallel was a devastating conflict—one that resulted in the deaths of more than thirty-five thousand Americans, more than four hundred thousand South Koreans, and possibly an even greater number of North Koreans.[17] It is also a war that is technically still ongoing, as the violence was brought to a temporary halt in 1953 with an armistice instead of a formal peace treaty. In seeking to personalize this difficult war, instructors might start by asking whether any students' family members or neighbors served in the war. Then, the class could engage in a debate about its causes and consequences. Provocative topics such as the Nogun Ri Massacre, in which Americans GIs shot and killed scores of Korean refugees before covering up the incident, may be effective in stimulating debate.[18] Students could "un-forget" the war by reading contemporary popular narratives, such as Richard Condon's *The Manchurian Candidate* (1959), which dramatizes a brainwashed Korean War veteran's attempt to assassinate a political candidate in the United States. One could compare this dark novel with John Frankenheimer's 1964 film adaptation, which, in typical Hollywood fashion, ends in a slightly more redeeming way.

Yet, in relying on American texts such as *The Manchurian Candidate*, one needs to be cautious about the representation of the Asian (and non-Western) world. As scholars often point out, many of them are Western-centered, "Orientalistic" portraits that reduce East Asians to crude stereotypes.[19] Depending too much on American resources could perpetuate a caricature of the Korean War as a war that solely concerned the likes of General Douglas MacArthur, President Truman, and US and UN soldiers. But, as recent studies have shown, the Korean War was in essence a *civil war* among competing Korean factions that drew the two superpowers into the peninsula. It is thus necessary to probe into the mindsets of the Koreans themselves, for instance, by turning to *Piagol* (1955), a classic South Korean film that depicts a band of communist fighters struggling to survive near the thirty-eighth parallel. One might also turn to *Tae Guk Gi: The Brotherhood of War* (2004), which dramatically portrays a pair of siblings tragically split by the war.[20] Additionally, we need to think of the war's impact on the antagonists' East Asian neighbors, most notably China. A few months after Douglas MacArthur led the UN troops into North Korean territory, Mao decided to counter the offensive by sending troops. This strategy would push back the UN forces to the thirty-eighth parallel but would result in the death of an estimated nine hundred thousand Chinese soldiers.[21] The Korean War was at once a local and an international war. Looking at it from a balanced perspective will prove fruitful to students.

Rethinking the Middle:
From the 1950s to the 1970s

The two decades that followed the Korean War ushered in a dynamic "middle" phase of the Cold War. A close look at this era—covering the mid-1950s through the 1970s—can be useful in challenging another common presumption: that the Cold War was a "long peace" that remained stable for nearly five decades.[22] This was, in fact, a highly volatile time in which the Cold War "consensus" was breaking down, even while East Asian leaders were endeavoring to solidify their alliances with superpowers. One can spot this, for example, in the tension that brewed between allies as well as the rise of popular protests that helped shape the "sixties revolution." What's more, there was the Vietnam War. Even though the world was able to avoid a World War III, the "long peace" came with death, damage, and high anxiety. The Asian context offers critical lessons on the Cold War and its most dangerous moments.

The fractures of the Cold War "consensus" become evident through a close study of individual societies. Japan offers a case in point. The San Francisco conference of 1951 helped bring an end to the US occupation, restore Japan's sovereignty, and strengthen the US-Japanese alliance through a bilateral security treaty, which allowed US troops to remain in Japan for strategic purposes. Yet the seemingly everlasting presence of the US military provoked considerable anger. In class, one might explore this "Japanese dilemma" by invoking the mass of protests that occurred around 1960, as the security treaty was under discussion for ratification.[23] MIT's highly useful "Visualizing Cultures" digital project offers a pair of essays ("Protest Art in 1950s Japan" and "Tokyo 1960: Days of Rage and Grief") that capture the ambivalent sentiments of Japanese artists, activists, and youth. These writings are peppered with photographs and paintings that capture the rage and disillusionment of many Japanese. Students could analyze these visual texts to probe into the mindset of popular protestors who challenged US practices on the ground.[24]

240

Another issue that could trigger a good deal of conversation is Okinawa. A site that remained under US control until 1972—two decades after the San Francisco Peace Treaty—and that still witnesses the presence of American military bases, this southern archipelago has given rise to a multitude of anti-American protests over the decades.[25] *Teahouse of the August Moon* (1956), a big-budget MGM comedy, seeks to counter this tendency by painting the occupation as an amicable partnership between the United States and the Okinawans. In the film, American administrators embark on a mission to erect a Pentagon-shaped schoolhouse in a remote village, but its residents manipulate the occupiers to build a teahouse that celebrates local customs and traditions (somehow at peace with the outcome, the US captain states, loud and clear: "I don't want to be a world leader"). This sanitized view of the Okinawan situation overlooks the resentment that brewed on the ground. After viewing this movie, students might conduct primary research on online databases (such as ProQuest) to explore the contemporary news coverage on Okinawan politics. It will not be difficult to find English-language reports that document the rise of fierce opposition to the US occupiers.[26]

South Korea is another intriguing case. From its founding in 1948, the Republic of Korea (ROK) was governed by Syngman Rhee, who ran an autocratic regime by courting conservative elites—many of whom "collaborated" with the Japanese during the colonial era. In this sense, Rhee might belong in the line of "friendly dictators" with whom the United States worked at the expense of its democratic idealism.[27] In class, instructors thus could ask: What do you think of Rhee's reign? Is it justifiable to support an undemocratic regime? What were the other alternatives? Weren't they more desirable? These questions will have greater meaning if one thinks of the ways in which a growing number of citizens—particularly students, military members, and political opponents—rallied against Rhee, until he was removed from leadership in 1960. Although the "April 19 Revolution" ended with the reign of another autocrat, Park Chung-hee, the South Korean desire for democracy remained alive and finally erupted again in the 1980s.[28]

The "united front" of the Cold War was deteriorating in the "second world," or communist-bloc nations, as well. In China, Mao actively challenged the Soviet Union in what is known as the "Sino-Soviet split." In 1956, three years after Stalin's death, Nikita Khrushchev officially criticized Stalin's purges and military strategies while calling for a "peaceful coexistence" with the United States. This prompted the Chinese premier to turn away from Moscow's leadership and chart its own course of "continuous revolution" with the Great Leap Forward (1958–60) and the Cultural Revolution (1966–76).[29] North Korea reacted similarly. In the months following Khrushchev's condemnatory speech, Kim Il-sung purged his more moderate opponents who appeared to be in favor of the new Soviet agenda.[30] Ever more skeptical of outsiders, the "fatherly leader" chose to keep his country cut off from much of the wider world while uniting its people around his cult of personality.[31]

The Chinese and North Korean reactions against the Soviet Union during this era provide a welcome opportunity for us to contemplate the agendas of the so-called second world. A good assignment for this is to craft a policy memo, working either in teams or as individuals, based on existing sources. In recent years, a growing number of primary documents have become available from Soviet, Chinese, and other second-world repositories. The Digital Archive of the Wilson Center's Cold War International History Project has a treasure trove of such materials, labeled the "Sino-Soviet Split," "Sino-Japanese Relations," "North Korean Public Diplomacy," "Purges in 1950s China," and so on (http://digitalarchive.wilsoncenter.org). The National Security Archive at George Washington University also holds a host of useful primary documents concerning East Asia and the Cold War (http://www2.gwu.edu/~nsarchiv/). Using these materials, the class could produce a productive simulation of intelligence gathering and analysis as done in government branches, think tanks, and other institutions of policymaking.

In addition, teachers could call attention to the Vietnam War. Given its complexity, it would be difficult to offer a comprehensive discussion of this far-reaching war in a session or two. But studying it in a class on East Asia is of value, because it can illustrate the fact that Vietnam was far more than an "American war."[32] Instructors could stress the war's transregional influence by pointing out the involvement of America's allies. For example, South Korea dispatched some three hundred thousand South Korean troops to Vietnam in response to US escalation; about five thousand of them perished in combat (the trauma of the experience surfaces in *R-Point* [2004], a rare horror film on Vietnam).[33] The Japanese did not put boots on the ground, as their constitution prohibits the possession of military force (hence Japan is armed with a Self-Defense Force), but the American bases in the island nation functioned as a launching pad for US bombers and soldiers. Antiwar protests, some of which turned violent, raged on the ground.[34]

China was another critical player in the war. An avid supporter of Ho Chi Minh's Democratic Republic of Vietnam from early on, it reacted to the Americans' involvement by providing an abundance of munitions and at least 320,000 soldiers to aid the North. The PRC's troops did not engage in physical combat but assisted the North Vietnamese by enabling them to penetrate the South.[35] Military action took place after US troops left Vietnam in 1973. The covert bombings during the Nixon administration drove many Cambodians to support Pol Pot's Khmer Rouge—the Cambodian Communist Party—which had a tense relationship with the Vietnamese. Shortly after Vietnam achieved unification as a socialist republic, the Khmer Rouge launched an attack and ignited a brutal war. This provoked China, an ally of Cambodia, to intervene against Vietnam.[36] A look at these developments could demonstrate that the "Vietnam War" consisted of many wars, involving the superpowers, the Vietnamese, and their neighbors. And, of course, Vietnam raises questions about the alleged "stability" of the Cold War itself.

Rethinking the End: From Détente to the North Korean Problem

The two decades that followed the Vietnam War traditionally constitute the "late" Cold War. This was yet another eventful era on a global scale, shaped by the Strategic Arms Limitation Talks, Ronald Reagan's New Cold War, the fall of the Berlin Wall, and—last but not least—the collapse of the Soviet Union. Yet here, too, East Asia mattered a great deal. Students can learn about this in looking at the hallmark event of détente: Nixon's meeting with Mao.[37] This shocking rapprochement of 1972 led to the establishment of official diplomatic relations between Beijing and Washington, while Taiwan was now perceived as a part of mainland China, even though the Taiwan Relations Act of 1979 allowed Taiwan to retain US military support (among other things). How and why did the United States and the People's Republic of China, previously hostile states, decide to bridge the divide that separated them? Teachers could provoke students by exploring their intentions. Was it primarily motivated by geopolitical interests? Or did it stem from America's desire for trade and commerce with the fabled "China market"? Did the two countries come together because of the domestic unrest that was hurting both societies?

Students could also ponder the long-term ramifications of the rapprochement. Much can be discussed here, as détente had a great influence on the political landscape of Asia. From the American perspective, the opening of official relations with China was a form of "triangular diplomacy" aimed at containing the Soviet Union.[38] At odds with the Soviet Union for many years, China would increasingly deepen its ties with the United States as Deng Xiaoping—Mao's successor—launched a modernization program that relied on private enterprises, foreign businesses, and joint ventures.[39] Initially taken aback by Nixon's surprising maneuver, Japan chose to take part in security cooperation with China and the United States vis-à-vis Moscow.[40] At the same time, Japan gradually deepened its economic and security ties with South Korea, with which it normalized relations in 1965.[41]

These developments may direct the classroom conversation toward emphasizing regional cooperation. Yet instructors need to be mindful that traditional Cold War frictions died hard, thanks to North Korea. Even as East-West relations seemed to thaw in the 1970s, the DPRK continued to blatantly antagonize its neighbors. It, for example, abducted scores of civilians from South Korea and Japan, thereby causing diplomatic frictions that still endure. As if to counter the superpower talks on arms reduction, Pyongyang also moved forward with its nuclear program. From the late 1950s, Kim Il-sung invested in atomic research and development at Yongbyon. In the 1970s, North Korea's nuclear reactors were modernized and updated, and it became increasingly evident that Pyongyang was aiming to produce nuclear weapons.[42] In recent years, North Korea has repeatedly played the game of "nuclear chicken" to gain attention and aid, thereby provoking the rage of the international community.[43]

As noted at the beginning of this chapter, the frustrating antics of North Korea offer us a chance to interrogate the "end" of the Cold War. Doesn't the enduring presence of the DPRK mean that the Cold War remains alive and well? Instructors can debate the question with students by assigning research topics on North Korea's military development, nuclear program, (failing) economic policy, and human rights abuses. To get a sense of "everyday life" in this self-isolated state (to the extent possible), students might read excerpts from Andrei Lankov's *North of the DMZ* (2007), a compilation of short essays on North Korean society and culture, and from Barbara Demick's *No Place to Envy: Ordinary Lives in North Korea* (2009), which seeks to recount the lives of a handful of North Korean defectors.

In thinking about the North Korean problem today, it is crucial to go beyond mainstream US perspectives, which often portray Kim Jong-un and his predecessors, Kim Il-sung and Kim Jong-il, as irrational and crazy leaders. To do so, students might dissect news coverage by the major TV networks and analyze how the media depict the current North Korean leader's actions and behaviors. Or students might be asked to decipher familiar Hollywood narratives such as *Team America* (2003), *Red Dawn* (2012), and *The Interview* (2014), which stereotype and ridicule the "fatherly leader" and his society. These exercises could be combined with a study of alternative texts such as "Escape to North Korea," a rap song by PacMan and Pe$o.[44] Using Kickstarter.com to raise production costs, the Washington, DC-based duo visited Pyongyang in 2014, posing as tourists, and shot this music video on location. For these African American men, North Korea turned out to be a revealing experience. Following their return to the United States, the duo, not unlike the former basketball star Dennis Rodman, interestingly claimed that Pyongyang was not as dangerous as their neighborhoods in Washington, DC. "Nine times out of 10 you get robbed on my streets more than out of North Korea," PacMan noted afterward.[45]

In addition, North Korean feature films can offer students valuable insights on the self-isolated state. Over the decades, North Korea has devoted a great deal of its resources to pump out propaganda narratives that would help mobilize the masses. It has even abducted prominent South Korean filmmakers—Shin Sang-ok and Choi Eun-hee—to achieve this goal.[46] Although seldom screened in US theaters, North Korea's cinematic products are readily available online (e.g., at YouTube) and on DVD. Perhaps the most iconic film is *The Flower Girl* (1972), which presents an impoverished young girl who suffers under Japanese colonialism until the Revolution Army (led by her brother) comes to the rescue. *A Traffic Controller on Crossroads* (1986) paints the iconic traffic controller in Pyongyang as a compassionate public servant who sacrifices personal pleasure for a higher (national) cause. These and other films should help us think of the political and international agendas of the North Korean government. They also point to the duties and roles that are expected of women in the "fatherly state."

The persistence of the Cold War milieu could be explored with South Korean texts as well. Over the past decade and a half, there have been a slew of South Korean feature films and TV shows that dramatize the "North Korean problem" as an ongoing matter. The most common genre concerns espionage, as seen in the likes of *Shiri* (1999), *Iris* (2009), *Commitment* (2013), *The Berlin File* (2013), and *Suspect* (2014). These narratives are more than entertaining; in contrast to mainstream US perspectives, they refuse to hastily caricature the North Koreans as an exotic or demonic Other but portray them as human beings with emotion and reason. They also treat the people of both countries as victims of a larger international struggle. After having the class watch any of these entertaining films, instructors could urge students to explore the South Korean perspective on the Korean crisis and devise solutions to the conflict. How might we end this unending confrontation—and thereby truly conclude the Cold War in East Asia? Should the two Koreas seek unification? If so, how? Can South Korea take on the North Korean "burden" immediately? Should it encourage and invest in North Korea's economic development before moving toward unification? How should the neighboring states, as well as the United States, deal with the Korean crisis? What are the diplomatic, economic, and cultural strategies?

To solve the Korean crisis would require students to grapple with the politics of East Asia in the present. Doing so, one would quickly realize that breakthrough ideas are difficult to find, thanks to long-lasting animosities that continue to fracture the region. Japan has played a leading role in aggravating this trend by failing to reconcile its differences with China and the two Koreas over its actions during the war. The nation's conservative leadership (from Yasuhiro Nakasone in the 1980s to Shinzo Abe in the past decade), the politicized debates over the content of school textbooks in the 1990s, the efforts to deny the existence of "comfort women" (*ianfu*), and the growth of anti-Korean and anti-Chinese sentiment have added fuel to the fire, thereby infuriating liberals as well as victims of Japanese imperialism.[47] Eager to boost its military capabilities and economic prowess in the global arena, China has increasingly taken a confrontational attitude toward Japan, for instance over the rights to control the Senkaku/Diaoyu Islands. These and other territorial disputes in East Asia—including the Southern Kuriles/Northern Territories (Russia and Japan), Dokdo/Takeshima (South Korea and Japan), and the Spratlys/Nansha Islands (China, Taiwan, Vietnam, Philippines, Malaysia, Brunei)—have moved to the forefront of state-to-state diplomacy and have widened the rifts among these entangled societies.[48]

The existence of these skirmishes suggests that the welfare of the region is influenced by local factors and motivations. They also make us wonder how the dynamics of the Cold War have influenced these developments. Discussing the "end" of the Cold War might raise more questions than answers. Yet it should be noted that these questions are necessary for us to fully comprehend this global struggle.

Conclusion

What can East Asia teach us about the Cold War? The answer: a great deal. From the atomic bombings of Hiroshima and Nagasaki, the rise of the PRC, the Korean War, the Sino-Soviet split, the Vietnam War, to the troubles involving North Korea, the region has harbored myriad dangerous events that have greatly affected the wider world. A close study of the region reveals the active role of national and regional actors in shaping global politics. It also sheds light on oppositional voices and movements that challenged the Cold War "consensus." These rich examples should help students understand that East Asia was a central site of the global struggle.

Furthermore, a course on East Asia complicates our common assumptions about the Cold War itself. When and where did the Cold War begin? Was it really a "long peace"? Did this global conflict homogenize local experiences, or did people in different places live the Cold War differently? Did the Cold War really end with the collapse of the Berlin Wall and the Soviet Union? Can we comfortably say that we are living in a post–Cold War world?

The 2010 assault on Yeonpyeong Island reminds us that we ought to keep grappling with these important questions. For much of East Asia at least, the Cold War is not a thing of the past but an experience that carries contemporary resonance. As William Faulkner once famously said: "The past isn't dead. It isn't even past." The continuity of experience makes it vital for students to focus greater attention on the region.

NOTES

1. Mark McDonald, "'Crisis Status' in South Korea after North Shells Island," *New York Times,* November 23, 2010, http://www.nytimes.com/2010/11/24/world/asia/24korea.html?pagewanted=all&_r=0.

2. Office of the Press Secretary, "Statement by the Press Secretary on North Korean Shelling of South Korean Island," November 23, 2010, https://www.whitehouse.gov/the-press-office/2010/11/23/statement-press-secretary-north-korean-shelling-south-korean-island.

3. Chico Harlan, "Yeonpyeong Attack Raised South Korea's Resolve," *The Japan Times,* April 16, 2013, http://www.japantimes.co.jp/news/2013/04/16/asia-pacific/yeonpyeong-attack-raised-south-koreas-resolve/#.VVpkEtfUdI.

4. Andrei Lankov, *The Real North Korea: Life and Politics in the Failed Stalinist Utopia* (New York: Oxford University Press, 2013).

5. This chapter focuses on "East Asia," which includes Japan, the People's Republic of China, Taiwan, the Republic of Korea, and the Democratic People's Republic of Korea.

6. See, for example, Odd Arne Westad, *The Global Cold War: Third World Interventions and the Making of Our Times* (New York: Cambridge University Press, 2007).

7. See, for example, Herbert Feis, *The Atomic Bomb and the End of World War II* (Princeton: Princeton University Press, 1961).

8. Gar Alperovitz, *Atomic Diplomacy: Hiroshima and Potsdam* (East Haven, CT: Pluto Press, 1994).

9. Kate Brown, *Plutopia: Nuclear Families, Atomic Cities, and the Great Soviet and American Plutonium Disasters* (New York: Oxford University Press, 2013), 81; Richard Rhodes, *Dark Sun: The Making of the Hydrogen Bomb* (New York: Simon & Schuster, 1995), 82–179.

10. For a succinct discussion of the key arguments, see J. Samuel Walker, *Prompt and Utter Destruction: Truman and the Use of the Atomic Bombs against Japan* (Chapel Hill: University of North Carolina Press, 1997), esp. 92–97.

11. *Embracing Defeat* is the best synthesis on the occupation of Japan. The most comprehensive study of the bureaucratic structures and functions of the occupation is Eiji Takemae, *Inside GHQ: The Allied Occupation of Japan and Its Legacy* (New York: Continuum, 2002).

12. Michael Schaller, *The American Occupation of Japan: The Origins of the Cold War in Asia* (New York: Oxford University Press, 1985).

13. Chen Jian, *Mao's China and the Cold War* (Chapel Hill: University of North Carolina Press, 2001), 38–48.

14. Joseph W. Esherick, ed., *Lost Chance in China: The World War II Dispatches of John S. Service* (New York: Random House, 1974).

15. Timothy Cheek, ed., *Mao Zedong and China's Revolutions: A Brief History with Documents* (New York: Bedford/St. Martin's, 2002); Mao Tse-Tung, *On Guerrilla Warfare,* trans. Samuel B. Griffith II (Chicago: University of Illinois Press, 1961).

16. Andrew Gordon, *A Modern History of Japan: from Tokugawa Times to the Present,* 3rd ed. (New York: Oxford University Press, 2013).

17. Bruce Cumings, *The Korean War: A History* (New York: Modern Library, 2010), 35.

18. Cumings, *The Korean War,* 167–68.

19. Christina Klein, *Cold War Orientalism: Asia in the Middlebrow Imagination, 1946–1961* (Berkeley: University of California Press, 2004); Edward Said, *Orientalism* (New York: Vintage, 1978).

20. Gregg Brazinsky, *Nation Building in South Korea* (Chapel Hill: University of North Carolina Press, 2007), 13–40. For other South Korean films about the Korean War, see Darcy Paquet, "South Korean Films about the Korean War

(1950–53): A Tool for Reference," *Koreanfilm.org*, http://www.koreanfilm.org/warfilms.html.

21. Cumings, *The Korean War*, 35.

22. On the "long peace," see John Lewis Gaddis, *The Long Peace: Inquiries into the History of the Cold War* (New York: Oxford University Press, 1989).

23. Michael Schaller, *Altered States: The United States and Japan since the Occupation* (New York: Oxford University Press, 1997), 143–62.

24. MIT, "Visualizing Cultures," http://ocw.mit.edu/ans7870/21f/21f.027/home/index.html.

25. Gavan McCormack and Satoko Oka Norimatsu, *Resistant Islands: Okinawa Confronts Japan and the United States* (New York: Rowman & Littlefield, 2012); Miyume Tanji, *Myth, Protest and Struggle in Okinawa* (New York: Routledge, 2006).

26. See, for example, Igor Oganesoff, "Teahouse Tempest: Okinawa Slaps at US Rule as Capital Elects a Red-Backed Mayor," *Wall Street Journal*, January 15, 1958, 1; Robert Trumbull, "Okinawa: 'Sometimes Painful' Lesson for Us," *New York Times*, April 7, 1957, 225.

27. For examples outside East Asia, see, for example, Eric Paul Roorda, *The Dictator Next Door: The Good Neighbor Policy and the Trujillo Regime in the Dominican Republic, 1930–1945* (Durham, NC: Duke University Press, 1998); Bradley R. Simpson, *Economists with Guns: Authoritarian Development and U.S.-Indonesian Relations, 1960–1968* (Stanford: Stanford University Press, 2008).

28. Brazinsky, *Nation Building in South Korea*.

29. Lorenz M. Luthi, *The Sino-Soviet Split: Cold War in the Communist World* (Princeton: Princeton University Press, 2008).

30. Lankov, *The Real North Korea*, 14–15, 17–19.

31. B. R. Meyers, *The Cleanest Race: How North Koreans See Themselves—and Why It Matters* (New York: Melville House, 2011).

32. Instructors looking for resources for teaching the Vietnam War can consult another book in the Harvey Goldberg Series: John Tully, Matthew Masur, and Brad Austin, eds., *Understanding and Teaching the Vietnam War* (Madison: University of Wisconsin Press, 2013).

33. Mark Philip Bradley, *Vietnam at War* (New York: Oxford University Press, 2009), 123.

34. Schaller, *Altered States*, 190.

35. Qiang Zhai, *China and the Vietnam Wars, 1950–1975* (Chapel Hill: University of North Carolina Press, 2000), 135–37.

36. Bradley, *Vietnam at War*, 177.

37. Margaret MacMillan, *Nixon and Mao: The Week That Changed the World* (New York: Random House, 2007).

38. Gordon H. Chang, *Friends and Enemies: The United States, China, and the Soviet Union, 1948–1972* (Stanford: Stanford University Press, 1990), 288–90.

39. Robert G. Sutter, *US-Chinese Relations: Perilous Past, Pragmatic Present*, 2nd ed. (New York: Rowman & Littlefield, 2013), 65–94.

40. Kenneth B. Pyle, *Japan Rising: The Resurgence of Japanese Power and Purpose* (New York: Public Affairs, 2007), 323.

41. Michael W. Chinworth, Narushige Michishita, and Taeyoung Yoon, "Future Challenges and Opportunities for Trilateral Security Cooperation," in Robert A. Wampler, ed., *Trilateralism and Beyond: Great Power Politics and the Koran Security Dilemma during and after the Cold War* (Kent, OH: Kent State University Press, 2012), 132.

42. Lankov, *The Real North Korea*, 147–48.

43. Gavan McCormack, *Target North Korea: Pushing North Korea to the Brink of Nuclear Catastrophe* (New York: Nation Books, 2004), 149–80.

44. The song is available on Youtube: https://www.youtube.com/watch?v=PDfThUsqpc.

45. "Washington 'More Dangerous' Than North Korea," *SkyNews*, January 13, 2014, http://news.sky.com/story/1193902/washington-more-dangerous-than-north-korea.

46. Paul Fischer, *A Kim Jong-Il Production: The Extraordinary True Story of a Kidnapped Filmmakers, His Star Actress, and a Young Dictator's Rise to Power* (New York: Flatiron Books, 2015).

47. Alexis Dudden, *Troubled Apologies among Japan, Korea, and the United States* (New York: Columbia University Press, 2008).

48. Kimie Hara, *Cold War Frontiers in the Asia-Pacific: Divided Territories in the San Francisco System* (New York: Routledge, 2007).

KEY RESOURCES

Brazinsky, Gregg. *Nation Building in South Korea: Koreans, Americans, and the Making of a Democracy.* Chapel Hill: University of North Carolina Press, 2007.

Cantelon, Philip L., et al., eds. *The American Atom: A Documentary History of Nuclear Policies from the Discovery of Fission to the Present.* 2nd ed. Philadelphia: University of Pennsylvania Press, 1991.

Chen Jian. *Mao's China and the Cold War.* Chapel Hill: University of North Carolina Press, 2001.

Condon, Richard. *The Manchurian Candidate.* 1959; reprint ed., New York: Thunder's Mouth Press, 1987.

Cumings, Bruce. *The Korean War: A History.* New York: Modern Library, 2010.

Demick, Barbara. *No Place to Envy: Ordinary Lives in North Korea.* New York: Spiegel & Grau, 2009.

Dower, John W. *Embracing Defeat: Japan in the Wake of World War II.* New York: W. W. Norton and the New Press, 1999.

Esherick, Joseph W., ed. *Lost Chance in China: The World War II Dispatches of John S. Service.* New York: Random House, 1974.

Kelly, Cynthia, ed. *The Manhattan Project: The Birth of the Atomic Bomb in the Words of Its Creators, Eyewitnesses, and Historians.* New York: Black Dog & Leventhal, 2009.

Lankov, Andrei. *The Real North Korea: Life and Politics in the Failed Stalinist Utopia.* New York: Oxford University Press, 2013.

Walker, J. Samuel. *Prompt and Utter Destruction: Truman and the Use of the Atomic Bombs against Japan.* Chapel Hill: University of North Carolina Press, 1997.

The Cold War
in Latin America and
the Caribbean

ANDREW J. KIRKENDALL

In teaching Latin America's Cold War, one needs to remember that many parts of Latin America had long
been part of the US sphere of influence and had experienced invasion,
occupation, and large-scale economic investment. (This was particularly
true for Central America, the Caribbean, and Mexico.) Many other parts
of the world were now experiencing dramatically higher levels of US
influence for the first time beginning in the 1940s. Between the signing
of bilateral trade agreements with the vast majority of Latin American
countries in the 1930s and the creation of and/or use of military bases in
most of them during World War II, the long-standing dream of US dominance throughout the Western Hemisphere had been accomplished.

US influence in Latin America, therefore, was stronger and more
widespread during the Cold War than it had ever been. (And certainly
in the early years, at least, the Soviet Union recognized this and was
willing to live with it.) And yet, paradoxically, US officials generally
tended to pay much less attention to the region during the Cold War
than they had before 1942, since the dangers seemed so much greater in
Europe and Asia. US officials tended to veer back and forth between
complacency about Latin America for much of the time and hysteria at
particular moments.[1] Consistent and positive policies could not be maintained. And, generally, US officials preferred Latin American leaders
who could provide stability, at whatever cost, so that they could focus
on issues they considered more important in other parts of the world.

Even as US officials were tending to ignore Latin America, the region as a whole was changing, industrializing to some degree and urbanizing to a greater degree than any other part of the developing world. Many countries were hoping to transform themselves socially and economically, embracing some economic nationalist measures while not abandoning the long-standing policies of welcoming free trade and foreign investment. They were still primarily providers of raw agricultural and mineral materials to a North Atlantic economy, but they aspired to be more than that. And Latin American countries were changing in ways that were promising (in that urbanization was accompanied by rising literacy rates and, to some degree, the growth of a middle class) and at the same time destabilizing (because urbanization was accompanied by more complicated political dynamics and higher rates of growth of an often desperately poor population that had no reliable access to decent food or shelter). And intermittent US attention to the region made it more difficult to devise beneficial responses when events in the region demanded US attention.

The first country to receive a great deal of attention from the United States during the Cold War was Guatemala during the presidency of Jacobo Árbenz, who had his own dreams of economic development in an unusually democratic period in his country's history. The Central American country was experiencing what has been called ten "years of spring in the land of eternal tyranny."[2] Although the Harry S. Truman administration had considered various means of removing the democratically elected leader, it would be during the presidency of Dwight D. Eisenhower that covert actions by the Central Intelligence Agency, inspired in part by success in Iran, would lead to Árbenz's resignation in June 1954.

The overthrow of Árbenz is a topic of vital importance in teaching Latin America's Cold War for several reasons.[3] One is that it enables students to engage the question of why the US government would choose to work toward the removal of a democratically elected leader. Many of our students are surprised to learn that the United States has ever acted in such a manner. It does not fit with their understanding of how the United States acts in the world. Moreover, it is a subject that has attracted a great deal of attention from historians, not all of whom are united, by any means, in their explanations of why the United States took the actions that it did. Instructors who are so inclined might choose to linger over the historiographical debates. Some authors argue that

Árbenz was removed because his land reform programs hurt the economic interests of a US-based multinational, the United Fruit Company.[4] (Árbenz hoped that his program would create a class of small- to medium-size landowners, which would move the country from what he understood to be a feudal society to a truly capitalist one.) That the United States acted to protect US economic interests is certainly the interpretation shared by many in Latin America. And historians also have long noted the close ties between Eisenhower administration officials, including Secretary of State John Foster Dulles and CIA director Allen Dulles, both former corporate lawyers at the Sullivan and Cromwell law firm, and the company. Ironically, in the weeks following the overthrow of Árbenz, the US Department of Justice finally moved forward with an antitrust suit charging United Fruit with anticompetitive practices. Therefore, the United States helped overthrow a government that was damaging US economic interests in the name of capitalist economic development and then chose to take action against those same interests itself.

Other historians have argued that the actions taken by the United States against Árbenz were inspired by his close ties to members of the small Guatemalan Communist Party. The United States assumed that Guatemalan communists were acting under orders from the Soviet Union, which was not an altogether unreasonable thing for them to believe, given the actions of Communist Party members elsewhere in the world. And many of these party members were also involved in implementing the land reform program, which would have enabled them to enhance the popularity of their party throughout the country. And though we now know that there were virtually no ties between the Guatemalan communists and the Soviet Union, nevertheless, given the Cold War context, Eisenhower administration actions were understandable if not necessarily admirable.

Still another reason to examine the case of Guatemala in a course on the Cold War is that the long-term costs for the country were so dire. Not only did the United States turn back the clock on a needed land reform program that was similar to programs the United States was encouraging in Asian countries, but also the United States would find here and elsewhere that it was far easier to destroy democracy than it was to promote it. And, in the long run and over the next few decades, no Latin American country during the Cold War suffered more due to political violence, with roughly two hundred thousand people in a country of ten million dying at the hands of military and security forces who perceived peasants, particularly those of Mayan origin, to be a threat.

For the United States, however, the cost of the intervention was small (although Guatemala would receive significant economic aid in the years after 1954). And Guatemala in 1954 was remembered as a success by the Eisenhower administration and the Central Intelligence Agency, leading, therefore, to a return to complacency among US officials.

The best book to assign in an undergraduate course on the Cold War on this subject is Nick Cullather's *Secret History: The CIA's Classified Account of Its Operations in Guatemala, 1952–1954*. I presume that anyone teaching about the Cold War will want to devote some time to the examination of the agency and to covert action. Researched and written during what now seems like a relatively brief period of openness regarding CIA operations in the 1990s, the declassified and "sanitized" history shows how "an intensive paramilitary and psychological campaign" replaced "a popular, elected government with a political nonentity"—a nonentity, it might be added, who had participated in previous attempts to undermine democracy and who bore an unfortunate physical resemblance in some pictures to Adolph Hitler. CIA psychological pressures (including the support for a small but well-funded proxy army) were effective in convincing Guatemalan army officers to act to remove Árbenz even though the United States did not at that time have close ties with top Guatemalan military officers themselves and even though the proxy army supported by the agency was fairly inept. The book is as interesting to students for what it omits as for what it contains, since they can puzzle over the blank spaces left by the redaction process, which are reproduced in the book. They may be amused or dismayed by the agency's attempts to classify information that comes from published materials. The book can inspire an interesting debate over the relationship between secrecy and national security in a democracy. (It also includes agency documents in the appendix that describe CIA perceptions of Árbenz, his advisers, and his land reform program, as well as the agency's eventual disappointment in Carlos Castillo Armas, whom the agency had put in power.)[5]

For Latin America, the Cuban revolution was the next major turning point in the Cold War, the event that made Latin America matter. As President John Kennedy, inaugurated during one of those moments of peak hysteria regarding Latin America, said, "Although the Cold War will not be won in Latin America, it may well be lost there." These concerns led not only to increased military aid and counterinsurgency training and greater efforts to improve ties between the US and Latin American militaries but also to enhanced funding for scholarly research on the region. "Thank God for Fidel Castro," as a colonial Latin American historian, no radical he, once said in a class I took in graduate school.

The lessons learned by the US government in Guatemala and by the CIA in particular would prove misleading in the case of Cuba, demonstrating that historical actors sometimes learn as little from their successes as from their mistakes. Fidel Castro, of course, would not prove as easy to remove as Árbenz had been. From 1959 to 1961, he initiated a revolution that transformed Cuban society. This was a popular revolution that received a great deal of support from the poor (a relatively neglected peasant rebellion in El Escambray notwithstanding) and that drove first the elite and then the middle class into exile. Castro definitively broke long-standing economic and political ties with the United States in a complex dynamic of action and reaction as Castro sought support from the Soviet Union for his revolution. An interesting exercise for students could involve an examination of the presidential rhetoric surrounding the revolution, drawing upon the *Public Papers of the Presidents of the United States of America*, which should be available in most libraries. President Dwight David Eisenhower, for example, sounded genuinely puzzled about what was going on in Cuba in his public comments in 1959, while indicating that, given the history of relations between Cuba and the United States, the Cubans should be good friends with the United States. He suggested that the Cubans didn't know what their true interests were and that they were, to say the least, ungrateful for the help the United States had provided. By 1961, President John F. Kennedy was claiming that the revolution was controlled by external forces and loyal to an extrahemispheric ideology.

US officials frequently portrayed the Castro regime as a satellite or a puppet of the Soviet Union, which had a degree of plausibility during the Cuban Missile Crisis, at least. But the inability of the United States to accept that Castro was an active agent is a good example of Cold War thinking. Students should be encouraged to try to understand how Castro sought to further revolution throughout the Western Hemisphere, frequently in opposition to the interests of the Soviet Union itself, which in the 1960s was seeking to forge normal diplomatic relations with Latin America countries of many different types. Castro and his associate Ernesto "Che" Guevara inspired, trained, and occasionally armed Latin America revolutionaries, many of them middle-class university students.

For some in Latin America, the Cuban revolution inspired dreams of egalitarian societies forged through revolutionary violence and popular mobilization. Cuba's increasing economic dependence on the Soviet Union was less important for many Latin Americans than the fact that it had broken free from the US orbit. Castro's Cuba, however, inspired a fear among Latin America's upper class and even its middle class that their traditional privileges would be lost, and the armed forces worried that they would be replaced by a revolutionary army.[6] Some undoubtedly feared as well that civil liberties where they existed would be curtailed, but most countries that experienced Castro-style insurgencies (Venezuela being a notable exception) did not enjoy them. Internally, Cold War alliances were often forged between the elite and the military (where they did not exist already), and sometimes the Latin American middle class as well gave their support to the establishment of military dictatorships. The Cuban revolution and its progeny led to a great fear of internal subversion. The United States briefly, during the administrations of Kennedy and Lyndon Baines Johnson, supported reform efforts in parts of Latin America under the Alliance for Progress to lessen the appeal of the Cuban revolutionary model. Long-term efforts to promote stability led to the aforementioned increased US military aid and counterinsurgency training under Kennedy and Johnson and, ultimately, by the late 1960s and 1970s, to support for some of the most brutal military dictatorships the region had ever seen. Despite the widespread (and understandable) concern with guerrilla movements in Latin America following Fidel Castro's dramatic left turn, officials rarely reflected deeply on the internal reasons for the insurgencies' widespread failure in countries not named Cuba or Nicaragua.

Threat perception is one of those issues that certainly need to be addressed in any course on the Cold War. Given that the US commitment to containing communism was usually perceived as a global one and that US resources were not limitless, when was it necessary for the United States to act and react, and how? Students should be encouraged to challenge themselves to understand why US officials found so many politicians of widely varying ideological persuasions, from populists to socialists, particularly those who had been democratically elected, to be so threatening during the Cold War.[7] Students also need to be challenged to address the question of why the United States was almost never committed to the nurturing of democratic traditions in Latin America. And, although certainly some of the nations had only limited experience with democracy, a country like Chile, whose political system seemed in the 1960s to be a model of constitutional longevity and legitimacy, pluralism, and military subordination to civilian authority, would see these traditions destroyed following a US-supported coup on the "other September 11," in 1973.

The government of Salvador Allende and its overthrow is a subject that needs to be addressed in a course on the Cold War. It has attracted plentiful attention from journalists and scholars. While we hardly know everything we would like to know about the coup itself, we can hardly ignore it if we are going to address the impact of the Cold War on Latin America. A lovely book about the revolutionary process that Allende's Chilean path to socialism ("with red wine and empanadas") exemplified, told through oral histories and from the bottom up, is Peter Winn's classic *Weavers of Revolution*. (Instructors may wish to consult this book for background purposes.) The most recent and most sophisticated treatment of the interaction between a number of historical actors, not only Chilean and US leaders but also Brazilians and Cubans, is Tanya Harmer's *Allende's Chile and the Inter-American Cold War*. It is one of the best examples of an international study that, for a change, actually demonstrates the necessity of taking seriously the agency of Latin Americans themselves during the Cold War. Whether it is too sophisticated for your undergraduate class I will have to leave it up to you to judge. Even after almost two decades of full-time teaching, I have been known to overestimate my students' abilities and willingness to read even straightforward historical accounts like Harmer's.

The nature of the Cold War military dictatorships that the United States supported in the 1960s and 1970s deserves as much attention as if not more than the Cuban Revolution because these dictatorships were far more numerous and affected far more people. For many of my students, the idea of a "pro-American dictator" is particularly hard to swallow. It is often a concept to which they have never been introduced, and it is one they find unsettling. For many it upsets an unquestioned world view. And, to judge from my experience, some never do accept the notion that such a thing as a pro-American dictator can exist. (Their use of historical evidence to refute it, of course, is not necessarily all that impressive.)

A related subject in this regard is the concept of human rights. It doesn't occur to my students that it could have ever not been an issue that a US ally tortures or murders its own people. Students find this unsettling as well, in some cases because they often believe that after the Holocaust there was a universal acceptance of the idea of human rights as enshrined in the United Nations declaration of 1948. And, for some, it helps if you have them view a movie that addresses the issue directly.

Many important events during Latin America's Cold War have not inspired particularly good movies. Nevertheless, there are a number of excellent films that help students understand aspects of Cold War Latin American history and often make what you have lectured about in class seem more real. It often helps, I have found, if the film tells a compelling individual's story. In this regard, the 1982 film *Missing*, by the left-wing Greek director Costa-Gavras, is well worth viewing with a class. It tells the story of a young US citizen named Charles Horman who was drawn to the Popular Unity attempt to create the peaceful path to socialism under Allende. Horman was one of two US citizens who disappeared after Allende was overthrown in 1973; the other was Frank Teruggi, who is also a character in the film. You might choose to ask the students to write a paper based on the movie and a collection of primary documents put together by Peter Kornbluh of the National Security Archive.[8] Kornbluh has a chapter on Horman and Teruggi in *The Pinochet File*. Students could be encouraged to write a paper examining what the documents can tell us and what they can't tell us about the coup and its aftermath in Chile in general and about Horman and Teruggi in particular. The documents Kornbluh is able to provide do not prove that US involvement in the coup was as direct as the filmmakers contend. This does not undercut the power of the film's portrayal of what happened to Horman and Teruggi themselves.

Another movie worth assigning in a class on the Cold War is the Brazilian film *Four Days in September*. Based on a memoir by Fernando Gabeira, a Brazilian author and politician, it tells the story of the kidnapping of US ambassador Charles Burke Elbrick in 1969. Students are often surprised to find themselves sympathizing with anti-American "terrorists" like Gabeira, who were seeking a way to break through the censorship of the mass media to get out their message about the military government's torture of Brazilian citizens and to win the freedom of some of their fellow guerrillas. The movie, released in 1997, definitely has a post–Cold War perspective in that many of the characters (kidnappers

and kidnap victims, torturers and tortured) are portrayed sympathetically, not least of all Elbrick himself, a likable man who is depicted as
having been personally opposed to US support for the Brazilian military government. The movie can be used in conjunction with the book
*We Cannot Remain Silent: Opposition to the Brazilian Military Dictatorship
in the United States* by James N. Green, which provides an important
contribution to the development of human rights as an issue in US
foreign relations.

It may be argued that most good movies set in Cold War Latin
America have a left-wing perspective. That I won't deny. But *Four Days
in September* and even a film like Oliver Stone's *Salvador* (1986) provide
their share of criticism of many sides in the conflicts they depict. And,
undoubtedly, many of our students now are able to "read" a film more
critically than they can a book or article.

The human rights paradigm promised to simplify foreign-policy
decision making. But few governments with international interests have
found it easy to limit their allies to only those with admirable human
rights records. Human rights and torture remain significant issues
worth discussing with our students. There is always the danger of suc-
cumbing to the twisted attractions of the actual practices of torture
themselves (what some people call torture pornography). We need to
address this issue as well and guard against it. In any case, the torture
and disappearance of thousands of people need to be factored into the
larger question of the costs of the Cold War, which were so often ob-
scured in the triumphalism that accompanied the collapse of the Soviet
empire in Eastern Europe and the implosion of the Soviet Union itself.

The last major turning point of the Cold War was the overthrow of
the long-standing Somoza dynasty (1936–79) in Nicaragua by the San-
dinistas. Coming as it did only months after the defeat of another pro-
American leader, the Shah of Iran, and only months before the Soviet
invasion of Afghanistan, it became part of the larger picture of a renewed
sense of threat in the Western Hemisphere and around the world as the
relaxation of tensions between the United States and the Soviet Union
ended. The focus of the United States in the hemisphere narrowed more
dramatically as the United States sought through various means to
influence (under Carter) or overthrow (under Reagan) the Sandinista
government, while trying to prevent a guerrilla victory in El Salvador.

The Central American wars of the 1980s inspired a wide variety of
political activities in the United States. There were direct protests of US

policy that drew heavily upon the Vietnam analogy (although one could argue that the "No More Vietnams" metaphor could have cut more than one way). I myself can remember marching through the streets of New York, chanting "No draft, no war, US out of El Salvador." There were also sister-city projects that reached out to municipalities in Nicaragua as well as the sanctuary movement, which provided shelter for Central American refugees. Depending upon where you teach, you may be able to encourage your students to engage in oral-history projects related to these activities. Or, for that matter, you may be able to find people who served as military advisers in El Salvador who would be willing to talk about what they did. (My own experience has been that they are proud of what they believe they accomplished.) Students may be interested to discover that the George W. Bush administration remembered 1980s El Salvador as a positive model for how to succeed in Iraq.

For those interested in making use of online primary-source documents, the best place to start is the National Security Archives website (www2.gwu.edu/~nsarchiv/). It has materials related to the topics discussed in this chapter: Guatemala, El Salvador, Chile, Nicaragua, and human rights policy, as well as the Cuban Missile Crisis and Iran-Contra. There also are collections devoted to Henry Kissinger's conversations.

A course on the global Cold War probably will not be able to cover the coups in Guatemala and Chile, the Cuban revolution, and the rightist military dictatorships, as well as the revolutions and civil wars in Central America. You will have to weigh which ones seem most essential to your course. (And you may want to ponder why the Cold War with Cuba continued even as the United States maintained good relations with China and even Vietnam.) But I hope that my exploration of these issues will help you sort out which ones cannot be ignored. We owe it to our students to not neglect the region as so many US officials did.

NOTES

1. Having assigned Gaddis Smith's *The Last Years of the Monroe Doctrine* recently, I was somewhat surprised to discover how much my understanding of Cold War US–Latin American relations still owes to this book, which is more a general history of the subject than a focused examination of the Monroe Doctrine itself.

2. The quotation comes from Piero Gleijeses, *Shattered Hope*, 3.

3. The literature on this subject is unusually rich. I most admire Gleijeses, *Shattered Hope*, and the relevant section of Paul Dosal, *Doing Business with the Dictators*.

4. See Stephen Schlesinger and Stephen Kinzer, *Bitter Fruit: The Untold Story of the Coup in Guatemala* (Cambridge, MA: Harvard University Press, 2005).

5. Cullather, *Secret History*, 7.

6. My treatment here is strongly influenced by Thomas C. Wright, *Latin America in the Era of the Cuban Revolution*.

7. A good source here is Peter Kornbluh, ed., *The Pinochet File: A Declassified File on Atrocity and Accountability*.

8. Ibid. The movie is based on Thomas Hauser, *The Execution of Charles Horman: An American Sacrifice*.

KEY RESOURCES

Cullather, Nick. *Secret History: The CIA's Classified Account of Its Operations in Guatemala, 1952–1954*. 2nd ed. Palo Alto: Stanford University Press, 2006.

Dosal, Paul. *Doing Business with the Dictators: A Political History of United Fruit in Guatemala, 1899–1944*. Wilmington, DE: Scholarly Resources, 1993.

Gleijeses, Piero. *Shattered Hope: The Guatemalan Revolution and the United States, 1944–1954*. Princeton: Princeton University Press, 1991.

Green, James N. *We Cannot Remain Silent: Opposition to the Brazilian Military Dictatorship in the United States*. Durham, NC: Duke University Press, 2010.

Harmer, Tanya. *Allende's Chile and the Inter-American Cold War*. Chapel Hill: University of North Carolina Press, 2012.

Hauser, Thomas. *The Execution of Charles Horman: An American Sacrifice*. New York: Harcourt Brace Jovanovich, 1978.

Joseph, Gilbert M., and Greg Grandin, eds. *A Century of War: Insurgent and Counterinsurgent Violence during Latin America's Cold War*. Durham, NC: Duke University Press, 2010.

Kornbluh, Peter, ed. *The Pinochet File: A Declassified Dossier on Atrocity and Accountability*. New York: New Press, 2003.

LeoGrande, William M. *Our Own Backyard: The United States in Central America, 1977–1992*. Chapel Hill: University of North Carolina Press, 1992.

Peace, Roger. *A Call to Conscience: The Anti-Contra War Campaign*. Amherst: University of Massachusetts Press, 2012.

Rabe, Stephen G. *The Killing Zone: The United States Wages Cold War in Latin America*. New York: Oxford University Press, 2012.

Schlesinger, Stephen, and Stephen Kinzer. *Bitter Fruit: The Untold Story of the Coup in Guatemala*. Cambridge, MA: Harvard University Press, 2005.

Sikkink, Kathryn. *Mixed Signals: US Human Rights Policy and Latin America*. Ithaca, NY: Cornell University Press, 2004.

Smith, Christian. *Resisting Reagan: The US Central America Peace Movement*. Chicago: University of Chicago Press, 1996.

Smith, Gaddis. *The Last Years of the Monroe Doctrine, 1945–1993*. New York: Hill & Wang, 1994.

Winn, Peter. *Weavers of Revolution: The Yarur Workers and Chile's Road to Socialism*. New York: Oxford University Press, 1986.

Wright, Thomas C. *Latin America in the Era of the Cuban Revolution*. New York: Praeger, 2000.

The Cold War in Africa

RYAN M. IRWIN

W here does Africa fit into a class about the Cold War? My first book examined African decolonization, and I'll be honest: I have a hard time with this question. In the classroom, Cold War Africa slips between the cracks. It is a subject that is taught everywhere, but, depending on the department and the faculty, it is covered differently, which tends to undercut a straightforward answer to the question.

As a teacher, I have engaged with Cold War Africa in several ways. I first taught African history in a survey-level course that was cross-listed in an African and African American Studies Department, where I emphasized African perspectives over the intrigues of great powers. My goal was to introduce students to Africa's diversity and to do so in a way that dispelled myths about the continent and its inhabitants. Today, as my department's US world historian, I cover Cold War Africa from a global perspective and tend to use episodes from Africa's past to substantiate arguments about the international system. In these two settings I have stressed different themes and turning points. Depending on your course's pedagogical objectives, the Cold War in Africa can reveal truths about everything from midcentury labor norms to late-century guerrilla warfare—and that's just scratching the surface.

If this chapter has an argument, it is that this diversity makes Africa critical to Cold War history, especially in the classroom. As a place and an idea, Africa provides unique insight into world affairs after 1945, and while it may seem like a challenge, you should teach a module about the continent in your Cold War class. This chapter explores some of the ways you could think about Africa and the Cold War and introduces a few techniques for engaging undergraduate students.

The Elephant

Let's begin by addressing the elephant in the room: Did Africa matter in the Cold War? The fact that I'm chapter 17 doesn't bode well. Covering Europe is a no-brainer—the Iron Curtain ran through that continent and German unification marked the end of the superpower contest. Asia matters for self-evident reasons as well. Beyond the Vietnam imbroglio, Mao Zedong's rise to power created rifts within the communist world and horrific periods of mass violence. Deng Xiaoping, in turn, facilitated the Sino-American rapprochement that shapes global politics today. Latin America saw the Cuban Missile Crisis and a string of covert American interventions, giving that region a natural place in your course, and the Middle East witnessed dramatic violence over . . . well, *everything*. From religion and war to oil and nationalism, that region was ground zero for intractable Cold War problems. You can't cover every topic in a single semester, and I recognize that it's tempting to cut Africa from your syllabus. At first glance, the continent simply lacks the urgency and relevance of these other places.[1]

Don't do it! Africa reveals crucial dimensions of the Cold War. Most obviously, it exposes the danger of lumping a whole continent together in a single analytical frame; Africa is a remarkably diverse place, and its peoples are linked in multifarious ways to the Americas, South Asia, and the Middle East. In the early decades of the superpower rivalry, Europe's commitment to ruling over this region divided the North Atlantic community, which is a topic that raises profound questions about Western unity and pan-European power. It is no secret that the United States struggled to walk the line between containment and decolonization after World War II, and in Algeria, Kenya, and South Africa, among other locales, nationalists and imperialists jockeyed for American support, forcing Washingtonians to ponder whether their country could be powerful and popular in the postcolonial age. After the 1960s, this road became tougher still, partly because the superpowers could not resist the temptation to meddle in Africa's affairs. Despite bloviating about noninterference, Washington and Moscow saw the same thing—a vacuum of continental proportions—and orchestrated interventions that were ignominious then and teachable now.

In fact, some of the Cold War's seminal events unfolded in Africa. Algeria's revolution, which raged from 1954 to 1962, brought down France's Fourth Republic and served as a clarion call for worldwide anti-imperial revolution. Farther south, the Congo crisis of 1960–65 led to a sprawling UN intervention that effectively destroyed that organization's peacekeeping credibility. Nigeria's Biafra War claimed one million lives and raised profound questions about postcolonial sovereignty, while Angola's civil war became the first proxy conflict of the post-Vietnam era. The horn of Africa was a hotbed of superpower intrigue during the 1970s, and the fight against apartheid vexed Ronald Reagan's administration as much as the Iran-Contra scandal during the 1980s. In fact, Nelson Mandela's victory over apartheid, which overlapped with Mikhail Gorbachev's fall from power in Moscow, had more influence on the intellectual horizon line of the 1990s than any of George H. W. Bush's thousand points of light.

When I explain Cold War Africa to my students, I tend to emphasize two themes. The first is decolonization, which shaped the context around the superpower conflict and presented Washington and Moscow with many opportunities but an equal number of headaches. On one hand, the United States and the Soviet Union were drawn to the Congo in the early 1960s because it provided a stage on which to present the merits of their respective ideologies. Whoever had the most partners abroad, the argument went, had the better system, and Africa, most of which became independent between 1958 and 1964, was critical to this wider contest. On the other hand, decolonization revealed contradictions that Washington and Moscow preferred to ignore. Americans agonized over the continent because independence there exposed the United States' racist past, while the Soviets fretted because they could not get money and weapons to their new African friends, foreshadowing the logistical ineptitudes that accompanied the Soviet Union's demise. It is impossible to understand the superpower rivalry without decolonization.[2]

My second theme is internationalism. The Cold War was important, but it was not the postwar world's only international discourse, and Africa reveals the alternative solidarities that thrived during the second half of the twentieth century. Many leaders of the Pan-African movement, including Kwame Nkrumah and Nnamdi Azikiwe, who became heads of state in Ghana and Nigeria, respectively, attended university in the Americas, where they were ensconced in an intellectual milieu that questioned European ideas about power and order. Rather than identifying with liberalism or communism, these individuals campaigned for diasporic unity and racial equality—especially in regions affected by

266

the transatlantic slave trade—and, in the process, established novel alliances and networks around the world. Their efforts cultivated critiques of pan-European authority, breathed life into theories of dependency and neocolonialism, and led to cultural breakthroughs, especially in the realms of music and art. Africa's diversity and vitality challenged the stifling bipolarity of the Cold War.[3]

Teaching students to see past the East-West paradigm is a lesson in itself. As historians, we distort the postwar period fundamentally if we ignore perspectives beyond those of Moscow and Washington, and Africa is particularly useful in explaining why the Soviet-American rivalry became global when it did and how that conflict affected people outside the Soviet Union and the United States. The Cold War's expansion beyond Eurasia overlapped with African decolonization, which, in turn, introduced new voices and ideas into the global arena. These developments matter as much as the German question and the Cuban Missile Crisis, and if students hope to understand the world created by the superpowers, there is no better place to study than Cold War Africa.

Your Toolkit

If you need a refresher on the particularities of African history after World War II, two books jump to mind: Frederick Cooper's *Africa since 1940* and Elizabeth Schmidt's *Foreign Intervention in Africa*. They explore Africa's recent history in complementary ways. More argumentative than your typical textbook and more synthetic than a scholarly monograph, they will leave you with an answer to that most basic of riddles: Who did what to whom—and when'd they do it?

Africa since 1940 is about Europe and Africa. Organized thematically, Cooper's narrative explains the crisis of midcentury colonialism and the rise of what he terms the "gatekeeper" state in Africa. The book begins with the premise that development, specifically government-backed, expert-led planning projects, captured the imagination of European imperialists after the 1940s. This infatuation facilitated debates about African labor, which, in turn, led to conversations about citizenship that African nationalists reshaped into the fight for self-government. As Cooper peels back the layers of this story, he pinpoints why so many national states resemble their colonial predecessors in Africa. Before and after independence, governments relied on recognition and resources from abroad; irrespective of who was in control, leaders could not reinvent local people as predictable, loyal citizen-workers. Africa's post-colonial difficulties, in other words, stem from expectations that were woven into decolonization.[4]

Conspicuously absent from Cooper's work is the Cold War, which *Foreign Intervention in Africa* covers in great detail. Schmidt provides a compendium of superpower flare-ups in Africa and argues that out-siders changed local affairs by escalating benign disagreements into hostile conflagrations. She points her critical eye in a very different place from Cooper. Each chapter is devoted to a specific region, touching on everything from the Suez Crisis of 1956 to Portuguese decolonization in 1975. There are pictures and maps galore, as well as up-to-date reading lists about American and Soviet foreign policy in Africa. The book skims over the peculiarities of postcolonial sovereignty and the logic of great-power diplomacy, which makes Schmidt's conclusions more predictable than Cooper's views in *Africa since 1940*: the bad guys are to blame. Yet *Foreign Intervention in Africa* excels as an overview of the high cost of hubris and convincingly documents the Cold War's effects across the continent.[5]

In terms of student reading, I'd recommend a few texts. If you use historical monographs in the classroom, two stalwart texts are Odd Arne Westad's *Global Cold War* and Piero Gleijeses's *Conflicting Missions*. Westad's book is wide ranging, and its first half, which outlines the author's ideas about modernization, stimulates students, even if the later chapters, which include case studies about Southern Africa and the Horn of Africa, leave them a little dazed.[6] *Conflicting Missions* is narrower in focus, covering Cuba's military escapades after 1960, and generally provokes quality classroom debate.[7] The downside of *Conflicting Missions* is that it's a big book, so it requires time to teach, which creates problems if your syllabus moves through the Third World quickly. Gleijeses's more recent *Visions of Freedom* has the same strengths and weaknesses; it's essentially a sequel to *Conflicting Missions*.[8] There are also monographs about Algeria and South Africa and terrific scholar-ship on Egypt and West Africa, but nothing with the same punch as *The Global Cold War*, *Conflicting Missions*, and *Visions of Freedom*.[9]

If you assign memoirs, there are many options. Nelson Mandela's *Conversations with Myself* is excellent. It is less polished than his acclaimed *Long Walk to Freedom*, and it includes primary sources that illuminate his evolving ideas about freedom and resistance and provide frank thoughts on racial justice and geopolitics.[10] Peter Goodwin's *Mukiwa* explores similar themes from a European-settler perspective. The book is a riveting account of Rhodesian colonialism, which explains how that world, anchored by racial paternalism and anticommunism, fell apart after the 1960s.[11] Helene Cooper also experiences hardship in *The House at Sugar Bay*. Born into Liberia's ruling class in the mid-1960s, she saw her life destroyed by civil war in the 1980s, and she provides her reader with powerful source material to talk about the human dimensions of Cold War Africa.[12] The list could go on, but these volumes do comparable things, namely encourage students to see the Cold War through non-American eyes.

There are also document collections. *The Cold War*, edited by Jussi Hanhimaki and Odd Arne Westad, includes some speeches by prominent African leaders.[13] If you'd prefer to burrow into a specific crisis, the Wilson Center's Cold War International History Project has materials about the Horn of Africa between 1977 and 1978, South Africa's nuclear program, and the Nonaligned Movement.[14] The US State Department's *Foreign Relations of the United States* series includes many volumes about US policy in Africa, which are available online through the State Department's webpage; the multivolume *From Protest to Challenge* is a documentary history of South Africa's freedom struggle, edited by Thomas Karis, Gwendolen Carter, and Gail Gerhardt.[15] The former is admittedly US-centric, and the latter is better suited for courses about the anti-apartheid movement, but both volumes offer quality insights about Cold War Africa.

Teaching Algeria

There are many ways to use these books. My own approach is a bit quirky. When teaching the Cold War as a stand-alone subject, I adopt an episodic classroom method, organizing the semester's first half around six turning points and the second half around a multistage student research project. Although the turning points vary each semester, they involve a Tuesday lecture, which explains the event's importance, and a Thursday activity that requires hands-on learning. As the course proceeds, students receive tutorials about the research process, and they complete assignments that encourage textual analysis and reading comprehension.

Eventually, students identify their own Cold War turning point. Once they have a topic, they craft an appropriate research question and create an annotated bibliography of primary and secondary sources. Students end the semester with a presentation to the class, as well as an essay that evaluates their research experience and explains how they would use their material to write a fifteen-page research paper. In this respect, my learning objectives inform the way I contextualize Cold War Africa. The class is about the research process first and foremost, and it is designed to leave students with a deep understanding of how to frame a question, obtain and evaluate relevant information, and organize a persuasive, evidence-backed interpretation.

At least one of my six turning points is always about Africa. Last time I taught the course, we looked closely at the Algerian revolution. This particular session came a week after I had covered the Cold War's origins, so, building on that previous activity, we began by discussing the West and East as constructed political categories, and I introduced a question: Could the United States prevent communism in the North Atlantic while creating new partnerships in Asia and Africa? The basic tension was obvious enough—Europe's empires needed America's money after World War II—which led to a conversation about anticommunism and anticolonialism, as well as a lecture about US foreign policy toward Japan, the Philippines, South Asia, and Indonesia during the early Cold War. My argument was fairly straightforward: Washington wanted to have its cake and eat it too. Specifically, the United States tried to walk a tightrope in these years, incorporating decolonized countries into an interdependent political order held together by collective security agreements, free trade pacts, and UN diplomacy, which would, theoretically, replace European imperialism but perpetuate Western power.[16]

Trouble came in Algeria. French *colons* saw the territory as home; Algerian nationalists wanted self-determination. As the conflict attracted more attention, Washington's tightrope became narrower, and, despite the best efforts of US officialdom, the United Nations evolved from a bulwark of US influence into a redoubt of postcolonial sentiment. New national states were interdependent, but few accepted the premise that liberation and liberalism were mutually constitutive. The lecture looked at this tension through the eyes of Washington and Paris and then turned to Algeria's National Liberation Front (FLN), which successfully made its fight into a cause célèbre at the UN General Assembly. Despite the FLN's defeat in Algiers, its support in New York paved the way for the 1962 Évian accords, which dramatized a teachable paradox: while no country had more power than the United States in these years, forging a new international order—finding that *perfect* balance between anticommunism and anticolonialism—proved to be nearly impossible.[17]

In the Thursday class, we explored this claim with a hands-on activity. The week's assignment was to watch *The Battle of Algiers*, which I uploaded to Blackboard, and the students read Peter Matthews's essay on the film, "The Battle of Algiers: Bombs and Boomerangs."[18] Using these sources and my lecture, the class came to Thursday's session with a five-paragraph essay in hand, which explained (1) the Algerian revolution's timeline, (2) the FLN's worldview, (3) its strategy for gaining independence, (4) the group's tactics or methods, and (5) the conflict's historical legacy. Rather than jumping straight into these papers, I opened the class with a curveball: Does morality have a place in history? The question was purposefully abstract, and the students responded well, sharing ideas about violence and religion and tackling the gap between past and present moral norms.

We chewed on this topic for about five minutes and then transitioned from the clouds to the trenches: Was the Algerian revolution a moral struggle? In search of answers, we watched a thirty-minute selection from *The Battle of Algiers*, specifically chapters 9–16 of the DVD, which begins with the barricading of Algiers's Muslim quarter and concludes with the arrival of French military forces in the city. In theory, the students were familiar with these scenes, which show the FLN's assassination campaign after the barricade's erection and the French authority's misguided retaliation against an innocent Muslim family. The movie continues with a famous scene in which several FLN women detonate explosives at different tourist destinations in Algiers, and it ends with the arrival of French paratroopers and an overview of France's counterinsurgency strategy. Taken as a whole, the clip shows the steady escalation of violence on both sides during 1956.

The ensuing discussion lasted for approximately forty minutes. Between the paper and preliminary chat, the students were primed, and we began by talking about *The Battle of Algiers* as a source, which gave me an opportunity to explain the film's history.[19] We then returned to morality, and I managed the discussion by bouncing between comprehension and opinion questions. I had the students interpret specific scenes—the false arrest of a Muslim peddler and the role of gender, among others—and used their responses to set up bigger questions:

Was the FLN a freedom movement and terrorist organization? Was conventional warfare different from guerrilla warfare? Was torture an acceptable method of counterinsurgency? The students were split on the role of violence, which I anticipated, with many people harking back to India's experiences to make an argument against the FLN's methods. With fifteen minutes to go, I introduced an excerpt from Frantz Fanon's *Wretched of the Earth,* specifically his opening paragraphs in "Concerning Violence."[20] The students responded, and I concluded the session with a riddle: Had I asked the wrong question on Tuesday? Did my question—which dealt with US grand strategy—fail to capture the true stakes of the Algerian revolution? Had I failed as an historian?

Taken together, the lecture and activity worked on two levels. First, they provided students with multiple perspectives on a complex event. Tuesday's lecture explained the context of the struggle in Algeria, while Thursday's activity put the class in Algiers. The paper was a bridge between these two activities, clarifying the FLN's worldview and strategy and setting up an exchange about the past's moral ambiguities. Second, the lesson got students to think about the relationship between the questions historians ask in the present and the stories they tell about the past. This lesson became more important during the semester's second half, when each student identified a turning point and articulated a research question, so the activity planted seeds that were nurtured as the course proceeded.

Teaching Angola

In previous years, I've taught Cold War Africa by focusing on the Angolan civil war. This session came later in the semester, and I took a slightly different approach by concentrating on the mid-1970s, not Angola per se. During the previous week, we had covered Vietnam, and my Tuesday lecture opened with this question: Why did the United States remain so powerful after that war? Washington had been defeated, after all, and that defeat had happened against the backdrop of rising energy costs, economic stagnation, and political crisis. Yet, within a decade, Americans were poised to win the superpower contest, which, I argued, represented one of the great mysteries of late-twentieth-century diplomatic history.

My lecture suggested two explanations. First, other countries failed to supplant the United States. This claim set up an overview of Mao's

China—picking up on an earlier lecture, I discussed the Cultural Revolution and the tumult following Mao's death in 1976—and it facilitated a discussion about Leonid Brezhnev's tenure as leader of the Soviet Union, which left Mother Russia in worse shape than Uncle Sam. Within the West, neither Europe nor Japan repudiated the United States, partly because the status quo worked so well for both. Despite squabbles with Washington, America's allies enjoyed access to the world's largest marketplace and protections by the world's biggest military. That left the third world, which, despite its many speeches at the UN General Assembly—and a divisive oil embargo—struggled on every front imaginable during the mid-1970s. The bottom line was that the Cold War was uniquely dysfunctional after Vietnam.[21]

Second, the United States found new ways to project its influence abroad. Most obviously, it became less ambitious, cutting foreign aid and abandoning dreams about liberal internationalism, while deepening its ties to states that behaved as American proxies in Africa, Asia, the Middle East, and Latin America. Many of these partnerships had been established in the early Cold War, but this approach became more critical to US grand strategy during these years—an argument I substantiated by explaining US foreign policy toward Congo, Saudi Arabia, Indonesia, and Argentina. In each case, I suggested, the US government built alliances with authoritarian military officials—despite concerns about human rights—and used these inroads to fund regional campaigns against communism. The Angolan civil war revealed this approach beautifully; rather than building dams or deploying GIs, the United States worked covertly with Kinshasa and Pretoria to destabilize the entire country. If the United States couldn't have its cake, it would create so much chaos that no one emerged victorious.

This cheerful thought became the starting point of Thursday's class. I had the students reflect on my claims by doing a role-playing activity. As a group, we transported ourselves to early 1976, with each student assigned a different character from that time. The week's reading included a one-page character sketch—which also explained that person's job description—and some common readings from Gleijeses's *Conflicting Missions*. Additionally, students received a modest packet of primary sources from Volume 28, *Southern Africa*, of *Foreign Relations of the United States (FRUS)*.[22] I had just under forty students that year, so I divided people into four groups and asked them to come to class with a five-paragraph overview of (1) their character's background, (2) the reasons their character cared about Angola, (3) their character's strategy for the region, (4) some tactics to advance that strategy, and (5) their character's worst-case scenario.

The activity required preparation. The characters included President Gerald Ford, Secretary of State Henry Kissinger, Secretary of Defense Donald Rumsfeld, Assistant to the President for National Security Affairs Brent Scowcroft, Chairman of the Joint Chiefs Joseph Brown, CIA Director George H. W. Bush, Undersecretary of State for Political Affairs Joseph Sisco, Assistant Secretary of State for African Affairs William Schaufele, and UN Ambassador Daniel Patrick Moynihan. My character sketches were written carefully, and each one provided historical context and some gossip. In theory, these sketches helped the students read the primary source packet more critically. I invited people to read the material closely and to consider the spirit of their character. When it came time to role-play, improvisation was fine, so long as it was plausible. It was unlikely, for instance, that Brown was a closeted pacifist, but not impossible that Sisco cared about congressional sentiment.

We began class by establishing some context. I told the groups that it was early 1976; two months earlier, Fidel Castro had sent soldiers to Angola, ostensibly because South Africa expanded had its military presence in the area after the collapse of Portuguese imperialism. In response to these developments, President Ford had authorized a covert CIA mission in Angola in late 1975 that essentially funneled money to anticommunist forces in the region, but the mission had not started well. Now, in early 1976, Washington's local allies were asking for more money, claiming that the fight was turning against them, and US intelligence, while inconclusive in many respects, indicated that the conflict was indeed *tilting* toward Cuba and the communists. The American public, for its part, was tired of war, and Congress would almost surely rebuke a US mission in Africa if Ford's actions became public. The president was sitting between a rock and a hard place. His popularity, hanging by a thread because of Watergate, would plummet if he sent US troops to Angola and evaporate if he lost a domino there.

The activity unfolded in two parts. To begin, each group's president was given an agenda for a thirty-minute meeting, with items that reflected the day's essay assignment. The president opened by asking some questions: What were the risks and rewards of expanding America's mission in Angola? Did the United States need to fight communism in southern Africa? If the group established consensus on the mission, the conversation segued to strategy and tactics: How could the United States win? What would victory look like? Should the mission be bigger—and who should get US aid? When the conversation lagged, the president called on individual members, and the primary sources gave each group some guidance and inspiration, so they had a vague sense of the situation and their character's talking points. Students labored with specific instructions: they would present a plan of action to the class at the session's halfway mark.

However, instead of proceeding with these presentations, I ambushed them with an announcement: Congress had just passed legislation that prohibited direct aid to Angolan rebels. It took them a few minutes to regain their bearings. As I walked around the class, I nudged each group to return to its worst-case scenario: Was this it? With about thirty minutes to go, I told the students that each group had to reformulate its action plan, which we'd share at the fifteen-minute mark.

The results were fascinating. Some groups decided to accept Congress's authority; others concocted plans that made Watergate seem lily white; still others announced they'd shift US aid from anticommunist rebels in Angola to leaders in Zaire, South Africa, and Zambia. At the end of class, I distributed additional *FRUS* documents that explained what actually happened in early 1976, and we finished class by returning to my thesis from Tuesday. Students tended to agree: I'd lied to them. Even if I had captured the big picture, US policymaking was more contentious and more complex than I had indicated two days earlier.

Mission accomplished. Like the Algeria activity, this project encouraged students to think about a complex event from multiple perspectives. However, students were beginning to research their individual projects at this point in the semester, so this time I opted for an activity that involved primary-source analysis, since they were beginning to collect primary sources for their annotated bibliographies. Role-playing forced them to read each document closely and to reflect on events through the eyes of an historical actor. No matter the student's preparation, at some point in the activity each student improvised, taking an educated guess about what his or her character would say in a situation, which reinforced lessons about imagination and empathy. These lessons blossomed as each student completed a unique research project at the end of the semester. Those who invested in the learning process left the course with a deep appreciation of historical thinking—of the art of balancing arguments and facts—and skills they then transferred to upper-level history courses as they proceeded through the major.

Conclusions

Where does Africa fit into a class about the Cold War? With a little creativity, anywhere you want! The continent's diversity makes it essential to postwar history, and as a place and an idea, Africa provides special insight into the superpower rivalry—into its geographic scope and its local impact. It may seem like a challenge to find a place for Africa on your syllabus, but dig deeper and you'll be rewarded handsomely. Looking at Cold War Africa encourages students to get beyond clichés about spies and walls and helps them rethink their assumptions about the world today.

NOTES

1. For representative texts, see Martin Walker, *The Cold War: A History* (New York: Holt, 1993); John Lewis Gaddis, *The Cold War: A New History* (New York: Penguin, 2006); and Carole Fink, *The Cold War: An International History* (Boulder, CO: Westview Press, 2013).

2. For an introduction, see Prasenjit Duara, ed., *Decolonization: Perspectives from Now and Then* (New York: Routledge, 2004); Leslie James and Elizabeth Leake, eds., *Decolonization and the Cold War: Negotiating Independence* (New York: Bloomsbury, 2015); Robert McMahon, ed., *The Cold War in the Third World* (New York: Oxford University Press, 2013).

3. For an introduction, see Patrick Manning, *The African Diaspora: A History through Culture* (New York: Columbia University Press, 2009); Minkah Makalani, *In the Cause of Freedom: Radical Black Internationalism from Harlem to London, 1917–1939* (Chapel Hill: University of North Carolina Press, 2011); Nikhil Pah Singh, *Black Is a Country: Race and the Unfinished Struggle for Democracy* (Cambridge, MA: Harvard University Press, 2005).

4. Frederick Cooper, *Africa since 1940: The Past of the Present* (Cambridge: Cambridge University Press, 2002).

5. Elizabeth Schmidt, *Foreign Intervention in Africa: From the Cold War to the War on Terror* (Cambridge: Cambridge University Press, 2013).

6. Odd Arne Westad, *The Global Cold War: Third World Interventions and the Making of Our Times* (Cambridge: Cambridge University Press, 2006).

7. Piero Gleijeses, *Conflicting Missions: Havana, Washington, and Africa, 1959–1976* (Chapel Hill: University of North Carolina Press, 2003).

8. Piero Gleijeses, *Visions of Freedom: Havana, Washington, Pretoria, and the Struggle for Southern Africa, 1976–1991* (Chapel Hill: University of North Carolina Press, 2013).

9. For an introduction, see Matthew Connelly, *A Diplomatic Revolution: Algeria's Fight for Independence and the Origins of the Post–Cold War Era* (New York: Oxford University Press, 2002); Ryan Irwin, *Gordian Knot: Apartheid and the Unmaking of the Liberal World Order* (New York: Oxford University Press, 2012); Jeffrey Byrne, *Mecca of Revolution: From the Algerian Front of the Third World's Cold War* (New York: Oxford University Press, 2016); Elizabeth Schmidt, *Cold War and Decolonization in Guinea, 1946–1958* (Athens: Ohio University Press, 2008); Salim Yaqub, *Containing Arab Nationalism: The Eisenhower Doctrine and the Middle East* (Chapel Hill: University of North Carolina Press, 2004).

10. Nelson Mandela, *Conversations with Myself* (New York: Farrar, Straus & Giroux, 2010).

11. Peter Goodwin, *Mukiwa: A White Boy in Africa* (Johannesburg: Picador, 1996).

12. Helene Cooper, *The House at Sugar Bay: In Search of a Lost African Childhood* (New York: Simon & Schuster, 2009).

13. Jussi Hanhimaki and Odd Arne Westad, ed., *The Cold War: A History in Documents and Eyewitness Accounts* (New York: Oxford University Press, 2004).

14. For an overview, see the Wilson Center's Digital Archive, available online at http://digitalarchive.wilsoncenter.org.

15. The *Foreign Relations of the United States* series is available online at https://history.state.gov/historicaldocuments. Thomas Karis, Gwendolen Carter, and Gail Gerhardt, ed., *From Protest to Challenge: A Documentary History of African Politics in South Africa, 1882–1990*, 6 vols. (Stanford: Hoover Institution Press, 1972–2010).

16. For an introduction, see G. John Ikenberry, *Liberal Leviathan: The Origins, Crisis, and Transformation of the American World Order* (Princeton: Princeton University Press, 2011).

17. For an overview, see Connelly, *Diplomatic Revolution*.

18. *The Battle of Algiers*, dir. Gillo Pontecorvo (Casbah Films, 1966), which is available online: https://www.youtube.com/watch?v=y-j4WVTgWc. Matthews's essay was published with the Criterion Collection's 2004 DVD edition of the film and is available online: http://www.criterion.com/current/posts/342-the-battle-of-algiers-bombs-and-boomerangs.

19. For useful commentary about the film, watch disks 2–3 of *The Battle of Algiers* (Criterion Collection, 2004).

20. Frantz Fanon, *Wretched of the Earth*, trans. Constance Farrington (New York: Grove Press, 1963).

21. For an introduction, see Niall Ferguson, Charles S. Maier, Erez Manela,

and Daniel Sargent, eds., *The Shock of the Global: The 1970s in Perspective* (Cambridge, MA: Harvard University Press, 2010).

22. Edward C. Keefer and Myra Burton, eds., *Southern Africa*, Vol. 28, *Foreign Relations of the United States, 1969–1976* (Washington, DC: US Government Printing Office, 2011), selections from documents 137–180.

KEY RESOURCES

Cooper, Frederick. *Africa since 1940: The Past of the Present*. Cambridge: Cambridge University Press, 2002.

Cooper, Helene. *The House at Sugar Bay: In Search of a Lost African Childhood*. New York: Simon & Schuster, 2009.

Gleijeses, Piero. *Conflicting Missions: Havana, Washington, and Africa, 1959–1976*. Chapel Hill: University of North Carolina Press, 2003.

———. *Visions of Freedom: Havana, Washington, Pretoria, and the Struggle for Southern Africa, 1976–1991*. Chapel Hill: University of North Carolina Press, 2013.

Goodwin, Peter. *Mukiwa: A White Boy in Africa*. Johannesburg: Picador, 1996.

Hanhimaki, Jussi, and Odd Arne Westad, eds. *The Cold War: A History in Documents and Eyewitness Accounts*. New York: Oxford University Press, 2004.

Keefer, Edward C., and Myra Burton, eds. *Foreign Relations of the United States, 1969–1976*. Vol. 28: *Southern Africa*. Washington, DC: US Government Printing Office, 2011.

Mandela, Nelson. *Conversations with Myself*. New York: Farrar, Straus & Giroux, 2010.

Pontecorvo, Gillo, dir. *The Battle of Algiers*. Casbah Films, 1966.

Reynolds, Jonathan T. *Sovereignty and Struggle: Africa and Africans in the Era of the Cold War, 1945–1994*. New York: Oxford University Press, 2015.

Schmidt, Elizabeth. *Foreign Intervention in Africa: From the Cold War to the War on Terror*. Cambridge: Cambridge University Press, 2013.

Westad, Odd Arne. *The Global Cold War: Third World Interventions and the Making of Our Times*. Cambridge: Cambridge University Press, 2006.

A Pox on Both Your Houses

Neutralism and the Cold War

MARY ANN HEISS

From the Cold War's earliest moments, US officials framed it in starkly black-and-white terms that left no room for shades of gray. President Harry S. Truman's famous March 1947 speech enunciating the doctrine that bears his name described a rigidly bipolar world and claimed that "nearly every nation must choose between alternative ways of life." Not choosing, which would have amounted to opting out of the emerging bipolar conflict, Truman implied, was not an option.[1] A succession of US policymakers made the same point, arguing insistently that the world was made up of only two kinds of nations, members of the US-led Free World coalition and states allied with the opposite camp, led by the communist Soviet Union. In June 1956, John Foster Dulles, who served for six years as secretary of state under President Dwight D. Eisenhower, even went so far as to decry efforts to avoid being pulled into the orbit of either superpower as not only "increasingly . . . obsolete" but also "immoral and short-sighted."[2] Despite such American denunciations, the first decades of the Cold War witnessed growing support for a neutral or nonaligned stance toward the bipolar conflict and eventually the emergence of a movement designed to counter bifurcation in international politics—and the dangers to the entire world that went along with it.

Efforts to steer a middle course in the Cold War were first manifest in Europe. Sweden and Switzerland, both relatively untouched by World War II, maintained their historically neutral positions vis-à-vis global affairs by eschewing alliance with either the Soviet Union or the United States. Other manifestations of European neutralism were directly tied to the developing Cold War. Pro-Axis Finland, for instance, avoided outright allegiance to the Soviet Union, with which it shared an eight-hundred-mile long border, through the Treaty of Friendship, Cooperation, and Mutual Assistance (1948), pledging resistance to hostile attacks on the Soviet Union but dodging a formal military or political alliance. It was able thereafter to maintain neutrality for the duration of the Cold War. Austria, a front-line state when it came to Nazi aggression, was subject to Allied occupation until the 1955 Austrian State Treaty restored its autonomy. Thereafter, it adopted strict neutrality in the Cold War, prevented from allying with either side in the bipolar conflict. The most interesting example of European Cold War neutralism, however, is arguably Yugoslavia. Alone among the European neutrals as a communist state, it broke from Soviet influence in 1948 and successfully steered an independent path between the two superpowers. In 1961, in fact, Yugoslavia's Marshal Josip Broz Tito helped to found the Non-Aligned Movement (NAM).

The importance of European neutralism during the early Cold War notwithstanding, the real focus of Cold War nonalignment was the developing nations of what was often called the third world. When Cold War tensions first developed in the wake of World War II, the key Western European powers still held sway over much of Asia and Africa, either through formal colonial rule or through informal influence and control. As the Cold War wore on, decolonization created dozens of new nations, most of which worked assiduously to avoid outright identification with either Cold War camp. Given their immense economic, social, and political needs, such states were naturally more concerned with internal developments than with global rivalries and had no desire to become entangled in—or, worse, pawns of—the East-West Cold War. Although they declined to form an actual organization, in 1961 the nonaligned states did create a movement that represented their collective identity as inhabitants of the global South and pursued an agenda that was often at odds with the more developed North. In addition to calling for measures that would improve the economic and educational lot of the developing world, they spoke out stridently against nuclear proliferation.

Classroom exploration of the ways European and especially non-European states sought to abjure explicit alignment with either side in the East-West Cold War has many advantages. One is to offer a corrective to the contemporary assertion of rigid geopolitical polarity of the sort Truman pronounced in 1947. Studying efforts toward neutralism and nonalignment reveals the presence of a third force that challenged superpower domination of international affairs and sought especially to lessen the chances of a devastating nuclear confrontation. A second is to highlight the agency that small, relatively powerless states were able to wield on the postwar global stage. Individually as well as collectively, the nonaligned nations successfully challenged both postwar superpowers' bids for allegiance and control, demonstrating that the United States and the Soviet Union were hardly all-powerful. Finally, studying the NAM's use of the United Nations as a vehicle for advancing its agenda serves as a reminder that there was a time when the world organization commanded international respect, especially among non-European nations. The remainder of this chapter provides a basic discussion of several key aspects of Cold War neutralism/nonalignment, along with some specific classroom strategies. In keeping with the historical profession's penchant for privileging contemporary voices, many of the activities that follow are based on readily available primary-source documents.

European Neutralism

European neutralism was never the real focus of Cold War avoidance, but the case of Yugoslavia offers up important insights into the conflict's early contours, particularly when it comes to the limits of Soviet control. Yugoslavia broke free of Soviet control after Tito grew disillusioned with what he perceived as Josef Stalin's Soviet-centered economic policy, formally casting his lot with neutralism in the spring of 1948 and thereafter pursuing a quasi-socialist domestic policy but an independent course when it came to foreign affairs. Yugoslavian neutralism belied the myth of a monolithic, Moscow-controlled communist enemy and revealed the limits of Soviet adventurism as well as the success one relatively weak state could have in challenging the Kremlin.

Exploring the Yugoslavian road to neutralism with students reveals much about both the state of affairs in Europe during the early Cold War and the exertion of local agency. Fueled in large measure by Tito's refusal to bow to Stalin when it came to foreign policy, matters came to a head in June 1948 when the Communist Information Bureau (Cominform), which Stalin had established the previous year to coordinate Soviet control over the European communist states, expelled Yugoslavia in a stinging and illuminating resolution that condemned Yugoslavia's "departure[s] from Marxism-Leninism," "unfriendly policy toward the Soviet Union," and "incorrect line on the main questions of home and foreign policy." Including "nationalism" among Yugoslavia's purported transgressions made clear Moscow's determination to maintain rigid control of its satellites—at least where it could—and foreshadowed the line of thought that would motivate later advocates of nonalignment as they sought to guard both their national interests and what they saw as larger international ones by rejecting the bipolar worldview that was coming to dominate world affairs.[3]

The Seeds of Nonalignment: Bandung, 1955

Although it is often described as a gathering of nonaligned states, the April 1955 Bandung Conference actually brought together representatives of twenty-nine Asian and African states of varying political orientations; not all were truly neutral.[4] Staunchly pro-Western attendees included the US client states Iran and South Vietnam; Japan and the Philippines, which had both concluded security pacts with the United States in 1951; and Turkey, a member of the North Atlantic Treaty Organization. Communist states such as the People's Republic of China and the Democratic Republic of Vietnam were also in attendance. Not surprisingly, much of the conference was taken up with economic, cultural, and political matters, as attendees sought strategies for improving their individual and collective positions. The speeches of key participants such as Indonesia's Ahmed Sukarno, Egypt's Gamal Abdel Nasser, and India's Jawaharlal Nehru illustrated, however, that geopolitical concerns also held a prominent place in the conference's proceedings. Sukarno spoke for all attendees when he lamented that "great chasms yawn[ed] between nations and groups of nations," forcing "the peoples of all countries to walk in fear, lest, through no fault of their own, the dogs of war [be] unchained once again." Nasser urged resistance to what he termed "the game of power politics in which the small nations can be used as tools" of the "selfish interests" of the larger states. And, in a clear articulation of the emerging non-aligned position, Nehru argued for true equality among all of the world's nations, large and small, rejecting the thought that the nations of Asia and Africa should be mere "'yes-men'" to one or the other of the great powers or "camp-followers of Russia or America or any other country."[5] Exploring the speeches of these key participants, as well as those of other attendees, can serve as a good introduction to the multiplicity of concerns that motivated the conferees; students might work in groups to dissect the texts, assigning broad categories to the issues each statesman identifies and then considering the speeches in comparison.

Guiding students through the conference's final communiqué, the teacher can help them see that it openly reflected two important contemporary concerns. One was the looming fear of nuclear war. Although only three nations—the United States, the Soviet Union, and the United Kingdom—had nuclear weapons capability at the time, conferees expressed grave concerns about the "danger of an atomic world war," recommending "disarmament and the prohibition of the production, experimentation and use of nuclear and thermo-nuclear weapons of war [as] imperative to save mankind and civilisation from the fear and prospect of wholesale destruction." If the total number of nuclear states was not large, the danger of nuclear war was real, particularly given the lack of international safeguards. The Asian and African states therefore considered it their "duty towards humanity and civilisation" to work for "the speedy establishment of the International Atomic Energy Agency."[6] A second important motivating factor for the Bandung conferees was the continued existence of colonialism. Dozens of states throughout Asia and Africa and elsewhere at the time were subject to "alien subjugation, domination and exploitation." Their lack of "freedom and independence" was not only unfair to them individually but also impeded "the promotion of world peace and co-operation." To remedy the situation, the Bandung final communiqué asserted that "all nations should have the right freely to choose their own political and economic systems and their own way of life, in conformity with the purposes and principles of the Charter of the United Nations." Juxtaposing the Cold War and the anticolonial contexts for the Bandung Conference helps students see that the nations of the emerging world both appreciated the dangers of the East-West conflict and recognized that that conflict was not the sole determinant of global affairs.[7]

Once students have gained a sense of the contemporary context from the final communiqué, they can then assess the document's prescriptive content, focusing on how the attendees proposed to rise above the present state of world tensions, effect improvements for the Asian and African states, and avoid the bipolar conflict. To those ends, the long body of the communiqué endorsed equality, mutual respect, regional cooperation, and the avoidance of war, both in the abstract and with regard to specific instances. In service to economic development, it called for all manner of cooperative endeavors, from technical and educational exchanges, to trade agreements, to "national and regional banks and insurance companies." And, in a nod to third world solidarity, it exhorted the United Nations to admit "all those States which [are] qualified for membership in terms of the Charter" in the belief that "effective co-operation for world peace" requires "universal" UN membership. Having students research, individually or in groups, whether the final communiqué's calls actually reached fruition will go some distance toward discerning the Bandung Conference's tangible accomplishments.[8]

The final communiqué closed with ten principles that, if implemented, "would effectively contribute to the maintenance and promotion of international peace and security." Working through these principles in the classroom, perhaps by breaking the students into groups, is another fruitful way to use the document as a lens for understanding the roots of the nonaligned movement. Although all ten of the principles are enlightening for what they say about the mindset that motivated the twenty-nine nations that gathered at Bandung, several may be singled out as central for the project of nonalignment. The call for "abstention from intervention or interference in the internal affairs of another country," for example, spoke to the growing sentiment in Asia and Africa that the superpowers had a tendency to meddle in other countries' business to suit their own purposes. The same may be said of the appeal for nations to abstain "from the use of arrangements of collective defence to serve the particular interests of any of the big powers" and "from exerting pressures on other countries" and to refrain "from acts or threats of aggression or the use of force against the territorial integrity or political independence of any country."[9] Without identifying any particular nation or nations, the signatories to these principles lobbed criticisms at what by 1955 had become a proclivity by both superpowers to shape the international environment to suit themselves, even at the cost of the local, popular will.

Creating the Nonaligned Movement:
Belgrade, 1961

In early September 1961, representatives of twenty-five states gathered in Belgrade, Yugoslavia, and officially created the Non-Aligned Movement (NAM).[10] Unlike the meeting at Bandung, which brought together states on a regional basis and thus included some that had overtly taken sides in the Cold War conflict, the gathering at Belgrade included only true neutrals that had eschewed outright identification with either of the Cold War superpowers. India's Nehru, Indonesia's Sukarno, and Egypt's Nasser reprised the leading roles they had played at Bandung, joined by Yugoslavia's Tito, who served as host. Given the tense state of world affairs at the time, with the failed superpower summit at Vienna, the US-led debacle at the Bay of Pigs, and the ongoing Soviet-American showdown over Berlin as background, it was not surprising that nuclear fears were high on the conference agenda. Indeed, one of the meeting's most notable outcomes was a direct message to President John F. Kennedy and Premier Nikita S. Khrushchev calling for the resumption of superpower disarmament discussions. The attendees also sketched a broadly anticolonial platform that affirmed the right of self-government, mutual respect for differences in political and economic systems, and national self-determination.

The criteria on which invitations to the Belgrade Conference were based illustrate the broad contours of the NAM as well as the way those principles seemed to tilt against the United States and toward the Soviet Union. In brief, conference planners equated the following positions with nonalignment: adoption of or movement toward coexistence with states of differing political and social systems; avowed and consistent support for ongoing efforts at national independence; and avoidance of explicitly Cold War military alliances or other arrangements of any kind.[11] The first, which amounted to the sort of peaceful coexistence Soviet leaders had been advocating since 1956, called upon nations to cease or avoid competition or other unfriendly activities, gestures, or words and to agree instead to live in peace and harmony. US officials viewed peaceful coexistence with suspicion, so the fact that it was included as part of the nonaligned agenda was certainly cause for concern in Washington. The same was true of the second broad requirement for invitation to Belgrade, support for wars of national liberation, which was another way of saying colonial independence movements. At the time, nationalists in Vietnam, Algeria, and Angola were struggling for independence, backed implicitly if not explicitly by the Soviet Union and opposed implicitly if not explicitly by the United States. So, again, US officials had reason to be concerned that the principles of nonalignment seemed to lean in favor of the Soviet Union. The last of the three basic ideas championed by the organizers of the Belgrade Conference, avoiding explicitly Cold War–oriented or –originated entanglements, was also directed against the United States more than the Soviet Union. By 1961, the United States was a member of or had played a major role in creating a number of anti-Soviet military alliances, most prominently the North Atlantic Treaty Organization (NATO), the Southeast Treaty Organization (SEATO), and the Central Treaty Organization (CENTO). Some members of those alliances, specifically Iran, Pakistan, the Philippines, and Turkey, had attended the Bandung Conference but were not invited to Belgrade. Neither were the close US ally Japan and the US client the Republic of Vietnam or the communist states the People's Republic of China and the Democratic Republic of Vietnam. Working with students to compare the attendance lists for the two conferences and to ponder the reasons for excluding these states can help students see the firmness with which leaders of the emerging NAM set about avoiding any contact with the bipolar conflict.

As at Bandung, the conferees at Belgrade issued a final declaration at the conclusion of their work, but, rather than constituting it as a mere statement of principles, they cast it as "A Program of Action for the United Nations General Assembly," thereby revealing their faith in that organization's singular ability to "lay a firm foundation of cooperation and brotherhood between nations" that was built around "freedom, equality and social justice for the promotion of prosperity." In a nutshell, the "Program for Action" framed the criteria used to determine attendance at the Belgrade Conference as universal principles, affirming the right of self-determination, calling for an end to colonialism, and advocating economic equality among nations. Far from simply advocating for these principles in the abstract, however, the attendees included specific references to contemporary conflicts that embodied what they believed was wrong with the world—in all cases setting themselves in opposition to the United States and its Western allies. In keeping with the Cold War focus of the conference itself, the "Plan of Action" devoted much attention to the current state of global tensions and implored the superpowers to adopt a "constructive approach" to resolving their differences, including the negotiation of "a general, complete and strictly and internationally controlled disarmament." Rejecting the view that "war, including the 'cold war,' [was] inevitable," the attendees touted nonalignment as "the only possible and indispensable alternative to the total division of the world into blocs and the intensification of cold war policies," policies that were "likely to result in world conflagration."[12] Having students compare the Belgrade "Plan of Action" with the Bandung final communiqué, noting both similarities and differences, is a useful strategy for revealing issues such as the rising state of global tensions, the growing activism of the nonaligned states, and those states' unwavering commitment to neutralism.

In an illustration of the long shadow the fear of war cast on the Belgrade gathering, the conferees also sent simultaneous messages to Kennedy and Khrushchev urging them to undertake "direct negotiations" to defuse "the international situation" and to remove "the prospect of war which now threatens humanity." With nothing less than "human survival" hanging in the balance, the twenty-five signatories expressed a universalist vision of peace that they believed both Kennedy and Khrushchev—and the nations they represented—shared.[13] Neither superpower response was particularly encouraging. In fact, each blamed the other for the state of world tensions and professed its own willingness to discuss disarmament questions. Each also downplayed the direct call for disarmament negotiations by introducing other issues, most notably the ongoing tension over Berlin, illustrating the emphasis both Washington and Moscow continued to place on their own national interests, a position that stood in direct contravention to the Belgrade Conference's intentions.[14] Studying these three communications with students, perhaps by dividing the class into three groups representing the three actors in the exchange, is a good way to reveal the gap that existed between the NAM and the superpowers, a gap that the superpowers' subsequent failure to pursue nuclear deterrence also illustrates.

Consolidating the Nonaligned Movement: Cairo, 1964

Three years after Belgrade, representatives from forty-seven nations gathered in Cairo, Egypt, for the second NAM summit. All of the states that had attended the Belgrade meeting were there save the Congo (Leopoldville); joining them were Angola, Burundi, Cameroon, the Central African Republic, Chad, the Congo (Brazzaville), Dahomey, Jordan, Kenya, Kuwait, Laos, Liberia, Libya, Malawi, Mauritania, Nigeria, Senegal, Sierra Leone, Syria, Tanzania, Togo, Uganda, and Zambia. Many of the attendees were newly independent states. Having students research and report on the recent history of each participant can help to drive home the role of decolonization in creating the NAM.

The long and detailed Cairo Declaration constituted the most comprehensive articulation to date of the nonaligned agenda. Given the makeup of the conference, it was not surprising that much of the document focused on reaffirming universal principles such as national self-determination, the complete equality of states in international affairs, and the peaceful resolution of disputes. It also repeated the NAM's by now well-known stance against nuclear weapons, calling for "the convening of a world disarmament conference under the auspices of the United Nations" and "urg[ing] all nations to join in the cooperative development of the peaceful use of atomic energy for the benefit of all mankind."[15] To gain an appreciation for the world tensions that provided the context for the drafting of the Cairo Declaration, students might be asked to annotate the document, researching the specific conflicts, disputes, and other contemporary developments that it mentions as a way of better understanding the prevailing state of world affairs in 1964, how the instances noted in the declaration were the result of or related to the bipolar conflict, and why the conferees might have made the proposals they did for resolving them. This exercise would be most fruitfully accomplished as group work, with different groups taking responsibility for different sections of the declaration. To develop a sense of the evolution of the NAM agenda, students might compare the Belgrade and Cairo conference declarations. What concerns from the first declaration were repeated in the second? What new concerns were evident in the second that did not appear the first? What new strategies for easing global tensions were advanced at Cairo?

The Cairo Declaration also provides an opportunity for considering the central role the United Nations played for the NAM. One way to drive this point home for students is to work through the document with them, noting its numerous references to the UN Charter and the similarities between the NAM's principles and goals and those of the international organization.[16] Another is to highlight the document's repeated calls for UN action as a way of easing international tensions and effecting the sort of global equality that lay at the heart of the NAM agenda and then determining whether the United Nations followed through on those issues at its 1964 and 1965 sessions. Among the most important issues the Cairo conferees considered as falling under UN purview were disarmament, economic development, and decolonization.[17]

Conclusion

Considering the foundational proclamations of the NAM as outlined in the preceding discussion and undertaking the suggested activities or developing others not included here should go some way toward illustrating for students that, despite the Cold War's importance, it did not entirely dominate global affairs during the early post–World War II period. Nations throughout Asia, Africa, and Latin America came together to challenge the bipolar worldview, calling for what amounted to a middle way in the superpower conflict that rejected the rigid bipolarity of the Cold War in favor of economic cooperation, mutual respect, and peaceful coexistence through UN-sponsored nuclear disarmament. Although the NAM did not succeed in easing East-West tensions, it did call attention to the plight of the global South and give voice to millions who had no desire to ally with either the United States or the Soviet Union. Including study of the neutral/nonaligned perspective in an overall consideration of the Cold War makes for a more complete— and thus more accurate—understanding of the true costs and consequences of the bipolar confrontation.

NOTES

1. Truman Doctrine speech, March 12, 1947, http://www.trumanlibrary
.org/whistlestop/study_collections/doctrine/large/documents/pdfs/5-
.pdf#zoom=100. For an insightful exploration of the rhetoric of Truman's speech see Denise M. Bostdorff, *Proclaiming the Truman Doctrine: The Cold War Call to Arms* (College Station: Texas A&M Press, 2008).

2. Dulles commencement address, Iowa State College, "The Cost of Peace," June 9, 1956, *Department of State Bulletin* 34, no. 886 (June 18, 1956): 999, 1000, https://archive.org/stream/departmentofstat3456unit#page/998/mode /2up.

3. "Cominform Communiqué: Resolution of the Information Bureau Concerning the Communist Party of Yugoslavia, June 28, 1948," http://legacy .fordham.edu/halsall/mod/1948cominform-yugo1.html.

4. The conference was attended by Afghanistan, Burma, Cambodia, Ceylon,

Egypt, Ethiopia, the Gold Coast, India, Indonesia, Iran, Iraq, Japan, Jordan, Laos, Lebanon, Liberia, Libya, Nepal, Pakistan, the People's Republic of China, the Philippines, Saudi Arabia, Sudan, Syria, Thailand, Turkey, the Democratic Republic of Vietnam, the State of Vietnam, and Yemen.

5. "Speech by President Sukarno of Indonesia at the Opening of the Conference," in The National Committee for the Commemoration of the Thirteenth Anniversary of the Asian-African Conference, *Asia-Africa Speaks from Bandung* (Jakarta: Ministry of Foreign Affairs, Republic of Indonesia, 1985), 6; Nasser speech, ibid., 54; Nehru speech ibid., 165, 166. Additional documents from the Bandung Conference may be found in George McTurnan Kahin, *The Asian-African Conference: Bandung, Indonesia, April 1955* (Ithaca, NY: Cornell University Press, 1956); and Richard Wright, *The Color Curtain: A Report of the Bandung Conference* (Jackson: Banner Books/University Press of Mississippi, 1995).

6. "Final Communiqué of the Asian-African conference of Bandung (24 April 1955)," http://franke.uchicago.edu/Final_Communique_Bandung _1955.pdf.

7. Ibid.

8. Ibid.

9. Ibid.

10. Attending were Afghanistan, Algeria, Burma, Cambodia, Ceylon, the Congo (Leopoldville), Cuba, Cyprus, Ethiopia, Ghana, Guinea, India, Indonesia, Iraq, Lebanon, Mali, Morocco, Nepal, Saudi Arabia, Somalia, Sudan, Tunisia, the United Arab Republic, Yemen, and Yugoslavia.

11. The criteria may be found in full at http://www.nam.gov.za/back ground/history.htm.

12. "A Program of Action for the United Nations General Assembly: Declaration of the Heads of State or Government of Non-Aligned Countries, Approved at Belgrade, September 5, 1961," in *American Foreign Policy: Current Documents, 1961* (Washington, DC: US Department of State, Historical Office, Bureau of Public Affairs, 1965), doc. 39, http://hdl.handle.net/2027/mdp .39015010323460.

13. "Belgrade Conference Appeal for Negotiations between the Heads of Government of the United States and the Soviet Union," September 6, 1961, in *American Foreign Policy: Current Documents, 1961* (Washington, DC: US Department of State, Historical Office, Bureau of Public Affairs, 1965), doc. 271, http:// hdl.handle.net/2027/mdp.39015010323460.

14. "United States Preference for the Use of 'Existing and Appropriate Channels' in 'Surmounting the Present Impasse' with the Soviet Union," September 13, 1961, and "'We Are Ready for Talks Any Time, Any Place, and at Any Level,'" September 16, 1961, both in *American Foreign Policy: Current Documents, 1961* (Washington, DC: US Department of State, Historical Office, Bureau of Public Affairs, 1965), docs. 273 and 276, http://hdl.handle.net/2027/mdp .39015010323460.

15. "Cairo Declaration," October 1964, http://namiran.org/wp-content /uploads/2013/04/Declarations-of-All-Previous-NAM-Summits.pdf.

16. The United Nations Charter is available at http://www.un.org/en /documents/charter/.

17. See *Yearbook of the United Nations, 1964* (New York: Office of Public Information, United Nations, 1966), http://www.unmultimedia.org/searchers /yearbook/page.jsp?volume=1964&page=1, and *Yearbook of the United Nations, 1965* (New York: Office of Public Information, United Nations, 1967), http:// www.unmultimedia.org/searchers/yearbook/page.jsp?volume=1965&page=1.

KEY RESOURCES

Brands, H. W. *The Specter of Neutralism: The United States and the Emergence of the Third World, 1947–1960*. New York: Columbia University Press, 1989.

Jackson, Richard L. *The Non-Aligned, the UN, and the Superpowers*. New York: Praeger, 1983.

Kullaa, Rinna. *Non-Alignment and Its Origins in Cold War Europe: Yugoslavia, Finland, and the Soviet Challenge*. London: I. B. Tauris, 2012.

Lawrence, Mark Atwood. "The Rise and Fall of Nonalignment." In *The Cold War in the Third World*, edited by Robert J. McMahon, 139–55. New York: Oxford University Press, 2013.

Lee, Christopher J., ed. *Making a World after Empire: The Bandung Moment and Its Political Afterlives*. Athens: Ohio University Press, 2010.

Mišković, Nataša, Harold Fischer-Tiné, and Nada Boškovska, eds. *The Non-Aligned Movement and the Cold War: Delhi-Bandung-Belgrade*. London: Routledge, 2014.

Parker, Jason C. "Small Victory, Missed Chance: The Eisenhower Administration, the Bandung Conference, and the Turning of the Cold War." In *The Eisenhower Administration, the Third World, and the Globalization of the Cold War*, edited by Kathryn C. Statler and Andrew L. Johns, 153–74. Lanham, MD: Rowman & Littlefield, 2006.

Rakove, Robert B. *Kennedy, Johnson, and the Nonaligned World*. New York: Cambridge University Press, 2012.

Tan, See Seng, and Amitav Acharya, eds. *Bandung Revisited: The Legacy of the 1955 Asian-African Conference for International Order*. Singapore: National University of Singapore Press, 2008.

PART FIVE

Archival Collections for Teaching the Cold War

The Global Cold War

Using the Resources of the Cold War
International History Project

CHRISTIAN OSTERMANN

"Cruising While High in Possession"—that is, "riding around high in possession of marijuana, smoking on the road, bumping loud music and enjoying life"—is, according to urbandictionary.com, the most frequently used meaning of the acronym "CWIHP." Yet for those interested in researching, teaching, and learning about Cold War history, the five letters can open up—a few scrolls down the Google search chain—a set of historical resources that is the result of a collective effort over more than two decades to access and analyze new documentation that has become available in the former communist world archives—and beyond. Complementing such invaluable resources as the *Foreign Relations of the United States* series published by the US Department of State[1] and the National Security Archive, a leading nongovernmental repository for US government documents released through the Freedom of Information Act, the resources of the Cold War International History Project (CWIHP) allow faculty, teachers, and students to look at the post–World War II confrontation from the perspectives of both—or, better, the many—protagonists and sides of the Cold War. Viewing the Cold War through the lens of the adversaries and the partners of the United States can help students to assess more accurately the impact of American actions in the world, to become more sensitive to other people's worldviews, interests, and intentions, and, for a few moments, to step outside the political-cultural paradigm that governs how Americans look at the world.

Background

In order to understand the nature of the documents available through the Cold War International History Project, it is important to understand its origins and history. Launched in 1991 with a grant from the John D. and Catherine T. MacArthur Foundation, the Project, based at the nonpartisan Woodrow Wilson International Center for Scholars in Washington, DC, has become a globally active clearinghouse for new and important archival evidence on recent international relations.[2] The idea behind the Project, conceived initially by historian John Lewis Gaddis, was to take advantage of the Russian and Eastern European archives that were then just opening in the wake of the "velvet revolutions" of 1989 and the end of the Soviet Union. Until the very early 1990s, most of the archival based historical scholarship on the Cold War was based largely on Western, in particular American, government sources that had become available since the 1970s. But this historiography was in many ways an example of "one hand clapping." While scholars had access to tens of thousands of US documents to help them to analyze American policies, when it came to understanding Soviet or communist world perceptions and actions, they had to rely on newspapers and publications, memoirs, and official document publications, testimony by defectors and the occasional document that could be smuggled out, and Western intelligence assessments of uncertain accuracy. A greater number of Soviet documents became accessible to selected scholars as the *glasnost* policies of Mikhail Gorbachev in the late 1980s opened up darker chapters in Soviet history, yet there was no systematic free access to the records of the ruling communist parties and governments until those regimes crumbled in the revolutions of 1989.

Suddenly the doors to these archives flung open—or, more accurately, were pried open by activists, scholars, and citizens eager to gain control of their past and bring perpetrators to justice. But few scholars in the East or West were positioned—linguistically, logistically, politically—to take advantage of the openings. No single individual or organization had the resources, staff, or funding necessary to open up, collect, translate, and publish the important materials from these archives in a systematic fashion, even on more limited subjects. This is where CWIHP came in: by providing resources to scholars to seize the archival opening; by facilitating the sharing and discussion of the new evidence emanating from the former Warsaw Pact archives; by providing emerging scholars from what used to be "the other side" opportunities to study archival practices, source materials, and literature in the United States through fellowships; and by translating and publishing important new documents and findings through its *Cold War International History Project Bulletin* and other publications, the Project helped to create a new international network of researchers, archivists, and journalists engaged in exploring the communist world archives and to internationalize the research and writing of Cold War history. This new international community was itself, as its first director Jim Hershberg has argued, a methodological revolution for the field: it is constantly trading information about new sources, new documents, new research opportunities, and new findings and cooperating to find ways to push for the most rapid possible opening and exploration of Cold War archives across the globe.

"A new generation of scholar began to sink its teeth into the Cold War's leftovers," as *Lingua Franca* put it. Over the years, new evidence published by CWIHP in its *Bulletin* and other publications has made the front pages of the *New York Times* and the *Washington Post* and received frequent coverage in other US and international media. "The contours of the Cold War change every time" CWIHP publishes an issue of the *Cold War International History Project Bulletin*, the late Harvard University historian Ernest May once said. Within a few years of the Project's launch, "This indispensable guide to the latest archival releases . . . mushroomed from a meager review into a four-hundred-page tome crammed with eye-catching entries."[3] Hundreds, perhaps thousands of books, PhD theses, and articles written on the post–World War II confrontation rely on, cite, and quote CWIHP materials. They include Pulitzer Prize–winning books such as Steve Coll's *Ghost Wars* (2004), William Taubman's *Khrushchev: The Man and His Era* (2003), and John Gaddis's *George F. Kennan* (2011). Henry Kissinger's *On China* (2011) relies heavily on CWIHP materials, and the former secretary of state acknowledged his own misperception of Cuban policy in Africa in the last volume of his memoirs after reading documents in *CWIHP Bulletin* 8/9. The Project helped inspire intellectually and served as a lead academic resource for CNN's twenty-four-episode *Cold War* television documentary, funded by Ted Turner and produced by Jeremy Isaacs and Pat Mitchell. The largest undertaking of its kind, the documentary, broadcast on CNN and BBC2 in 1998, reached vast audiences across the globe.[4]

Central to its clearinghouse mission were CWIHP's efforts to collect, translate, and publish new archival evidence, initially through its *Bulletin* and Working Papers series, later increasingly through its Digital Archive. In collecting the materials, CWIHP engaged journalists, scholars, civic activists, and archivists and sponsored conferences that served as occasions for new document releases. Early on it exploited Russian president Boris Yeltsin's "archival diplomacy"—his practice of presenting batches of hitherto secret documents to former allies or foes during state visits. Documents on the 1956 Hungarian Revolution or the assassination of President John F. Kennedy, for example, came the Project's way as a result. But, most importantly, it obtained documents through a quickly growing network of often younger scholars working on the archival frontlines for which the Project's publication platforms provided a first outlet. CWIHP's collections of Cold War–era documents are therefore primarily driven by the research agendas, the priorities, and the situational possibilities of its network of individuals across the globe. Even as these collections cover most major crises, events, and dimensions of the Cold War, they were not originally created to represent a comprehensive sampling of Cold War–era records.

One of CWIHP's most important roles is that of archival access and research catalyst. The Project actively promotes the value of archival openness and transparency through publications and cooperation and direct contacts with archives, government ministries, universities, and NGOs around the world. CWIHP recognizes that national security and foreign-policy documents, the core of CWIHP's collections, are among the most closely guarded government records and therefore employs several mutually reinforcing approaches to further reasonable access. One of the most effective ways of accessing the contents of closed archives is by looking for the information, for counterpart documentation, in more open ones: diplomatic correspondence, memoranda of conversations between foreign leaders and diplomats, and a host of other types of archival materials necessarily involve multiple persons, stakeholders, and countries. Though collections on a given subject in one country may be closed, the more accessible archives of its allies or rivals may be "back doors" into the history of the former. CWIHP and its partners, including the Parallel History Project based at the ETH Zurich, fruitfully employed this strategy when they sought to document Warsaw Pact decision-making, operations, and planning in the face of closed doors at the Russian military in Podolsk in the late 1990s. Based on systematic and collaborative efforts by the network, we now have access to nearly complete sets of transcripts and further documentation on the Warsaw Pact's main consultative bodies—the records of the Committee of the Ministers of Defense (1969–90) and the records of the Committee of Foreign Ministers (1976–90). Prior to the declassification of Chinese foreign policy records, archival records in the Albanian State Archives, made accessible through the valiant efforts of the Cold War Studies Center in Tirana (led by Ana Lalaj), provided a fascinating glimpse into Chinese foreign relations and politics given the two isolated countries' exceptionally close and unique relationship during the Cultural Revolution era. The Bulgarian, Czech, East German, Hungarian, and Polish party and state archives served as archival back doors into Soviet policy on important Soviet bloc crises, beyond their role in documenting Eastern Europe's role in the Cold War. Perhaps not surprisingly, dissonances within the Soviet empire emerged as a central finding from the research. During key moments, the tail often seemed to wag the dog: the Soviet Union's junior allies drove alliance dynamics more often than previously assumed. Through its Digital Archive collections, CWIHP provides a platform for scholars to piece together information from dozens of archives to learn about the perceptions and motivations that undergird countries' national security decision making.

A corollary to this "back door" strategy has been the use of local and provincial archives when central state archives remain closed. While local archives may contain only the final results of decisions passed down from the central authorities and may generally lack information about the internal decision-making processes that lead the enactment of particular policies, they are often considered less sensitive and are therefore more accessible. Not a substitute for central decision-making files, records in local or provincial archives can contain new insights on how macro-level policies affected and were affected by individuals and grass-roots movements at the local or regional level. The importance of this approach has only grown as new research emphasizes the significance of domestic and regional political dynamics for international affairs. Given the closed doors to the central archives in Beijing throughout the 1990s, this strategy was important for new work on Chinese policy, particularly the Korean and Indochina wars. With the help of local partners in Azerbaijan, Armenia, and Georgia, CWIHP also used this approach to document Soviet policy vis-à-vis Iran and Turkey: records in the "local" Baku archives proved exceptionally insightful on the run-up to the 1946 Iran crisis.

Continual and direct engagement with government and archive officials in countries and organizations whose archives remain closed or only partially accessible has also proven to be an effective means of opening new collections around the world. National authorities and communities have a vested interest in seeing their views and perspectives reflected in the emerging global narrative. By subtly appealing to national pride and interests, CWIHP has leveraged the opening of archival collections on international history in one country to prompt greater access in those of its allies and especially its rivals: after all, what country would want its foreign-policy history researched, written, and taught through the lens of foreign documents alone? One example is the Indian archives. While the government of India could not be bothered by the release of US and even Russian documentation pertaining to India history, what got under its skin was the—as we now know, temporary—opening in the archives of its most important strategic competitor, the People's Republic of China. The developments in China— persistently highlighted by CWIHP *Bulletin* issues—likely contributed to major tranches of Cold War–era materials becoming accessible in the National Archives of India since 2012.[5]

During the early 1990s, CWIHP's activities focused on the Russian and Eastern European archives. To this day, Russian records constitute the largest number of documents in the collections. But this "golden period" of access in the archives proved exceedingly short lived. A few months after CWIHP's first major international conference in Moscow in 1993, officials in the Russian Security Ministry (the successor to the KGB) initiated a sudden clamp down on scholarly access, charging that hordes of foreign researchers were looting Russia's "national patrimony." Some Russian archivists, devastated by the disappearance of state subsidies, had indeed begun to auction off documents to foreign television stations, often granting them exclusive access to materials that Russians had never seen. Compounding the problem, some publishing houses struck similar deals. Political embarrassment over unseemly revelations contributed to the regression in access. The Western press published stories on a sensational document discovered by an Australian researcher that implied there were substantially more American prisoners of war in Vietnam than Hanoi had officially claimed, leading to inquiries from the Clinton administration. Defensive Russian officials soon abandoned their open-drawer policy.[6] The rise of neo-communism and anti-Western sentiments spurred in part by NATO expansion, the breakdown of academic support systems amid socioeconomic crisis, and democratic backsliding reinforced the retrenchment in the archives. As a result, the archives of Moscow's erstwhile Warsaw Pact allies became a "back door" into Soviet and Warsaw Pact policy.

All along Yeltsin had set tight limits on access and had in fact never opened several of the most important archives: the Presidential Archive (formerly the Politburo Archive), the KGB archive, the foreign intelligence archive, and the military intelligence archive. To this day, none of these archives has ever been made accessible to ordinary researchers. Further setbacks occurred in early 1993, when the Center for Preservation of Contemporary Documentation (TsKhSD), now the Russian State Archive of Contemporary History (RGANI), which preserves many of the post-1952 documents of the Communist Party of the Soviet Union, closed for several months, only to open with many of the records that had been previously accessible reclassified. In the late 1990s, the Russian Foreign Ministry Archive also became more restrictive in its access policies (though there have been some improvements since about 2007). A good number of Russian documents available through CWIHP were later reclassified and are no longer available to Russian or foreign researchers in the Moscow archives.[7]

With echoes of the conflict in the more recent confrontation over Ukraine and the West's deteriorating relations with Russia more generally, the Cold War continues to reverberate powerfully through the Russian archives. The status of the archives in the Putin era has been a "mixed bag," as Mark Kramer, a frequent CWIHP contributor, director of the Harvard Project on Cold War Studies, and the leading expert on the Soviet bloc archives, has aptly put it, as key files from the Russian State Archive of Socio-Political History (RGASPI, containing the records of the pre-1952 period) were closed in 2003, only to be reopened in 2008. While some new collections at RGASPI (particularly some valuable personal papers, or *lichnye fondy*, of top leaders and the important *osobye papki* documents that were discussed or reviewed at Stalin-era Politburo meetings) and even RGANI (particularly the crucial Malin notes and related documents from Khrushchev-era Communist Party Presidium meetings) have become available, the political climate has sharpened. Most notably, in May 2009 President Dmitry Medvedev (with Putin's

301

strong support) established a presidential commission to "counter attempts at falsifying history against Russia's interests."[8] Though authoritarian trends in Russia suggest that access will remain volatile, researchers have been surprised by dramatic new openings in the Moscow archives since late 2014, including access to the Communist Party of the Soviet Union Politburo and International Department records for the Brezhnev period (1964–82) at RGANI.

After a pioneering CWIHP conference on the Cold War in Asia, hosted in January 1996 by the University of Hong Kong, Asia moved further into the focus of the Project, initially through the lens of Russian and European documents, then increasingly through documentation from archives in Asia itself. In the early 2000s, CWIHP became the first NGO-like organization the Chinese government turned to when it made the unprecedented decision to provide limited access to its Foreign Ministry Archive. Following on a formal agreement with the Foreign Ministry Archive, CWIHP started to translate and publish documents on key moments in post-1949 Chinese diplomacy, including the 1954 Geneva Conference, the Bandung Conference, and the Sino-American ambassadorial talks that preceded the 1972 Sino-American opening. Based on this cooperation, along with contributions from its international network, CWIHP had amassed a wealth of archival materials by the time the Foreign Ministry Archive abruptly closed in 2012. The closure was likely a reaction to the publication of Foreign Ministry documents on the highly sensitive Senkaku-Diaoyu territorial dispute in Japan in late 2012. The worsening research environment also reflects a widespread crackdown on civil society and freedom of information amidst a general tightening of the political climate since President Xi Jinping came to power in November 2012. Once again the CWIHP collections—in this case its Chinese Foreign Policy database—contain documents, obtained legally at the time, that are no longer accessible to researchers and the public at the Foreign Ministry Archive. The Communist Party, military, and intelligence "central archives" have not been accessible to the research community at any point.[9]

For twenty-five years, CWIHP has navigated the strong national or ideological sensitivities and often highly charged politics that surround previously hidden, classified, or otherwise inaccessible documentation on Cold War international affairs. Its mission has grown to encompass inaccessible or difficult-to-access foreign-policy documentation around the globe and well beyond the Cold War. From holding freedom-of-information workshops in Ulan Bator to partnering with like-minded research organizations in Eastern Europe to engaging archival authorities in Algeria or, more recently, Burma,[10] CWIHP seeks to apply its resources to foster access to and research on foreign-policy documentation (writ large) in international archives; to help train the next generation of Cold War experts; to harness the intellectual energy of its global network for archival inroads and relevant historical context; and to improve public policy and international understanding and reconciliation through openness and a multiperspective history of post–World War II international politics. One indication of its success may be the spawning of similar projects around the world over the last two decades. From Budapest and Sofia to Shanghai, from Moscow to Tirana, these groups work in close cooperation with CWIHP to advance a common agenda. Similarly, CWIHP's sister projects, such as the North Korea International Documentation Project and the Nuclear Proliferation International History Project, like CWIHP part of the History and Public Policy Program at the Wilson Center, use the CWIHP formula for capacity-building and database expansion and policy impact.

CWIHP Resources

The Cold War International History Project offers a number of resources for teachers and students. In addition to regular seminars at the Wilson Center at which new Cold War findings and publications are discussed, occasional briefings for visiting high-school classes, professional training sessions for high-school teachers, and the "Summer Institute for Conducting Archival Research" for PhD students preparing to do field research (organized with George Washington University), CWIHP disseminates its findings through a number of publications, available at www.cwihp.org. The Project's flagship publication, *CWIHP Bulletin*, provides significant new documentation from archives around the world, alongside introductions and commentaries by experts. Working Papers are article-length analyses that reflect ongoing research in the archives. The CWIHP e-Dossier series provides introductions to new accessions to the CWIHP collections. Hard copies are available free upon request while stock is available; copies of the *CWIHP Bulletin* are also available at about a thousand US universities and public libraries.

Since the mid-1990s CWIHP has increasingly contributed to the emerging field of digital history—"the study of the past using a variety of electronically reproduced primary source texts, images, and artifacts as well as the constructed historical narratives, accounts, or presentations that result from digital historical inquiry."[11] CWIHP built its first website in 1995—predating the Wilson Center website. This early website included a "Cold War Virtual Archive," which featured English translations of historical documents made available with rudimentary metadata and basic HTML formatting. The Virtual Archive went through several iterations as the CWIHP's website moved from host servers—first at George Washington University and later at the Smithsonian Institution—to, finally, the Wilson Center's own dedicated website. In 2003, CWIHP relaunched the Virtual Archive as part of the Wilson Center's website. A Google search plugin on the website offered basic full-text search. Supported by grants from the Leon Levy Foundation (New York), the MacArthur Foundation, private donations, and Wilson Center federally appropriated funds, the Project began a complete redesign and relaunch of its online archive. As Laura Deal, the Project's catalog specialist, has emphasized, "One of the Project's key goals was the development of user-friendly browse tools that would make it easy and fun for new users to explore the diverse collections of the Digital Archive."[12] The unique and idiosyncratic nature of CWIHP's collections, as detailed above, make them particularly challenging for new, non-expert users to explore.

CWIHP launched its "Digital Archive: International History Declassified" (digitalarchive.org) in January 2013. The state-of-the-art digital platform provides advanced search capabilities, enhanced navigational structures, and curated access to thousands of translated and increasingly original-language documents from more than 150 different archives and pioneers an integrated document management system that serves as the backbone of the Project's core objective—the rapid and solid cataloging, translation, and dissemination of significant new international documentation. The front end features powerful new search and visualization tools in an intuitive user interface, including time lines, educational tools such as analyses by leading experts, and biographies of significant Cold War figures. While the Digital Archive's previous interface allowed only browsing across artificially created thematic "collections" or an alphabetical list of geographic locations, the new site allows users to search by date, subject, location, language, authorship, and collection, even by the originating archive. Much more than just an archive with a sophisticated search engine, the site curates a variety of topics into compelling narratives, time lines, and images.

"Theme" pages provide broad overviews of historical subjects and explanatory educational resources related to the raw primary documents featured in the main site. Among the themes are "Cold War History," "Nuclear History," and a "Modern Korean History Portal." A new "Chinese Foreign Policy Database" features more than 1,500 translated documents from the archives of the People's Republic of China and other archives—and new documents are being added on a weekly basis. The multiple interfaces, including an interactive map, proactively engage researchers from various backgrounds to make their own pathways through the vast archive.

The Digital Archive website is based on hypertext preprocessor protocol (PHP) and imports content for the Web to a MySQL database. Both the website and the offline database are backed up daily by a third-party server. The Digital Archive's download feature allows researchers to save archival records—including their scanned original, an English translation, and accompanying citation data—as a single PDF in a single click. Original documents are scanned at 300 dpi or higher to ensure legibility and are made searchable through Adobe Acrobat Pro's OCR function. The Digital Archive's metadata is based on the Dublin Core schema of fifteen core "elements" for describing digital objects. Subjects and author vocabulary terms are drawn from the Library of Congress Subject Headings and Name Authority File. The Digital Archive website is fully indexable by search engines, and its data are also exposed via Web services (http://digitalarchive.wilsoncenter.org/srv/). The website is responsive and its interface dynamically resizes to fit mobile and tablet screens.[13]

The Digital Archive's 115 collections (thus far) contain selected sets of historical documents related to specific topics, regions, or events, including the 1956 Hungarian and Polish Crises; the 1980–81 Polish Crisis; Anti-Communist Asia; the 1955 Bandung Conference; the Berlin Wall; Brazilian Nuclear History; China and the Korean War; China and the Soviet Union in Xinjiang; China-North Korea Relations; Cold War Origins; Cuba and Southern Africa; the Cuban Missile Crisis; and the East German Uprising. While many of the documents are focused on diplomatic, military, and political history, other collections, such as "Cold War on Ice," "The 1988 Seoul Olympic Games," and "Mass Media and Censorship," open up sociocultural and economic dimensions of the Cold War. The Digital Archive's front page highlights new document additions to the collections, features specific collections, and showcases the Digital Archive's Twitter feed. In late 2013, the CWIHP Digital Archive won the Roy Rosenzweig Prize for Innovations in Digital History, awarded by the American Historical Association.

CWIHP's Digital Archive has replaced the *Bulletin* as the Project's primary publication and dissemination platform. Since the launch, more than 550,000 users have visited the site. In 2014 alone, two hundred thousand people accessed the Digital Archive—a 60 percent increase in traffic since the site's launch in 2013. Longer than average user sessions suggest exceptionally deep engagement of users with the materials on the site. Documents in the CWIHP collection have been downloaded more than seven hundred thousand times, and some individual documents have been downloaded more than forty thousand times. When a document release on the KAL 007 shoot-down incident in 1983 went viral after being posted on the popular Reddit site, demand nearly brought down the Wilson Center website. Another popular set of documents on the 1954 transfer of Crimea to Ukraine—linked to a front-page *New York Times* article in the wake of the Russian annexation of the peninsula in 2014—quickly became by far the most popular publication ever released by the Wilson Center, exceeding fifty thousand page views (at the time of writing).[14]

Teaching (and Researching) the Cold War with the CWIHP Digital Archive

According to historian Austin Jersild, "The Digital Archive is a wonderful resource for instruction in undergraduate courses and graduate seminars, and even appropriate for advanced high school students. The internet potentially makes this material globally accessible, from rural Montana to the distant corners of Armenia."[15] Indeed, students can now to sift through an enormous amount of documentation at the tip of their finger. Documents in the CWIHP Digital Archive are now hyperlinked into hundreds of college syllabi around the world and are more and more frequently used in teaching and research at the university level. But to a nonexpert visitor, especially students, the wealth of information and documentation in the Digital Archive can be overwhelming and intimidating. The most difficult challenge for university and high school instructors is to get a handle on the thousands of available primary documents in the CWIHP collection, how to direct students to the documents most pertinent to a given subject, and how to contextualize the materials so students can conduct their own research. In designing the Digital Archive, CWIHP has tried to make this task less daunting by creating a more effective and meaningful pedagogical interface, by providing curated access to the documents in the Digital Archive through collections, themes, chronological and geographic browsing, and improved search filters. But for high school teaching especially, the challenges remain formidable: historical content knowledge deficiencies tend to limit students' ability to properly contextualize the available sources. Moreover, the Digital Archive's intent in design is still primarily archival, not pedagogical. Hence the sources it makes available "can be difficult to find, hard to manipulate, and of limited value for students who are doing the kind of short-term inquiries that are common in high school social studies." High school instructors in particular must therefore develop robust sets of pedagogical devices to mediate student interaction with the Digital Archive.[16]

Methodologically, the difficulties run more deeply: unlike in the physical archives where most of the documents originate, researchers cannot see the documents in the Digital Archive in their original archival context, which might indicate which documents (or drafts or notes) preceded or followed a document in the file, which in turn might lead to interpretative insights. Facsimiles of the original documents are of uneven quality (given different situational possibilities for those who donated documents), and translations are be open to debate and vary in quality, despite the enormous editorial efforts by the CWIHP team to ensure accuracy, consistency, and, of course, authenticity. As a database largely driven by archival users and individual research priorities, as mentioned earlier, the CWIHP Digital Archive collections are necessarily uneven and idiosyncratic in nature. They mirror the historiographic trends rather than a systematic sampling. Constantly expanding, they reflect the fact that archival access and the field of Cold War international history at large are still very much in flux, influenced by, among other things, a changing political and academic environment. Take, for example, the Ukrainian law "On Access to the Archives of Repressive Organs of the Communist Totalitarian Regime 1917–1991," which has recently provided access to one of the world's largest collections of original documents from the Soviet period. With an estimated one to four million documents, Ukraine's collection of Soviet archival materials is likely to be by far the largest among the former Soviet republics. The new possibilities for access will over time spur new research. CWIHP is already actively exploring the new documentation, and in time new collections will be posted to the CWIHP Digital Archive. Or take the recent historiographic trend to give the Global South greater agency in the history of the Cold War. Ongoing research in this direction is reflected in new accessions to the Digital Archive from the Algerian and Burmese archives.[17] Teachers and students should be aware of the selection bias inherent in the CWIHP collections.

These weaknesses of the CWIHP Digital Archive are balanced by the opportunity to read and analyze thousands of high-grade documents in English (and increasingly also in their original language, for those able to do so) that it would be nearly impossible for most people to access otherwise. Some even are no longer accessible in their original archive! And the very evidently "work-in-progress" nature of the Cold War history "project" can be an empowering point of departure for student inquiries: with some basic tools and guidance, students can become— to paraphrase the historian Carl L. Becker—"their own historian." Rather than confronting students with a "preset" narrative, the documents in the CWIHP collections can help sharpen critical thinking, foster deductive, analytical, and synthesizing skills central to historical reasoning, and encourage students to question common wisdom and long-standing assumptions. Cold War history is history in the making, and, taking advantage of the CWIHP Digital Archive and other resources, students can become active participants in this process.

Transcripts of leadership discussions in the Digital Archive allow students to be "flies on the wall" during key moments of the Cold War. In contrast to textbook narratives, these documents allow students to get a sense for the relative openness of these historical situations, for the role of personality and human agency but also the importance of the structural context. Questioning these records can allow students to develop empathy, a critical skill both in historical understanding as well as statecraft: to be able to put yourself into the shoes of the historical actors, especially those "on the other side." Based on the transcripts and supporting materials teachers might devise role plays that give students the opportunity to construct historically informed alternative scenarios and outcomes in an effort to sharpen students' sense of the fluidity, conditionality, and contingency of the historical process.

The Digital Archive collections can also teach students to question official government publications. The Russian and Eastern European sources, for example, have served as a powerful corrective and context for the selective document publications produced in Beijing. The most famous case is Mao's October 2, 1950, cable. It came in the wake of the successful US-UN landing at Inchon and the ensuing retreat of North Korean forces northwards, raising the specter of UN Command troops crossing of the demarcation line along the thirty-eighth parallel. Threatened by complete defeat, the leadership of the Democratic People's Republic of Korea (DPRK) reluctantly but urgently appealed to Stalin and Mao Zedong for direct intervention in the war. In a telegram to Mao Zedong on October 1, Stalin urged the Chinese to "move at least five to six divisions toward the 38th parallel at once." Thus, at the most crucial moment of the Korean War, the PRC leaders, only a year after coming to power, were forced to decide whether they would take on the burden of defending North Korea against the world's most powerful armed forces.

In 1987, in the first volume of *Jianguo yilai Mao Zedong wengao* (Mao Zedong's Manuscripts since the Founding of the People's Republic), an official but internal *neibu* publication, the Chinese government published what it claimed was Mao's response to the North Koreans' desperate plea for help—a telegram to Stalin dated October 2, 1950, declaring that the Chinese leaders had "decided to send a portion of our troops, under the name of [Chinese People's] Volunteers, to Korea, assisting the Korean comrades in fighting the troops of the United States and its running dog Syngman Rhee." According to this text, Mao told the Soviet leader that "we must be prepared for an American declaration of war on China. We must be prepared for the possible bombardment by American air forces of many Chinese cities and industrial bases, and for attacks by American naval forces on China's coastal areas." The record thus suggested China's unambiguous willingness to come to the fraternal support of its embattled North Korean comrades—a version of history that suited the contemporary political needs of the PRC's alliance with the DPRK.

It therefore came as a great surprise when, in 1995, scholars affiliated with CWIHP discovered among newly released Russian archival documents in Moscow a sharply different version of Mao's message to Stalin on October 2, 1950. In the telegram actually received in Moscow (which now can be found in translation in the CWIHP Digital Archive), Mao declared that, while the Chinese leadership had originally planned to move several volunteer divisions to North Korea to assist its Korean comrades if the enemy advanced north of the thirty-eighth parallel, "having thought this over thoroughly, we now consider that such actions may entail extremely serious consequences." Pointing to the risk of a global conflagration, "many comrades in the CC CCP [Central Committee of the Chinese Communist Party] judge that it is necessary to show caution here. Of course, not to send our troops to render assistance is very bad for the Korean comrades, who are presently in such difficulty, and we ourselves feel this keenly; but if we advance several divisions and the enemy forces us to retreat; and this moreover provokes an open conflict between the USA and China, then our entire plan for peaceful construction will be completely ruined, and many people in the country will be dissatisfied."

CWIHP's publication of this sharply different Russian document created a major debate among historians and officials within China and abroad. In response, Party archivists in Beijing searched Mao's documents in the Central Party Archives and confirmed that the original of the published Chinese version of Mao's October 2, 1950, message, in Mao's own handwriting, did indeed exist and was kept there. However, while other telegrams usually (but not always) carried Mao's office staff's signature indicating how and when the telegram was dispatched, this telegram did not. Thus, while Mao's telegram published in 1987 was in fact genuine, that telegram was apparently never dispatched. Sometime later the PRC released a facsimile copy of the original document that the Project had published. This document, handwritten by Mao Zedong, suggested that Mao had been well ahead of a majority within the CCP leadership in his readiness to come to the aid of the Korean comrades: most within the Chinese leadership, including senior military commanders, were initially opposed to entering a military confrontation with the US-UN in early October 1950. That decision would come only after several weeks of lengthy deliberations and consultations: only at the end of October 1950 did Chinese "volunteer" troops join the fighting. The October 2 cable episode illustrates the danger in relying solely on official document publications to interpret China's Cold War experience—or, for that matter, any country's foreign policy.[18]

In the context of other Cold War primary-source collections, such as those in the National Archives, the National Security Archive, and the *Foreign Relations of the United States* (*FRUS*) series, the relative value of the CWIHP archives lies in the possibility of juxtaposing Eastern bloc and other sources with the US documentation available at these other outlets. Thus, students can compare George F. Kennan's March 1946 seminal "Long Telegram," which, along with the famous "Mr. X Foreign Affairs article," laid the conceptual foundation for early American containment strategy vis-à-vis the Soviet Union, with the influential September 1946 telegram sent by Soviet diplomat Nikolai V. Novikov that assessed the future direction of US foreign policy for the Soviet leadership around Josef Stalin. The juxtaposition of the two documents can elucidate how starkly differing perceptions on the part of American and Soviet governments about each other's intentions contributed to the rise of the Cold War. This combination of sources—particularly related to events such as the Berlin Ultimatum Crisis of 1958–62 and the 1962 Cuban Missile Crisis, the Korean and Vietnam Wars, the Soviet invasions of Hungary, Czechoslovakia, and Afghanistan, the Sino-Soviet split, the 1983 War Scare, and the origins and ending of the Cold War, for which substantial fresh documentation on the policies of the "other (communist) side" is available—should enable student to write papers that assess and compare the motives, perceptions, and actions of US and Soviet/communist foreign-policy decision makers. Given the growing strength of CWIHP's document collections on actors other than the two superpowers, such assignments can highlight the role of second- and third-tier powers and nongovernmental organizations and groups.

NOTES

1. See Todd Bennett's contribution to this volume.

2. Over the sixteen years that I have led the Project, I have benefited from the counsel of the Project's Advisory Committee chaired by Professor William Taubman of Amherst College and comprising John Lewis Gaddis (Yale University), Samuel F. Wells Jr. (Wilson Center), the independent historian Michael Beschloss, Warren Cohen (University of Maryland–Baltimore County), James H. Billington (recently retired Librarian of Congress), Sharon Wolchik (George Washington University), and former (1991–96) CWIHP director James Hershberg (George Washington University). Robert Litwak, the Wilson Center's Vice President for Programs, has been crucially involved in overseeing and securing funding for the CWIHP over the years. I have also appreciated the cooperation of former (1997–98) CWIHP director David Wolf and the support of the Project's amazing staff—Martha "Dee" Beutel, Pieter Biersteker, Laura Deal, Ryan Gage, Charles Kraus, Allison Lylakov, Nancy Meyers, Timothy McDonnell, Mircea Munteanu, James Person, Evan Pikulski, and Kristina Terzieva.

3. Eyal Press, "The Archive Eaters: A New Generation of Scholars Sinks Its Teeth into the Cold War's Leftovers," *Lingua Franca* 8, no. 3 (1998), http://linguafranca.mirror.theinfo.org/9804/archiveeaters.html.

4. On the controversy over the series, see Richard Pipes, Robert Conquest, and John Lewis Gaddis, "The Cold War over CNN's *Cold War*," *Hoover Digest* 4 (1999), https://web.archive.org/web/20091011040407/http://www.hoover.org/publications/digest/3522116.html.

5. In fact, the first major release was announced at an international conference organized by the Institute for Defense and Strategic Analysis (New Delhi) and the Program in New Delhi in October 2012.

6. Press, "The Archive Eaters."

7. I draw on the best recent survey of the Russian archival situation, Mark Kramer's "Archival Policies and Historical Memory in the Post-Soviet Era," *Demokratizatsiya* 20, no. 3 (Summer 2012): 204–15. See also his "Archival Research in Moscow: Progress and Pitfalls," *CWIHP Bulletin*, no. 3 (Fall 1993): 1, 18–39.

8. "Ukaz Prezidenta Rossiiskoi Federatsii o Komissii pri Prezidente Rossiiskoi Federatsii poprotivodeistviyu popytkam fal'sifikatsii istorii v ushcherb interesam Rossii," Ukaz Prezidenta RF No. 549, May 15, 2009, in *Rossiiskaya gazeta* (Moscow), May 20, 2009, 2, cited in Kramer, "Archival Policies," 212.

9. For an excellent overview on research in the Chinese archives, see Charles Kraus, "Researching the History of the People's Republic of China," CWIHP Working Paper, no. 79 (April 2016), http://www.wilsoncenter.org/publication/researching-the-history-the-peoples-republic-china.

10. See Christian Ostermann, Sergey Radchenko, and Charles Kraus, "Report on the National Archives Department of Myanmar," *CWIHP Bulletin*, no. 19 (Summer 2016): 383–90.

11. John K. Lee and W. Guy Clarke, "High School Social Studies Students' Uses of Online Historical Documents Related to the Cuban Missile Crisis," *The Journal of Interactive Online Learning* 2, no. 1 (Summer 2003): 2.

12. Thanks to my colleague Laura Deal for chronicling this development in "Visualizing Digital Collections: Creating User-Friendly Search and Browse Tools," *Technical Services Quarterly* 32, no. 1 (2015): 14–34.

13. See unpublished version of manuscript by Laura Deal, "Visualizing Digital Collections: Creating User-Friendly Search and Browse Tools."

14. Mark Kramer, "Why Did Russia Give Away Crimea Sixty Years Ago?," *CWIHP e-Dossier*, no. 47 (March 2014), https://www.wilsoncenter.org/publication/why-did-russia-give-away-crimea-sixty-years-ago.

15. Austin Jersild, "The Digital Archive of the Cold War International History Project," http://uncpress.unc.edu/browse/page/862.

16. A 2003 study of sixty-four eleventh-grade students using the former, now defunct CWIHP Virtual Archive and another online repository to answer a set of questions about the Cuban Missile Crisis detailed some of the difficulties

encountered by students: "Referring to the Cuban Missile Crisis, [one student] said, 'We should have known the whole situation and understood it.' Another student worried that 'in order to apply the information found on the CWHIP web site, you will need to have previous knowledge about the Cold War.' Still another student thought that if she 'knew more about the Cold War it would have made more sense.' Other students were less direct. One student claimed that 'the sites were hard to understand and get the answers from. I never could discover any methods to find answers.' Some students implied their lack of content knowledge by mystifying the information on the site. Several students complained that the vocabulary was too difficult. A student complained that a specific document he used was 'confusing to read and the wording was weird and hard to understand.' Another student grumbled that she 'could not comprehend the way things were said.' All of these students distanced themselves from taking responsibility for answering the questions by claiming that they lacked the prior knowledge needed to properly understand the documents." Students lacking the appropriate skills-based historical knowledge "did not understand that they needed to make inferences, weigh alternatives, and generalize as they pieced together the answers. Instead, they were too rigidly focused on finding the right answers to the questions. . . . Another student was very direct when complaining about her problems finding answers. 'Almost all the documents were extremely long and after skimming about 5, I got discouraged and frustrated because I could not find any answers.' Still another student expressed the same sentiment saying, 'Nothing really gives facts just what the speakers thought.' . . . Several students thought that the questions required too much opinion. They were unable to make arguments using supporting details from the documents. Other students were confused by the choices they had to make when confronted with alternatives. For example, a student said she 'searched through many documents and looked for key words and phrases that I thought would pertain to the questions, but I did not find any answers.' This student like others was unable to extract useful pieces of information that could be synthesized into answers." Lee and Clarke, "High School Social Studies Students' Uses of Online Historical Documents Related to the Cuban Missile Crisis," 5–6.

17. Odd Arne Westad, *The Global Cold War: Third World Interventions and the Making of Our Times* (Cambridge: Cambridge University Press, 2007).

18. The episode is documented in "The Cold War in Asia," *CWIHP Bulletin*, no. 6–7 (1996–97).

KEY RESOURCES

Cold War International History Project *Bulletin*. https://www.wilsoncenter .org/publication-series/cwihp-bulletin.

Cold War International History Project Digital Archive. http://digitalarchive
    .wilsoncenter.org/.

Coll, Steve. *Ghost Wars: The Secret History of the CIA, Afghanistan, and Bin Laden,
    from the Soviet Invasion to September 10, 2001.* New York: Penguin Books, 2004.

Gaddis, John. *George F. Kennan: An American Life.* New York: Penguin Books,
    2011.

Taubman, William. *Khrushchev: The Man and His Era.* New York: W. W. Norton,
    2003.

Teaching with the Tapes

Presidential Recordings and the Cold War

MARC J. SELVERSTONE

Secret presidential taping began with the recording of Franklin D. Roosevelt's press conferences in August 1940, but the vast majority of White House tapes—upwards of 99 percent, in fact—come from the administrations of John F. Kennedy, Lyndon B. Johnson, and Richard M. Nixon. Stretching from 1962 through 1973, these recordings of private telephone conversations, Oval Office meetings, and Cabinet Room sessions cover some of the most dramatic moments of the Cold War, from the high-stakes showdown over Soviet missiles in Cuba, to the introduction of US ground forces in Vietnam, to America's engagement with China and the emergence of a détente in superpower relations. More broadly, these tapes span a crucial era in that twilight struggle—one that began, purportedly, with so much promise, as a self-proclaimed new generation set out to conquer new frontiers. Although tragedy would befall the nation in Dallas a thousand days later, Americans would soon reach for even greater glory in the building of a great society. Yet that heady, historical moment ended in spasms of violence and a shattered consensus over much of what had long seemed settled in national life. The tapes chronicle these struggles of time and place, but they also speak to more enduring questions about power and purpose, including those about America's role in the world, the rights of its citizens, and the health of its democracy.

This history is uniquely accessible via the presidential recordings. The tapes offer the immediacy of the moment, the fly-on-the-wall perspective that no other source can provide, allowing the past to unfold in real time. But they do more than simply narrate the affairs of the Oval Office. Among their virtues, they break down the artificial boundaries between foreign and domestic policy, revealing the intersecting demands of geopolitics and partisan politics that presidents confront every day. They document the starts and stops inherent in the making of national policy, as presidents seek to overcome obstacles by stroking, vilifying, or accommodating a range of personalities. They highlight the sheer magnitude of the top job in the land, as the nation's chief executive tacks from one set of challenges to countless others on a daily basis. And they remind us that presidents are human—whether they're taking time out to order a pair of pants, interrupting the business of state to play with their children, or watching pro football games on the weekend with family.[1]

While the recordings add tremendous value to teaching as well as to scholarship, they also have their limitations—as do other primary sources—and instructors should acknowledge and address these weaknesses when using the tapes in the classroom. Remarks made in a telephone call or in a meeting may well be indicative of a president's true feelings or policy preferences, but they may also reflect the simple need to blow off steam; sensitivity to context is therefore essential when listening to the tapes. Likewise, users should consider the identities and motivations of the public officials and private citizens captured on tape, as presidents often make different arguments on the same topic to different people for different reasons. Conversations may also be so laden with oblique references and verbal shorthand that they defy easy comprehension. Deeper research into these sources, therefore, is not only a valuable but also an essential part of the pedagogical process.

Value

One of the great merits of the presidential recordings is their ability to refine the historical record. On the most fundamental level, the tapes can augment a written summary of a meeting or a telephone call, providing information that a note taker failed to include or correcting a scribe's account in ways large and small. An example from the Kennedy tapes is illustrative. In the fall of 1963, Secretary of Defense Robert S. McNamara and General Maxwell D. Taylor, chairman of the Joint Chiefs of Staff, traveled to South Vietnam to assess Saigon's progress in its war against the communists. Prior to their departure,

McNamara and Taylor met with President Kennedy and proposed a number of measures they hoped would prod South Vietnamese president Ngo Dinh Diem into prosecuting the fight with greater energy. One of these measures included the withdrawal of US military advisers from South Vietnam. According to the written memorandum of conversation (memcon), published in the State Department's *Foreign Relations of the United States* (*FRUS*) series, Taylor was the lone official who raised the matter of a deadline for US participation in the war.[2] Yet the meeting tape reveals that McNamara, too, sought to use an American departure as leverage against Diem, intimating that military progress was a precondition for US withdrawal: "I think we can tell [Diem] we have plans for withdrawal of our forces when military success warrants it. If you like to get them out, just—why don't you see about getting them out. We hope that before the end of the year, we can withdraw military, [if the] situation improves. We hope—believe we can."[3] McNamara's comment is a significant piece of evidence in the enduring debate about US planning for a Vietnam troop withdrawal, since the defense secretary had long argued that a force reduction was in no way contingent on military success.[4] But his statement is also a reminder that memcons, often the only contemporaneous account of a presidential meeting, are imperfect documents of record.

The tapes also capture the human drama of these moments as policymakers weighed the life-and-death decisions of war and peace. Again, drawing on the Kennedy tapes, the following vignette offers a window into the emotional valence of these interactions. Upon their return from Vietnam, McNamara and Taylor debriefed Kennedy on their trip and detailed the measures they thought would increase Diem's chances of winning his war against the communists; as they had indicated prior to their departure, one of these measures was the withdrawal of US military advisers. Accordingly, the report they submitted to the president called for a program "to train Vietnamese so that essential functions now performed by U.S. military personnel can be carried out by Vietnamese by the end of 1965," noting further that "it should be possible to withdraw the bulk of U.S. personnel by that time."[5] No memcon exists for the meeting at which McNamara and Taylor presented these findings to Kennedy, but a tape of their exchange reveals the heightened pitch of the discussion. After National Security Adviser McGeorge Bundy questioned the rationale for a troop withdrawal, Secretary McNamara, his voice rising, launched into an ardent defense: "We need a way to get out of Vietnam and this is a way of doing it. And to leave forces there when they're not needed, I think, is wasteful and it complicates both their problems and ours."[6] Although knowledge of the proposed troop reduction stretches back to the publication of the Pentagon Papers in 1971 and to the relevant *FRUS* volumes for 1990 and 1991, it was not until the release of this tape in 1997 that the public could hear McNamara making his impassioned plea. By injecting this emotional element into the mix, the tapes add greater nuance to the history preserved in the textual record. And, as is the case with this recording, they can raise new questions or suggest new arguments about a person's motivation or depth of conviction as it relates to matters of policy.

This emotional dimension of policymaking is particularly evident on the White House tapes of Lyndon Johnson. It is one thing, for instance, to read about Johnson bemoaning the choices he was confronted with in Vietnam; it is another thing altogether to hear him anguishing over the responsibility that, ultimately, he alone would bear in committing combat troops to the fight. Students, therefore, benefit greatly from listening to LBJ engage Cabinet officials, lawmakers, presidential aides, and private individuals in conversation about wartime policy and politics. His May 1964 conversation with Senator Richard B. Russell provides a good example of these exchanges; we hear LBJ wonder, "what the hell are we going to get out of" sending soldiers to Vietnam.[7] It is further arresting to hear Johnson acknowledge that Hanoi was probably never going to "quit" the war and yet lament that his own strategy for victory rested on little more than forcing the communists to do just that.[8]

The tapes also help to reframe the often self-serving renditions of events that appear in the memoirs and oral histories of policymakers. Aside from the previously mentioned case of Robert McNamara, another example comes from the Johnson collection and involves a telephone conversation between LBJ and his vice president, Hubert H. Humphrey, at a pivotal moment in the 1968 presidential campaign. Humphrey, by then the Democratic candidate for the White House, had called to tell Johnson that he was departing from the administration's line on a bombing halt in North Vietnam—a line that Johnson had essentially forced Humphrey to observe but that Humphrey was now abandoning in the hope that a more dovish approach to Vietnam would appeal to more voters. As he described the call in his autobiography, published in 1976, Humphrey told Johnson that he would soon be breaking with the president in a tape-delayed speech broadcast on television.[9] Yet,

President Lyndon Johnson on the phone in the summer of 1965. (LBJ Library photo by Yoichi Okamoto)

contrary to claims made in his book, the tapes reveal that Humphrey failed to give Johnson advance warning of the speech and never did receive from Johnson a grudging acknowledgment of his own policy independence. Nor did he inform Johnson that he had discussed the terms of his speech with the president's own negotiators in Paris, as Humphrey himself later wrote.[10]

The tapes of President Richard M. Nixon likewise highlight the gap between what appears on the recordings and what shows up in the published recollections of policymakers. The fate of Cambodia offers a particularly noteworthy case of real-time insight conflicting with post hoc rationalization. Both Nixon and his national security adviser, Henry Kissinger, long maintained that their secret bombing of Cambodia, which began in March 1969, bore no relation to the killing fields that would later claim much of its population; the raids, they said, neither undermined the existing government of Prince Norodom Sihanouk nor pushed the North Vietnamese further into Cambodia and weakened the Sihanouk government as a result. Yet Nixon's White House tapes suggest that both men understood there to be a direct connection between the bombing and the destabilization of the country.[11] It was this upheaval that ultimately paved the way for the murderous regime of Pol Pot.

Access

Given the breadth of the presidential recordings and the challenges of separating the wheat from the chaff, educators may find it daunting to identify the most illuminating tapes and then use them effectively in a classroom setting. Fortunately, teachers and students can avail themselves of several print and digital sources that provide audio clips, transcripts of conversations, or both. These materials began to emerge in the 1990s with the publication of Michael Beschloss's book of selected and abridged Johnson transcripts and also through the work of Ernest May and Philip Zelikow on Kennedy's Cuban Missile Crisis tapes.[12] Thereafter, scholars brought forth several compilations of presidential "greatest hits" as well as comprehensive volumes on the history of presidential taping. William Doyle and John Prados were among the first to write about the tapes, and each produced expansive accounts of presidential recording from Roosevelt through Bill Clinton, replete with transcript snippets; Doyle also released an accompanying

CD in 2008, while Prados packaged CDs of the corresponding audio files with his original publication in 2003.[13] Ted Widmer later narrowed the historical focus by publishing selections of Kennedy transcripts on a variety of topics in 2012.[14] Much heftier volumes of Nixon transcripts, edited by former Nixon aide John Dean and by the duo of Douglas Brinkley and Luke Nichter, appeared in 2014 and 2015, respectively.[15]

While these print works and digital extras can help teachers navigate this large mass of data, several websites offer an additional and more technologically efficient means of identifying usable clips and deploying them for classroom use. The State Department's online edition of *FRUS* includes transcripts of Kennedy, Johnson, and Nixon recordings, with the largest collection covering Nixon's handling of arms control with the Soviet Union (https://history.state.gov/historicaldocuments). Although these transcripts are freely accessible, none of them is joined to the associated audio files. The presidential libraries, on the other hand, have focused on making the raw audio more easily discoverable. Visitors to the Kennedy Library's online portal can search the site and download mp3s of Kennedy tape on topics such as Vietnam or Soviet relations through a series of highlighted links (http://www.jfklibrary.org/). Nevertheless, the site is most helpful to users who know precisely what documents they want, as it lacks a dedicated and user-friendly webpage for the tapes.[16] The Nixon Library, in contrast, provides a more intuitive landing page for the recordings, especially from an Internet search (http://www.nixonlibrary.gov/virtuallibrary/tapeexcerpts/). The library makes these files available in mp3 or flac formats, offering finding aides for the recordings and samples of conversations on specific topics. The Johnson Library provides users with two ways of accessing the LBJ tapes: through a menu (http://www.lbjlib.utexas.edu/johnson/archives.hom/Dictabelt.hom/content.asp) that ultimately directs listeners to the holdings of the University of Virginia's Miller Center (http://millercenter.org/presidentialrecordings) and through a search portal that generates pages that integrate sound, images, finding aids, and daily diary entries (http://digital.lbjlibrary.org/).

In addition to these federally sponsored efforts, nongovernmental initiatives are helping to get the tapes into the hands—and ears—of teachers, students, and the interested public. Nixontapes.org offers raw audio files and associated resources for the nation's thirty-seventh president; these include contextual essays and Nixon's daily appointment calendars, though relatively few transcripts are available on the site (http://nixontapes.org/). The National Security Archive also provides links to audio files and associated transcripts via interpretive essays on several subjects (https://www2.gwu.edu/~nsarchiv/). These span a range of presidencies and address topics such as the Cuban Missile Crisis, the Vietnam War, and the 1965 deployment of US Marines to the Dominican Republic.

The University of Virginia's Miller Center, which established the Presidential Recordings Program (PRP) in 1998, houses the most ambitious effort to transcribe the once-secret White House tapes. Having published its initial transcripts in print format, PRP now offers two online portals for accessing more than twenty volumes of materials in the Kennedy, Johnson, and Nixon collections. The *Presidential Recordings Digital Edition* includes a comprehensive and fully searchable interface supported by the University of Virginia Press (http://prde.upress .virginia.edu/), while the Miller Center's own website serves up downloadable files of all declassified presidential recordings, as well as synchronized audio and transcript clips geared primarily to teachers, students, and the general public (http://millercenter.org/presidential classroom). These clips highlight some of the more compelling recordings across a range of Cold War topics, rendered in a format suitable for classroom use.

Scholarship

Since a critical mass of tapes became available to the public only during the second half of the 1990s, their impact on scholarship has been slow to emerge. Nevertheless, historians are now locating the presidential recordings at the center of their writing and are doing so with increasing frequency. George Herring, Robert David Johnson, Mitchell Lerner, Alan McPherson, and Thomas Alan Schwartz, to name just a few, have used the White House tapes to great effect in studies on US relations with Israel, Latin America, and Vietnam, as well as in books and articles on the interplay between domestic politics and foreign policy.[17] In addition, scholars who have spent years transcribing and analyzing the tapes are leveraging them in works that have revised our understanding of key historical episodes. Sheldon Stern, the former historian at the Kennedy Library, has used the tapes extensively in three volumes on the Cuban Missile Crisis, while David Coleman, Max Holland, and Ken Hughes, all of whom have been associated with the

Miller Center, have incorporated the tapes in studies, respectively, of the Cuban Missile Crisis, the Kennedy assassination, and the linkages among Nixon, Vietnam, Watergate, and the presidential elections of 1968 and 1972.[18] Monographs and articles from Howard Jones, Jeffrey Kimball, and Fredrik Logevall, as well as biographies from Robert Dallek and Randall Woods, have added to an expanding literature on Cold War topics that continues to draw on the White House tapes for insight, texture, and new discoveries.[19]

While teachers would benefit generally from consulting these works, educators may find them unwieldy for identifying bite-sized chunks of text and audio that are suitable for classroom use. Pedagogically, the most versatile may be the Herring and Hughes books, as conversations cited in these volumes are linked directly to online portals featuring the tapes and associated transcripts; e-book versions of these studies (the Herring work is offered only as an e-book) provide an even more seamless experience of toggling between the narrative text and the transcript/audio pages.[20] The roughly 250 prepackaged snippets available via the Miller Center website may grant teachers the most flexibility in customizing their classroom activities. Suggestions for how teachers might use these clips are also available through the Miller Center and in related articles and essays centering on the tapes.[21]

Activities

Comparative approaches are often effective tools for enhancing the learning environment, and, as already noted, tapes can highlight the gulf between public and private accounts of historical episodes. The gap between events and their treatment in popular culture may offer particularly ripe opportunities for promoting student engagement. One episode that has come in for repeated treatment by filmmakers has been the Cuban Missile Crisis, and activities that place the White House tapes from those thirteen days alongside cinematic accounts of their unfolding can help to clarify the record and explore the connections among history, memory, and popular representation.

Several aspects of the crisis are worthy of closer study, but the relationship between JFK and his military advisers—captured through one moment in particular—is well suited to classroom analysis.[22] On the morning of October 19, 1962, President Kennedy informed the Joint Chiefs of Staff that he intended to blockade Cuba and thereby induce

Moscow to crate its missiles and warheads and return them to Russia. The Chiefs, who had been lobbying for a more aggressive response since the start of the crisis three days earlier, voiced their displeasure with Kennedy's proposed action. According to Robert Kennedy's *Thirteen Days*, the conflict reached a climax when Marine Corps commandant Gen. David M. Shoup, recognizing the magnitude of the moment, summarized JFK's predicament with the cheeky observation "You are in a pretty bad fix, Mr. President." Without missing a beat, Kennedy countered with his own wry remark: "You are in it with me." In RFK's telling, his brother's comment elicited laughter from "everyone" in the room. Differences of opinion certainly remained, but the president's quip and the Chiefs' response to it suggested a muted, if no less acknowledged, atmosphere of tension.

In the hands of Hollywood screenwriters, such macabre humor gave way to posturing, sermonizing, and a much darker mood. *The Missiles of October*, based on Bobby's book and broadcast on television in 1974, preserved Shoup as the author of the "pretty bad fix" remark. But its Kennedy now glowered at Shoup and at the rest of the Chiefs, disparaging their simplistic plans for military action, and there were no laughs—nervous or otherwise—in the offing. That same spirit infused the feature film *Thirteen Days* (2000). In this stylized, big-budget, and post–Cold War version of the episode, Kennedy and the Joint Chiefs are joined in the Oval Office by key administration and national security officials, with some of them circling the room as they explore the potential meaning and impact of the blockade. Now, however, it is General Curtis E. LeMay, the hawkish Air Force chief of staff, who provokes a contemptuous JFK by referencing the president's "pretty bad fix." Walking away from LeMay, Kennedy looks over his shoulder and delivers the stinging riposte "Well, maybe you haven't noticed—you're in it with me." LeMay responds with a look that is equal parts resignation and bemusement.[23] The mutual disdain felt by the president and the military brass is hard to miss.

These contrasting versions of the episode provide an opening for teachers and students to explore its representation during different cultural and historical moments. But our ability to consult a recording of the meeting—which reveals that it was, in fact, LeMay who uttered the "pretty bad fix" remark and that it indeed prompted laughter within the room—shines a light on how the exchange really happened, adding yet another dimension to consider. While the two Hollywood versions alter historical reality in various ways, the filmmakers' revisions are arguably less significant than their interpretive approaches to civil-military relations, to the presumed consequences of military action, and to the rendering of the characters themselves. Moving beyond this example, teachers might encourage students to use the tapes when evaluating dramatic accounts of other historical episodes and then to explore the resulting gap between factual rhetoric and fictionalized reality.

The tapes can also alert students to the way that interpretations of history change with the introduction of new source material. Recordings made during the Tonkin Gulf incident, for instance, when North Vietnamese vessels allegedly fired on US warships in two separate engagements in August 1964, were unavailable to the scholars who wrote the first accounts of the affair; they would remain inaccessible for decades. Once the Johnson Library began to release these materials in the 1990s, scholars could factor their revelations into monographs as well as into classroom texts. A comparison of the way that historians have treated the incident prior to and after the declassification of the tapes would allow students to investigate the ways that changes in the evidentiary base can alter treatments of presidents, their advisers, and historical events.[24]

While the tapes lend themselves to creative use in the classroom, they also support straightforward approaches to supplementing lectures and lesson plans. Whether the goal is to highlight illustrative episodes or to explore aspects of presidential behavior, teachers can use audio clips, transcript snippets, or both in a variety of formats, including teacher-directed presentations, group-based learning, or individual assignments. Sound recording analysis worksheets, developed by the National Archives, outline pre- and post-listening activities, prompting students to consider the purpose of a conversation, the mood or tone of the conversation, and information transmitted via the recording that might not be available through other sources. These tools also ask students to reflect on broader aspects of American life germane to the era, as well as to consider information not conveyed in the recording that would have been of value to the conversation participants.[25]

Tapes, in short, can enliven the classroom experience just as meaningfully as they can enhance the scholarly enterprise. They offer insight into myriad dimensions of national and international life—as key actors in those dramas experienced them—and provide further grist for exploring the personal lives of the presidents themselves. Indeed, no other resource captures the way that power is used and policy is made quite like the presidential recordings. They illuminate in rich and candid detail the means by which presidents have shaped and been shaped by events large and small, offering case studies in executive leadership—both good and bad—and providing users with a better understanding of diverse yet related decision-making environments. For all of us engaged in teaching and understanding American life, and particularly its texture during the Cold War, they are singular and invaluable and will likely remain so for a long, long time.

NOTES

1. Lyndon B. Johnson to Joe Haggar, August 9, 1964, WH6408.16, Citation #4851, Lyndon B. Johnson Library (hereafter LBJL), http://millercenter.org /presidentialclassroom/exhibits/lbj-orders-some-new-haggar-pants; John F. Kennedy, Dictated Memoir Entry, Dictation Belt 52.1: Cassette M, Side 2, President's Office Files, Presidential Recordings Collection, John F. Kennedy Library, http://millercenter.org/presidentialclassroom/exhibits/jfks-memoir-dictation-on-the-assassination-of-diem; Camp David 235-014, Richard Nixon Presidential Library and Museum, Yorba Linda, California, https://www .youtube.com/watch?v=RYCoRU_BNo.

2. "Memorandum for the Record of a Meeting," September 23, 1963, in Edward C. Keefer, ed., *Vietnam: August–December 1963*, Vol. IV, US State Department, *Foreign Relations of the United States* (hereafter *FRUS*), *1961–1963* (Washington, DC: Government Printing Office, 1991), 281.

3. Meeting Tape 112, September 23, 1963, John F. Kennedy Library (hereafter JFKL), President's Office Files (hereafter POF), Presidential Recordings Collection (hereafter PRC). Transcript by author.

4. Robert S. McNamara, *In Retrospect: The Tragedy and Lessons of Vietnam* (New York: Vintage, 1995), 96–97; see also McNamara Oral History, Library of Congress, McNamara Papers, Speeches and Writings, Interviews, Office of the Secretary of Defense Historical Office, 1986.

5. "Memorandum from the Chairman of the Joint Chiefs of Staff (Taylor) and the Secretary of Defense (McNamara) to the President," October 2, 1963, *FRUS*, 4:338.

6. Meeting Tape 114/A49, October 2, 1963, JFKL, POF, PRC. Transcript by author.

7. "Lyndon Johnson and Richard Russell on May 27, 1964," Tape WH6405.10, Citations #3519, #3520, and #3521, *Presidential Recordings Digital*

Edition (hereafter *PRDE*) [Toward the Great Society, vol. 6, ed. Guian A. McKee] (Charlottesville: University of Virginia Press, 2014-), http://prde.upress.virginia.edu/conversations/9060283.

8. Lyndon Johnson and Robert McNamara, June 21, 1965, WH6506-05, Citations #8168, #8169, LBJL.

9. Hubert H. Humphrey, *Education of a Public Man: My Life and Politics*, ed. Norman Sherman (Garden City, NJ: Doubleday, 1976), 403.

10. See Ken Hughes, *Chasing Shadows: the Nixon Tapes, the Chennault Affairs, and the Origins of Watergate* (Charlottesville: University of Virginia Press, 2014), 19–23.

11. Hughes, *Chasing Shadows*, 90–91. See also "Richard Nixon, John Connally, H. R. 'Bob' Haldeman, and Henry A. Kissinger on 4 May 1972," Conversation 334-044 (*PRDE* Excerpt A, PRDE), *PRDE* [Chasing Shadows, ed. Ken Hughes] (Charlottesville: University of Virginia Press, 2014-), http://prde.upress.virginia.edu/conversations/4006729.

12. Michael R. Beschloss, *Taking Charge: The Johnson White House Tapes, 1963–1964* (New York: Simon & Schuster, 1997); Ernest R. May and Philip D. Zelikow, eds., *The Kennedy Tapes: Inside the White House during the Cuban Missile Crisis* (Cambridge, MA: Belknap Press of Harvard University Press, 1997). Beschloss and May/Zelikow followed these publications with additional and updated volumes of transcripts; see Beschloss, *Reaching for Glory: Lyndon Johnson's Secret White House Tapes, 1964–1965* (New York: Simon & Schuster, 2001); May and Zelikow, eds. *The Kennedy Tapes: Inside the White House during the Cuban Missile Crisis* (New York: W. W. Norton, 2002).

13. William Doyle, *Inside the Oval Office: The White House Tapes from FDR to Clinton* (New York: Kodansha International, 1999); John Prados, *The White House Tapes: Eavesdropping on the President* (New York: New Press, 2003).

14. Ted Widmer, *Listening In: The Secret White House Recordings of John F. Kennedy* (New York: Hyperion, 2012), with DVD of recordings included.

15. John W. Dean, *The Nixon Defense: What He Knew and When He Knew It* (New York: Viking, 2014); Douglas Brinkley and Luke A. Nichter, *The Nixon Tapes: 1971–1972* (Boston: Houghton Mifflin Harcourt, 2014); Douglas Brinkley and Luke A. Nichter, *The Nixon Tapes: 1973* (Boston: Houghton Mifflin Harcourt, 2015). Widmer, *Listening In*, includes two CDs of corresponding audio files.

16. See also http://www.jfklibrary.org/JFK/JFK-in-History/White-House-Tape-Recordings.aspx.

17. George C. Herring, *The War Bells Have Rung: The LBJ Tapes and the Americanization of the Vietnam War* (Charlottesville: University of Virginia Press, 2014), http://prde.upress.virginia.edu/content/herring; Robert David Johnson, "Lyndon Johnson and Israel: The Secret Presidential Recordings," S. Daniel Abraham Center for International and Regional Studies, Tel Aviv University, Research Paper #3 (July 2008), http://www.tau.ac.il/humanities/abraham

/publications/johnson_israel.pdf; Mitchell Lerner, "History and Haggar Pants: The Cold War on Tape," *OAH Magazine of History* 24, no. 4 (October 2010): 19–24; Alan McPherson, "Misled by Himself: What the Johnson Tapes Reveal about the Dominican Intervention of 1965," *Latin American Research Review* 38, no. 2 (June 2003): 127–46; Thomas Alan Schwartz, "'Henry, . . . Winning an Election Is Terribly Important': Partisan Politics in the History of US Foreign Relations," *Diplomatic History* 33, no. 2 (April 2009): 173–90.

18. Sheldon M. Stern, *Averting the "Final Failure": John F. Kennedy and the Secret Cuban Missile Crisis Meetings* (Stanford: Stanford University Press, 2003); Sheldon M. Stern, *The Week the World Stood Still: Inside the Secret Cuban Missile Crisis* (Stanford.: Stanford University Press, 2005); Sheldon M. Stern, *The Cuban Missile Crisis in American Memory: Myths versus Reality* (Stanford: Stanford University Press, 2012); David G. Coleman, *On the Fourteenth Day: JFK and the Aftermath of the Cuban Missile Crisis* (New York: W. W. Norton, 2012); Max Holland, *The Kennedy Assassination Tapes* (New York: Knopf, 2004); Hughes, *Chasing Shadows*; Ken Hughes, *Fatal Politics: The Nixon Tapes, the Vietnam War, and the Casualties of Re-election* (Charlottesville: University of Virginia Press, 2015).

19. Howard Jones, *Death of a Generation: How the Assassinations of Diem and JFK Prolonged the Vietnam War* (New York: Oxford University Press, 2003); Jeffrey Kimball, *The Vietnam War Files: Uncovering the Secret History of Nixon-Era Strategy* (Lawrence: University Press of Kansas, 2004); Fredrik Logevall, "Presidential Address: Structure, Contingency, and the War in Vietnam," *Diplomatic History* 39, no. 1 (January 2015): 1–15; Robert Dallek, *An Unfinished Life: John F. Kennedy, 1917–1963* (Boston: Little, Brown, 2003); Randall Woods, *LBJ: Architect of Ambition* (New York: Free Press, 2006).

20. Herring, *The War Bells Have Rung*, http://prde.upress.virginia.edu/content/herring. Stand-alone portals for the Hughes books, which allow users to access the associated tapes and transcripts free of charge, are available at http://chasing-shadows.org/ and http://fatal-politics.org/. Full disclosure: this author contributed to the editing of these volumes and the production of their associated resources.

21. Stephanie Van Hover, Marc J. Selverstone, and Patricia Preston-Grimes, "Window into the White House," *Social Education* 72, no. 3 (April 2008): 130–35; Mitchell B. Lerner, "'We Must Bear a Good Deal of Responsibility for It': The White House Tapes and the War in Vietnam," in John Day Tully, Matthew Masur, and Brad Austin, eds., *Understanding and Teaching the Vietnam War* (Madison: University of Wisconsin Press), 75–95; Lerner, "History and Haggar Pants."

22. For a clip dramatizing an additional one of those moments—the concern over trading Soviet missiles in Cuba for NATO missiles in Turkey—see Meeting Tape 41, POF, PRC, JFKL; Philip Zelikow and Timothy Naftali, eds., *The Presidential Recordings: John F. Kennedy*, Vol. 3 (New York: W. W. Norton,

2001), 397–99, http://millercenter.org/presidentialclassroom/exhibits/missiles-in-turkey.

23. Robert F. Kennedy, *Thirteen Days: A Memoir of the Cuban Missile Crisis* (New York: W. W. Norton, 1969), 36–37; *The Missiles of October*, dir. Anthony Page (1974; Maljack Productions/Viacom Productions); *Thirteen Days*, dir. Roger Donaldson (2000; New Line Cinema).

24. See "Lyndon B. Johnson—Gulf of Tonkin Recordings," http://miller center.org/presidentialrecordings/johnson/tonkin, and Marc Selverstone and David Coleman, "Gulf of Tonkin, 1964: Perspectives from the Lyndon Johnson and National Military Command Center Tapes," Miller Center, http://miller center.org/presidentialclassroom/exhibits/gulf-of-tonkin-1964-perspectives.

25. http://www.archives.gov/education/lessons/worksheets/sound _recording_analysis_worksheet.pdf.

KEY RESOURCES

Filipink, Richard M., Jr. "A Necessary Reinterpretation: Using the Kennedy and Johnson Tapes as a Biographical and Historical Source." *Journal of Historical Biography* 3 (2008): 87–97. http://www.ufv.ca/jhb/Volume_3 /Volume_3_Filipink.pdf.

Powers, John. "The History of Presidential Audio Recordings and the Archival Issues Surrounding Their Use." CIDS Paper, National Archives and Records Administration. July 12, 1996.

Rushay, Samuel W., Jr. "Listening to Nixon: An Archivist's Reflections on His Work with the White House Tapes." *Prologue* 39 (Fall 2007): 3. http://www .archives.gov/publications/prologue/2007/fall/tapes.html.

Teaching the Cold War with the *Foreign Relations of the United States* Series

M. TODD BENNETT

I may not have infiltrated the Communist Party as an undercover Federal Bureau of Investigation agent, as does the protagonist of the Cold War B-movie *I Was a Communist for the FBI* (1951). But in a former professional life I was a documentary editor for the *Foreign Relations of the United States* series, or *FRUS*, that is, the official documentary record, produced by the Department of State, of US foreign policy. Hollywood will not be releasing an adventure based on the working life of a *FRUS* editor anytime soon. But by sharing my insider account of the *Foreign Relations* series, I hope to help teachers make better classroom use of a world-class but underutilized Cold War history resource that can take students inside the foreign policymaking process at the click of a mouse.

Defining *FRUS*

Produced by the State Department's Office of the Historian, the *Foreign Relations* series presents, through documents, the official record of major US foreign-policy decisions and significant diplomatic activity. Now comprising more than 450 volumes, *FRUS* (rhymes with "Bruce") has matured since premiering in the early days of Abraham Lincoln's presidency. At first *FRUS* published little aside from State Department cables, and early volumes appeared almost contemporaneously with the events they documented: published in December 1861, the very first volume covered the Union's foreign relations during the opening year of the American Civil War.[1] Just nineteen volumes sufficed to document the relatively limited foreign relations conducted by both the Lincoln and the Andrew Johnson administrations, from 1861 to 1868. But as the US role in the world expanded, international issues multiplied, and the American foreign policy bureaucracy swelled, the *Foreign Relations* series grew as well to accommodate such developments. By the Cold War, *FRUS* volumes no longer published just State Department telegrams but also included memoranda, meeting minutes, policy studies, and similar documents generated by the Defense Department, the National Security Council, the Central Intelligence Agency, and other institutions involved in the formulation and implementation of US foreign policy. Consequently, it required sixty-five volumes, each of which includes hundreds of documents, to cover US foreign relations during the eight years, 1961–68, of the John Kennedy and Lyndon Johnson administrations.

Today, *Foreign Relations* enjoys a reputation as "the global gold standard in official documentary history."[2] And that is not just because the series is the world's oldest or largest publication of its kind. It is also because *FRUS* acts as an important force on behalf of government transparency. Most of the records that make up a published *Foreign Relations* volume were classified, often highly so, when that volume went into production. *FRUS* editors possess the requisite need-to-know and security clearances to conduct research in classified records housed in the vaults of presidential libraries, the US National Archives, and government agencies, among other repositories. And they routinely discover documents that portray US foreign actions in unflattering light and/or contain closely guarded national secrets. Backed by a 1991 congressional act empowering the *Foreign Relations* series to provide the public with a "thorough, accurate, and reliable" account of US diplomatic activity, *FRUS* editors select those documents for publication that best tell that story. They then submit those documents for declassification through an established multiagency process. To be sure, the Historian's Office does not win every declassification battle. Claims that the release of even decades-old historical information will irreparably harm US interests regularly trump calls for greater transparency. And critics sometimes accuse *Foreign Relations* of publishing whitewashed accounts of US diplomatic history. Two *FRUS* volumes published in the 1980s inadequately documented US involvement in coups that toppled democratically elected governments in Iran and Guatemala in 1953 and 1954, respectively, for instance, causing a public outcry that culminated with the passage of the 1991 law and the publication of a special retrospective volume in 2003 that provided more complete coverage of events in Guatemala.[3] Yet *Foreign Relations* has earned a reputation as a force for openness because it declassifies and publishes (often for the first time) once-secret documents that take readers inside CIA headquarters, the State Department, the Pentagon, the White House, and wherever else US foreign policy was made at the highest levels of the US government. Users can thus see (and judge) for themselves what the director of central intelligence did, the secretary of state recommended, the national security adviser advised, and the president decided. The picture is not always pretty—Richard Nixon's White House tape transcripts, many of which appear in *FRUS*, reveal Nixon at his racist, sexist, anti-Semitic, and foul-mouthed worst—but the fact that such a portrait is available at all is what makes *FRUS* such a valuable asset to diplomatic historians as well as to the general public.

Cutting *FRUS* Down to Size

Which is to say that teachers can trust *FRUS* to provide students with the most "thorough, accurate, and reliable" account of US diplomatic history available. All that thoroughness, accuracy, and reliability come at a cost, however. The scope of *Foreign Relations*, all 450-plus volumes of it, presents the biggest obstacle to using the series in the classroom. If one accepts the textbook definition of the Cold War as a global competition between the American and Soviet superpowers, their allies, and their proxies that began not long after World War II and ended in 1989 or so, then more than two hundred volumes now in print document various aspects of US Cold War activity. As if that were not enough, more volumes are on the way. Unlike in Lincoln's day, *Foreign Relations* volumes now routinely appear three or more decades after the events they document. There are many reasons for the delay, the biggest of which has been heightened concern about protecting national security, something that has dramatically lengthened the declassification process. As a result, the series' coverage currently extends only into the late 1970s. Some thirty volumes dealing with the Jimmy Carter years are now being published. Fifty volumes covering Ronald Reagan's two terms are in production. Work on volumes documenting the George H. W. Bush administration has yet to begin. The *Foreign Relations* series' coverage of the Cold War will thus not be complete until the 2020s, at the earliest, when volumes documenting the 1989 collapse of communism throughout Eastern Europe and the 1991 disintegration of the Soviet Union are scheduled to appear.[4]

How is a busy teacher, much less a student, supposed to make sense of it all? In the old days, that is, before the Internet, *Foreign Relations* volumes were published only in hard copy, and people who wanted to research them had just two options. Either they trudged back and forth to the library—uphill both ways, often in the snow of course—or they sent a check to the US Government Printing Office in Washington, DC, and waited weeks for a copy of a volume to arrive in the mail. However, thanks to the Historian's Office's well-regarded website—www.history.state.gov—everything the office has to offer is available to today's users virtually anywhere, anytime, at the click of a mouse. Teachers can view suggested teaching activities geared toward middle and high school students. Students can read brief histories of US relations with individual countries. They can also explore the portion of the website devoted to the State Department's history, which provides short biographies of the secretaries of state, identifies the department's principal officers and chiefs of mission, and lists the travels of the president as well as the secretary of state. Or they can view "Milestones in the History of U.S. Foreign Relations," a collection of concise essays written by experts that provides an authoritative but accessible overview of US diplomatic history. The chapter covering the period 1945–52 includes several pieces on the early Cold War, for example, that discuss topics such as the Truman Doctrine, the National Security Act of 1947, and the Marshall Plan. Because entries refer readers to additional resources such as *FRUS* volumes, the "Milestones" collection can serve as an entry to the study of US diplomatic history, orienting students even as it guides them to project ideas and research materials. Most important, students and teachers can access electronic versions of each and every *FRUS* volume ever published. Although the Historian's Office continues to publish print editions of select *Foreign Relations* volumes, it started posting electronic versions of printed volumes on the Web in the late 1990s. And today every *FRUS* volume is digital, searchable, and available online, including the entire library of legacy volumes going all the way back to 1861.[5]

Whether one reads *FRUS* online or in print, understanding the idiosyncratic way in which the series is organized helps to narrow things down. The *FRUS* volumes for the years before 1952 are organized annually. The 1951 subseries includes eleven volumes, for example. Since 1952 the series has been subdivided according to presidential administration. The first such administrative subseries, 1952–54, covers the end of the Harry Truman administration and the beginning of Dwight Eisenhower's first term in twenty-seven volumes. The 1955–57 subseries and the 1958–60 subseries, comprising fifty-seven volumes, round out the Eisenhower years. The thirty volumes in the 1961–63 subseries document the entirety of Kennedy's tenure in office, as the thirty-five in the 1964–68 subseries do Lyndon Johnson's. Totaling fifty-four volumes, the 1969–76 subseries encompasses both Nixon's presidency and that of Gerald Ford. The 1977–80 subseries covers Carter's one term, and the 1981–88 subseries documents Reagan's two. Knowing that individual volumes in each annual or administrative subseries deal with specific topics or geographical areas further reduces *FRUS* to just those volumes most germane to the Cold War. Twenty-eight volumes currently in print document either US national security policy or US relations with the Soviet Union since the end of World War II.

Teaching with *FRUS*

Those twenty-eight volumes do not encompass the totality of the Cold War. But they do capture the essence of the superpower rivalry that lay at the heart of the Cold War. Together, they provide a relatively complete documentary record of the Cold War from the US point of view, and from them teachers can select any number of individual documents as the bases for class discussions or writing assignments.

Teachers could begin by selecting the document that helped set the United States on a collision course with the Soviet Union, the "Long Telegram" of February 22, 1946 (printed in *FRUS, 1946*, Volume VI), in which the chargé d'affaires of the US embassy in Moscow at the time, George F. Kennan, gave a lengthy response to a State Department request for an interpretative analysis of Soviet behavior and intentions in the world. Given just weeks earlier, Josef Stalin's "election" speech, in which the Soviet premier spoke of inevitable conflict between communism and capitalism, was one of several actions (pressure on Turkey and Iran were others) taken by the Soviet Union in the months since the end of World War II that, collectively, raised a basic question in the West: Did the Kremlin seek cooperation or conflict? Conflict, answered Kennan, who characterized the Soviet Union as "a political force committed fanatically to the belief . . . that the internal harmony of our society [must] be disrupted, our traditional way of life be destroyed, the international authority of our state be broken, if Soviet power is to be secure."[6]

Highly influential in Washington, Kennan's telegram did not make a policy recommendation. Kennan rectified that in July 1947 when he published an article in *Foreign Affairs*, a quarterly widely read among the foreign policy establishment. Known as the "X" article because the author, Kennan, did not identify himself as he had since accepted a prestigious position directing policy planning at the State Department and therefore wished to remain anonymous, the piece concluded that Soviet expansion could be "contained by the adroit and vigilant application of counter-force" on the part of the United States. In November 1948, the National Security Council (NSC), a cabinet-level committee established only the previous year to advise the president on foreign-policy matters, issued a report, designated NSC 20/4, that endorsed Kennan's recommended method of countering the Soviet Union's perceived threat to US security. Days later, President Harry Truman approved NSC 20/4 (printed in *FRUS, 1948*, Volume I), making containment the centerpiece of US Cold War strategy. Teachers might open a discussion by asking who Kennan was and what he proposed. Why did containment win such acceptance in Washington? Was it simply because containment was superior to other potential Cold War strategies? Or, as the diplomatic historian Frank Costigliola argues, did Kennan's alarmist rhetoric play a role as well?[7]

Selecting the Long Telegram reveals a limitation of *FRUS*: the series documents only US policy, thus providing a one-sided view of world affairs. Were students to read only Kennan's words, they might well come away with the impression that, in adopting policies such as containment, the peaceful United States was merely (and justifiably) defending itself from aggression by the Soviet Union, the instigator of the Cold War. However true or false that orthodox interpretation of the Cold War's origins may be, it does not leave much room for discussion. Which is why I pair Kennan's Long Telegram with a similar telegram that Nikolai Novikov, the Soviet ambassador to the United States, sent to Moscow a few months later, in September 1946. Available online via the Wilson Center's Cold War International History Project—a key source of non-American documentation and one that pairs well with *FRUS* to provide the broadest possible perspective—the Novikov Telegram concluded that the United States sought "world domination."[8]

What led Novikov to reach such a damning conclusion, teachers might ask. How does Novikov's conclusion compare to that of Kennan, who wrote that the Soviet Union was "committed fanatically" to America's destruction? Does the existence of such diametrically opposed world-views suggest that each superpower perceived the other as the aggressor, thereby lending credence to revisionist or postrevisionist interpretations of the Cold War's origins? Students could address such questions either in a class discussion or in short papers comparing the telegrams.

Teachers might also select an equally influential document, NSC 68, from *FRUS, 1950*, Volume I. Students may be familiar with the general outlines of NSC 68. Despite containment, momentum in the Cold War appeared to have swung against the United States by 1949. The Soviets successfully tested an atomic bomb, and Mao Zedong's forces won the Chinese Civil War, leading Truman's right-wing critics to charge him with losing China to communism. The president responded in January 1950 by directing the NSC to conduct a thorough reappraisal of US strategic plans and objectives. That April, the council issued NSC 68. Like Kennan's Long Telegram, the lengthy document spoke logically as well as apocalyptically, claiming that a Cold War victory by the Soviet Union and its allies could lead to the "destruction not only of this Republic but of civilization itself." To prevent such a calamity, NSC 68 recommended a buildup of US military strength that went well beyond what Kennan had proposed.[9]

Students may be less aware of the backstory behind NSC 68, and this is where *FRUS* proves especially valuable. Principally drafted by Paul H. Nitze, Kennan's successor as the State Department's director of policy planning, NSC 68 initially met stiff opposition from some of the most powerful figures in Washington. Now the department's counselor, Kennan believed that Nitze's draft mistakenly reduced the Soviet threat to "just a military problem." Only a "patient" and broad strategy that also incorporated political, economic, and cultural measures, that is, containment, could meet the vast Soviet challenge, Kennan maintained.[10] Ordinarily, the Pentagon would have welcomed the additional resources NSC 68 recommended. But Truman appointed Secretary of Defense Louis Johnson to trim the US defense budget, and Johnson stormed out of a meeting with Nitze after hearing what NSC 68 proposed. The president played it cooler, sitting on NSC 68 until Bureau of the Budget and Treasury Department officials reviewed the study's fiscal implications, but still nothing happened for months.

Then, in September 1950, Truman approved NSC 68's conclusions "as a statement of policy to be followed over the next four or five years, and agreed that the implementing programs will be put into effect as rapidly as feasible."[11] Defense spending tripled as a percentage of the gross domestic product between 1950 and 1953, rising to 14.2 percent from 5 percent, and NSC 68 would go on to guide US strategy for the better part of the Cold War. What caused Truman to change his mind? North Korea's invasion of South Korea in June 1950 ended talk of cutting the Pentagon down to size during the Korean War. But deft bureaucratic maneuvering by Nitze and Secretary of State Dean Acheson also played a role. Acheson chose Nitze rather than, say, Kennan to chair the committee charged with drafting a response to the president's directive. Nitze then handpicked the members of that committee, stacking it with hawks and leaving fiscal conservatives and Johnson loyalists in the minority. As the draft document took shape, Nitze outmaneuvered Johnson, keeping the defense secretary in the dark about the study's conclusions until the last minute and also quietly meeting with key stakeholders to obtain their support.[12] Finally realizing that he stood almost alone, Johnson quietly dropped his opposition and reluctantly got on board the NSC 68 bandwagon. And NSC 68's findings—supported by Nitze's careful reasoning and apocalyptic language—put Truman in a political box. If the president failed to approve a US military buildup after being warned about the consequences of not doing so by a government study that top experts almost unanimously endorsed, then he would be even more vulnerable to charges of being soft on communism as the country headed into that autumn's congressional elections. "Without the Korean War," the diplomatic historian Ernest R. May explained, "defense spending would probably not have shot so quickly to such levels. Indeed, it might never have gone so high. But given all the support that Nitze and Acheson had mustered for a document warning that the alternative to a military buildup was enslavement for the free world, Truman would nevertheless have found it difficult, perhaps impossible, not to spend substantially more money for ready military power." As such, NSC 68 "provides an example of how officialdom can force a president to follow policies that are against his inclinations."[13]

Which is to say that NSC 68's backstory demonstrates how US foreign policy is sometimes made. Like sausage making, foreign-policy making may not always be pretty. But it is important nonetheless to understand the process, and the *Foreign Relations* series can take students inside the policymaking factory, so to speak, where bureaucratic politics often play an outsized role.[14] *FRUS* documents every stage in NSC 68's production, from Truman's January directive to his September decision. By pointing students to such documents, teachers can develop a class discussion or writing project dealing with questions such as: What did NSC 68 recommend and why? How and why did NSC 68 develop into "a statement of policy" that governed US strategy throughout much of the Cold War? What role did foreign and domestic affairs play in gaining wider acceptance of the study's conclusions? Looking at NSC 68 itself, does the study's appeal to reason or its emotional tone better explain its persuasiveness? While some diplomatic historians criticize NSC 68 as an overreaction to Soviet behavior that militarized and made the Cold War costlier and more dangerous than it otherwise would have been, others hail it as a document that helped win the Cold War. Should we remember NSC 68 as a cautionary tale or as a success story?

As for a bigger writing project, consider the one I assign in my undergraduate diplomatic history courses. It asks students to step into the past, assume the identity of a foreign-policy expert, and write a paper on a major problem in US diplomatic history from that expert's perspective. The paper (the ones I assign are ten to twelve pages long, though they could just as well be shorter or longer) could take any one of several forms—newspaper editorial, think-tank piece, or personal letter— addressed to anybody in a position to affect foreign policy. But the exercise works best when students address a memorandum to a foreign-policy principal—from the president down to the secretary of state, national security adviser, or below—recommending a course of action with regard to a pressing problem of the day. Providing detailed guidance reduces student anxiety about this unorthodox assignment, and so I specify that the paper should mimic an official options paper, which typically includes three sections. (Students appreciate seeing actual examples such as a memorandum the NSC staffer Winston Lord sent to National Security Adviser Henry Kissinger in May 1972 weighing whether the United States should risk President Nixon's upcoming summit with Soviet premier Leonid Brezhnev in Moscow by bombing the North Vietnamese cities of Haiphong and Hanoi.)[15] Subtitled "Background" or "The Problem," the first section describes the issue, situation, or crisis facing the United States and specifies the country's stake in it.

The second, "Options," lists the options available to the United States in response to that issue, situation, or crisis and weighs the relative advantages and disadvantages of each. And the third, "Recommendation," recommends a course of action and justifies why it is the best approach given the realities outlined in the first two sections.

Teachers everywhere want to improve students' critical thinking skills but are not always sure exactly how to do that. Assigning an options paper arguably teaches critical thinking better than having students write traditional research papers. (That options papers are idiosyncratic enough to be less susceptible to Information Age plagiarism is a bonus.) A role-playing exercise, the assignment encourages students to view the wider world from the perspective of a foreign-policy principal and to weigh the competing interests and complex factors, both foreign and domestic, that decision makers necessarily take into account. To the extent that students do their homework and stay within the historical moment—we all have 20/20 hindsight, and some Monday-morning quarterbacking inevitably creeps in despite my discouragement—they learn, in a hands-on, experiential way that a traditional research paper cannot effectively duplicate, just how challenging good decision making can be. Working under pressure and with incomplete information, US foreign-policy makers often had at their disposal only a limited menu of imperfect policy options, all of which were likely to lead to less-than-ideal outcomes. Often the trick, students come to realize, was to choose the least bad option. That is not to excuse the poor choices US foreign policymakers made—Nixon's deadly decision to bomb North Vietnam in 1972 led to protests both at home and abroad—but to illustrate the decision-making process. And that lesson in critical thinking extends to the student's selection of an authorial voice. Which policymaker role will the student choose? That of diplomat or soldier, secretary of state or defense, or perhaps a lesser official with a specific portfolio such as human rights coordinator? Whichever role the student assumes, he or she may come away with a better appreciation of how bureaucratic politics can shape foreign policy, specifically of Miles' Law ("where you stand depends on whether you sit"), which holds that officials' attitudes reflect the organizations they represent.

Better yet, everything about the papers—from the expert's identity to the problem he or she faced to the solutions at his or her disposal to the conclusions that the expert drew—comes from historical research, mostly in primary sources of the type published in the *Foreign Relations* series. Here is where the series shines brightest, serving as a source of documents as well as ideas, all at the click of a mouse. Paper topics are as limitless as the events *FRUS* documents, so is it important to provide students with some direction. For example, I encourage students to imagine that it is June 1950 (the exact date is fungible in many cases, and choosing it is part of the exercise). How should the United States respond to the North Korean invasion of South Korea? (To address that question, students can reference *FRUS, 1950,* Volume VII: *Korea.*) The Cuban Missile Crisis and the Vietnam War consistently rank as popular topics among students. How should Washington respond to the discovery of Soviet missiles in Cuba in October 1962? (See *FRUS, 1961–1963,* Volume XI: *Cuban Missile Crisis and Aftermath.*) Should the United States escalate its involvement in Vietnam? (Five administrations debated that question in one way or another, as any one of the twenty volumes documenting US actions in Vietnam from 1954 to 1975 attests.) Or fast forward to 1977, the first year of the Carter administration. Should the United States make human rights a centerpiece of its foreign policy? (See *FRUS, 1977–1980,* Volume II: *Human Rights and Humanitarian Affairs.*)

While the list could go on, the *Foreign Relations* series clearly presents teachers of the Cold War with an overabundance of resources. Wrapping one's arms around *FRUS* can prove challenging, which probably explains why the series remains underutilized in the classroom. But, thanks to the Office of the Historian's website, teachers and students can unlock— anywhere, anytime—a treasure trove of primary documents that enrich class discussions and paper projects designed to teach students not only what but also how to think about the Cold War.

NOTES

1. *Message of the President of the United States to the Two Houses of Congress at the Commencement of the Second Session of the Thirty-Seventh Congress* (Washington, DC: US Government Printing Office, 1861), http://digital.library.wisc.edu /1711.dl/FRUS.FRUS1861v01.

2. William B. McAllister, Joshua Botts, Peter Cozzens, and Aaron W. Marrs, *Toward "Thorough, Accurate, and Reliable": A History of the Foreign Relations of the United States Series* (Washington, DC: Office of the Historian, US Department of State, 2013), 8, http://history.state.gov/historicaldocuments/frus-history.

3. Carl N. Raether and Charles S. Sampson, eds., *Iran, 1951–1954,* Vol. X, *Foreign Relations of the United States* [hereafter *FRUS*], *1952–1954* (Washington, DC: US Government Printing Office, 1989); N. Stephen Kane and William F.

Sanford Jr., eds., *The American Republics*, Vol. IV, ibid. (1983); Susan Holly, ed., *Guatemala, 1952–1954,* ibid. (2003).

4. The Historian's Office maintains a *FRUS* status report on its website: http://history.state.gov/historicaldocuments/status-of-the-series.

5. The Historian Office's website sometimes redirects users of pre-1952 volumes to the University of Wisconsin library's Digital Collections Center: http://uwdc.library.wisc.edu/collections/FRUS.

6. George F. Kennan to Secretary of State, telegram, February 22, 1946, in Rogers P. Churchill and William Z. Slany, eds., *Eastern Europe, the Soviet Union*, Vol. VI, *FRUS, 1946* (Washington, DC: US Government Printing Office, 1946), 706. The Long Telegram is printed in its entirety on pp. 696–709; http://digicoll.library.wisc.edu/cgi-bin/FRUS/FRUS-idx?type=header&id=FRUS.FRUS1946v06.

7. "X" [Kennan], "The Sources of Soviet Conduct," *Foreign Affairs* 25 (July 1947): 566–82; Report to the President by the National Security Council (NSC), November 23, 1948, in Ralph R. Goodwin and Neal H. Peterson, eds., *General; The United Nations*, Vol. I, pt. 2, *FRUS, 1948* (Washington, DC: US Government Printing Office, 1976), 662–69, http://digicoll.library.wisc.edu/cgi-bin/FRUS/FRUS-idx?type=header&id=FRUS.FRUS1948v01p2; Frank Costigliola, "'Unceasing Pressure for Penetration': Gender, Pathology, and Emotion in George Kennan's Formation of the Cold War," *Journal of American History* 83 (March 1997): 1309–39.

8. Nikolai Novikov to the Soviet Leadership, telegram, September 27, 1946, Woodrow Wilson International Center for Scholars, Digital Archive, http://digitalarchive.wilsoncenter.org/document/110808.

9. Harry Truman to Dean Acheson, January 31, 1950, in John P. Glennon, Ralph R. Goodwin, David W. Mabon, Neal H. Petersen, and William Z. Slany, eds., *National Security Affairs; Foreign Economic Policy*, Vol. I, *FRUS, 1950* (Washington, DC: US Government Printing Office, 1977), 141–42; A Report to the President Pursuant to the President's Directive of Jan. 31, 1950 [NSC 68], April 7, 1950, in ibid., 238. NSC 68 is printed in its entirety on pp. 235–92, http://digicoll.library.wisc.edu/cgi-bin/FRUS/FRUS-idx?type=header&id=FRUS.FRUS1950v01. For a history of NSC 68 and teaching suggestions, see Ernest R. May, ed., *American Cold War Strategy: Interpreting NSC 68* (Boston: Bedford Books of St. Martin's Press, 1993), esp. 1–19.

10. Kennan to Dean Acheson, draft memo, February 17, 1950, *National Security Affairs; Foreign Economic Policy*, Vol. I, *FRUS, 1950*, 160–67.

11. James S. Lay Jr. to the NSC, report, September 30, 1950, ibid., 400.

12. The records of the meetings of February 27, March 2, March 10, March 16, and March 20, 1950, are found in ibid., 168–82 and 190–201.

13. May, *American Cold War Strategy*, 15.

14. J. Garry Clifford, "Bureaucratic Politics," in Michael J. Hogan and

Thomas G. Paterson, eds., *Explaining the History of American Foreign Relations,* 2nd ed. (New York: Cambridge University Press, 2004), 91–102.

15. Winston Lord to Henry A. Kissinger, memorandum, May 1, 1972, printed as document 177 in David C. Geyer, Nina D. Howland, and Kent Sieg, eds., *Soviet Union, October 1971–May 1972,* Vol. XIV, *FRUS, 1969–1976* (Washington, DC: US Government Printing Office, 2006), http://history.state.gov /historicaldocuments/frus1969-76v14.

KEY RESOURCES

Clifford, J. Garry. "Bureaucratic Politics." In *Explaining the History of American Foreign Relations,* 2nd ed., edited by Michael J. Hogan and Thomas G. Paterson, 91–102. New York: Cambridge University Press, 2004.

Foreign Relations of the United States. Washington, DC: US Government Printing Office, 1861–). http://history.state.gov/historicaldocuments.

May, Ernest R., ed. *American Cold War Strategy: Interpreting NSC 68.* Boston: Bedford Books of St. Martin's Press, 1993.

McAllister, William B., Joshua Botts, Peter Cozzens, and Aaron W. Marrs. *Toward "Thorough, Accurate, and Reliable": A History of the* Foreign Relations of the United States *Series.* Washington, DC: Office of the Historian, US Department of State, 2013. http://history.state.gov/historicaldocuments/frus-history.

Contributors

LAURA A. BELMONTE is the department head and a professor of history at Oklahoma State University. She is the author of *Selling the American Way: US Propaganda and the Cold War* (2010) and editor of *Speaking of America: Readings in US History* (2006). She has coauthored *Global Americans: A Transnational US History* (2017) and is working on two additional major projects. The first examines US global policy on HIV/AIDS. The second synthesizes the history of the international LGBT rights movement. She is a member of the US Department of State's Historical Advisory Committee on Diplomatic Documentation.

M. TODD BENNETT is an associate professor of history at East Carolina University. He is the author of *One World, Big Screen: Hollywood, the Allies, and World War II* (2012). From 2002 to 2009 he served in the US Department of State's Office of the Historian, where he edited several volumes in the *Foreign Relations of the United States* series.

DAVID BOSSO, a social studies teacher at Berlin High School in Berlin, Connecticut, is the 2012 Connecticut Teacher of the Year and 2012 National Secondary Social Studies Teacher of the Year. Over the course of his teaching career, he has traveled to Africa, Asia, the Middle East, and Europe as part of educational delegations for global understanding. Bosso holds an EdD from American International College; his areas of expertise include teacher motivation and morale, education policy, and social studies education.

WARREN I. COHEN is Distinguished University Professor Emeritus of History at the University of Maryland, Baltimore County; University Professor Emeritus at Michigan State University; and Senior Scholar with the Asia Program at the Woodrow Wilson International Center for Scholars in Washington, DC. His most recent book is *Challenges to American Primacy, 1945 to the Present* (2013). In 2004 he received the Laura and Norman Graebner Prize of the Society for Historians of American Foreign Relations, granted biennially to a senior scholar for excellence in teaching, scholarship, and service.

ANTHONY D'AGOSTINO is a professor of history at San Francisco State University. He is the author of *Soviet Succession Struggles* (1988), *Gorbachev's Revolution, 1985–1991* (1998), *The Rise of Global Powers: International Politics in the Era of the World Wars* (2012), and other works on international politics. He is currently working on an international history of the era of globalization, 1968–2008.

MARIO DEL PERO is a professor of international history at the Institut d'études politiques/SciencesPo of Paris. His research has focused on the history of US foreign relations, particularly during the Cold War. Among his most recent publications are *Libertà e Impero: Gli Stati Uniti e il Mondo, 1776–2011* (Empire and liberty: The United States and the world, 1776–2011; 2011, 2nd ed.) and *The Eccentric Realist: Henry Kissinger and the Shaping of American Foreign Policy* (2009). He is writing a book on the presidency of Barack Obama that will appear in early 2017 and is working on research on US evangelical missions in early Cold War Italy.

JESSICA ELKIND is an associate professor of history at San Francisco State University. Her book *Aid Under Fire: Nation Building and the Vietnam War* (2016) examines the role of American aid workers in implementing nation-building programs and development efforts in South Vietnam between 1955 and 1965. She is currently working on a study of US-Cambodian relations in the 1970s.

CAROLE FINK, Humanities Distinguished Professor Emerita at the Ohio State University, is the author of *Cold War: An International History* (2017, 2nd ed.). Two of her other books, *Defending the Rights of Others: The Great Powers, the Jews, and International Minority Protection 1978–1938* (2004) and *The Genoa Conference, 1921–1922* (1984), were awarded the George Louis Beer prize of the American Historical Association; and her *Marc Bloch: A Life in History* (1989) has been translated into six languages. She taught European international history for more than four decades at several colleges and universities and most recently was a guest professor at the University of Jena.

MARY ANN HEISS is an associate professor of history at Kent State University, where she teaches courses on US foreign relations and the history of the Cold War. The author of *Empire and Nationhood: The United States, Great Britain, and Iranian Oil, 1950–1954* (1997) and numerous journal articles and book chapters, she is currently completing a book on the United Nations and decolonization.

RYAN M. IRWIN is an associate professor at the University at Albany, SUNY. His *Gordian Knot: Apartheid and the Unmaking of the Liberal World Order* (2012) explores decolonization's effects on the Cold War. His articles and book chapters have explored many aspects of decolonization and the Cold War. He is currently writing a book about liberal internationalism.

ANDREW J. KIRKENDALL is a professor of history at Texas A&M University. He is the author of *Class Mates: Male Student Culture and the Making of a Political Class in Nineteenth-Century Brazil* (2002) and *Paulo Freire and the Cold War Politics of Literacy* (2010). He teaches a course on the history of the world since 1918 that was taught for decades by Betty Unterberger. He created the history department's course on inter-American relations. He is currently at work on a book on the Kennedy brothers, liberal Democrats, and Latin America.

HIROSHI KITAMURA is an associate professor of history at the College of William and Mary. He is the author of *Screening Enlightenment: Hollywood and the Cultural Reconstruction of Defeated Japan* (2010) and has published a number of essays on Hollywood and Japanese cinema. At William and Mary, he teaches classes on the Cold War, America in the world, and international relations from disciplinary perspectives.

SHANE J. MADDOCK is a professor of history at Stonehill College in Easton, Massachusetts. His publications include *Nuclear Apartheid* (2010), *American Foreign Relations: A History* (2014, 8th ed., coauthor), and *The Nuclear Age* (2000, editor and contributor).

MATTHEW MASUR is a professor of history at Saint Anselm College in Manchester, New Hampshire. His publications include "Historians and the Origins of the Vietnam War" in *America and the Vietnam War: Re-Examining the Culture and History of a Generation* (2010, ed. Andrew Wiest, Mary Kathryn Barbier, and Glenn Robins), "Exhibiting Signs of Resistance: South Vietnam's Struggle for Legitimacy, 1954-1960" published in *Diplomatic History*, and, with coeditors John Day Tully and Brad Austin, *Understanding and Teaching the Vietnam War* (2013).

KENNETH OSGOOD is a professor of history and the director of the McBride Honors Program at Colorado School of Mines. He is the author or editor of five books on propaganda, foreign policy, and politics, including *Total Cold War: Eisenhower's Secret Propaganda Battle at Home and Abroad* (2006), *The United States and Public Diplomacy: Toward a New International History* (2010, edited with Brian C. Etheridge), *Selling War in a Media Age: The Presidency and Public Opinion in the American Century* (2010, edited with Andrew K.

Frank), and *Winning While Losing? Civil Rights, the Conservative Movement, and the Presidency from Nixon to Obama* (2014, edited with Derrick E. White).

CHRISTIAN OSTERMANN directs the Woodrow Wilson Center's History and Public Policy Program, which includes the Cold War International History Project (CWIHP) and the Nuclear Proliferation International History Project (NPIHP). He is the editor of the *CWIHP Bulletin* and the executive editor of the Digital Archive. Before joining CWIHP, he worked as a research fellow at the National Security Archive, a nongovernmental research institute and repository based at George Washington University. He is a coeditor of *Cold War History*, a member of the editorial board of the *Journal of Cold War Studies*, and a senior research fellow at the National Security Archive (George Washington University).

PHILIP PAJAKOWSKI is a professor of history at Saint Anselm College, where he teaches courses on the history of Eastern Europe and, together with Matthew Masur, the Cold War. His field of research is the political and legal history of the Habsburg Empire.

BRENDA GAYLE PLUMMER teaches in the departments of history and Afro-American studies at the University of Wisconsin–Madison. Her publications include two books on Haiti, an edited anthology on civil rights and foreign affairs, and a book about African American engagements with international issues during the period 1935–60. Her most recent book is *In Search of Power: African Americans in the Era of Decolonization, 1956–1974* (2013).

J. SIMON ROFE is senior lecturer in Diplomacy and International Studies in the Centre for International Studies and Diplomacy at SOAS, University of London. His research interests focus on US foreign relations in the twentieth century with a specific focus on US postwar planning and the diplomacy of sport. The author of numerous books and articles, including *The Embassy in Grosvenor Square: American Ambassadors to the United Kingdom 1938–2008* (2012, with Alison Holmes) and *Franklin Roosevelt's Foreign Policy and the Welles Mission* (2007), Simon is also series coeditor of Key Studies in Diplomacy and is on the editorial board of *Diplomatic History*.

MARC J. SELVERSTONE is an associate professor and chair of the Presidential Recordings Program at the University of Virginia's Miller Center. He is the author of *Constructing the Monolith: The United States, Great Britain, and International Communism, 1945–1950* (2009), the editor of *A Companion to John F. Kennedy* (2014), and general editor of the *Presidential Recordings Digital Edition* (2014–). He is currently writing *The Kennedy Withdrawal: Camelot and the American Commitment to Vietnam*.

MOLLY M. WOOD is a professor of history at Wittenberg University in Springfield, Ohio, where she teaches modern US history and US foreign relations. She has published articles in journals including *Diplomatic History* and the *Journal of Women's History*, as well as numerous pieces on pedagogy. She is serving a second term on the Teaching Committee of the Society for Historians of US Foreign Relations.

THOMAS W. ZEILER is a professor of history and the director of the Program in International Affairs at the University of Colorado Boulder, where he teaches a course on American history through baseball. He is the author, most recently, of *Jackie Robinson and Race in America* (2014) and is currently working on a history of capitalist peace doctrine and free-trade philosophy and policy.

Index

Olmstead, Kathryn, 147
Olympic Games, 191
One, Two, Three (film, 1961), 165–66
On the Beach (film, 1959), 163
Operation Tempest, 208
Oppenheimer, J. Robert, 55
options paper, 338–40
oral history interviews, 105, 108, 185
oral history projects, 261
Organization of Petroleum Exporting
    Countries (OPEC), 78
origins of Cold War, 39–52, 206–11, 224–29;
    East Asian perspective, 236–40
Orwell, George, 16, 69
Ostpolitik (Brandt), 21

Paley, William, 149
pamphlets, use for propaganda, 123–24
Pan-African movement, 266–67
paragogy, 228
Parallel History on Cooperative Security
    (Parallel History Project on NATO and
    the Warsaw Pact, PHP), 94, 298
Park Chung-hee, 241
Patriotism (2003), 58
patriotism, issue of, 200
peace: in Cold War rhetoric, 126–32; and
    nuclear arms race, 65
peaceful coexistence, 36, 127, 131, 241–42,
    285, 289
Pearl Harbor, Japanese sneak attack on,
    237
pedagogical interface, CWIHP and, 303,
    306–11
People's Century (PBS documentary series,
    1999), 160, 165
People's Republic of China. *See* China/
    People's Republic of China (PRC)
perestroika, 23, 80
periodization, 223; of Cold War, 224–29;
    and teaching of civil rights movement,
    179–82
Pershing II missiles, 154
Philippines, 282
photographs, classroom use of, 44–45

Piagol (film, 1955), 239
Pipes, Richard, 73, 80
"Plan of Action for U.N. General Assem-
    bly" (1961), 286–87
Point Four Program, 49–50
Poland, 205–20; and end of Cold War,
    24; and Solidarność (Solidarity),
    21–22, 95. *See also under* international
    relations
Polish October, 217
Polish United Workers Party (PZPR), 211
Pol Pot, 243
Pompidou, Georges, 21
popular culture, 143, 147, 154–55, 159–68
popularity of archival resources, CWIHP
    and, 306
population shift, Polish-German, 210
post-9/11 generation, 100–115, 174–75
posters, use for propaganda, 123–24
postwar diplomacy, 46–51
Potsdam Summit (1945), 16
PowerPoint presentations, 160, 183, 186
Prados, John, 320–21
Prague Spring, 19–20
presidential libraries, and presidential re-
    cordings, 321
Presidential Speech Archive, 94
primary sources, 40, 61, 93–94, 106, 129,
    143, 150, 159–60, 180, 184–86, 224, 229–
    32, 242, 273–76, 281; sale of, 300–301
primers, 93
prisoner exchange (Cuba), 3
"pro-American dictator," 258
propaganda: baseball and, 193–94; in Cold
    War history, 119–38; ideological, 132–
    34; introducing and defining, 120–23;
    materials, 107, 109; popular culture as,
    164–65; techniques, 122–23
protest movement, 240, 260–61. *See also*
    antiwar movement
Pry, Peter Vincent, 154
publications, African American, 183–84
public diplomacy, 119
purges, 241–42
Putin, Vladimir, 25

The Harvey Goldberg Series
for Understanding and Teaching History

Understanding and Teaching the Vietnam War
Edited by John Day Tully, Matthew Masur, and Brad Austin

Understanding and Teaching U.S. Lesbian, Gay, Bisexual, and Transgender History
Edited by Leila J. Rupp and Susan K. Freeman

Understanding and Teaching American Slavery
Edited by Bethany Jay and Cynthia Lynn Lyerly

Understanding and Teaching the Cold War
Edited by Matthew Masur